Obsessions
with the Sino-Japanese
Polarity in Japanese Literature

Atsuko Sakaki

University of Hawai'i Press
Honolulu

Library of Congress Cataloging-in-Publication Data
Sakaki, Atsuko.
  Obsessions with the Sino-Japanese polarity in Japanese literature / Atsuko Sakaki.
    p. cm.
  Includes bibliographical references and index.
  ISBN-13: 978-0-8248-2918-6 (hardcover : alk. paper)
  ISBN-10: 0-8248-2918-2 (hardcover : alk. paper)
  1. Japanese literature—Chinese influences. 2. Japanese literature—History and
criticism. I. Title.
  PL720.55.C6S35 2005
  895.6'09—dc22
                            2005009469

A part of chapter 2 first appeared in "Japanese Perceptions of China: The Sinophilic
Fiction of Tanizaki Jun'ichirō," *Harvard Journal of Asiatic Studies* 59, no. 1 (June
1999): 187–218, and is reprinted here in modified form with the permission of the
editors.

A part of chapter 3 was originally published as "Sliding Doors: Women of Letters in
the Heterosocial Literary Field of Early Modern Japan," *U.S.-Japan Women's Journal*,
English Supplement 17 (December 1999): 3–38, and is reprinted here in modified
form with the permission of the editors.

A part of chapter 4 was originally published as "*Kajin no kigū*: The Meiji Political
Novel and the Boundaries of Literature," *Monumenta Nipponica* 55, no. 1 (Spring
2000): 83–108, and is reprinted here in modified form with the permission of the
editors.

University of Hawai'i Press books are printed on acid-free
paper and meet the guidelines for permanence and durability
of the Council on Library Resources.

Designed by University of Hawai'i Press production staff

Printed by The Maple-Vail Book Manufacturing Group

Contents

Acknowledgments • vii

Introduction
Scenes from within the Fold • 1

Chapter 1. Site Unseen
Imaginary Voyages to China and Back in
Classical Japanese Fiction and Theater • 18

Chapter 2. From the Edifying to the Edible
Chinese Fetishism and the China Fetish • 65

Chapter 3. Sliding Doors
Women and Chinese Literature in the
Heterosocial Literary Field • 103

Chapter 4. The Transgressive Canon?
Intellectuals on the Margins and the Fate of
the "Universal" Language • 143

Coda
Folding the Subject into the Object • 177

Notes • 191

Glossary • 229

Bibliography • 239

Index • 261

Acknowledgments

The longest journey is the hardest to end.

This book is as uncannily autobiographical as any book can be. I wrote the first chapter without revisiting China for the purpose; the second, while grappling with the chasm between the textual and the physical/material China; the third, while sliding doors were constantly being opened or closed in front of or behind me; the fourth, while trying to come to terms with gaps in my knowledge of the Chinese language that I had not been able to overcome. The introduction was written with the self-reflection of a comparativist, while the conclusion was written with the anticipation of liberation from the stake of the Sino-Japanese polarity.

The completion of this project gives me an occasion to recall gratefully and fondly my teachers of Chinese: Mr. Matsuyama Yōichi, who first introduced me to *kanbun* in junior high school; Mr. Katō Bin, who in senior high school recited classical Chinese poetry with the "authentic" modern Chinese pronunciation and let me write short stories inspired by Li Bai and Cen Shen in place of essay assignments; Li Laoshi of Beijing Yuyan Xueyuan, who as a visiting instructor at the University of Tokyo taught me first-year Mandarin; Professor Takeda Akira of the University of Tokyo, with whom I read *zhiguai*; Mr. Kō (Ch. Jiang), with whom I read *Shuihuzhuan* at the University of Tokyo; and Dr. Jerry Schmidt of the University of British Columbia, with whom I read Su Shi and Huang Tingjian.

I am also grateful to the two anonymous readers of this work for their support and constructive criticism. Pamela Kelley at the University of Hawai'i Press has been most conscientious, supportive, and professional since our first contact and has helped me complete the book to its full potential. I am most grateful to the dedication and professional guidance provided by Bojana Ristich, my copy editor. My managing editor, Cheri Dunn, has always been there for me, to pave the road to completion steadily and sensibly. My indexer, Baryon Tensor Posadas, has proven to be unflaggingly responsive to my demands, which were many and urgent. My proofreader, Cynthia Lowe, has helped me in the home stretch. I am fortunate to have been offered such high morale from the entire production team.

Many people have contributed their thoughts, knowledge, expertise, and votes of confidence. This book would not have been completed without Andre Schmid, Andy Gordon, Carl Sesar, Daisy Ng, David McCann, Edwin Cranston, Ellen Widmer, Emanuel Pastreich, Emi Shimokawa, Emma Teng, Faye Kleeman, Hal Bolitho, Helen Hardacre, Hill Anderson, Howard Hibbett, Ivo Smits, J. Thomas Rimer, James Cheng, Jay Rubin, Joanna Handlin Smith, John Timothy Wixted, Joshua Mostow, Judith Zeitlin, Karen Thornber, Kate Nakai, Larry Marceau, Leo Ou-fan Lee, Linda Hutcheon, Mariel O'Neill-Karch, Matthew Fraleigh, Noriko Murai, Norma Field, Ohki Yasushi, Patrick Hanan, Paul Rouzer, Rebecca Waese, Rick Guisso, Robert Campbell, Robert Khan, Shang Wei, Shiamin Kwa, Sonja Arnzen, Steve Owen, Thomas Hare, Thomas LaMarre, Thomas Rohlich, Wiebke Denecke, William Johnston, Wilt Idema, and Yoshiko Yokochi Samuel.

I benefited tremendously from opportunities to present my ideas and receive audience feedback, first and foremost from courses I have taught at Harvard University (Japanese Literature 130) and the University of Toronto (East Asian Studies 235). I thank the following, who have offered venues of intellectual exchange: the Midwest Association of Japanese Literary Studies; at Harvard University, the Harvard Asian and Asian-American Gender Studies Forum and the Chinese Cultural Studies Workshop; the Ford Foundation Workshop on Visual and Material Representations of Modern Japan; the Humanities Center; the Department of East Asian Languages and Civilizations; and a workshop on New Approaches to Early Japanese Textuality: Functions, Occasions and Genres of *Kanshibun;* the Mansfield Freeman Center for East Asian Studies and the Department of Asian Languages and Literatures, Wesleyan University; the Association for Asian Studies; the Department of East Asian Studies, University of Toronto; the New England Association for Asian Studies; the Association of Japanese Literary Studies; the Department of East Asian Languages and Civilizations, University of Chicago; and the International Congress for Asian Scholars.

I gratefully acknowledge the following institutions, which granted me funding support for this research: the Japan Foundation (Short-

Term Research Fellowship); the University of Toronto, Faculty of Arts and Science (Dean's Travel Fund and the Connaught Start-Up Fund); Harvard University: the Faculty of Arts and Sciences (the Cooke Fund, the Clark Fund, and a Junior Faculty Research Assistant Grant); the Edwin O. Reischauer Institute for Japanese Studies (Reischauer Institute Grant for Individual Research and Reischauer Institute Grant for Workshops); and the Department of East Asian Languages and Civilizations (the Japan Fund). I am delighted to acknowledge the individual sponsors and staff members who facilitated the awarding of the respective grants and to repay them for their help with the publication of this book.

Introduction
Scenes from within the Fold

Every perception is hallucinatory because perception has no object.
—Gilles Deleuze

This is the story of the changing but still vital collusion between privilege and knowledge, possession and display, stereotyping and realism, exhibition and the repression of history.
—Mieke Bal

This locality [of culture] is more *around* temporality than *about* historicity.... The focus on temporality resists the transparent linear equivalence of event and idea that historicism proposes; it provides a perspective on the disjunctive forms of representation that signify a people, a nation, or a national culture.... It is the mark of the ambivalence of the nation as a narrative strategy—and an apparatus of power—that it produces a continual slippage into analogous, even metonymic, categories, like the people, minorities, or "cultural difference" that continually overlap in the act of writing the nation.
—Homi Bhabha

In this study, I shall discuss several aspects of Japan's literary negotiations with China that have been evident in texts from the tenth to the twentieth centuries. I shall focus on how Japanese writers and readers revised or in many cases even devised rhetoric to present "Chineseness" and how this practice has helped form and transform the discursive self-fashioning of the Japanese. In so doing, I hope to reveal that contrasts between China and Japan that had been tenaciously drawn out in Japanese literature were contingent and yet haunting. That is, even though the referents that bear the names of China and Japan have been diverse and ever changing, the desire to propose and/or authenticate the binary between the two seems to be explicit and persistent. Rather than simply renouncing the stability of the ethnic/national essence that Japan or China was thought to embody, I examine the way that the dialectic formulation of the subject-object dyad was validated. I do this within a framework inspired by the theories of Mieke Bal, among others. I argue that the China/Japan polarity, manifested in a variety of contrastive images, persists throughout the period with which I deal. The force behind these comparative representations is the subject of this study.

This focus may appear to have much in common with what David Pollack maps out in the introduction to his study of the Sino-Japanese literary relationship, *The Fracture of Meaning: Japan's Synthesis of China from the Eighth through the Eighteenth Centuries:*

> For the Japanese, what was "Japanese" had always to be considered in relation to what was thought to be "Chinese"—and I must stress from the outset that I am not dealing here so much with the "objective" facts of cultural influence so much as with the history of its interpretation, with what was "thought" to be. In other words, this study falls within the field of critical interpretation, of the ways in which men have represented their cultures to themselves. If I say that the notion of Japanese-ness was meaningful only as it was considered against the background of the otherness of China, then, it is clear that I am no longer speaking of "China" and "Japan" in the usual senses of those words. Rather, I am considering them only as they existed in relation to each other as the antithetical terms of a uniquely Japanese dialectic to which the Japanese gave the name *wakan*, "Japanese/Chinese."[1]

Whereas I acknowledge the imagined-ness of the "Japanese" and "Chinese" dialectic that is apparent in the above quotation, I do not acknowledge Pollack's subsequent definition of the essence of the dialectic as "form (Chinese) versus content (Japanese)."[2] Pollack's efforts to unravel the heterogeneity in Japanese culture during the period of the purported isolation, while rightly intended, result in much too neat a polarization of the perceived Chineseness and Japaneseness in the Japanese cultural products he analyzes. By assigning the former to form and the latter to content, Pollack seems to be entrapped in the nativist dichotomy of "Japanese spirit, Chinese art" *(wakon kansai)*, on the one hand, and the structuralist binary (content versus form) on the other. I intend instead to complicate the binary, while acknowledging its persistence, by attending to Japanese writers of the past who sought to advance and showcase the rhetoricity and figurativeness of Japanese written discourse. Some of them took China or Chineseness as their theme (i.e., "content"), while others engaged with Chinese discourse ("form") to the effect of blurring lingual boundaries. The ubiquitous dialectic had many facets that cannot be reduced to a unitary and sustaining contrast between form and content.

Many have criticized the arbitrariness, as well as the persistence, of the *wa/kan* dialectics. Thomas LaMarre, a recent example, successfully reveals the contingency of the dyad, demonstrating instead a "coordination" of "Japaneseness" and "Chineseness" that was not originally contrastive, let alone competitive.[3] LaMarre's argument becomes particularly persuasive when it comes to an examination of the art of calligraphy, which exemplifies the materiality and technicality of the text. He points out that the Japanese script *(kana)* and Chinese script *(mana)* were not distinct from each other—as if the former represented orality/immediacy/emotions and the latter, conceptuality/mediatedness/intellect—for two reasons. First, characters in calligraphy were selected as much for graphic effect as for representation of the text (its pronunciation and meaning) and were coordinated with the quality of paper and placement of visual design. Second, many *mana* were interspersed with *kana* not because they represented concepts that were essential to the texts but often because they stood for sounds and looked nicer than the corresponding *kana*. Thus, the neat contrast drawn between *kana* and *mana* needs to be eliminated because they are only two of the players in the game where many other factors (tactile, visual) participate and also because they have different functions from those ordinarily imagined. By locating both the Japaneseness (ordinarily thought to be manifested in *kana*) and Chineseness (ordinarily so thought in *mana*) within the art/practice of calligraphy, where the significance of materiality has been more obvious than in the art/practice of literary composition, LaMarre effectively dismisses the pat association between the Chinese exterior and the Japanese interior. Inasmuch as LaMarre's work engages technical specifics, his thesis inspires us with a different model for the way in which Japanese and Chinese elements are identified, arranged, and associated with each other.

In the 1970s, Imai Yasuko traced the origins of the term *wakon kansai* and revealed its contingency.[4] In more recent years, Nakajima Wakako titled an essay "Karafū ankoku jidai" (The Dark Ages for the Chinese style), a play on "Kokufū ankoku jidai" (The Dark Ages for the Japanese style), a catchphrase for the ninth-century heyday of *kanshibun* in Japan. Her point was, first, to renounce the dominant/conventional theory that the primacy of indigenous Japanese literature (*kokufū* or *wabun*), had been temporarily obscured by Chinese literature's claim of canon, and, second, to undermine the contrast itself between Japanese and Chinese (*karafū*) literature. Hasegawa Michiko problematizes the pat contrast between Chinese instrumentality (*kara-zae*) and Japanese spirituality (*yamato-gokoro*) by swapping the idiomatic combinations of ethnicity and essence in the title of her book, *Karagokoro: Nihon seishin no gyakusetsu* (The Chinese sensibility: The paradox of the Japanese spirit).

Stefan Tanaka has written on the modernity and constructedness of Japanese views of China. Japan's autonomy from China was established in academic discourse as that of a modern nation-state that rewrote or invented the perceptions of its past relationship with China.[5] Naoki Sakai, in his rigorous study of the implications of questioning the phonetic aspects of Chinese writing, suggests that the questioning process was first set in motion in eighteenth-century scholarship in philosophy and philology. The convention of privileging the original sound of language, and thus an imagined interiority and immediacy, which was first theorized by scholars such as Ogyū Sorai, needed only to be politicized in the wake of the modern nation-state of Japan.[6] That brings us back to LaMarre's above-cited work, in which he—inspired by Benedict Anderson—invalidates the premises of the national imagination, including linguistic homogeneity, in the modern enterprise of inventing early Japan.[7] The ethnicization of the Chinese language inevitably entails conscious and systematic differentiation of Japanese from Chinese, which has led to the objectification of China in the name of scientific research.

Structure and Methodology

Japanese literary writers/readers employed a number of metaphors for China; against these—and almost exclusively against them, in the imagined vacuum of other countries—all things Japanese had to be defined as representative of Japan. The following four such metaphors, which qualified China not as just another country, but also as the cultural Other, seem particularly dominant, sustaining and thus deserving extended attention: the foreign and exotic (as opposed to the domestic and indigenous); the intellectual, conceptual, and abstract (as opposed to the sentimental, spontaneous, and material); the masculine (as opposed to the feminine); and the traditional and rigid (as opposed to the modern and variable). For this study I have selected topics that should permit us to review the validity of such metaphors and to articulate the mechanisms that promote them in order to produce specific interpretations of the cultural identity of Japan. Thus, chapter 1 examines imaginary portraits of China and the Chinese presented by Japanese characters either traveling in China or hosting Chinese guests in genres written in *wabun*—specifically fiction and theater, which were less codified by the Chinese lexicon and less informed by the empirical knowledge of historical returnees from China, who composed primarily in Chinese. Chapter 2 turns to the emergence of the Japanese attention to the material aspects of Chinese culture, which used to be taken as ideological and intellectual, and to the subsequent negotiations with the codified material and materially informed and formed text, that undermine the simple binary between form and content. Chapter 3 explores women Sinophiles who fashioned themselves and were received by their colleagues according to Chinese (i.e., then universal and cultural) standards and then were scrutinized according to non-/anti-Chinese (i.e., nationalistic and essentializing) standards. Chapter 4 looks at the function of the Chinese canon in Japan in the wake of nationalism. I have selected cases that best demonstrate the configurations involving China and Japan in Japanese rhetoric. Hence, this is neither a survey nor an inventory in the sense of an extensive enumeration of facts that prove Chinese elements in Japanese literature—an approach that has been taken by many scholars, especially in Japan, and that has produced substantial results. Instead, this is a showcase of outstanding examples that I hope will offer readers formulae that they will be able to apply to other cases.

For several reasons I have not shaped this study as a succession of chapters recounting what transpired during a given historical period. One reason was to avoid duplication. One can find many books in Japanese that chronologically list Chinese writers, Sinophiles, and books on China and hypothesize or confirm Chinese sources for Japanese writers.[8] While such painstaking and informative works help substantiate my work, here I do not offer my version of this type of enterprise. Another and more compelling reason for my decision not to "survey the field" is that I wish to nuance chronology. Whereas periodization has been viewed as contingent, chronology has been taken for granted as a property of knowledge shared by the subjects, objects, and audience of any historical analysis, as though it were tangible, coherent, and static.

Instead of the concept of chronology as an evenly paced and unidirectional template for time—a transparent measure that goes unnoticed by the participants in and observers of all events—I suggest that it is pliable, its pace, direction, and density subject to variance at any time.

While this work slowly shifts toward the contemporary, the movement is neither entirely linear nor even paced, as each theme requires a varied amount of time that may overlap with the time needed for another issue. Even within chapters, selected texts are not placed at equal distance from one another. Furthermore, the narrative present in which I write does not form a static relationship with the moment of production or reception of a given text, let alone all of the texts discussed here. The way I am connected with one text that inspired another is informed by my relationship with the latter, which is informed by my relationship with the former. It is not only impossible to draw a straight line of evenly spaced texts, but it is simply pointless to envision one. As Walter Benjamin puts it,

> Historicism contents itself with establishing a causal connection between various moments in history. But no fact that is a cause is for that very reason historical. It became historical posthumously, as it were, through events that may be separated from it by thousands of years. A historian who takes this as his point of departure stops telling the sequence of events like the beads of a rosary. Instead, he grasps the constellation which his own era has formed with a definite earlier one.[9]

Linda Hutcheon also articulates the contingency of history writing by encapsulating a historian's active involvement in the making of historical "facts" out of "events": "Events are configured into facts by being related to 'conceptual matrices within which they have to be imbedded if they are to count as facts.'…Historiography and fiction…constitute their objects of attention; in other words, they decide which events will become facts."[10] I thus resist identifying the "past" as a unified entity distinct from the "present." I refrain from privileging contemporaneity over antiquity or vice versa as though they were two distinct entities and critiquing reworkings of earlier texts uniformly as the homogenization of a national culture and construction of its continuity. Instead, I let engagements with the past emerge at various historical points; these may all have occurred in the "past" from where I stand, but each was in "the present" vis-à-vis its *own* "past." As Benjamin puts it, "History is the subject of a structure whose site is not homogeneous, empty time, but time filled by the presence of the now [Jetztzeit]."[11]

I also illustrate the conditions under which the subject of cultural analysis presents an object under investigation from the past and the effects of such an action. Chino Kaori, in her highly acclaimed essay on engendering in Japanese art history, comments on the perceived neutrality of the historian: "None can represent history 'objectively.' The scholarship of art history does not exist in a vacuum or germ-free room that is 'objective,' 'universal,' and evenly distanced from every object of study."[12] Rather than purporting to observe and articulate chronology at a distance and in the right perspective, as though it were an autonomous artifact, I propose to look at chronology as something that we all sense and yet cannot quite figure out, as we are all caught up within it. This study is not written from the height of the omniscient narrator but "from within the fold."

NEGOTIATION WITH ARCHIVAL FALLACIES

Inasmuch as China was and still often is equated with the past, whether simply as a forerunner that set a standard for the rest of East Asia or as a representative of an abstract entity vaguely called "tradition," I will have to discuss the newer (mostly Japanese) writers' attention to the older (mostly Chinese) texts. Even so, my interest is more in the *vector* (constituted by force and direction) of such approaches than the respective *locations* of the origins and offspring. It is my aim to frame the traces of the past as forces, or enactments of desire, rather than as archived facts. In Mieke Bal's words,

> Instead of "influences," the past is present in the present in the form of traces, diffuse memories. The stake of the productive, ethically responsible, and politically effective baroque aesthetics, then, is cultural memory as an alternative to traditional history. Memory is a function of subjectivity. Cultural memory is collective yet subjective by definition. This subjectivity is of crucial importance in this view, yet it does not lead to an individualist subjectivism.[13]

I also hope that my study will sufficiently show the presentness of the reworking of the past. It goes without saying that what may be termed a nostalgic gesture belongs to contemporaneity rather than antiquity, as it reveals as much of the subject of the gesture as its object. Bal again has a guiding remark on "conservation": "The inevitable inscription of the present in what is taken to be the conservation of the past as past is more often than not obliterated."[14] I would like to save the work of the later artists/critics from said obliteration.

In her articulation of "preposterous history," Bal, in a position distinct from traditional iconographic art historians, distinguishes between their practice of source studies and her theory of intertextuality. I validate two of her three points in the study of literature as I envision and undertake it. First, while in the former framework, the new artist "implicitly or explicitly declares his allegiance and debt to [his] predecessor," the latter reverses "the passivity" and "consider[s] the work of the later artist as an active intervention in the material handed down to him or her."[15] Second, source studies more often than not avoid "interpreting the meaning of the borrowed motif in their new contexts," whereas intertextuality implies a transmission of the sign's meaning—not in the sense that the later artist has to "endorse" it but that "he or she will have to deal with it." In this view, "the process of meaning-production over time (in both directions: present/past and past/present)" is traced as an "open, dynamic process" instead of "map[ping] the results of the process."[16] In deconstructionism, "what the quoting subject does to its object" is emphasized, as "reaching the alleged, underlying, earlier speech" is impossible. Bal cites Derrida and paraphrases his argument that the quoted word "never returns [where it was before it was quoted] without the burden of the excursion through the quotation."[17] This view of the reworking of an earlier work in a newer work has two advantages. First, it neutralizes the unidirectional chronology that locates the "origin" and the "offspring" in static positions and defines the latter's approach to the former only as regressive. It also alerts us to the slippery hierarchy between the subject and the object being constructed on the site of such reworkings.

The Japanese literary imagination tried to objectify China, the hegemonic other; it was a conceptual attempt at toppling the political and cultural hierarchy of power. I have found that postcolonialist theories are not parallel to but chiasmatic with the paradox that Japan saw itself in relation to China, simply because the Japanese were able to take recourse to Japanese, a language that their cultural Other did not and would not understand. Thus, Japanese perceptions of China did not engage any response or reaction from China not because it was deprived of power, but because it was deprived of access to the texts written in Japanese. Even when the Japanese wrote in Chinese, their texts were rarely distributed to Chinese readers. The overwhelming hierarchy of value in which China could afford not to know anything that Japan produced worked in favor of Japan's intent to comment on and devise China as it saw convenient. Thus, the "descendants" were in control of the "ancestors," as they should always be in ontological terms.

NEGOTIATION WITH ANTHROPOLOGICAL FALLACIES

Precisely because of the contemporaneity of quotation and historicization, we should be careful not to claim the authenticity of our discourse over the past. Knowing is not a state in which one possesses facts that are transmitted from the referent to the referee. Knowing instead is a dynamic process that involves staging, framing, and displaying by the subject of knowledge production.

Joan Scott cuts directly into the self-righteousness of the subject of analysis who authenticates "experience" as autonomous from the politics surrounding the production of his/her text. She begins with a quotation from Theresa de Lauretis: "Experience [de Lauretis writes] is the process by which, for all social beings, subjectivity is constructed":

> The process that de Lauretis describes operates crucially through differentiation; its effect is to constitute subjects as fixed and autonomous, and who are considered reliable sources of a knowledge that comes from access to the real by means of their experience. When talking about historians and other students of the human sciences, it is important to note that this subject is both the object of inquiry—the person one studies in the present or the past—and the investigator him- or herself—the historian who produces knowledge of the past based on "experience" in the archives or the anthropologist who produces knowledge of other cultures based on "experience" as a participant observer.[18]

Scott elaborates on her definitions of subjectivity, agency, and discourse as follows:

> Subjects are constituted discursively, but there are conflicts among discursive systems, contradictions within any one of them, multiple meanings possible for the concepts they deploy. And subjects have agency. They are not unified, autonomous individuals exercising free will, but rather subjects whose agency is created through situations and statuses conferred on them. Being a subject means being "subject to definite conditions of existence, conditions of endowment of agents and conditions of exercise." These conditions enable choices,

though they are not unlimited. Subjects are constituted discursively, experience is a linguistic event (it doesn't happen outside established meanings), but neither is it confined to a fixed order of meaning. Since discourse is by definition shared, experience is collective as well as individual. Experience is a subject's history. Language is the site of history's enactment. Historical explanation cannot, therefore, separate the two.[19]

The subjectivity of engagement in a process has been foregrounded in metacritical studies in anthropology, among other fields. An increased awareness of the narrative agency helps problematize authentication of the content of stories. Telling the other's story in the third person, for example, neutralizes the position of the narrator and thus is authenticated as scientific, while the confessional mode of telling tends to be granted "naturalness." Mieke Bal, in her metacritical study of museums, exhibitions, and anthropological discourse, cogently argues that "expository writing" exposes the subject of writing as well as the object. One of the theorists whom Bal engages is Karen J. Warren, who comments justly on the use of "we," employed by critics to uncritically assume a shared privileged status between the writer and reader of cultural analysis, distinct from the object of analysis:

> The pronoun appeals to a solidarity between the speaker, the "I" who is a member of the group, and the other members. Thus it absorbs the position of the "you." The addressee is no longer the "you" whose task it is to confirm the "I"'s subjectivity, but who might also take his or her distance from what the "I" is saying. Instead the "you" becomes "one of us," a member of the group. The "I" no longer speaks to the "you" but in "you"'s name. The addressee loses the position from which he or she could criticize or disavow the speaker's utterance and is thereby manipulated into accepting the speech as her own. That acceptance is not rational but subliminally emotional; moralistic discourse works primarily through sentiment. The vague "we" is more often than not semantically fleshed out with moral superiority. The discourse of "we," lacking a "you," becomes binary, and the structure of "us" versus "them" is in working order.[20]

It would be presumptuous of "anthropologists" to assert that they themselves are exempt from the objectification that is conducted upon the objects of analysis. This very writing should not be exempted from this principle. I thus define my study not as a work of annotation, or "show-

ing," but as one of argumentation, or "telling." I do not purport to esoter-
ically present a body of knowledge that has been safely restored and
retrieved as though I were a select mediator. I instead try to reconfigure
information that has been known to many, in the hope of identifying several apparatuses in operation that produce and promote some perceptions of China and repress others. The narrative presented below is not
monolithic, as it consists of several stories corresponding to the apparatuses that partly conflict with or are irrelevant to one another. Instead of
matching each chapter to a distinct historical period and proposing a
metanarrative overarching all the chapters, I resort to a network of subjects that are defined and act according to different variables, while I am
invariably concerned with an imagined dyad between China and Japan in
Japanese literature. Consider the chapters that follow to be "scenes" witnessed from within the fold where I am also caught up.

NEGOTIATION WITH COMPARATIVIST FALLACIES

This study is not meant to compare Japanese literature with Chinese
literature in order to uncover similarities and differences between the
two, although it traces many attempts at such bifurcation. Such a comparison would necessitate essentialism, presuming, on the one hand, a distinct and sustained essence of each "entity" to be compared with the
other, and, on the other hand, a contextual vacuum in which I would assume a position transcending the respective conditions that informed
Japanese and Chinese literary theories and practices. The binary maintains a strong presence in this study, but it is not because I myself believe
in its validity; it is because the persistence and ubiquity of the binary as a
working hypothesis in Japanese literature is such that ignoring it would
only do injustice to the texts. It is not "polarity" itself that I maintain; it is
a sense of "twosomeness" in the texts themselves that needs to be acknowledged. I am not contradicting myself; I am simply willing to negotiate with the textual instances that contrast with my own beliefs.

Karen J. Warren has succinctly identified the problems of comparative rhetoric. She elaborates on the vital effects of binarism, or what she
terms "value dualism and subsequent disjunctive argumentation," as follows: "First, the multiple issues and positions, values and possibilities involved in a debate are reduced to two groups (reduction). Second, these
are polarized into two opposites (polarization). Third, the opposites are
hierarchized into a positive and negative (hierarchization). None of these
three moves is 'natural' or inevitable, yet all three are so commonly

applied that they easily appear so."[21] Another problem of the pervasive and yet arbitrary Sino-Japanese contrast is that it is placed in a contextual vacuum. The perceived *wa/kan* contrasts are so pervasive that they more or less exclude other players in the field such as Korea or Vietnam (to name two of the most relevant examples in the Japanese literary imagination) from the network of cultural exchange.[22] Furthermore, if there has to be a contrast, it does not have to involve competition. Binary oppositions are not givens; they are envisioned and proposed by agency. However, when one chooses to focus on a pairing and perceives a difference, it tends to be defined as a contrast, though it does not have to be. Instead of envisioning China and Japan as two discernible and opposing entities, I opt to imagine them as "two mobile positions," as Mieke Bal puts it, in an "entanglement"[23]—two processes of self-fashioning with or without constantly varying degrees of consciousness of the imagined cultural other(s), or, to put it differently, objectifications (including a lack thereof) that, in effect, invent self-consciousness and self-definition.

Such positioning of the self and the other precedes the establishment of identity on either side. Indeed, the desire to envision, evaluate, and relate (in both of the meanings of "relate" suggested by Ross Chambers— "connect" and "narrate")[24] seems to me primary, while the substance of the subject and object becomes secondary, constructed, and contingent. The "essence" of the subject does not precede its "entanglement" with the object but is only imagined from the operation of the contrasting act. Gilles Deleuze notes the following regarding the historical Baroque, and it is applicable to operations from any historical period: "The Baroque refers not to an essence but rather to an operative function, to a trait. It endlessly produces folds....Yet the Baroque trait twists and turns its folds, pushing them to infinity, fold over fold, one upon the other. The Baroque fold unfurls all the way to infinity."[25] The subject of observation is always already enfolded within the object, which presents itself invariably with the subject within it. Or one might echo Emmanuel Levinas and state that the Other, as opposed to the other, is not autonomous from the self, as alterity is supposed to be within the self.[26] The contrast between China and Japan should not be envisioned as a distance between two distinct entities but rather as an entanglement from which the subject and object are constructed as identifiable a priori.

Inspired by Bal's model of "two mobile positions in an entanglement" and drawing upon Gilles Deleuze as she does, I propose that Japan is like a sensitive subject wrapped in a blanket; it can and does change the shape of the blanket, its temperature, smell, and shade. It is hard to determine where the warmth and other sensual effects come from—whether from "China," the blanket, or "Japan," the body. Though it may feel as though the sensual effects are produced by the blanket and that these effects define the blanket, in fact they are coproduced by the blanket and the body—the object/subject. As the body tosses and turns, folds are made and unmade in the blanket. While the blanket might be feeling the warmth, sensing the smell, and seeing the color of the body (who knows?), its inanimate state is taken for granted and is not questioned.

A valid question is why I do not deal with perceptions of Japan in Chinese literature when I am inspired by Bal's metaphor of "two mobile positions in an entanglement." I do not do so precisely because of Bal's warning in *Double Exposures* against the complacent assumptions of neutral spectatorship; I resist the position of an omniscient and objective narrator of stories that both Japan and China have to tell about each other. Instead, I confirm my location on the plane of Japan (which itself is moving and changing), from where I look at "China" in its various and varying manifestations. Since "Japan" views its relationship with "China" while enclosed within "China," rather than standing at a point from which it commands an unrestricted and "perfect" view, its observations are not even, smooth, or structured so as to conform to one single norm. I am mindful of the disparity of the themes of the four chapters and the transactive nature of the Sino-Japanese knot.

Above I mentioned studies of the China-Japan binary, but I wish to stress that this work does not aspire to become their descendant and that there is no predecessor for what I am trying to achieve in this study. I do not contest any specific scholar's past work so as to draw attention to my work. Instead, I have listed a variety of possible approaches that I could have taken and decided not to take owing to the limitations that I illustrate. Contrasts are *hypothetically* made in order to define my work against what it is not. Furthermore, while I have strived to stay away from chronicling, archivalization, anthropologization, and comparison, I need to deal with numerous and recurrent such attempts throughout the Japanese literature that I tend to cover. There are constant references to Chinese influences, Chinese stereotypes, and comparative definitions of Japaneseness and Chineseness. Hence, the title "*Obsessions* with the Sino-Japanese Polarity in Japanese Literature." I suggest that it is not I (Sakaki) who is responsible for archivalization, anthropologization, or comparison. To differentiate myself from the speakers, narrators, and authors that I discuss, I hope that it will be sufficient if I simply identify the agents of such attempts. Since I quote frequently from the texts under discussion and cite the exact locations of the quotations, I trust that concerned readers will be able to see that I am no ventriloquist.

Overview of the Chapters

Chapter 1 examines how Japanese travelers in China and Chinese travelers in Japan are portrayed, viewed by other characters, and in turn observe themselves and members of their respective host countries in literary works by writers who did not themselves travel to China. We will see how contrasts and comparisons are made on little factual ground, to some epistemological effect, intended or otherwise, in texts such as *Tosa nikki* (A Tosa Journal, 935); *Hamamatsu chūnagon monogatari* (The tale of Middle Councilor Hamamatsu, ca. 1060); *Matsura no miya monogatari* (The tale of Matsura, 1201); *Kokusen'ya gassen* (The battles of Coxinga, 1715); and *Honchō Suikoden* (the Japanese version of *Shuihu zhuan* [The water margin], 1773).[27] The Sino-Japanese dyad, we will see, is at times presented in hierarchical or confrontational terms to serve Japan's claims to cultural autonomy and at other times to highlight its resilience in and adaptability to cultural transactions. The constructed contrast or alliance is constantly modified as the Chinese reception of Japan, as imagined by the Japanese authors, changes from sheer ignorance/indifference to antagonism to competitiveness. What is almost intrinsically involved in this bifurcation is the making and unmaking of the masculine/feminine dyad. Since the above-mentioned works center on Japanese male protagonists who encounter Chinese men and women, the last being potential romantic objects, they challenge the conventional contrast between the Chinese language as masculine and the Japanese language as feminine. Stories allow a variety of configurations of gender and ethnic elements as opposed to the stable dyad. When the theme of miscegenation in particular is introduced, the validity of specifying the two ethnic poles is itself radically put into question. I will show textual evidence of the concern with hybridity, even though the theme may appear to be typically contemporary, addressed by modern theorists such as Homi Bhabha. While the writers' notions of boundaries between China and Japan are obviously not informed by the modern ideology of nationalism or the modern discipline of geography—and it is important to note the epistemological difference—a distinction between the two countries, often (and aptly) visualized as the two shores of an ocean, had already been encoded in the minds of the authors from the tenth through the eighteenth centuries. The above-mentioned texts were already concerned with Chineseness and Japaneseness even when they problematized them.

An increasing awareness of the diversity of Chinese culture on the part of the Japanese forms a premise for chapter 2, which investigates Japan's objectification of the Chinese and their works of art from the eighteenth century onward. The Japanese gaze—scholarly or consumerist—is more noticeable when the focus of observation is not the literary canon, which had been taken as synonymous with Chinese culture. We will see how China, which had taught the Japanese how to fetishize objects of art, was itself changed into the object of fetishist adoration. In turn our study will illustrate both the changes and the persistent effects of the past in Japan's self-definition vis-à-vis China. With the introduction of a new element, the "West," into the entanglement, China became equated with the historical past, making the Japanese connoisseurs' position even more ambiguous regarding the conservation of literary topoi and the development of tourism. We will briefly examine the case of Aoki Masaru, a modern scholar of Chinese material culture who unveiled the slippery footing of the Japanese observer of China. The irony of the subject-object relationship is most eloquently captured by Tanizaki Jun'ichirō's work in the early twentieth century; it actively involves the fetishization of the Chinese female body as well as material goods. We will see that opportunities to visit and travel in China, which were not available to the authors examined in chapter 1, called for a revision rather than a renunciation of rhetorical configurations of Chineseness.

The intervention of gender as an inevitable factor in the formation and transformation of the Sino-Japanese dyad, which occasionally surfaces in chapters 1 and 2, is the theme of chapter 3. The chapter reveals how women Sinophiles were misrepresented or underrepresented in modern Japanese literary scholarship and journalism in order to establish a nativist and essentialist view of women's literature in accordance with nationalism, anti-intellectualism, and the male centrism of the time. I first examine both contemporary and later receptions of three women of Chinese letters—Murasaki Shikibu, Arakida Reijo, and Ema Saikō—who were active in fiction, historical narrative, and Chinese verse respectively, representing some of the fields in which women were not necessarily expected to be competent. In contrast with their contemporary male Sinophiles, who responded positively to their accomplishments, the nativist and nationalist reception of their work shows how Chineseness became engendered as masculine in the process of the formation of the literary canon as indigenous, natural, and feminine. We will then see how Mori Ōgai, a modern Sinophile, took advantage of the new equation of the feminine with the indigenous and painted a picture of the "New Woman" by drawing upon the legends of a Chinese intellectual woman. In the 1980s, when the engendered China/Japan dyad was almost neutralized, quotations from Chinese texts became instrumental to Kurahashi Yumiko, a contemporary female novelist who resisted the literary establishment's bias against women writing eruditely and engaging foreign literatures. A variety of factors surrounding female intellectuals and their positions vis-à-vis Chinese literature reveals both the contingency and tenacity of the Japanese association of Chineseness with masculinity.

While the dynamics of the Sino-Japanese dyad might have changed over time, the Japanese reception of Chinese literature does not necessarily rest upon the nostalgic glorification of a thing of the past. In fact, some Japanese took recourse to the Chinese literary tradition in order to resist modern nationalism's insistence upon the state's monopoly of culture and language. Chapter 4 focuses on early modern and modern Japanese representations of male and female intellectuals who would have been central in premodern cultural production and consumption but who were marginalized because of their insistence on the value of the classical Chinese canon and literary Chinese. The title of the chapter, "The Transgressive Canon?" aims at a displacement of the common definition of the canon—namely, the textual corpus that conforms to and confirms the establishment's doctrine. Once legitimized as such, the classical Chinese canon was dismissed in modern Japan as irrelevant to changing reality and as incommensurate with its mimetic representation, which was now defined as the mission of literature. However, the classical Chinese canon was exploited, effectively in some cases, by those who resisted the nationalist discourse and transcended national boundaries, now (unlike in the period covered in chapter 1) drawn by territorial consciousness. The term "transgressive" in the chapter thus suggests resistance both to the political institutional power that is normally thought to help form the canon and to the dominant rhetoric of "one nation, one language" that was behind canon formation in Meiji Japan. Shiba Shirō's *Kajin no kigū* and Nakamura Shin'ichirō's *Kumo no yukiki* are representative works of transnationalist intellectuals in the modern nation-state of Japan, both within and outside the text, whose diasporic positions are best manifested (rather than checked) by their mastery and exhibition of the classical Chinese heritage. They reveal the awareness of literary composition as a cultural, and thus transnational, practice rather than a transparent representation of "the natural" in one's mother tongue.

In place of a conclusion I offer a fast-paced coda to revisit the critical points I made in chapters 1–4 and to relocate them in yet another possible venue to test their validity—namely, in several pieces of Tanizaki Jun'ichirō's fiction that are better known than the short stories covered in chapter 2 or, for that matter, than any other text I visit in this study. The formulae showcased in the preceding chapters will shake the kaleidoscope, if you will, and will paint a different picture of these familiar texts. I expect the reader to realize that the functions of quotations from Chinese sources have been largely ignored or inaccurately labeled as part of Tanizaki's appreciation of the quintessential Japanese literary and artistic tradition. Instead of being noncodified references to things that happen to fill the backdrop of a story, Tanizaki's choice and use of Chinese sources prove to be strategic and ready to be theorized. The discovery of the production of effects in those well-known texts should lead the reader to review other examples with which he or she is familiar in order to renounce the widely accepted assumptions based on the Sino-Japanese dyad. The coda is thus intended as an invitation to a journey that each reader can now take in his or her own direction with the map that I have provided.

CHAPTER 1

Site Unseen

Imaginary Voyages to China and Back
in Classical Japanese Fiction and Theater

To see is to have seen. . . . A seer has always already seen. Having seen
in advance he sees into the future. He sees the future tense out of the
perfect.
—Martin Heidegger

Literature becomes the truth, essence, or self-consciousness of all other
discourses precisely because unlike them, it knows that it does not
know what it is talking about.
—Terry Eagleton

I n this chapter, I examine instances of the exoticization of China and
Chinese figures in fiction and theater written in *wabun* from the tenth
through the eighteenth centuries in order to identify reasons for
specific tropes of Chineseness where knowledge of China in the empirical sense was largely inaccessible.[1] This is not to say that Japan had no
contact with China; contrary to the conventional understanding, Japan
was hardly isolated from the continent. Although there was some political isolation, Japan maintained diplomatic relations with Parhae (Ch.
Bohai; J. Bokkai; today part of northeastern China and northern Korea;
698–926) and Korea, and these yielded many poetic exchanges among
diplomats and their hosts in Japan. Drifters and refugees flowed in from
the continent, especially at times of unrest (e.g., at the beginning of the
Yuan [1271–1368] and Qing [1616–1912] dynasties).[2] Japan pursued
mercantile relations, which were under the vigilance of the government
in the Muromachi and Tokugawa periods. And Zen (Ch. Chan) and
Ōbaku monks came from China, either invited by the Japanese government or sent by the Chinese authorities; among them were Mugaku
Sogen (1226–1286) and Issan Ichinei (1247–1317) in the Song (960–

18

1279) and Yuan dynasties and Yinyuan (J. Ingen; 1592–1673) in the Qing dynasty. Japanese visits to China, however, were limited to exceptional cases, such as those of selected Zen monks. Writings by travelers and their hosts in Japan are mostly in the genre of classical Chinese poetry, the shared literary language.

The authors of fictional travelogues whom I discuss in this chapter were neither authorities in Chinese nor travelers in China. Their textual and empirical resources being limited, they projected their own exotic infatuations onto the thoughts of their fictional Japanese sojourners, who were allegedly more educated in Chinese and more equipped with firsthand knowledge of China than they themselves. Instead of pointing a finger at the authors' erroneous understandings of Chinese geography and literature, as has been done in the past, I suggest identifying two layers of speech, the authors' and the characters', and concentrating on the latter so as to articulate the rhetorical configuration of China. Below I will briefly consider the authors, in theoretical rather than in historical terms, before moving on to the texts and the characters.

In considering authorial intent, we should account for the point of imagined referentiality when there is no object to which to refer. Instead of dismissing textual production in this period as fabrication, I suggest that we see it as the purest form of rhetorical configuration of China, a cognitive operation that may not be easily visible when overshadowed by business or diplomatic relations that may stand as "real" in the empirical sense.[3] That anthropological writing, in which "truth" is claimed, is rhetorical has long been noted. Take the following observation from Stephen Greenblatt:

> The sightings are important only in relation to what Columbus already knows and what he can write about them on the basis of that knowledge. If they fail in their promise, they will be demoted from the status of signs and not noticed any longer. It was, after all, the *known* world that Columbus had set out to discover, if by an unknown route: that was the point of reading Marco Polo and Mandeville. As Todorov writes, Columbus "knows in advance what he will find; the concrete experience is there to illustrate a truth already possessed, not to be interrogated according to preestablished rules in order to seek the truth."
>
> The paradox of the meaningful—or perhaps we can simply say the full—sign is that it is empty in the sense of hollow or transparent: a glass through which Columbus looks to find what he expects to find, or, more accurately

perhaps, a foreign word he expects to construe and to incorporate into his own language....The sign that Columbus cannot enfranchise, that is irreducibly strange or opaque, is *en route* to losing its status as a sign. For opacity here can only signal an obstacle standing in the way of the desired access to the known.[4]

What may appear to be firsthand, scientific, and authentic observation thus has to be construed within the language that precedes the experience. It is then not the anthropological writing (e.g., travelogues written by students and monks who actually visited China) that is transparent; it is the fantastic writing that is transparent, in the sense that it relies first and foremost on language, the primary experience for the authors. Thus, a study of quasi-travelogues should offer a most abstract theoretical model for studying other types of writing that retell the foreign.

The importation of Chinese classics and poetry had made the Japanese reading public familiar with China in rhetorical terms. Kawase Kazuma, one of the most proficient and prolific scholars of Sino-Japanese literature, says the following: "The creation of the so-called world of dreams and fantasy in the last years of the Heian period, represented by the author of *Sarashina nikki,* is inseparably tied with translation literature. An aspiration for the unseen, foreign land is an adoration for the world of fantasies."[5] Perhaps unwittingly, Kawase in effect suggests that a range of Sino-Japanese negotiations in translation and fantasy are framed by the same rhetoricity. While a translation of Chinese literature may be taken as a serious endeavor, aiming at accuracy and transparency, it is, like fantasies are, yet another impossible enterprise of configuring the other. Fantasies, on the other hand, are not generated out of nothing but out of a repertoire of rhetorical configurations made available by a variety of reading practices, including translation. That the Japanese reading knowledge of China varied from Chinese self-knowledge is not a matter of technical error but a matter of course: not only did the Chinese not compose their verse or prose so as to be understood by the Japanese, but the Japanese also became Japanese only in their entanglement with the Chinese, who represented the norm and thus stood at degree zero without requiring any definition. Japan located its own place by inventing a distance from China.

Kawase's statement reminds us of another important though obvious point involving the readership of the fictional travelogues in *wabun.* We can safely eliminate the Chinese, the objectified, from the list of expected and actual readers of such travelogues. In these stories the "contact zone" (to use Mary Louise Pratt's term) was mostly set in the land that was conventionally deemed the originator of cultural values and was thus superior, but the site of textual production and distribution was Japan.[6] The language of distribution was not that of the cultural center, but that of the cultural periphery, thus drawing an entirely different picture from that of colonial and postcolonial literature coming from the former European colonies. These fictional travelogues are unlike the anthropological literature in the age of imperialism, which was written in the language of the "civilized," who assumed that the perceived "primitives" that they studied would not be among their readers. Nor are they like postcolonial literature written in the colonizer's language by the colonized. That they were written in Japanese in effect denied the Chinese access to the texts. Japanese was of limited currency simply because it was not much needed, if at all, rather than being restricted for the use of only the privileged or being too difficult for the Chinese to learn. Few if any Chinese would deign to read Japanese travel fantasies; the Japanese authors knew that and took advantage of the virtual absence of a counterresponse from their object of study.

At the character layer of the texts, the gaze that dominates is not that of a colonizer, a connoisseur, or an ethnographer from the center of cultural hegemony—as is the case with colonial literature of the nineteenth and twentieth centuries—but that of a very select visitor from the cultural periphery.[7] This visitor has to submit to the judgment of the Chinese elite, who determine whether or not he meets cultural and social standards and is civil enough for their company. Praise for the individual who qualifies for honorary citizen status is often extended to his home country owing to the rarity of visitors from Japan. The alien nonetheless exoticizes and objectifies those he believes are superior. He has been granted a rare opportunity and is thus motivated and obligated to observe the cultural Other in order to repay his community of origin for the privilege that has been bestowed upon him. In his attempts to portray China, the traveler inevitably begins to define Japaneseness as well as Chineseness.

Attempts to define given attributes as typically Japanese predate the Japanese search for a cultural identity in the age of nationalism, as I will show by detailed commentaries on the texts. Characters in fiction and theater frequently made statements such as, "This is how the Japanese do this, unlike the Chinese," prior to the advent of nationalism. Whereas national territories were not delineated as they are in modern geography, the boundaries between the two "countries" were clearly drawn. I am not suggesting that there were essential entities that were distinct from each other as "Japan" and "China" (in fact I am opposed to that understanding), but I will reveal that, inconsistencies and inaccuracies notwithstanding, there was an obsession with contrasting what was Japanese from what was Chinese. My goal here is not to authenticate the theory that Japan and China were contrastive, but to reveal the persistence of the theory despite its flaws.

From the tenth to the eighteenth centuries, China remained the Other as Japan produced its many faces, corresponding to the faces of Japaneseness. Japan's relative political isolation helped accelerate the objectification of China as the symbolic Other. Tropes for China and the Chinese were elaborated, and the symbolic codes to manipulate the foreign were refined. Below we will see some examples of this compositional practice; they are consistent with the issues at stake, but they vary from one another in the way they negotiate with these issues. Inconsistencies, fluctuations in the intensity of engagement, and ambiguous implications do not mean a lack of negotiations but simply suggest the complexity, magnitude, and persistence of both confusion and a will to sort it out. The "fold" has not been even, consistent, or homogeneous, as it should not be.

Waves from Coast to Coast

A fictional memoir of a journey taken by a governor of Tosa and his company as he returns to the capital, *Tosa nikki*[8] plays with binary oppositions: male and female; Chinese and Japanese languages; public and private. While these pairs of oppositions may appear to simply parallel one another, it has been suggested that a closer look at the text reveals subtle transitions and inflections in subjectivity and diction that complicate the pat binary contrasts.[9] The alleged author, Ki no Tsurayuki (ca. 868–ca. 945), is known to have written a *kanajo*, the Japanese preface to *Kokin wakashū* (Anthology of Japanese poems old and new, 905);[10] in this preface he compares the functions of Chinese poetry (*shi*) and Japanese poetry (*yamato uta*), drawing upon ancient Chinese poetics such as those mapped out in *Maoshi daxu* (Great preface to the classics of poetry, sixth century BC). Scholars have recently revised if not refuted one longstanding interpretation of Tsurayuki's agenda—that is, that he tried to defend the position of Japanese poetry compared to Chinese poetry. John Timothy Wixted suggests that there may not be anything uniquely Japanese about the thesis Tsurayuki presented, while Thomas LaMarre argues that Tsurayuki aimed at coordination rather than hierarchization (as has often been interpreted) of the two poetic practices.[11] It is true that nothing in Tsurayuki's text goes beyond a defense of Japanese poetry according to Chinese poetics, nor does he suggest an outright rejection of the "Chinese influences" over the "indigenous." Nevertheless, the obvious fact that a comparison with Chinese poetry was called for in defense of Japanese poetry, while such a comparative operation did not take place in any manifesto of Chinese poetry (if ever it was felt needed), reveals the contingency of the binary between Chinese and Japanese poetic theory and practice. The awareness of the binary was felt only by the Japanese and not reciprocated by the Chinese.

The uneven entanglement manifests itself most prominently in a reference to Abe no Nakamaro (698–770), a Japanese student-turned-officer who visited Tang China during the reign of Emperor Xuanzong (685–762; r. 712–756), who kept him in China beyond his expected stay out of excessive favor. In the following passage, the speaker (an attendant of the governor who is set to leave for the capital) talks to the local residents who are seeing him off about the time when Nakamaro was about to return to Japan:

> The twentieth night's moon rose. With no mountain rim around, it came out of the sea instead. Indeed, it must have been something like this that a man called Abe no Nakamaro saw long ago. When he was to return to Japan from the China [Morokoshi] that he had visited, the Chinese people [kano kuni hito] gave a farewell party and composed Chinese poems [kashiko no karauta] at the port of departure. They must yet have been to be satisfied, as they stayed until the twentieth night's moon rose. The moon did come out of the sea. Seeing that, Nakamaro remarked: "This is a kind of a poem that deities in mythical times and human beings of all ranks compose on occasions like this, delighted or saddened, in my country [waga kuni]." And the poem read:
>
> Aounabara / furisake mireba /
> Kasuga naru / Mikasa no yama ni / ideshi tsuki kamo
>
> (As I gaze over / the blue expanse of the ocean / I find the moon—
> the moon that rose over Mount Mikasa / in Kasuga!)
>
> Though he thought the Chinese would not understand the concept, he wrote down the outline in Chinese characters and had the person who knew

Japanese [koko no kotoba] mediate the essence of the poem, and they seem to have understood the meaning and appreciated the poem beyond expectation. Though the languages are different in China and Japan [kono kuni], the moonlight is the same, so human emotions must be the same. Imagining how things must have been in the past, a certain person composed a poem as follows:

> Miyako nite / yamanoha ni mishi / tsuki naredo
> nami yori ide te / nami ni koso ire
>
> (In the capital / I saw the moon / above the mountain ridge;
> here it rises from waves / and sets into waves).[12]

While the speaker's slightly patronizing tone indicates the cultural hierarchy between the capital and the countryside within Japan, this version of Nakamaro's story attempts to reverse the hierarchy between China and Japan. Nakamaro, as portrayed here, speaks with the confidence of knowing more than his Chinese listeners, instructing them in the value of Japanese poetry (waka), which they have not been trained to appreciate, let alone compose. In this version of the story, China is characterized as culturally poorer than Japan, lacking the art of waka composition. The Chinese, who are monolingual, are regarded as lacking the versatility of the Japanese, who are bilingual. This neutralization of the hierarchy between the cultural center and the periphery is reconfirmed when the contrast between the miyako (capital) and hina (rural areas; specifically Tosa) is superimposed on the contrast between kono kuni (this country) or koko (here; in this case, Japan) and kano kuni (that country) or kashiko (there; i.e., China) as the departure point and destination of travel.

This is not to say that the speaker suggests Japan is superior to China; rather, he states that the Chinese and Japanese hold the same ideals, just as they both appreciate the moon. It is not as though Japan were the country from which the moon rises; the moon rises "from the sea," the neutral zone between the two distant shores. Still, given that China could afford to be monolingual while Japan could not, the proposed universality of Japanese poetry is a trace of the Japanese desire to move from the status of inferior to equal. Thus, the elevation of Japanese poetry is obvious in terms of the trajectory of the movement rather than in the position that it aspires to occupy.

The suggestion in this text that Abe no Nakamaro composed both Japanese poetry (waka) and Chinese poetry (kanshi), to which Chinese poets responded with *shi,* tends to be ignored. Nakamaro was instated into the community of Chinese literati precisely because of his mastery of the Chinese language and his ability to compose in it. Far from being respected for his advocacy of the value of Japanese poetry, as is suggested in *Tosa nikki,* Nakamaro was a cosmopolitan intellectual who transcended national boundaries. His departure for Japan occasioned the composition of a farewell poem by Wang Wei (699–759), and his reported death in a shipwreck was elegized by Li Bai (701–762), a fact registered in both China and Japan and showing that Nakamaro's status was high enough to draw the attention of China's most prominent poets. Moreover, *Wenyuan yinghua* (Flowers of distinction in the garden of literature, 987), an imperially commissioned anthology of Chinese poetry from the Liang (502–557) through the Tang (618–907) dynasties, has a poem by Nakamaro in Chinese.[13] The piece, a five-character, eight-line regulated poem, expresses the speaker's profuse gratitude for the Chinese emperor's favors and adds a small mention of his parents in Japan, which is only appropriate, given that the poem was composed in Chinese and in China.

We now turn to a Chinese-language text produced in Japan, *Gōdanshō* (early twelfth century), a collection of episodes about historical Japanese figures recounted by Ōe no Masafusa (1041–1111).[14] It too does not portray Nakamaro as a *waka* advocate but as a culturally Sinified individual entrapped in the rivalry between the Chinese and Japanese. In this version, instead of failing to return to Japan because of a shipwreck (as is documented in the sources noted), Nakamaro was imprisoned in a tower in China and starved to death. Kibi no Makibi (695?–775), visiting China as ambassador (as documented in history), meets with the same treatment by the Chinese authorities. The Chinese are ashamed because Makibi demonstrates a superior mastery of Chinese literature and art, so much so that they decide not to let him return to Japan and instead lock him up in the same tower so that he will die of starvation. The ghost of Nakamaro exerts his supernatural powers to tell Makibi that the Chinese plan to test him with Chinese texts and helps him fly to the site at which Chinese scholars discuss *Wenxuan* (Literary collection, sixth century), a book that, *Gōdanshō* tells us, was not yet known to the Japanese, so that he can prepare for the test.[15] Makibi manages to pass the test, so he is further challenged with Buddhist texts and games of chess. He surmounts these challenges one way or another, once with the help of Sumiyoshi, the god of the military and of Japanese poetry whose defense of the Japanese recurs in Japanese literary history, as we will see below in this chapter. Whereas the implicit rivalry in *Gōdanshō* between the Chinese and Japanese may resonate with the Nakamaro episode in *Tosa nikki*, the fact that none of the texts used for Makibi's tests are indigenously Japanese tells us that it was not an issue whether or not Nakamaro was able to exhibit his mastery of the Japanese arts, let alone defend the value of Japanese poetry vis-à-vis Chinese poetry.

Another episode in *Gōdanshō* functions as an even more explicit antithesis to the portrayal of Nakamaro as an advocate of *waka*. Recounted in the format of a dialogue between a master and his disciple, the episode quotes the *waka* by Nakamaro that we noted above and then questions the propriety of Nakamaro's composing in Japanese, as there may have been "a taboo" that one must not compose *waka* while in China.[16] The episode does not cite any regulation against the practice, but the very fact that it struck mid-Heian Japanese Sinophiles (including the author of *Gōdanshō* and its prospective readers) as odd for Nakamaro to compose a *waka* reveals their understanding of this Japanese historical figure: he was the embodiment of proficiency in Chinese literature rather than an advocate of the ethnolingual.[17]

One condition that notably persists in these anecdotes surrounding Abe no Nakamaro (among other Japanese historical literati who were known to the Chinese either in reality or in the Japanese literary imagination) is the fact that the site of an encounter, whether materialized or not, is often a shore—either in China or in Japan. This suggests that national boundaries were envisioned as coastlines rather than as a complete delineation of territories—understandably so, as these stories were written before the time of cartography. As LaMarre argues, drawing upon Benedict Anderson, the concept of territoriality is historically modern.[18] The title words of *Hamamatsu* and *Matsura* in the texts to be discussed below also denote points of departure/arrival. This cognition of spatiality allows individuals of dual loyalty to redefine their identities as they embark or disembark from a ship—as happens repeatedly in the texts discussed below.[19]

A Beautiful Stranger

In the *wabun* fiction and theater pieces under discussion here, a newcomer from Japan is put to initial "tests" of his adaptability to the society of the Chinese elite, though the tests are not as excruciating as were the ones in the *Gōdanshō* episode about Kibi no Makibi. The visitor must meet Chinese expectations in poetic composition, musical performance, and physical appearance in order to be welcomed into the circle of the privileged. The protagonists in such classical Japanese works excel in the arts and are exceedingly handsome, and thus they pass the tests with flying colors. The hero of *Hamamatsu chūnagon monogatari* (hereafter *Hamamatsu*) is no exception.[20] His reception in China is most enthusiastic, possibly recalling the way Abe no Nakamaro might have been received in reality (rather than the way he was received in the episode we saw). Once having passed the "tests" with his extraordinary individual merits, he makes the hearts throb of Chinese men and women alike. In this way, he differs radically from his literary successor, the lieutenant in *Matsura no miya monogatari*, who, as we will see below, disturbs the peace of the Chinese rather than fascinating them.

"Hamamatsu" (which also appears in the tale's alternative title, *Mitsu no Hamamatsu*), is a poetic word literally meaning "pines on the shore," and, with the pun of *matsu* also meaning "to wait," it implies both a Japanese beach as a stage of Sino-Japanese travels and longings felt by those who are left there, if not those who have left from there.[21] The title thus suggests that this story is about a Japanese man who visits China and is missed by his loved ones in Japan. Despite the connotations, however, the focus of the story, at least in the currently available version (which is missing its first book), appears to be more on the protagonist's relationships with people in China, which affect him deeply, even after his return to his native land. This is partly because the protagonist's associates in China are not exclusively Chinese but are partly of Japanese ancestry, and partly because lingual boundaries are often crossed and recrossed. The Sino-Japanese contrasts are thus not as articulately staged as in *Tosa nikki* and are instead complicated with themes of miscegenation, transnational reincarnation, and the shared practice of composition and reception of literature in Chinese.

The protagonist, the Middle Councilor, decides to travel to China out of filial piety in order to find the reincarnation of his deceased father, who is now an imperial prince of China. Though the Middle Councilor thus does not formally represent Japan as government-sent students and diplomats did, he nonetheless goes through a similar appraisal once in China and is deemed distinguished in three areas: the composition of *wen* (high literary prose), musical performance, and physical (specifically facial) appearance, which the Chinese emperor considers more handsome than that of the legendary Chinese beau, Hakukan (commonly annotated as a misromanization of Pan Yue 潘岳 [247–300], whose standard Japanese reading is "Han Gaku") of Kōyō (likewise a mistranscription of Heyang, which should be read in Japanese as "Kayō," 河陽 or, in an even more domesticated reading, "Kaya"). If correctly cited, the analogy with the literary topos and icon foreshadows the location of the Middle Councilor's encounter with his reincarnated father and the prince's mother, Kōyō Ken no Kisai (Consort in the District of Heyang) and the possibility that the story will develop into romance.

These "errors" in transcribing Chinese proper nouns are usually attributed to the alleged author's (or any of the copiers') shaky knowledge of the language; the alleged author, Sugawara no Takasue no musume (Daughter of Sugawara no Takasue, 1008–?), is a sixth-generation offspring of Sugawara no Michizane (845–903), a paragon of Sinophilia accomplished in poetry, learning, and bureaucracy, as dictated by the Chinese. The Sugawaras were a family of scholars (monjōdō), one of three families from which university professors of Chinese poetry, prose, and history were normally appointed by the imperial government from the late Heian period on. The author's family history and upbringing are conflicting factors that we need to consider in order to determine her proficiency in Chinese. Not only was she deprived of opportunities to study Chinese institutionally because she was a woman, but she was also brought up partly in the countryside (in Hitachi, where she lived with her father, who was governor), where resources to study Chinese informally may have been limited.[22] Since much of her life remains unknown beyond the contents of her memoir, Sarashina nikki (Memoir of an aging woman, mid-eleventh century) and since the attribution of authorship of Hamamatsu to her remains hypothetical, if quite likely, I suggest that we interpret the "errors" in terms of their effects on the audience rather than the results of authorial deficiencies.[23] The "mispronounced" names could also attest to attempts to reproduce the foreignness, which had been erased in the process of domesticating the words' readings. Once incorporated into the Japanese vocabulary, "Han Gaku" and "Kayō"/"Kaya" ceased to sound as exotic as they used to. To refer to Pan Yue as "Haku Kan" or to Heyang as "Kōyō" would restore the exotic sounds of the proper nouns, especially for the ears of an audience less proficient in Chinese. Authenticity might have been lost, but it was still projected and perceived.

Indeed, Kayō or Heyang was so familiar to the Japanese readers of Chinese poetry that they bestowed the name on the Japanese place of

Yamazaki (in present-day Otokuni-gun, Kyoto), considering it equivalent to Kayō as a place of interest.[24] *Bunka shūrei shū* (Anthology of poetry of distinction, 818), an imperially commissioned three-volume anthology of *kanshi,* has a sequence called "Kayō jūei" (Ten poems on Kayō/Heyang), consisting of poems composed by Emperor Saga (786–842; r. 809–823) at and about Yamazaki Imperial Villa (Yamazaki Rikyū), which was also called Kayō Kyū (Heyang Palace).[25] The palace was a site of many *kanshi* and *waka* compositions and was visited by Ariwara no Narihira (825–880), among other men of letters of the day. While Narihira is known to have been inadequate in Chinese learning, many of his contemporary *waka* poets were also proficient in *kanshi* composition, as their poems in this anthology attest.[26] Given that *Hamamatsu* was intended for readers who may or may not have been proficient in *kanshibun,* the place name, if rightly spelled, must have evoked for them Yamazaki rather than Heyang, thus in effect making them feel as though a place name had been exported from Japan to China. "Kayō" or "Kaya" is thus not simply the historical place name in China, but also an example of the "fold"—once again to use Gilles Deleuze's terminology—with the Japanese reinvention of the place enclosed in the word as an anticipation of the audience's response. The unorthodox romanization of the place name, however, gives yet another twist to the fold as the spelling reexoticizes and defamiliarizes the name for the audience.

Another "fold" in which Japanese subjectivity and Chinese objectivity are lost and found only in an entanglement" with each other is the Middle Councilor's observation of Chinese women's recitation of *fumi,* or Chinese texts. He says: "I wonder if Chinese women do not compose Japanese poems *(uta)* as men do; the women recite from literature in Chinese when they see blossoms."[27] While this interior monologue may immediately propose a gender/language, competence/function dichotomy (men-bilingual-poets versus women-monolingual [native language only]-readers), a closer look at the texts recited by the Chinese women redirects our attention. Young ladies-in-waiting who serve the Heyang consort recite a phrase, "Ransei-en no arashino" (the storm in the garden of fragrant orchids), which is excerpted from a poem composed by Kan Sanbon, the Sinified pen name of Sugawara no Fumitoki (also called Funtoki; 899–981), a Japanese poet and courtier. Two lines of the same poem, including the quoted phrase ("After the storm in the garden of fragrant orchids crushed the purple flowers, the moon shone on these [flowers: chrysanthemums] among the frost in the Immortals' Palace"), are collected only in Japanese sources such as *Wakan rōeishū* (ca. 1012) and *Gōdanshō*.[28] In reality it was not expected that Chinese women would be familiar with this text, or for that matter any texts written by Japanese authors, even in Chinese. Indeed, there are no *kanshi/shi* in *Hamamatsu* other than those collected in anthologies edited in Japan (including those originally composed by Chinese poets). This "misrepresentation" might in effect showcase a "counter-importation" of Chinese composition practice mastered by the Japanese. That this may simply be a reflection of wishful thinking on the part of the author is beside the point in our context. The point is that Chinese figures observed by the Japanese are already accustomed to Chinese poems authored by the Japanese, who had previously acquired the Chinese language. This is an exemplary case of the "fold" in Deleuzean terms.

Yet another example of neutralizing the evaluative dichotomy between the Japanese and Chinese materializes as *Hamamatsu*'s Chinese characters are described as able to compose *waka*. While this is in part to cater to an audience less competent in Chinese and in part to compensate for the alleged author's lack of reading knowledge in Chinese, it also contributes to a uniquely hypothetical platform on which the Chinese and Japanese can communicate with each other in a language/literary practice other than the then universal Chinese. The earliest example of *waka* composition in *Hamamatsu* appears right after the above-mentioned recitation of a Japanese-composed *shi* line. The Middle Councilor wonders whether or not Chinese women compose poems as men do. With that question in mind, he challenges the Heyang consort to see if she can compose an impromptu *waka* in response to one he composes. His poem says something to the effect that his homesickness is assuaged by *kono hana*, or "this flower," which is an allusion to a chrysanthemum, the flower that he submits to the consort with his poem. The allusion was made famous by lines from a poem by Yuan Zhen (779–831), collected in *Wakan rōeishū*, which singled out the chrysanthemum as the last flower remaining in bloom until the end of autumn.[29] The consort then responds by offering both a fan to accept the flower (a gesture that strikes the Middle Councilor as Japanese) and a *waka* that answers his question.[30] This scene offers another example of the fold, suggesting that Japanese is also a universal language, and it renounces the *Tosa nikki* thesis that the monolingual and Japanese-illiterate Chinese are culturally more limited than the bilingual and Chinese-proficient Japanese.

Such intricacies of the entanglement in translingual practice are eclipsed on the textual surface by ostentatious Sino-Japanese contrasts in which the two cultures are portrayed as essentially contrastive entities. The character who exhibits Chineseness most evidently is the minister's fifth daughter, who falls for the Middle Councilor. She is not alone in wishing for a relationship with him; the Japanese man's distinction, which, as noted, has even impressed the emperor, makes him popular among members of the nobility who have eligible daughters. High-ranking courtiers wish to marry their daughters to him "even though he is a temporary resident from another country" (takoku no karisome no hito naritomo).[31] The reincarnated father of the Middle Councilor is concerned that any bonding may result in keeping him in China, despite his responsibilities back home, and counsels him against becoming involved with Chinese women. The Minister, however, tries to coax him into marrying his fifth daughter and treats him to an extravagant feast. Perplexed, the Middle Councilor questions the Minister's third son, who tells him outright that his sister is lovesick for him and has said that a glimpse of the Middle Councilor would cure her of the ailment. The Middle Councilor is appalled by the direct mode of speech and compares this lack of reserve with Japanese manners and customs, which are characterized by euphemism. He tries to let the daughter down gently, and in the process he observes that unlike Japanese women, she is not shy about exposing her figure beyond the screen and that she speaks only in Chinese. Unfavorable comparisons are made with the Heyang consort, whose remarkable qualities are defined as Japanese, as we saw briefly and will see in more detail below. He tries to stay on the fifth daughter's good side, giving her his flute and sending her letters, partly in consideration of her father's infamous temper. The failure to make a match is taken surprisingly lightly by the Chinese side: the daughter feels better after seeing the handsome Japanese man, and the Minister is thankful to him for helping improve his daughter's health. Throughout, the tone employed to portray the Chinese characters in the Minister's family is amicable and yet comedic, with little reverence for the candor of the Chinese. The contrasts made between Japanese and Chinese customs also seem to suggest a reversal of the cultural hierarchy: in contrast to the established ladder of value, Japan is viewed as civilized, elaborate, and complex and China as unsophisticated, rough, and simple.

That the protagonist's father is reincarnated as a Chinese child is also a microcosmic metaphor of the Japanese mastery of the Chinese arts (a mastery embodied by the Middle Councilor), placing Japan on a par with China, if not implying that Japan has become superior. Ancestors, biological or cultural, have become intellectually inferior to or incompatible with their descendants. Though the prince is superior in rank and is also portrayed as bright and thoughtful for his age, such a judgment is made by the Middle Councilor, the grown-up and well-educated observer. Genealogy is thus inverted; the cultural descendant (Japan) is equipped with the wisdom and judgment that comes with age. Precocious as the prince/father may be—as is evident in his discretion in keeping secret his previous life and in the composure with which he reveals the truth to his mother in this life—he cannot develop any further meaningful relationship with the Middle Councilor.

The focus of the story thus shifts to the prince's mother, the consort of Heyang District. The theme of Sino-Japanese relations is developed further as the consort admits to the Middle Councilor that she is half Japanese; she was born to a member of the Chinese royalty visiting Japan on a diplomatic mission and a daughter of a Japanese minister exiled in Tsukushi.[32] The consort is portrayed first as pleasing to the eye *despite* her Chinese coif and clothes, which make other Chinese women too formal and magnificent to be personable, and then, after the revelation of her hybridity, as outstandingly Japanese.[33] She is feminine (*taoyaka*), personable (*natsukashi*), forgiving (*yawaraka*), and enticing (*namameki*)[34]— characteristics that are accounted for by her upbringing: she was raised by her Japanese mother until she traveled back to China with her father at the age of five.

The emperor's favoring of the consort predictably elicits the jealousy of the other consorts—so much so that the consort retreats from the imperial palace and into the Heyang District. The emperor's devotion to the Heyang consort is said to "almost compare to the old instance of Yang Guifei" (Yōkihi to iu mukashi no tameshi hiki ide nu bekari keru o).[35] This is an almost verbatim repetition of a phrase in the "Kiritsubo" chapter of Lady Murasaki's *Genji monogatari* (Yōkihi no tameshi mo hiki ide tsu beku nari yuku ni), in which courtiers express their concern with the Kiritsubo consort's monopoly of the emperor's love by comparing her with Yang Guifei, who distracted Emperor Xuanzong from his duties as a ruler, to disastrous effect.[36] Thus, textually, the Heyang consort is more closely associated with the Kiritsubo consort in *Genji* than with the original Chinese archetype. This is another instance of the counterimportation of a Chinese literary model domesticated in Japanese literary practice: while it seems only consistent with and confined within a Chinese domestic literary imagination for Chinese courtiers to compare the Heyang consort to Yang Guifei on the diegetic level, the comparison in effect invites the Japanese reader to identify the allusion specifically as the one in *Genji monogatari,* where the almost precise phrasing of the analogy with Yang Guifei originates. The Chinese characters share a rhetorical expression that was (re)made within Japanese literary practice and counterimported.

In fact the Heyang consort's fortunes seem less closely akin to those of Yang Guifei than to those of Lingyuan Qie (Concubine at the Imperial Grave) or Shangyang Baifaren (Gray-Haired Lady in Shangyang Palace), two consorts who were assigned to parts of the imperial properties that were not visited by the emperor.[37] The Heyang consort's story, however, differs from that of the two deserted concubines, as she does not spend the rest of her postwithdrawal life in sheer isolation. The emperor pays frequent visits to her and to the prince that she has taken with her; the Middle Councilor sees these visits as a display of freedom not allowed Japanese royalty. What is more reminiscent of Japanese romance—suffice it to cite as an example *Ise monogatari,* which narrates Narihira's adulterous and blasphemous transgressions involving an imperial consort-to-be and a great priestess of the Ise Shrine—and is undoubtedly of greater importance in this story is that the consort becomes involved with the Middle Councilor. Though *Ise monogatari* is often thought to be a quintessentially Japanese classic that defined aesthetic sensibility for the works to come,[38] its negotiations with Chinese texts such as *Benshi shi* (Tales of poems, 886) and *You xian ku* (Excursion to the Immortals' Cave, end seventh century?; attributed to Zhang Wencheng [ca. 660–ca. 740]) are well known.[39] The last is particularly relevant in our context, as it tells of a male traveler's fleeting affair with two mysterious women. Thus, we might say that the *Ise*-reminiscent affair in *Hamamatsu* presents another example of the counterimportation of Japanese renditions of Chinese texts, though the link is much more subtly suggested.

The double enclosure of Chinese and Japanese cultural products is appropriate as the pretext for the Middle Councilor's affair with the mysterious Chinese woman, later identified as the Heyang consort incognito. First, the beautiful setting of San'in (Ch. Shan'yin) reminds the Middle Councilor of Wang Ziyou (?–388?) who is said to have lived in a place of the same name and enjoyed looking at the moon. According to legend, Wang took a boat to visit a friend so as to share with him the pleasure of moon viewing while the moon's beauty (and his interest) lasted, but he left, without meeting his friend, when daylight came. The legend epitomizes the prioritization of aesthetics over socialization.[40] The reference is another example of domesticated Chinese sources being brought back again to China, as the story is known to *waka* and *wabun* readers in Japan through the venue of *Kara monogatari* (Tales of China, twelfth–thirteenth centuries), an anthology of twenty-seven anecdotes whose partial function is to educate Japanese readers who are less competent in Chinese about Chinese legendary figures who are commonly the subjects of poems.[41]

The Middle Councilor then recollects a similar occasion with his first love, Ōigimi, and her father back in Japan. The nostalgic longing for the lover at home, as well as the native land, leads to his fatal attraction to an unidentified woman who "looks nothing short of like a woman of his own country" (waga yo no hito ni tsuyu bakari tagau tokoro naku) in that she is feminine *(taoyakani)*, personable *(natsukashiku)*, and enticing *(nama-meki)*[42]—the same epithets previously used to describe the consort. Since the woman is indeed the consort, the choice of attributes is only natural. The point here is that while Japaneseness and Chineseness are identified as contrastive qualities, they can be evoked in an individual who, as is the case here, may happen to be *understood* as Chinese. The nationality of the subject does not predetermine his or her characteristics in cultural terms; cultural attributes go beyond national identities.

The Middle Councilor's attachment to this unidentified woman makes it difficult for him to set out for Japan as initially planned. Concurrently, the Heyang consort suddenly leaves her remote palace and hides in a place called Shokuzan with her father, a retired minister. Her unaccounted for action is owing to her pregnancy, a result of her clandestine affair with the Middle Councilor. She plans to give birth to the baby in secret before she returns to court. The emperor invites the Middle Councilor on the seventh night of the seventh month—the night of the yearly tryst of star-crossed lovers in East Asian tradition—to join him in poetic composition and musical performance to disperse the emperor's loneliness now that his favorite mistress is gone—a sentiment that is well understood by the Japanese man who wishes he could see the mysterious "Chinese" woman again. Little does he know that the two men are in fact missing the same woman. This fact, which only the narrator and reader know, is ironically illustrated when the two men compose *waka*, drawing upon oft-quoted lines from Bai Juyi's (772–846) "Changhenge" (The song of lasting sorrow): "In the sky let us be a pair of birds flying together with each other's wings parallel / On earth let us be a pair of boughs entwining each other."[43] From the emperor's viewpoint, the association of Yang Guifei with the Heyang consort is obviously appropriate because separation is involved in both cases. The analogy also echoes the earlier quotation of Yang Guifei.[44] Here the Middle Councilor as the immediate audience for the emperor's poem is not unlike the wizard in the Bai Juyi song: he is a third party sympathetic with the lover longing for the departed soul. When the Middle Councilor composes his own poem, however, his role in the allusion to the legendary romance shifts from observer to protagonist. Even though his poem is to be understood by his audience (the emperor) as a vicarious composition, representing the emperor's position, the reader knows the Middle Councilor's own emotions inspired the poem. His association of the mysterious woman with Yang Guifei is also appropriate; he feels as though the poignancy of his separation from his lover is comparable to Xuanzong's dismay that he is separated from his favorite concubine by death. Without knowledge of the true situation, however, the Middle Councilor is only echoing the emperor's analogy between the Heyang consort and Yang Guifei.

Indeed, the parallel between Yang Guifei and the Heyang consort sheds light on the latter's past and future. It is predicted that she will be reborn in Japan as the child of her Japanese half-sister. According to Japanese popular legends, Yang Guifei was the reincarnation of a Japanese deity and then reincarnated again after her death in China as yet another Japanese deity. Thus the suggested hybridity of Yang Guifei matches the biographical background and fortune of the consort.

The ambiguous identity of the consort is masked, however, by the emperor during a farewell party for the Middle Councilor on Middle Autumn Night, the Fifteenth Night of the Eighth Month. The Heyang consort has been recalled to the palace after having delivered a son. The emperor regrets that the Middle Councilor has not seen anything remarkable while in China and that he will have nothing to say in praise of China to his fellow countrymen in Japan. Then the emperor conceives the idea that the Heyang consort's skills in playing the *kin* (Ch. *qin*) would do honor to China if presented to the foreign guest. Thus, the arrangement is made but on one condition: the consort must not reveal her identity. The emperor is concerned that it may be considered inappropriate in the foreign country that the imperial consort entertained the foreign guest. Thus, the consort plays the *kin* in the guise of a low-ranking lady-in-waiting. The emperor is satisfied with the consort's performance and the success of the masquerade, while he does not know that he has unwittingly presented the Middle Councilor's lover as *herself*; had the emperor presented her as the consort, then the Middle Councilor would have simply confirmed a remarkable resemblance between the *two* women. The Middle Councilor, who does not know that the woman with whom he had an affair is the consort, is shocked to see the woman he loves miraculously before his eyes. While he is struck with her resemblance to the consort in terms of both physical appearance and performance style, he cannot see the two as identical simply because the woman playing the *kin* is presented as a servant, and he would not expect the consort herself to perform in his honor. The consort is the only one who knows that she is playing the role of a low-ranking woman for both of the men but for quite different effects: to conceal her true identity from the Middle Councilor upon the emperor's command and to *reveal* her false identity to him.

The guest of honor, emotionally moved, accompanies the consort on the *biwa* (Ch. *pipa*), which highly impresses the emperor. His words of praise—"The Middle Councilor must be the best and unparalleled man in Japan; the consort, incomparably beautiful in my country"[45]—implies much more than he is aware: the Middle Councilor, as the best Japanese man, and the Heyang consort, as the best *Chinese* woman, are paired together. The emperor fails to recognize the consort's dual identity, in terms of both ethnicity (half Chinese, half Japanese) and relationships (involved with both of the men). He displays her as an emblem of the best of Chinese culture while viewing the Middle Councilor as her Japanese counterpart. Ironically, the emperor's attempt to match the Japanese guest's distinction with the pride of China is hollow in intention and effect, despite the brilliantly successful performance. The Middle Councilor and Heyang consort had an affair that was triggered by the consort's Japanese qualities, which are ignored, if not denied, by the emperor. Furthermore, the emperor's phrase, "as though seeing the sun and the moon parallel to each other" (tsukihi no hikari o narabete min kokochi shite),[46] betrays his intent, as it echoes Fujitsubo and Genji's parallel brilliance as described in the "Kiritsubo" chapter of *Genji monogatari*.[47] The allusion functions both to confirm the adultery between the two characters and to signal another instance of the neutralization of the China-Japan dichotomy: in the resonance of the Fujitsubo-Genji pairing, the consort *becomes* Japanese.

As the part of the story set in China nears its close, another bonding of the Middle Councilor with China is introduced so as to tighten the linkage among chapters. He is given new reasons to long for China even after accomplishing his initial goal of reuniting with his father. A female

relative of the consort finally reveals to the Middle Councilor the identity of the hitherto unidentified woman, as well as her secret delivery of
the illegitimate son. While slightly annoyed by her lack of discretion, a
trait he considers distinctly Chinese ("waga yo no hito naraba ima ni
nari te kaku arawashi ide zara mashi o": a Japanese would not reveal that
at this point),[48] the Middle Councilor reasons that his resolve to visit
China (despite the fact that he had to desert his lover and his mother) is
owing to Buddhist retribution from a previous life and is manifested in
the birth of a son in China. He decides to take the son to Japan with him,
just as the Heyang consort's father decided to take his daughter with
him from Japan when he returned to China. The theme of a parent's separation from a child, a fate that the consort's mother had to endure, is
now to be repeated. In such an application of Buddhist karmic reincarnation, retribution and bonding between parent and child, the distance
between China and Japan is paralleled with the distance between this
life and the previous one and with the distance among generations. The
axis of temporality is superimposed onto that of spatiality, as is often the
case with Japan's positioning of China, except that in this case China is
not necessarily cast in the older/ancestral role. Hierarchy by age is re-
versible, and precisely because of that, bonding and separation repeat
themselves, oscillating between the poles of China and Japan.

The minister's fifth daughter, who earlier functioned only to illustrate foreignness with her forwardness and incompetence in Japanese, re-
appears now to demonstrate her compositional skills in Japanese poetry
as well as musical skills in playing the *biwa*. She responds to the Middle
Councilor's *waka* with another *waka*. The Middle Councilor's *waka* is a
parody of Abe no Nakamaro's:

Hinomoto no / yama yori iden / tsuki mitemo /
mazuzo koyoi wa / koishikaru beki

(I shall longingly remember this evening
when I see the moon rise over the hills in Japan)

While Nakamaro's *waka* is about the homesickness he feels when seeing
the moon, which he once saw rising from the tip of Mount Mikasa in Japan, the Middle Councilor's is a poem predicting that even when he is
back in Japan and sees the moon rise above Japanese mountains, he will
be fondly reminded of the fifth daughter and the evening they spent

together watching the moon rise in China.[49] One *waka* is simply nostalgic, recalling the past, while the other is hypothetically and prospectively
nostalgic, imagining how the speaker might feel about the present moment, which will be a part of the past in the future. In spatial terms, the
earlier poem is again simply nostalgic—the poet misses his home when
he is far from there—while the newer poem reverses the direction of nostalgia by hypothesizing a longing for a foreign land when the poet has returned to his place of origin. Thus, the Middle Councilor's parody of the
Nakamaro poem effectively renounces the order of value between the
homeland (Japan) and the foreign land (China), as well as the chronological order that puts the past and the future at opposite poles.

Upon returning to Japan, the Middle Councilor takes great pains to
hide his son from the public eye and searches clandestinely for the consort's
mother, who now lives in the mountains of Yoshino, to give her a keepsake
(letter box) with which he has been entrusted. The discretion and reserve
that he exercises are the very qualities he did not find in his Chinese acquaintances. Ironically, despite his Japaneseness, he feels isolated from the
Japanese and attached to his lover in China. He shares secrets with his Chinese lover and keeps them from his Japanese friends. His homecoming
does not release him from the tensions of being in a foreign country but
charges him with new duties that he must assume for the sake of his foreign
friends. The location of his loyalty and belonging is thus ambiguous.

The Middle Councilor's first meeting with the Japanese emperor
upon his return illustrates his new status in the court as a result of his
journey. The emperor is particularly impressed by the councilor's aston-
ishing and divine appearance (asamashiu kono yo no mono narazu).[50]
While the emperor is overwhelmed with joy to see the Middle Councilor,
whose exceptional talents were missed at court, the returnee is brimming
with mixed emotions: gratitude for the emperor's favor, a longing for
home he felt while in China and that he now remembers, and a longing
for China, as a musical performance in the emperor's presence reminds
him of the occasion when he first heard the consort play the *biwa*. In the
subsequent exchange of *waka* between the emperor and the Middle
Councilor, the latter's "multifolded" mind comes across to the reader, in
contrast with the emperor's straightforward appreciation of the reunion
with the returnee, which is evident in the emperor's poem:

> Wakare te wa / kumoi no tsuki mo / kumori tsutsu /
> ka bakari sume ru / kage mo mi zari ki

(Since you left, even the moon in the sky tended to be clouded
I did not see such a luminous moonlight [as tonight])

The emperor uses the moon as a metaphor for the Middle Councilor, stating that the moon, which was clouded during his absence from Japan, is now brilliant. In reply, the courtier composes an allusive variation on the famous Abe no Nakamaro poem:

Furusato no / katamizokashi to /
Amanohara / furisake tsuki o / mishi zo kanashiki

(It makes me sad to remember that I looked in the sky at the moon,
thinking it was a keepsake of my native land)[51]

The precedent, Nakamaro's poem of homesickness, is reworked into a poem of longing for the foreign land, from which one used to long for one's homeland. While it was sad to remember the homeland (and the lover there) while viewing the bright moon in China, it is even sadder to remember the occasion now at home, as the councilor has a woman in China for whom he longs. Nostalgia becomes twofold and the vector of longing bidirectional. The old/new and the familiar/foreign are no longer stably stationed characteristics but instead vacillate between the poles of China and Japan. The only constant is transposition and isolation from the place where one feels one belongs at a given moment. Indeed, the Middle Councilor does not belong anywhere any longer: in China he has left behind his father's reincarnation and his son's mother; in Japan, he has been reunited with his first lover, who gave birth to his daughter, but is yet to meet with his son's grandmother and half-sister, who is destined to give birth to the consort's reincarnation. He is thus inescapably entrapped in the entanglement involving both China and Japan. The prediction that the consort will be reborn Japanese does not resolve the entanglement but rather sustains and develops it.

Many Japanese are anxious to obtain from the Middle Councilor information about the foreign land that they are not allowed to visit. His relative value in society has increased tremendously because of his exceptional experience, and others are ready to translate it into public property. For them, the Middle Councilor's status is further enhanced by his physical appearance: an exotic fragrance and magnificent attire brought from China.[52] The Middle Councilor tries to maintain a difficult

balance between protecting his privacy and satisfying his audience with
details, so he talks about what is really on his mind (the consort's distinction) by saying that he is impressed with the distinguished women
of China; the audience is more than willing to listen.[53] He sticks to the
story the Chinese emperor devised about the *kin* performer at the farewell party and occasionally takes recourse to talking about the fifth
daughter of the minister instead of the Heyang consort. While he would
never expose the consort's correspondence to the public, the Middle
Councilor does not mind showing letters from the fifth daughter. Her
talent in both Chinese and Japanese poetic composition—an inconsis-
tency in her character that we noted above and that remains unaccounted for—offers a convenient topic for conversation.[54] In contrast,
his relationship with the consort remains a deeply hidden secret and as
such causes unbearable agony and longing. The Japanese courtiers sense
the councilor's higher esteem for the *kin* performer; however, instead of
suspecting a serious relationship with her, one of them concludes that
the Middle Councilor's love for his Japanese lover must have been sincere because he would not otherwise have deserted such a distinguished
woman. Just as he did not have anyone in whom to confide his affection
for his Japanese lover while he was in China, the Middle Councilor has
to suppress his wish to "fly back to China as a bird" in the company of
his Japanese acquaintances.[55] The courtiers' interest in Chinese women
comes only from their reading knowledge of legendary beauties, including Yang Guifei, Wang Zhaojun, Li Furen, and Shangyang Baifaren.[56] The
Middle Councilor affirms his countrymen's lustful interest in Chinese
women by describing the incomparable beauty of the *kin* performer, em-
phasizing the contrast between "magnificent" (*uruwashi*), an attribute
he assigns to Yang Guifei and Wang Zhaojun, and "personable" (*natsukashi*), a quality that best describes the *kin* performer/consort.[57] It is evident here that the Middle Councilor values the hybridity embodied by
the consort, while the others harbor exotic fantasies about Chinese
women. We shall see that the cultural hierarchy is confirmed in the next
subject of study and then challenged in works that follow.

When an Alien Invades

While often compared with *Hamamatsu* for the shared theme of a Japanese nobleman in China and the romantic relationships he has there,
Matsura no miya monogatari (hereafter *Matsura*) reveals quite another

set of issues surrounding the Sino-Japanese entanglement.[58] For one thing, all the characters strongly and constantly feel the political strains in China that eventually lead to war. The tense and competitive environment affects the Japanese visitor's actions; he is mindful of how the Chinese court views his personality, his political function, and his loyalty. As an alien, he is under tighter scrutiny than a native and needs to act with the utmost discretion in order to protect himself from accusations of espionage. These restrictions consequently circumscribe his range as a romantic hero.

Occasional touches of jingoism, in which China's disorder is contrasted with Japan's justice and stability, need to be carefully assessed according to both the time in which the story is set (the eighth century) and the time in which the text was written (the thirteenth century). In the former period Japan was in the midst of building a new state, but the latter period was a time of trial for the imperial oligarchy, as the first military government had just been installed. Many disturbances, riots, and rebellions are known to have occurred in the Nara period (710–794). The civil wars between the Taira and Minamoto clans (each claiming that an imperial family member authorized their legitimacy) and between the abdicated Go Toba emperor and the Kamakura shogunate impelled Fujiwara no Teika (1162–1241), the alleged author of *Matsura,* to issue a famous statement in his *kanbun* diary, *Meigetsuki* (Diary of the bright moon, 1180–1235): "Kōki seijū waga koto ni arazu" (Warfare is not my business).[59] While it is true that Song China suffered from the successful and sustained invasions of northern nomads around the same time and the government was forced to move south in 1127, it is mere fiction to portray Japan as a pacified state. Whatever the authorial intent may have been, the positive portrait of Japan in contrast to the negative one of China and the disparities between the story and the real circumstances in Japan suggest that constructing the binary opposition was a prioritized agenda.

Unlike the Middle Councilor, who leaves Japan for China on a personal quest, the protagonist, a lesser lieutenant who is the son of a minister and a royal princess, is chosen by the government to visit China as deputy ambassador, as would have been possible in the Nara period. While he demonstrates outstanding accomplishments in learning and the arts (as the Middle Councilor does and as would any hero of classical Japanese romance for that matter), these are first and foremost considered essentials for a successful bureaucrat rather than simply proofs of personal distinction. This confirms the Japanese acceptance of the

Chinese civil service system, and it foreshadows the more overtly political nature of the story and the hierarchical relationship between China
(origin/model) and Japan (offspring/copy).

The romantic dimension of the tale is also informed by its hierarchical
value judgments. Like the Middle Councilor, who leaves a lover behind in
the native country, the Lesser Lieutenant has an object of affection (Princess Kannabi) whom he has clandestinely adored and is reluctant to leave
behind. Her name is the same as a place name in Nara that is often referred
to in ancient songs, so it contributes more to the creation of an archaic ambience than to illustrating the attributes of the loved one; Princess Kannabi is of even less significance than was the Middle Councilor's first love
(Ōigimi) in *Hamamatsu*. She is ignored during the hero's stay in China and
remains completely off his mind even after his return to Japan. Unlike in
Hamamatsu, where China and Japan hold different yet equal value, the
cultural superiority of China is made obvious in *Matsura*.

The Lesser Lieutenant's parents are also not happy about his assignment. In order to best cope with the separation from their only son, his
mother has a palace built on the shore nearest to the continent—Matsura
(hence the title)—so that she can wave to him from there. Matsura
(meaning the "pine shore"), in northern Kyūshū, is known from ancient
songs in which women wave to loved ones who have left them to go to
China. As in *Hamamatsu*, this literary topos helps paint the liminal space
where Japan ends and China begins.

The Chinese emperor likes the Lesser Lieutenant for his excellence
in arts and letters and favorably defines his personal characteristics as
typically Japanese. The emperor justifies his support for the young Japanese as a meritocratic practice with precedents going back to Emperor
Wu (Wudi, 156–87 BC; r. 141–87 BC) of the Early Han dynasty (202
BC–AD 8), who brought a Korean student of distinction to court.[60] The
emperor's Chinese subjects, however, are concerned about the unprecedented intimate treatment of the "traveler from afar" (harukanaru sakai
yori watari maireru tabito) who is "not old enough" (yowai itaranu)
for such an honor.[61] The reservation of the courtiers, in part due to the
lieutenant's alien status, represents opposition to and antagonism toward his increasingly significant presence in the imperial court.

Painfully aware that his remarkable advancement has caused strains,
the lieutenant strives to conform to "the customs of the country" to which
he has been sent (kuni no narai, a key phrase used throughout the text in
order for the Lesser Lieutenant to account for the otherwise inexplicable

actions of the Chinese). Hence, his celibacy in the first stage of his stay reflects his fear that "the slightest transgression will be seriously chastised in light of the formal manners and customs of the country."[62] The Lesser Lieutenant's reserve impresses the emperor, who thinks to himself that "the Japanese man is more faithful than I thought previously."[63] In *Matsura,* a formality is now detected in Chinese behavior, whereas in *Hamamatsu* it was a quality visible only in Chinese women's clothes; on the contrary, the Middle Councilor observed a lack of reserve and greater freedom. Because he feels that the Chinese make rigid ethical judgments, the Lesser Lieutenant does not mingle with them as much as the Middle Councilor did. He and his Chinese associates are thus distinctly separated from each other along the lines of their countries of origin, rather than being united by a shared universal language and arts.

A very important new phase in the Sino-Japanese relationship is that an interest in the other is now mutual. Chinese characters in *Matsura* pay more attention to Japan than did those in *Hamamatsu,* and they are ready to draw conclusions about the Japanese from observations of the Lesser Lieutenant, who is well aware of the scrutiny cast upon him and is anxious to make himself worthy of his country. This reciprocity of observation is matched by the terms of address used for the other country. *Hito no kuni* (the country of others), a phrase coined by the Japanese for a foreign country (most significantly China) from the Japanese perspective, is employed here by Chinese characters to refer to Japan. So are *nami no hoka, kumo no yoso* (the country across the waves, beyond the clouds), *shiranu kuni* (the unknown country), and *aranu kuni* (the country that is not this one). Thus, foreignness is felt to be relative rather than inherent in China. The two-directional interactions set a new standard for the works to come. Japan becomes a player in the game, rather than being just an observer who can exploit its insignificance so as to claim neutrality.

While the Lesser Lieutenant's celibacy is necessitated by political considerations, it effectively lends a blank backdrop to the two love affairs in which he is involved. The first evolves around the secret teaching of the art of musical performance, an important theme in the tradition of classical Japanese romance.[64] Destiny guides the lieutenant to learn the *kin,* taught first by an old recluse and then by a young imperial princess called Kayō Kōshu (Ch. Huayang Gongzhu; Princess Huayang), the most accomplished practitioner of the art; eventually the Lesser Lieutenant falls for her. He visits her for instruction on the Fifteenth Night of the Eighth Month and the Thirteenth Night of the Seventh Month, both dates established in East Asian literary convention as special occasions on which to appreciate the beauty of the full moon.

The Lesser Lieutenant's attraction to the princess is for reasons distinct from the ones we witnessed in *Hamamatsu*. The princess does not look "extravagant" or "distant" as Chinese women with unusual hairpieces and coiffures did in *Hamamatsu;* instead she is lovely, familiar, pure, and pretty.[65] To highlight her beauty, he compares her both with Chinese dancers, whom the Lesser Lieutenant saw previously ("they seem earthen now"), and with Princess Kannabi, who now appears to him as "rustic and unkempt."[66] Unlike the Middle Councilor's attraction to the Heyang consort, accounted for by her quasi-Japanese attributes, the Lesser Lieutenant's infatuation with Princess Huayang results from a cultural hierarchy in which the best Chinese traits clearly are placed above the best of the Japanese.

It is Princess Huayang who suggests a joining of the two cultures that appear so distinct to the lieutenant. Before her untimely death, she confirms their bond by entrusting him with a crystal ball and asking him to have a Buddhist ceremony conducted at Hatsuse Temple in Japan, a place of reunion for long-lost family members and lovers according to ancient Japanese myths. (She was prepared for death because a wizard had predicted that her mastery of the *kin* would lead to her early demise.) She tells her Japanese lover that she would rather die for the time being so that she can be reincarnated sooner and then establish an everlasting relationship with him.[67] She pleads with him not to forget her "even in the country other than this" and vows that she will meet with him again in a different form "across the waves, beyond the clouds."[68] As we saw above, these phrases were normally used to refer to places other than Japan. They now become referents for Japan when used by a Chinese character, revealing that Japan might appear exotic and distant to the Chinese. While the hierarchy between China and Japan has been restored, the reciprocity of the gaze between the two is newly instated.

The princess' wish for a memorial service in Japan has to be put on hold, however, as military emergencies arise after the death of the emperor. On his sickbed the emperor confides in the Lesser Lieutenant his premonition that there will be disturbances in China after his death. He thus asks the Lesser Lieutenant to support the crown prince. The Lesser Lieutenant need have no fear, the emperor tells him, as he will be able to pacify the nation and then return to Japan. Despite his enormous trust in the Lesser Lieutenant, however, the emperor swears him to secrecy in "the country of origin" (*moto no kuni*). The emperor is aware that relationships can suffer as a result of physical distance and (perhaps more important) from the context in which one party remembers the other. As soon as the Lesser Lieutenant arrives in Japan, the bond between him and the emperor may disintegrate, and it may seem pointless to remain loyal to him. In order to maintain the integrity of their relationship, the emperor further predicts their future reunion in Japan owing to retributions from their previous lives.[69] Thus, both Princess Huayang and the emperor procure the permanence of their bonds with the Lesser Lieutenant by suggesting reunions in their next lives.

The emperor's premonition soon proves right: a group opposing the crown prince, led by a fellow called Ubun Kai (Ch. Yuwen Hui) and allied with the northern nomads, raises a large force, and the Japanese traveler finds himself in the center of a steadily diminishing group of supporters for the legitimate successor to the throne. The Lesser Lieutenant repeatedly expresses his ignorance of military affairs, as he has never been trained in the martial arts or military planning. However, Tō Kōgō (Ch. Deng Huanghou; Empress Deng), the crown prince's mother, urges him to stay in the service of the crown prince so as to repay the emperor's favors, although she admits that as a foreigner, he has no obligation to do so. The empress further argues that Japan, though small in size, is a country of fierce warriors and that the Lesser Lieutenant should be able to devise strategies to defeat the enemy.[70] Thus persuaded, the Lesser Lieutenant decides to stay on, even if it means dying an honorable death on the battlefield.[71]

Sumiyoshi, the god of martial arts, exhibits his power by instantaneously increasing the crown prince's forces tenfold.[72] With his aid, the crown prince succeeds in defeating the rebel forces. The loyal Chinese subjects who previously berated the Lesser Lieutenant as a person from the unknown country now rejoice in his achievement.

The way the lieutenant is treated after the war reveals how Sinocentric the Chinese are. Having succeeded in his mission, the Lesser Lieutenant thinks it is time for him to leave. However, the Chinese courtiers are strongly opposed, offering the rationale that there is "no precedent of even a low-ranking foreigner returning to his native land."[73] Indeed, the empress has bestowed upon the Lesser Lieutenant the rank of Grand General of Ryōbu (Ch. Longwu), honoring the deceased emperor's principle that individuals should be rewarded for their merits regardless of their nationalities.[74] While this is a gesture that transcends national boundaries, it causes a reaction against the concept behind it. Many suggest that the Lesser Lieutenant, a mere foreigner, is not entitled to refuse such an honor and return to a land that is, in their view, undoubtedly inferior to China.

The plot of the story capitalizes upon this Sinocentric logic, which serves to postpone the Lesser Lieutenant's return until he is involved with yet another woman. The empress, who even-handedly offers reasons for and against the Lesser Lieutenant's departure, adds to the dilemma for herself and for him. On one hand, she suggests he should stay in China, as it is solely owing to the Lesser Lieutenant that her nation successfully overcame the threat it faced, and he could not be thanked enough even if he was given half of the country. On the other hand, she admits that the Chinese would not be rewarding the Lesser Lieutenant for his service if they prevented him from going home as he wishes. She adds yet another reason that the Lesser Lieutenant should be granted leave: divine aid was offered during the warfare because of the Lesser Lieutenant's deference to the deities of his native land.[75] Although she employs the somewhat compromising term *onigami* (demons, spirits), as well as a more respectful *kunitsukami* (deities of the native land), to refer to the Shinto deities, she suggests clearly that China has no equivalent to them.[76] Such reverence toward Shinto gods as binding forces for an individual to his native land is not found in *Hamamatsu* but is predominant in *Matsura*. It is the principal, if not the only, measure in which Japan is considered superior.

The supernatural again comes into play as the Lesser Lieutenant becomes involved with an unidentified woman whose body is imbued with the fragrance of plums. Bearing a remarkable resemblance to the empress—and she is later revealed to be the empress herself in disguise—she seduces him into repeated and yet fleeting nights together. She disappears without trace each time after love making, and the Lesser Lieutenant's inquiries into her identity lead nowhere. Overcome with the mysterious woman's charms, the Lesser Lieutenant feels as though supernatural beings are dictating the course of his life ("onigami nado no, hakari tsuru ni ya": Could this be engineered by demons and spirits?).[77] It is obvious from the use of the term *onigami* that the suspected deities are definitely not Sumiyoshi or the Great Goddess of Amaterasu, who are mentioned in the text as the Lesser Lieutenant's guardians. He wonders if the woman is a demon in disguise or a deception devised by either the goddess Wushan or the goddess of Xiangpu, both known to have allured ancient Chinese emperors. The hero's romance is evidently imbued with the mystical and erotic experience of encountering the divine, a ubiquitous theme in poetry during the Warring States (403–221 BC) and Three Kingdoms periods (220–280).[78]

Multiple identities are manifest in the theme of transnational reincarnation that drives the plot.[79] There is no character of mixed blood in this story, though both the emperor and Princess Huayang hint at their reincarnations in Japan. As is well known, *Matsura* is not complete, ending with a colophon stating that the following pages are missing. Whether the note is authentic or fictive, we are left without learning about the reincarnations. As it stands now, the story evolves around a clearly drawn distinction between China and Japan and occasionally portrays hostility, rivalry, and confrontation. While Japan's sacredness is demonstrated through the miraculous powers of the Shinto gods, Chinese women are portrayed as heavenly, beautiful, and accomplished, as opposed to Japanese women, who are earthly and rustic. Part of the reason for this distinction may be that Chinese characters in Japanese literature are polarized into either the villainous or the virtuous, while a wider spectrum of Japanese characters was available to the Japanese literary imagination. The vulgarity of the Japanese versus the nobility of the Chinese becomes a persistent theme, as we will see in the next section.

A Good Son

Kokusen'ya gassen (1715; hereafter *Kokusen'ya*) is a *jōruri* play (traditional puppet theater) from the eighteenth century and was thus written for a distinctly different audience in a different historical period.[80] Nonetheless, it shares many important premises with *Matsura* in its specific model of the Sino-Japanese entanglement: disturbances in China are caused by tensions between the Han and the non-Han (the Manchus in the present case); the Japanese protagonist acts honorably and effectively in service to the Han; Matsura is again the setting from which "China" becomes distinct from "Japan" and connotes journeys to the continent and the longings of the loved ones left behind; and Japan is a divine country protected by the power of Sumiyoshi. Given the utter difference between the two works in terms of the periods in which they were written, the genre, the expected primary audience, and the wealth of information on China available to the author of *Kokusen'ya,* it is rather surprising that many fundamental presuppositions are merely reconfirmed.

Though deprived of the opportunity to travel to China, the playwright, Chikamatsu Monzaemon (1653–1724), was granted much greater access to, and was more seriously compelled to consult, extraliterary sources than were the previous three authors. Contemporary military affairs involving Ming loyalist forces (or "rebels," depending upon one's loyalties) during the transitional period from late Ming to early Qing China were registered in numerous historical records.[81] The Ming dynasty's dissolution and fall in 1644 and the establishment of the Qing dynasty were closely monitored by the Tokugawa shogunate, especially through the Nagasaki Bugyō, an office that, since 1603, had been commissioned to interview Chinese and Dutch merchants on international matters and submit reports to the shogunate. Even after the shogunate forbade all international trade and transportation (except for authorized and limited Dutch, Chinese, and Korean merchants and vessels) as of 1639, Japan could not be impervious to its neighbor's political turmoil. Sometime around 1649, Zheng Chenggong (1624–1662), the model for the protagonist of *Kokusen'ya* who had left Japan for China to join his father, Zheng Zhilong (1604–1661), to resist the Manchu, wrote in vain to Japan for military aid. Soon afterward the father and son split, the former reconciling with Qing China and the latter continuing in the anti-Manchu military campaign in Amoy, Nanjing, and Taiwan. The son relied financially on Japanese connections as he maintained saving accounts in Nagasaki (a source of dispute among his descendants after his untimely death in 1661). Given these circumstances and general pro-Ming (or pro-Han) feelings among the Japanese, it is not difficult to imagine keen interest in the subject. In fact, Chikamatsu is not the only playwright who used Zheng Chenggong as a subject. Nor did he write only one play on the topic: in 1717, he completed *Kokusen'ya gonichi gassen* (The later warfare of Kokusen'ya) and in 1723, *Tōsen banashi ima Kokusen'ya* (Present-day Kokusen'ya: Tales collected from Chinese ships). The piece under discussion is the most successful and oft-performed of the plays; it had a seventeen-month continuous run in Osaka and was subsequently performed in Kyoto and Edo.[82]

For our study of the rhetorical configuration of Sino-Japanese relations, it is more to the point to see how Japan is positioned in the text in relation to the Han and the Manchu (rather than assessing the documented facts and incidents in the story). As we saw in *Matsura* (and as I have discussed elsewhere concerning Japan's fascination with legends about Wang Zhaojun),[83] the Japanese literary imagination tended to define Japan as a reliable and worthy ally of Han China while relegating nomads (of any ethnic identity) to the rank of barbarians. In contrast, the Japanese, who were deemed just another barbarous people by the Han Chinese, were elevated to a civilized status. *Kokusen'ya* expounds on this theme to the extent that it seems to be out of a desperate need for self-redemption. Immediately after the play begins, Wu Sangui (J. Go Sankei; 1612–1678), the grand general and in this play a loyal subject of the Ming emperor, refutes a recommendation by the conniving villain, Li Daotian (J. Ri Tōten)—who behind the scenes conspires with the Manchu to eradicate the Ming—that grain should be allotted for and sent to the Manchu. Wu Sangui defines China as a country of Confucian ethics, Japan of Shintoist ethics, and the Manchu of no ethics, a "land of beasts" *(chikushō koku)*. The insulting term "land of beasts" is thereafter applied by different parties to various others: the messenger from the Manchu, upset by the insult, so calls China because it has failed to observe a previously arranged contract; Li Daotian says that it is shameful that his country has been so called, and he theatrically scoops his eye out, claiming that his act will redeem China's name (the act is in fact coded, secretly sending a message to the Manchu that he will collaborate with them). The recurrence and reciprocity of insults suggest both an obsession with hierarchies among countries and the relativity thereof.

Poetic composition was a measure by which one's degree of civilization was evaluated in the texts we have discussed above. Princess Zhantan (J. Sendan), the emperor's younger sister, says, "I have heard that *uta* in Japan soften relationships between men and women. It is the same here: [poetry] mediates love." She herself composes *shi (kanshi)*.[84] This reference to the Japanese preface to *Kokin wakashū* is a little out of context, as the subsequent passage tells us how immaculately virtuous and disciplined the princess is, rather than how romantically inclined she is. Thus, it appears that the point of the statement is to emphasize China and Japan's shared culture, exemplified by poetry, the universal language of the emotions, rather than to focus on the speaker's character.

The princess' knowledge of Japanese poetry is one of the many fictional constructs that set the stage for a Chinese interest in Japanese affairs (as they did in *Matsura*). The interest resurfaces when the emperor, fooled by Li Daotian's theatrics, considers marrying Princess Zhantan to him. In an attempt to change his mind, Wu Sangui reminds the emperor—and thus informs the audience—that Zheng Zhilong offended the emperor by recommending the removal of Li Daotian in the narrative past. Wu reveals his concern that China will be put to shame if Zhilong, now forlorn in Japan, hears that the emperor is again favoring

Li. While Li has expressed his (false) concern that the Manchu may think of the Han Chinese as beastly, Wu is worried that the Japanese might think that China is unjust. The relative elevation of Japan's status vis-à-vis China, evident here in a manner similar to that in *Matsura*, effectively anticipates a later development in the story, when the half-Japanese protagonist comes to bear a lot of significance as a rightly concerned Ming loyalist. The first act of the play closes in a series of drastic turns: Wu's worries about the future of the Ming dynasty materialize with Li Daotian's rebellion; the Manchu military forces invade Ming China's territory; Li's brother murders the emperor; the pregnant empress dies on the battlefield; Wu kills his own baby and substitutes him for the baby that he retrieves from the empress' corpse; and Wu's wife defends Princess Zhantan and helps her escape alone on a boat without knowing her destination.

The second act is set in Hirado, a seaside village in Matsura. While it is a historical fact that Zheng Chenggong lived in Hirado, the significance of the area as a literary topos, as noted above, cannot be ignored. The cultural entanglement is deepened by the ambiguity of the protagonist's identity: he is only half Japanese. The fictional name of the protagonist, Wa Tōnai—three characters representing "Japan," "China," and "within" respectively—is appropriate, if not too pat, for a hybrid individual whose father is Chinese and whose mother is Japanese.[85]

In a long soliloquy by Wa Tōnai, which draws heavily on the Chinese classics to reflect upon the current state of affairs in East Asia, we see an interesting classification of diverse ethnic groups. The Han and the Manchu are grouped together as "Daimin Dattan" (Great Ming, the Tartar).[86] While Wa Tōnai recognizes "Daimin Dattan" as two distinct polities, as is obvious in the phrasing *ryōkoku* (both countries),[87] his expressed ambition to pacify "both countries" seems to be incongruous with the understanding that the Ming are legitimate and the Manchu are usurpers. Rather than attributing this contradiction to the author's lack of knowledge, I would propose that different configurations of allies and enemies—the ingroup and the out-group—are emerging almost simultaneously in Wa Tōnai's speech.

While Wa Tōnai's identity is made evident at the beginning of the act, by identifying his father as Zheng Zhilong, the narrator reinforces the point by inserting his own commentary after the soliloquy: "Indeed, this is the man—Coxinga, the king of Yuanping, who went over to China, pacified both the Ming and the Tartar, and earned a reputation in both that country and this one; it is none other than this young man."[88] In the guise of a reminder or presentation of historical facts, the playwright distorts history, which he must have known from sources in Nagasaki, even if his prospective audience did not. Though Zheng Chenggong was successful in the first stages of his military expedition, to the extent that he almost captured Nanjing, his realm never encompassed China or the Northern Territories, as is suggested in the narrator's comment. In fact, he was eventually compelled to retreat from mainland China to Taiwan, from where he pleaded for Japan's military aid. Since sources were available to Chikamatsu that recounted the events in detail, one may conclude that the digression is intentional, reflecting the author's choice to conclude the play with the hero's triumph, perhaps as a redemption in theater for the disappointment in reality. The narrator's comment foreshadows the happy ending, in which the hero realizes his ambitions and serves poetic justice.

Wa Tōnai and his wife, Komutsu, are a fisherman and fisherwoman (ama), a profession often considered to be on the borders of the Japanese constituency because it is least rooted in the native soil and is of a fleeting nature. In poetry anthologies, ama often appears near topics such as "Senkyū" (the Immortals' Palace), "Tōjin" (the Chinese people), or specific Chinese iconic figures, an arrangement that suggests that ama are on the borderline of the otherworldly and the exotic. The liminality of the major characters is thus confirmed by their occupation as well as their location.

Wa Tōnai and Komutsu find a deserted boat and in it a beautiful but exhausted young woman who, judging from her hairstyle and clothes, appears Chinese. The audience should immediately know that this is Princess Zhantan. Drawing upon conventional rhetoric, the narrator portrays her as having "a face comparable to a lotus" and "eyebrows comparable to willow leaves,"[89] attributes belonging to Yang Guifei and Wang Zhaojun respectively.[90] The analogy of "a blooming flower soaked in the rain"[91] also reminds us of Yang Guifei, whom Bai Juyi compared to "a branch of pear blossoms soaked in spring rain."[92] The literary associations continue as Komutsu thinks of the lady on the boat as a Chinese consort exiled because of lascivious acts, while Wa Tōnai hypothesizes that she is the ghost of Yang Guifei. Komutsu expresses jealousy, saying that Tōnai might have slept with a Chinese woman like that had he been in China, but Tōnai assures her that he would not have. His reason for not doing so illustrates a Japanese image of China: Chinese women all look like a deity (benzaiten) and thus make him feel unworthy and tense. Though this rationale is in part an invention to assuage his wife's unfounded jealousy and in part a foreshadowing for the revelation of the Chinese woman's lofty identity, it also coincides with and reconfirms the common prejudice of Chinese formality, as opposed to Japanese familiarity, which we saw in *Hamamatsu*.

As the princess begins to communicate with the couple, her speech is represented in *hiragana*, so that it sounds Chinese but makes no sense in either Japanese or Chinese. As we shall see in the next section and in the next chapter, the Japanese had long been accustomed to Chinese as a written language, but they recited Chinese texts in a Japanese pronunciation. Thus, when they heard Chinese spoken in the authentic pronunciation, it sounded exotic, if not barbarous. Here the princess' speech is not even an accurate transcript of anything said in Chinese but mimicry that appears to be Chinese. However, that would do for an audience who, in the early eighteenth century, did not have much knowledge of spoken Chinese and thus could not detect a fabrication. The anticipated effect on the audience was for the speech to sound funny or silly. Such is the effect within the text as well as far as Komutsu is concerned: rolling with laughter (to the extent that her stomach begins to hurt), she asks, "What kind of Buddhist scripture is this?" (Buddhist scriptures are recited phonetically and do not make obvious sense to the Japanese ear.) Komutsu's rhetorical question thus reveals the effect of reciting a text written in a literary language.

Wa Tōnai, on the other hand, comprehends the princess' speech and shows his reverence and loyalty toward her in both gesture and Chinese word. This provokes Komutsu, who tries to attack Zhantan for being a seductress. As soon as Wa Tōnai stops her and reasons with her, however, Komutsu's attitude changes. Her sudden burst of sympathy involves another contrast that is made between Japan and China. She says to Zhantan: "Even within this country of Japan princesses of royalty and nobility are supposed to be shielded from rough winds. You are even more undeservedly tried, as you are from the royalty of the unseen land of China."[93] Because it is far away and foreign, China is given a higher rank than Japan in Komutsu's speech. She then cries and even begins to repeat some of the words she heard spoken by the princess, without understanding their meaning at all. Language is not a tool for communication but itself constitutes a communicative act; without intending to mean anything, Komutsu shows loyalty by simply parroting the words she has heard.

After further misunderstandings are resolved, Zheng Zhilong and his Japanese wife depart on a boat for China, while Wa Tōnai temporarily leaves his wife and Princess Zhantan behind to go to China on another boat. The two women, who are to join him later, see him off longingly, as references are made to Hirefuri Saki (the cape from which shawls wave), a Japanese topos of a woman waving her shawl to her husband at sea, as well as to Wangfu Shan (the hill from which one gazes toward one's husband; also known as Wangfu shi, or, the rock from which one gazes toward one's husband), the site of a similar story in China that is collected in the aforementioned *Kara monogatari*.[94] From this point on, as the bond between the two women deepens, things Chinese and Japanese are often introduced as parallel to each other. The fourth act presents the procession (*michiyuki*) of the two women and confirms the transnational camaraderie while it continues to show the contrasts between Chinese and Japanese clothes, hairdos, and other attributes. The comparative and contrastive permutations thus authenticate the binary between China and Japan.

Komutsu crossdresses as a man to further display the binary opposition between her and Princess Zhantan, who represents femininity.[95] The pairing thus transgresses the conventional assignment of genders for China (masculine) and Japan (feminine), and it is even noted by Chinese women in the text when they remark that Japan, which is called a country of "great harmony" (*yamato*), must be a good country for women.[96] The transnational transvestism encapsulates the text's subversive effects: Chinese feminine frailty ("yowaki wa Morokoshi onna no fū," or being frail is how Chinese women are) is contrasted with Japanese (implicitly male) warriors' resolve ("nakanu wa Nihon bushi no fū," or not crying is how Japanese warriors are), a quality shared by Japanese women in honoring bonds with friends ("Nihon wa otoko mo onna mo gi wa sutezu," or in Japan, men and women alike would not renounce bonding).[97] Wa Tōnai's mother in particular is portrayed as concerned with Japan's honor, which she thinks she could compromise if she, as a Japanese woman, were not to conduct herself properly (such as acting out of personal enmity toward her stepdaughter, Jin Xiangnü [J. Kin Shōjo]).

The universality of values such as loyalty alternates with perceived irreconcilable differences between China and Japan throughout the play. For example, Wa Tōnai, having successfully converted pro-Manchu Chinese into pro-Han "Japanese" subjects, triumphantly mounts a horse, standing up "over the saddle with his feet positioned as though he had one foot in the foreign land and the other in the homeland" (ikoku honchō ni fumimatagitaru kura abumi);[98] Jin Xiangnü, Zheng Zhilong's daughter, who was left behind by her father and raised in China, tells her long-lost father of how torn she has been, "unfolding the map of the world [and pointing], 'This is China, that is Japan'" (sekai no zu o hiraki kore wa Morokoshi kore wa Nihon).[99]

Wa Tōnai's sense of honor and shame is so closely tied to the home-land that he sounds confrontational, if not hysterical, when he addresses the issue of nationality. Whenever he is challenged with hardships in China, he takes it as an offense against the Japanese, and he often vows to prove Japanese perseverance or resourcefulness and demolish any hint of their being otherwise. Hence, when he and his mother get lost in a vast bamboo grove, he is convinced that "Chinese foxes fool us chartless Japa-nese";[100] when he first encounters Chinese soldiers, who call him "a way-farer," he responds, "My native land is Great Japan; I don't deserve to be called that!";[101] when he fights off their leader, he addresses the rest of the group: "You despise Japan as a small country, but are you not impressed with the martial art of the Japanese, which even a tiger fears?"[102] Wa Tōnai's preoccupation with Japanese national pride cancels out his two-fold ethnic identity, which makes *Kokusen'ya* different from *Hamamatsu* in terms of the handling of hybridity.

The patriotic emotions aroused in the narrative present are rein-forced by references to mythical incidents that suggest Japan's superiority over China. Hence, mention is made of Empress Jingū's failed attempts to conquer Silla,[103] which were known from *Kojiki* (Records of ancient mat-ters, 712) and *Nihon shoki* (Chronicles of Japan, 720); mention is also made of Bai Juyi's poetic challenges to the Japanese, which are success-fully met by Sumiyoshi, as told in a popular legend that is immortalized in Zeami's *nō* play, *Haku Rakuten*.[104] National boundaries are so irrevocably entrenched in the characters' minds that even if at times transnation truces are called, each individual is expected to embody and demonstrate distinct national characteristics and to act on behalf of his own country. This expectation is particularly evident in the case of Wa Tōnai: while he is primarily and rightly defined as bicultural and hybrid, his speeches and actions in China clearly and exclusively represent Japan. His loyalty to the Ming imperial house is justified merely as filial piety.

The domestication and "purification" of Wa Tōnai is underlined by some deprecatory remarks he makes against hybrids or that the narrator makes on his behalf. In Hirado, suspicious individuals around the geo-graphical borders are called "chikuramono" (those who are neither

Japanese nor Chinese).[105] When the Han Chinese warriors who were previously united with the Manchus are defeated and converted into Ming loyalists by Wa Tōnai and his mother, the warriors' jumbled appearance, which encapsulates their political conversion, is mocked as follows: "Atama wa Nihon, hige wa Dattan, mi wa Tōjin" (their hairstyle is Japanese, their beards are Tartar, and their bodies are Chinese); it makes "the mother and son burst into laughter" and give them silly sounding Japanese names.[106] His lack of sympathy toward individuals of ambiguous identity blatantly shows how nation-bound the protagonist in fact is. This relentlessly jingoistic position—which does not exist in *Hamamatsu* and which was not articulated in *Matsura*—recurs in the subject of the next section.

Such a distinct national awareness, prior to the emergence of nationalism in the modern era, is also evident in Hiraga Gennai's (1728–1779) *Fūryū Shidōken den* (A biography of Shidōken, a man of taste, 1763), a comical and fantastic account of the fictive eponymous protagonist's visit to China. As Marcia Yonemoto points out, the protagonist tends to identify himself as "a Japanese" while in China and to portray Japan favorably, if not hyperbolically so, in order to impress or intimidate the Chinese. For example, when the Chinese mention the Five Sacred Mountains of China (Wushan), Shidōken could have responded that Japan had adapted the Chinese system of identifying the top five Buddhist monasteries and granting them special privileges in Kyoto and Kamakura in the Kamakura and Muromachi periods. In fact, that would have been the most relevant subject to bring into the conversation. Instead, Shidōken boasts about the height and magnificence of Mount Fuji which, in his opinion, is more impressive than all the Five Sacred Mountains of China put together. The protagonist's (if not the author's) competitiveness and search for uniqueness rather than commonalities reveal the work's jingoistic propensities and represent a new dimension in Japanese sentiments toward China that are already evident in *Kokusen'ya gassen*.[107]

Honor the Language of Their Own

Honchō Suikoden, a parody, as the title suggests, of the Chinese novel *Shuihu zhuan,* is set in the Nara period (roughly contemporaneous with Emperor Xuanzong's reign in the Tang dynasty).[108] Thus it is well prior to the time in which *Shuihu zhuan* is set (during Emperor Huizong's reign [r. 1100–1125] in the Song dynasty) or was written (in the early

ELPME.

Ming). While it is necessary to define the historical backdrop as Nara in order to justify the historically specific content, the story's anachronism helps to create the illusion that the parody predates the original. As the parody becomes primary and the parodied object secondary, the cultural hierarchy is also reversed: the periphery (Japan) has conquered the center (China). Thus, the conventional parallel between temporality and spatiality (the geographically defined China as the origin, Japan as the descendant) is destabilized as merely contingent.

The ambiguous Sino-Japanese relations implied in the tale may be examined against another historical backdrop—namely, the date of authorship/publication. The author, Takebe Ayatari (1719–1774), is primarily known as one of the pioneers of *yomihon,* a genre of fictional or historical narratives with elaborate plots and an ornate style that can best be appreciated by readers with narrative competence and literary knowledge. Among the authors who were active in this genre, Ayatari is roughly a contemporary of Tsuga Teishō (1718–ca. 1794), a Confucian scholar and medical doctor who wrote sophisticated adaptations of Chinese fiction; by a few decades he predates stellar writers such as Santō Kyōden (1761–1816) and Kyokutei Bakin (1767–1848), who brought the genre to its full potential. As we shall see in the next chapter, it was not uncommon for skilled writers in this period, who may not necessarily have composed Chinese verse or prose, to write adaptations of Chinese fiction. Many, including Ayatari, benefited from the abundance of annotations and Japanese translations of stories originally written in literary or vernacular Chinese. Ayatari was also a dilettante who dipped into *kokugaku* (nativism). His life span partly overlaps with those of Motoori Norinaga (1730–1801) and Ueda Akinari (1734–1809), two of the scholars in the field. Unlike Norinaga or Akinari, who in many of their works of criticism addressed issues of Sino-Japanese literary interaction directly (as we saw in passing in the case of Akinari's "Kaizoku" and shall see in detail in chapter 3), Ayatari may not have articulated his ideas as to how to position texts in Japanese vis-à-vis those in Chinese. Yet in *Honchō Suikoden,* we shall see a problematization of the binary in the unique setting of the transnational travel and relocation, which one might say anticipates the scholarly sophistication and ideological charging of the dichotomy that was yet to fully materialize.

The text is divided into two books, the first comprising twenty chapters and the second, fifty; it remains incomplete owing to the untimely death of the author. Travels to and from China appear in chapters

42–50 in the second book. Fujiwara no Kiyokawa (?–779), a historically known envoy from Japan, is about to set out from China to Japan when Abe no Nakamaro, who has been in China for a long time in an official capacity, is allowed by Emperor Xuanzong to finally return to Japan with Kiyokawa's group. Thus is presented another version of a well-known scene, hitherto told in *Tosa nikki,* among others. Nakamaro tells Kiyokawa: "I came to China at an early age and have since studied only Chinese. I have never composed a poem from my country of origin. However, when I am away from the shore, I will be Japanese. Shouldn't I then compose *waka* instead?"[109] Nakamaro's statement points to what are considered the markers of one's ethnic identity: it is defined both by one's current place of residence and by the language one employs in poetic composition. While one is in China, one is Chinese; when one is Chinese, one writes in Chinese. The same applies to Japanese identity. For high-ranking courtiers like Nakamaro, being/working in China involves serious engagement in poetic composition in Chinese. Thus the two gauges of residence and language are by and large interchangeable. One's race and place of birth, two markers that are conventionally considered irreducible, natural, and original, are viewed as irrelevant to the formation of identity in this picture. Cultural identity, in Nakamaro's view, is constructed on the site of cultural practice rather than out of biological essence or the native land. Radically in contrast with Tsurayuki's portrait of Nakamaro as a nativist advocate of the poetry of his motherland, Ayatari's Nakamaro defines himself by what he does at a given moment rather than by where he happened to be born.

Nakamaro and Kiyokawa then each compose a poem. Nakamaro's is a slightly different version from both the one in *Kokin wakashū* (its first line being "Amanohara," or the Field of Heaven) and the one in *Tosa nikki* (starting with "Aounabara," or the Field of the Blue Sea):

Ōunabara / furisake mireba
Kasuga naru / Mikasa no yama ni / ideshi tsuki kamo

(Gazing across the vast extension of the sea,
I see the same moon that rose over the hill of Mikasa in Kasuga)[110]

Kiyokawa's poem is in fact not his own but one that predates him, composed by Yamanoue no Okura (660–ca. 733) (it is collected in *Man'yō shū* [Anthology of ten myriad leaves], later than 759):[111]

Iza kodomo / hayaku Yamato e
Ōtomo no / Mitsu no hamamatsu / machi koinuran

(Children, let's rush to Yamato;
The pines on the shore of Mitsu of Ōtomo must have been pining for us)[112]

The staging of this exchange recalls the practice of fictional *uta awase* (poetry contests), textually matching poems on the same topic regardless of the contexts in which the poems were originally composed. The practice is validated by a faith in the timelessness of human emotions, such as a longing for home (the topic of both poems in question), as well as— contradictory as it may seem—by an experimental intent to relocate poems in a new context so as to produce new effects—an instance of the "baroque" (in Mieke Bal's terminology) that we saw in the introduction. The particular topic, premised on the spatial distance between the speaker and the object of his attachment, ideally embodies, and is embodied by, the nostalgic practice of neutralizing the temporal distance between the past and the present. The spatial distance is reconfirmed outside the text of the *waka* by the fact that "the Chinese could not even comprehend the meaning of the first *waka*" (Tōjin wa kiki mo waka zari kere ba), and then it is overcome, if not neutralized, by the work of "interpreters" (kototoki no hitobito); the Chinese company is moved to tears by a translation of the first poem and applauds that of the second.[113] In other words, the Chinese have overcome the linguistic barrier and reached a sense of commonality regardless of nationality. To place this in our context, poems about spatial distance that are arranged so as to diminish temporal distance work to diminish the spatial distance between different audiences, with the help of translation. Instead of capitalizing on nostalgia, which is premised upon a spatial distance, the translingual practice produces communicability in the present.

The poems about the excitement of returning home make for irony later, as Kiyokawa and Nakamaro are shipwrecked and sent back to China. From this point on the story ostensibly becomes original. An important departure from the historical facts in our context begins when Kiyokawa and Nakamaro are found and protected by a reclusive uncle of Yang Guifei, Yang Meng (J. Yō Mō), a fictitious character, during the An Lushan Rebellion, before which the shipwreck happens. Nakamaro is then escorted by Yang Meng's trusted friends back to Chang'an, while Kiyokawa stays on with the host. Kiyokawa is eventually entrusted with Yang Guifei, who, contrary to what both history and legends tell us, did not die at Mawei; owing to the wit of Yang Meng, she faked her death (by smudging her clothes with mud and leaving them behind) and has since lived clandestinely with her uncle.[114] Kiyokawa then crosses the ocean with Guifei and this time returns safely to Japan. In fear that his political opponent, who has since seized power, may arrest him, he stays incognito in Matsura.[115] (The opponent, Dōkyō (?–772), a Buddhist monk, is known historically as the seducer of Empress Shōtoku and a traitor who attempted to usurp the throne.)

Yang Guifei has the same problem in Japan as did Princess Zhantan in *Kokusen'ya*: her speech sounds like gibberish to the local residents. Kiyokawa easily convinces them that her speech is impaired (*koto domori*, or stammering). The locals laugh at Guifei when she recites poems in Chinese "as though birds were chirping," saying, "Listen to the handicapped sing."[116] This handling of Yang Guifei's "strangeness" showcases the relativity of the intercultural hierarchy: the language of the cultural superior is not appreciated as superior if the listener is not competent in the language. The language of the civilized can sound barbarous to the ears of "barbarians." This message resonates more loudly if we consider the fact that Takebe was a Sinophile. In order to further substantiate the point, he exploits three manifestations of linguistic hybridity involving Chinese and/or Japanese. One is the *rubi*, the Japanese transcription system that provides a reading—phonetic or semantic—of Chinese characters alongside the *kana*. Another is the Japanese practice of reciting Chinese texts in the Japanese pronunciation. The third is the coexistence of literary and vernacular languages within China. Yang Guifei's remarks are accompanied by *rubi*, which represents the sound of the Chinese rather than giving their domesticated reading or a translation of their meaning into Japanese. This creates a sardonic effect similar to the one we saw in Komutsu's reaction to Princess Zhantan's speech in *Kokusen'ya* because the imagined canonicity/formality of the Chinese text is juxtaposed with the obvious "vernacularity"/vulgarity of the unintelligible sounds.[117] The reader sees that the speech sounds like gibberish, without being so told, simply by looking at the nonsensical reading.

Since Yang Guifei is a political refugee whose protector, Kiyokawa, also has to live under cover, her purported speech impairment functions conveniently to shield her from possible interactions with local residents or potential suitors.[118] Kiyokawa, an eligible bachelor himself, starts courting a local woman over the course of time. He is attracted to the local woman rather than to the beautiful Yang Guifei because the latter does not communicate in Japanese; Kiyokawa has to convey messages to her in writing in Chinese, and thus she is "like a woman in a portrait."[119] This image of Yang Guifei confirms the conventional inaccessibility and elusiveness of Chinese women that we saw aptly captured in Wa Tōnai's metaphor for Princess Zhantan in *Kokusen'ya*.

China is transformed from an abstract model to a real entity as suitors' unsuccessful approaches to Yang Guifei and her reactions to them flesh out her role beyond her beautiful facade. When a local man, Asomaru, an accomplice of Dōkyō, tries to woo Yang Guifei and realizes that he cannot read a single letter in the book she is reading, he concludes that she must be the illegitimate daughter of a "hairy Chinese fellow" (Kara no Keyakko) and suggests that the emperor would be interested in seeing someone like her.[120] Kiyokawa is compelled to protect Yang Guifei by fabricating her life story: she is his younger sister, and she was educated according to their deceased parents' wishes. She is further handicapped by lacking a vaginal opening and urinating through her belly—a heavy vulgarization of the legendary beauty.[121] That Yang Guifei is not even capable of knowing that she has been disparaged to this extent is again a lampoon of Chinese monolingualism.

The subsequent transformation of Yang Guifei from monolingual to bilingual is indicative of the complexity of the Sino-Japanese lingual entanglement. Kiyokawa runs into an old comrade, Tamana, who suggests that they should use Yang Guifei as a decoy to manipulate Asomaru indirectly. In order to carry out this plan, they teach her how to speak Japanese. Here another lingual distinction—between elegant and vulgar diction—becomes important. Kiyokawa checks Guifei for her foul mouth when she uses *gaizi* (fool), saying, "The word's Japanese equivalent would be *baka,* but it's not used among the nobility."[122] It is not just national boundaries but also social boundaries that need to be attended to in speech, a fact that is appropriately addressed by the author, who mediated both between Chinese and Japanese and between vernacular and literary languages.

Once Yang Guifei has mastered the spoken language, the next subject of her education is naturally *waka*. As she has studied Japanese by learning the Japanese equivalents of Chinese words, she legitimately asks how *waka* presents the lines from a Li Bai poem.

雲 想 衣 裳 花 想 容   Un san e shō hō san yō   Yun xiang yi zhuang hua xiang rong

春 風 拂 檻 露 華 濃	chan hon fu kan ru ha non	chun feng fu jian lu hua nong
若 非 羣 玉 山 頭 見	shaku hi kyan yo san tō ken	ruo fei qun yu shan tou jian
會 向 瑤 臺 月 下 逢	e hyan yō dai e hyō hon	hui xiang yao tai yue xia feng

(The clouds are like a jacket and skirt, a flower, a countenance /
The spring breeze brushes the rail where dewdrops shine shimmering /
If not to see you on the top of Mount Qun'yu
Then we shall meet under the moon, toward the jade palace)[123]

This is a *yuefu* (rhapsody) called "Qingping diao" (A suite in the ch'ing-p'ing mode), one of three composed by Li Bai upon the command of Emperor Xuanzong and in the presence of Yang Guifei when they were still together in the imperial palace.[124] Despite the elegance of the original text and context, the lines, accompanied by the approximate phonetic transcriptions of *rubi* in *katakana* (given above in romanization in the second column), again end up sounding like gibberish. Though within the text Yang Guifei does not write down the lines, let alone transcribe them, the original Chinese pronunciation sounds funny to Tamana, his wife, and Kiyokawa's wife, all three of whom cannot help laughing. Notably, the effect is not lost on Yang Guifei: "She seems to find it funny herself now."[125] Now that she has become accustomed to Japanese literary conventions, whether by composing in Japanese or reading Chinese poetry in Japanese, Yang Guifei has *become Japanese* enough to appreciate the comical effect of the Chinese sounds.

In a notable view of Japanese poetry in *Honchō Suikoden*, Kiyokawa makes the technical point that *waka*, consisting of thirty-one syllables divided into five lines, can convey a much less substantial message than Chinese verse, which consists of more characters (each bearing meaning) and more lines (in the case of the above excerpt, seven characters per line and four lines); moreover, *waka* is meant to focus on one essence instead of developing a narrative and thus cannot support the same content as *shi*.[126] Having reasoned out his thesis, Kiyokawa attempts to compose a poem in order to capture the general ambience of the Chinese lines: "Omokageno / hanani kumonimo / taguinaba / haruno yamabeni / aubekarikeru" (If her image could be compared to a blossom or a cloud, then I could meet her in the spring field). Then he adds a disclaimer: "Its meaning falls short of the original."[127]

This lesson on theory and practice prompts Guifei to compose a *waka* of her own, inspired by another famous poem by Bai Juyi, "Changhenge."

Ten ni ara ba / hiyoku to chigiri /
chi ni ara ba / renri to nori shi /
kimi zo koishiki

(If we are in the sky / we shall make our wings overlap /
On earth / we shall cross our boughs, /
I miss you who has so declared!)[128]

With this Guifei begins to cry, which moves the people around her.[129] As we saw above, in "Changhenge" Xuanzong misses the deceased Yang Guifei so much that he sends a wizard to seek her spirit; Guifei's spirit tells the wizard of the pledge of love exchanged between her and the emperor, information that the messenger needs to prove that he has completed his mission for the emperor. At the time of the composition of this poem, Yang Guifei is destined to live under cover and apart from her lover, without any means of letting Xuanzong know that she is alive. The geographic distance between China and Japan serves as an alternative for the divide between life and death.

Yang Guifei longs for the days in China with her lover, and she is having some difficulty completing the transition from one persona to another as she attends a party to which she has been invited by the villain Asomaru (as Kiyokawa and Tamana have engineered). Given her rank in her "previous life," she is accustomed to being treated as the most important guest at any gathering; thus Kiyokawa and Tamana have to keep her from taking the seat reserved for such a guest, who in this case is Asomaru; the effect is comical.[130] When she sees women on boats plucking flowers, Guifei is reminded of such activities in Taiye Pond in the Huaqing Palace, where she used to live, and she sheds tears of nostalgia.[131] Then in order to get Guifei to seduce Asomaru, Kiyokawa offers a music and dance performance. He plays the flute to Li Bai's "Qingping diao"; it is meant to accompany a dance called "Rainbow Skirts, Feathery Dress," which portrays heavenly beings in the attire in the title. Historically known as a talented dancer, Yang Guifei is ready to perform, except she realizes that the sleeves of the Japanese clothes she wears now are too short to create the intended effect. When she requests that a robe, skirt, and fan be provided, she fails to pronounce the items' names in Japanese.[132] Despite the potentially fatal error,

Guifei's charm wins out. Her sudden burst of Chinese contributes to her otherworldly appearance; the audience is taken with her beauty, which, it says, excels that of the heavenly maiden who descended in Yoshino out of admiration for Emperor Tenmu's *kin* performance.[133] The parallel of the China-Japan dyad and the Heaven-Earth dyad is repeated here, except that this time China is Heaven and Japan, Earth. This transposition points to the sheer lack of a Chinese audience; unlike in the scene of the *waka* composition, in which Yang Guifei's Japanese poem diminishes the distance between China and Japan by capturing the sentiment of the Chinese poem and transmitting it to the Japanese audience, a cultural distance is created in the dance scene, as intended by Kiyokawa's strategy and as desired by the audience. Precisely because Guifei appears unearthly and foreign, she makes a strong impression and helps along the scheme of seduction. None of those present desires commonality across a distance; what is produced and appreciated is an exoticism that capitalizes on the cultural distance.

While the analogy between nations (China and Japan) and cosmological spheres (Heaven and Earth) is made only tangentially, it foreshadows the later revelation of Yang Guifei's identities in her previous life and afterlife respectively. Japanese popular legends, such as one in *Kojiki,* have it that Yang Guifei was a reincarnation of Miyazu Hime, who was a wife of Yamato Takeru (a controversial warrior who conquered other tribes on behalf of the Japanese emperor only to be labeled later as a rebel) and the founder of Atsuta Shrine. She had a mission to distract Xuanzong from his intention of conquering Japan.[134] Takebe's text gives a different account of the reincarnation: Yang Guifei tells her protectors that her mother dreamed of a foreign-looking woman (i.e., non-Chinese) who told her that she would rent her womb so as to be born into China for the time being. When her term was over, she would return to Atsuta Shrine, where she belonged.[135] The theme of transnational reincarnation, prominent in *Hamamatsu* and important in *Matsura,* is again manifest in this story, where Japan is seen as the country of deities and China, that of humans charged with earthly desires.

The subversion of course does not stop with the caricaturization of this legendary beauty. As noted above, the bilingualism of the cultivated Japanese (which was in reality a necessity for survival in a Sinocentric civilization) is revealed to be superior to the monolingualism of the Chinese, although initially one could dispense with any language other than Chinese, the only civilized language. In addition, Kiyokawa has acquired vernacular Chinese. A command of not only the literary language, which by definition should be acquired by any citizen of the Sinocentric world, but also the vernacular language, which is meant to belong to native speakers, disturbs the whole binary of the native/foreign, the spoken/written, and the natural/cultural. As I will show in the next chapter, at the time *Honchō suikoden* was written, vernacular Chinese was being studied by the Japanese literati, although they still did not have many opportunities to visit China.

Conclusion

In the fictional travelogues discussed in this chapter, the problem of communicating with the residents of the land of destination, a problem that real travelers inevitably encounter, is either resolved owing to the primary characters' excellence in Chinese or exaggerated in order to exoticize China. In the former cases, the exemplary characters, while garnering honorary citizenship in the Sinocentric civilization, are also instrumental in promoting the virtues of bilingualism and suggesting that one's identity be based on the language (and its corollary, cultural practices) in which one writes at a given moment. In this light, one might say that Sino-Japanese travel, like miscegenation, is a metaphor for the heterogeneity inherent in identity that is continuously formed and dissolved, depending upon the occasion.

As Japanese writers became increasingly familiar with colloquial Chinese, however, the language contributed to a concept of ethnic uniqueness of the Chinese in the Japanese mind—as though the psychological distance had grown wider as the perception of geographical distance had declined. Especially with the participation of lower-class characters, who were not knowledgeable in the classical Chinese canon, the local color of the foreign land, most obvious in the conversational language, was blatantly foregrounded. The effect was that China became just another foreign land that, despite what a sharing of the universal literary language might have suggested, was indeed ethnically distinct from Japan.

The awareness of China's ethnic identity is not identical with the portrayal of China as either a hegemon or a blank slate against which Japan struggled to mark its own presence. Indeed, the emerging awareness of the diversity of Chinese culture compelled the Japanese to reconfigure their relationship with the Chinese. Given the arrival of yet another cultural hegemon (the "West"), this proved to be a complex process of self-redefinition, as we shall see in the next chapter.

CHAPTER 2

From the Edifying
to the Edible

Chinese Fetishism and the China Fetish

It is not the passion (whether of objects or subjects) for substances that
speaks in fetishism, it is the passion for the code.
— Jean Baudrillard

The function of the tour is the estrangement of objects—to make what
is visible, what is surface, reveal a profound interiority through
narrative. This interiority is that of the perceiving subject; it is gained
at the expense of risking *contamination* . . . and the dissolution of the
boundary of that subject.
— Susan Stewart

From the mid-eighteenth to the mid-nineteenth century, the Japanese had acquired a broad knowledge of Chinese culture, which
until then had been considered primarily the source of ideological,
intellectual, and literary texts. Three newer dimensions of Japan's entanglement with China were vernacularism (corresponding to the rise of
baihua, the vernacular Chinese, as opposed to the predominance of *wenyan,* the literary language of the classical canon); an academic discourse
of Sinology, or *kangaku* (as opposed to the immersion in Chinese learning mandated for every man of letters); and the codification of Chinese
goods (as opposed to the production and reception of "meaning" in the
text). Irrelevant to and incongruous with one another as they may seem,
these three manifestations of the newer kind of contact were inter-
locked. Ibi Takashi maintains that Sinology changed its course almost
simultaneously with the explosion in popularity of the poetry on things

(*eibutsu shi;* Ch. *yongwu shi*), while Hino Tatsuo directs our attention to the concurrent popularity of the connoisseurial collecting of stationery (*bunbō aigan*) and kōshōgaku (Ch. *kaozhengxue*), a Qing scholarly approach to empiricism that involves the collection of information on a given term/topic for the purpose of historicizing references.[1] I would further argue that the concurrent ethnocentric, scholarly, and materialist approaches to China were not coincidental but indeed interrelated, if not mutually consequential. They even suggest a significant revision of Japan's self-definition, for which its diversifying and tightening involvement with Chinese culture was instrumental.

The shift of focus from the spiritual/intellectual to the material had run its course by the Taishō period (1912–1926), when urban, transnational consumer culture had reached its maturity. In addition to Japan's familiarity with Chinese goods, which had much increased in the advent of the modern international trade system and the normalization of transnational travel and transportation, the Western Orientalist appreciation of things Chinese, or *chinoiserie,* found a "colony" in Japan, especially in the wake of the Russo-Japanese War in 1905. Just as the assimilation of Chinese connoisseurship affected the Japanese acquisition and appreciation of Chinese objects and then of China itself, so the assimilation of Orientalism led to Japan's "orientalizing" of China, in which Japan's own position—whether object or subject—was made ambiguous. The confluence of the two trends, one since the eighteenth century and the other since the nineteenth, played out against the backdrop of Japan's aggression toward China. While military, capitalist, or other invasive actions may have been taken toward other Asian countries, action against China had two special symbolical meanings: the Japanese had either finally mastered the appreciation of artistic objects following the model of the Chinese connoisseurs, or they had transformed themselves into a version of the Western colonizers, for the majority of whom Chinese thought and literature meant little.

In this chapter, I will first illuminate the interconnection of the three developments, which contributed to the undoing of the older rhetoric that constituted Chineseness, and reveal how Japanese recipients of Chinese cultural products distanced themselves from them instead of fashioning themselves after the Chinese model. I will then show how the newly acquired critical distance was accommodated to the map of power and knowledge involving the "West" in post–Russo-Japanese War Japan, where physical proximity, realized by modern transportation, promoted a Japanese aestheticization of the China of the past against the backdrop of the China of the present.

"Read as They Speak": Vernacularism and the Birth of the "Barbarians"

Ogyū Sorai (1666–1728), who, as we shall see, is primarily known as a leading authority in the pro–High Tang Kobunji-ha school (Ch. Guwenci-pai) of Sinology, was also known to be an enthusiastic advocate of vernacularism. Sorai contended that Chinese texts (and the range of texts he had in mind still consisted of Confucian classics and poetry) should be recited in Chinese, honoring the authentic Chinese pronunciation (*tōin*). He renounced *kundoku* (or *yomikudashi*), the long-established practice of reading Chinese texts by rearranging the word order so as to reconstruct sentences in accordance with Japanese syntax. It is undeniable that the practice, which had domesticated Chinese texts, had curtailed the Japanese Sinophiles' oral skills and listening comprehension in Chinese. Two pieces of evidence are particularly relevant in our context. First, it is documented that in the sixteenth century, Ishikawa Jōzan (1583–1672), one of the most distinguished Sinophiles of his time, could not speak with Kwŏn Ch'ik, an officer accompanying the Korean envoy (*Chōsen tsūshinshi*), in either Korean or Chinese and yet was able to communicate with him by means of *hitsudan*, or brush talk. The topic of their conversation was classical-style Chinese poems that Jōzan had composed. The Korean offered a typical compliment—that Jōzan was the "Japanese [equivalent of] Li Bai or Du Fu."[2] That the presentation and evaluation of a Japanese man's thoughts had to be mediated by inscription in literary Chinese and by references to classical Chinese icons speaks loudly for the reasons of Sorai's frustration. The flip side of the "universality" of literary Chinese is the sheer incapability of East Asian intellectuals to communicate orally in each other's languages.

The other example of the overemphasis on the written language is in the different titles of the professional interpreters of Chinese and Dutch in the port of Nagasaki. The former is *tsūji*, literally meaning "translating things"; the latter, *tsūshi*, or "translating words." Ishizaki Matazō contends that the titles varied because "one could still understand what the Chinese were saying if it was written, while one couldn't comprehend the Dutch texts."[3] Against the backdrop of a shared knowledge in written Chinese, the specific deficiency of the Japanese in oral and aural skills was even more apparent.

Within a hundred years from the early Tokugawa, however, the status of spoken Chinese changed. There was a remarkable increase in human and material resources for the study of vernacular Chinese, a language that had not been taught in schools because it was considered unnecessary for, if not harmful to, serious students of classical essentials. Ishizaki relates that Yanagisawa Yoshiyasu (1658–1714), the chief political adviser for the fifth shogun, Tokugawa Tsunayoshi (1646–1709; r. 1680–1709), who employed Ogyū Sorai, studied colloquial Chinese with a Chinese immigrant monk and was able to comprehend conversations in Chinese between Chinese delegates from Nagasaki and their Japanese interpreters.[4] Yoshiyasu's acquisition of proficiency was not an isolated case that was possible only for those of power and means. Interpreters in Nagasaki were often relocated to other areas of Japan and published textbooks and dictionaries that made spoken Chinese more accessible to the Japanese. Among the most famous was Okajima Kanzan (1675–1728), whose works include *Tōwa san'yō* (Guidelines of spoken Chinese, 1716), a widely distributed textbook. Okajima was invited to teach in Edo and Osaka and was instrumental in Ogyū Sorai's advocacy of vernacularism. Okajima's accomplishments extend to translations of Chinese vernacular fiction, such as *Chūgi Suikoden* (Loyal Shuihu zhuan, 1728).[5]

The trend of studying Chinese as a foreign tongue, as opposed to the ostensibly universal literary language in which canonical texts were written, came hand in hand with a demand for Chinese vernacular fiction, or *hakuwa shōsetsu* (Ch. *baihua xiaoshuo*), a burgeoning genre in China itself. Given the Japanese readers' still shaky command of vernacular Chinese, they still required devices to domesticate these texts, which appeared more ethnically specific (as written in the native tongue of China) and "foreign" than did the Confucian classics or classical poetry, which had been read in the *yomikudashi* style and which thus appeared accessible, however deceptively so. For that reason a mode of negotiation with Chinese fiction was devised: *kun'yaku,* or supplying Japanese readings of characters, which inevitably provided a word-by-word translation into Japanese. Another way for the Japanese to engage Chinese fiction was with loose translations of the texts into Japanese. Such products typically added the term *tsūzoku* (popularized) as a prefix to the original titles (e.g., Okajima's *Tsūzoku chūgi Suikoden* [Loyal Shuihu zhuan: Popular version, 1757]). Even more remote from the original were parodies of Chinese fiction in Japanese. Many works in this genre have remained popular to date; among these, Takebe Ayatari's *Honchō Suikoden* is particularly renowned for a varied appropriation of Chinese sources not limited to the literary canon.[6] Many of the parodies reveal the authors' familiarity with the classics written in literary Japanese (*bungo*) and thus are examples of translingual practices not only between Chinese and Japanese, but also between the literary and vernacular languages.

It may appear only legitimate and sensible that the Japanese learned to do justice to the reading of Chinese texts. Ironically, however, the new recognition and observance of the distinct sounds of nonliterary (spoken and vernacular) Chinese had ramifications that would not have been so flattering to the Chinese. Authentic Chinese pronunciation sounded so odd to ears used to hearing the *sodoku* (recitation of Chinese texts in Japanese) of high-flown *kundoku*-style Japanese that many fiction writers opted to mock the speech of Chinese characters as though they deserved ridicule from the Japanese characters. As the idiom *Tōjin no negoto* (the sleep talk of a Chinese) suggests, Chinese speech was taken as nonsensical. As we saw in chapter 1, in *Honchō Suikoden* Yang Guifei successfully conceals her identity because the local residents of Matsura are ignorant enough of spoken Chinese to accept the excuse that she is speech impaired. Yang Guifei's speech is transcribed in *katakana* in an attempt to honor the original and authentic pronunciation as much as possible, yet the net effect is that her speech is highlighted as nothing but barbarous. The average Japanese response that Chinese pronunciation was comical was not simply fictitious. Marcia Yonemoto tells us that according to a travelogue entitled *Saiyū zakki* (1783), by Furukawa Koshōken (1726–1807), Chinese speech was considered strange by the Japanese in Nagasaki. Yonemoto analyzes a passage from the text that includes the phrase *chin-pun-kan* (unintelligible): "'Chin-pun-kan' was a generic mimicry of foreign languages as nonsensical babble, and it underscores the way in which language, for Koshōken, and perhaps universally, has been a prime distinguishing feature of cultural difference."[7]

That Chinese speech sounds to the Japanese too odd to be normal human speech is the whole premise of a *sharebon* (comic fiction) appropriately entitled *Wa Tō chinkai* (Hilarious translations between Japanese and Chinese, 1785). A parody of *Kokusen'ya gassen,* it places the original play's major characters in the pleasure quarters of Maruyama in Nagasaki.[8] Wa Tōnai, a.k.a. Coxinga, the half-Chinese, half-Japanese hero and potential savior of the Ming imperial house in Chikamatsu's play, is here an interpreter and accompanies a Chinese client Li Daotian (J. Ri Tōten, originally the villain who was instrumental in the demise of the

Ming dynasty) because he does not understand Japanese. Characters refer to Wu Sangui (J. Go Sankei), the faithful subject of the Ming emperor, as a handsome client who is popular among Japanese courtesans. Princess Zhantan (J. Sendan), whom Li Daotian was intent upon marrying and who later flees to Japan, is here a beautiful Japanese courtesan with whom Wa Tōnai has been sleeping in secret as he deceives the resourceless Daotian. The Chinese speeches of Daotian and Tōnai are given in Chinese characters, with *rubi* on both sides of the vertical lines of the main text: on the right side the approximate Chinese pronunciation of the words is transcribed in *katakana,* and on the left, rough Japanese translations are represented in *hiragana.* The courtesans and their apprentices, who are half amused and half horrified by the (to them) unusual physical appearance and manners of the Chinese customer and his black servant from Malaysia, Konrondo, keep asking Tōnai questions about the sounds Daotian makes (including nonwords, such as sneezes), taking it for granted that the object of their discussion and teasing will not understand a word they say about him.[9]

The exoticization of Chinese speech manifest in works such as *Wa Tō chinkai* coincides with the unabashedly domesticated and vulgarized readings of Chinese canonical texts. Domestication is embraced in the abundance of phonetic transcriptions of Chinese enunciation, as is evidenced in *Tōshisen ōkai: Gogon zekku* (Distortion of a rake's tea brush: Five-character quatrain, 1770), a comical commentary of classical Chinese poetry.[10] The first three letters of the title are obviously meant to be a parody of *Tōshisen,* an anthology of Tang poetry compiled in the Ming era (conventionally attributed to Li Panlong [1514–1570]) and widely distributed in Japan since its arrival in the early Tokugawa, while the two compounds are pronounced differently in Chinese (*Dangzi quan* and *Tangshixuan* respectively). The parody relies on translations of literary Chinese into colloquial Japanese and the interpretation of high-brow content via the manners and customs of the demimonde. Owing to the increased dissemination of commentaries and scholarly works on classical Chinese poetry, the range of moderately competent readers had widened, to the extent that comic writers, such as Shoku Sanjin (a.k.a. Ōta Nanpo; 1749–1823), could publish parodic commentaries and translations (*kyōshi*) and expect commercial success. The scholarly works, which show a formidable familiarity with the classical Chinese canon, challenge both the established *kundoku* method and the quest for ethnic authenticity that Sorai's allies rigorously sought.

Hino Tatsuo attributes the fact that many intellectuals well-versed in Chinese classics turned to *sharebon* and *kyōshi* to the intellectual and existential conflicts that emerged in the late Tokugawa period. Hino first articulates two stages in the transformation of literature: a distancing of literature from Confucianism in the early Tokugawa and a departure from the old rhetoric in the late Tokugawa. While it was possible by the late Tokugawa to write literature without a Confucian ideological framework, a way to represent ideas outside the scope of the classical poetic vocabulary was still being sought. Hino then notes the dilemma of late Edo literati—the desire to express themselves freely and the need to conform to the norm of high literary rhetoric—and he hypothesizes that one solution was to take recourse in ostensibly vulgar genres such as *kyōshi* and *gesaku* (comic fiction). The choice of such genres was possible as writers abandoned the status of literati and accepted the use of the vulgar language.[11] In our context, however, the explicit popularization of Chinese canonical texts does not contradict the rigorous restoration (or invention) of the exotic in Chinese discourse. In fact, the two operations are precisely the flip sides of each other, as both are premised on the linguistic distance between Japanese and Chinese, whereas Chinese as the written language was previously thought to be an essential and even formative part of Japanese.

China under Scrutiny: Things and Their (Textual) Companions

Sinology in Japan developed rapidly. Not only did the shogunate have Neo-Confucianism taught at its official school of Shōheikō, but also Japanese scholars published annotations and criticisms of Chinese works that, though distributed only in Japan, were as up to date and sophisticated as that of Chinese scholars on their own literature. An exposure to current Chinese scholarship was accelerated owing at least in part to the promotion of trade with Qing China encouraged by the eighth shogun, Tokugawa Yoshimune (1684–1751; r. 1716–1751). It is of course not as though the Japanese had never studied contemporary Chinese literature. There were notable scholarly endeavors, such as Kūkai's (774–835) works on poetics, as well as practical guides that helped Japanese students to familiarize themselves with Chinese literature. Moreover, Japanese scholars of Chinese had formed opinions of specific Chinese literary works. To take the most prominent example, the works of Bai Juyi were read with enthusiasm by the poet's contemporaries in Japan in the ninth century. It is also evident that the Japanese readings of Bai's works, especially poems of social criticism or satire, varied significantly from the Chinese readings thereof.[12] Nevertheless, the Japanese scholars of earlier generations did not form a school whose critiques were deemed independent of and comparable to those of the Chinese. Notable contributions to scholarship had to be claimed via the genres of *waka* and *karon* (theories of *waka*), rather than in Chinese studies. Even the invention of *kundoku* did not seem to have inspired Japanese students of Chinese toward autonomy or innovation.

It can be argued that among the earliest examples of critical evaluation of Chinese poetry is that of Ishikawa Jōzan, who, in collegial consultation with the Neo-Confucian authority Hayashi Razan (1583–1657), selected thirty-six poetic immortals (*shisen*) from the history of Chinese poetry.[13] A critical distance from Chinese poetry is evident in the classical Japanese practice of identifying thirty-six immortals to form the Chinese canon, as well as the seemingly independent evaluative standard of screening thirty-six poets and making eighteen pairs. Although Jōzan's project turned out to be the isolated personal pursuit of a reclusive dilettante of independent means, Tokugawa Sinology was much more communal, if not institutional.

The scarcity of direct contact with Chinese colleagues did not prevent Japanese Sinologists in the Tokugawa period from consulting scholarly works imported from China or refining their own theories by keeping abreast of recent interpretations and trends in the field. The time lag between the initial publication and distribution (and possible Japanese edition) of Chinese scholarly works kept diminishing toward the end of the Tokugawa period, while the autonomy of Japanese scholars grew. The development of the publishing industry and marketing helped disseminate scholarly works beyond an author's immediate colleagues and disciples. Increases in literacy and the demand for education also propelled the publication of Japanese editions of Chinese texts (*wakokubon kanseki*).[14]

In the early Tokugawa period, the Ming poetics of the Guwenci school, which canonized High Tang poetry (such as that of Du Fu and Li Bai) and most prominently represented by Li Panlong and Wang Shizhen (1526–1590), dominated Japanese scholarship on Chinese poetry, with Ogyū Sorai and Hattori Nankaku (1683–1759) as its most vocal advocates. Nineteenth-century Japanese scholars were more in agreement with the *xingling* theory advocated by Qing scholars such as Yuan Mei (1716–1797, whom we will see in the next chapter in yet another context) and discouraged the reproduction of Tang rhetoric while promoting the spontaneous expression of one's own observations.[15] The two critical stances are not to be simplified as one privileging language and the other, spirit. The High Tang poetry privileged in the Ming poetics tends to focus on intense emotions, such as patriotic concerns, homesickness, and longing for a lost lover, weaving what may appear to be hyperbolic rhetorical patterns to effectively convey passion. Thus, one of the predominant genres in the High Tang is the *yonghuai shi* (J. *eikai shi*), or poems on what one has on one's mind. In contrast, Qing poetics honors an attention to quotidian details. The predominant method of the time was *kaozheng* (J. *kōshō*), which was the collection and exhibition of empirical information on a given topic—as opposed to *xungu* (J. *kunko*), a lexicographical study based on the annotations of Tang criticism, or *lixue* (J. *rigaku*), a philosophical and theoretical study prevalent in the Song dynasty. In the words of Jean Baudrillard, who claims that "we live in a world where there is more and more information, and less and less meaning," these writings might be termed "the staging of meaning" rather than the production of meaning, in which information can "exhaust itself."[16] The act of reading, which used to be a *medium* to master the classics and gain virtue, became a symbolic act of status, on one hand, and a pastime, an indulgence in itself, on the other. Collected and displayed words are commodities, and owning many of them—either metaphorically (i.e., holding an encyclopedic knowledge) or literally (i.e., possessing a large personal library)—means one has wealth and power, a highly sought status. Hino Tatsuo differentiates thing-oriented connoisseurship *(shumi)* from text-oriented connoisseurship *(kyōyō)*. Whereas the former is based upon aesthetic tastes/ judgments exerted upon things, the latter is predicated on a body of fetishized knowledge—that is, knowledge not for the sake of the things to which it pertains but for its social value, knowledge not as a vehicle for the understanding of things but as a demonstration of knowing itself, an emblem of a higher social status, or, in Pierre Bourdieu's terms, "symbolical capital."[17] If we focus less on the body of knowledge than on the *function* of knowledge, it is obvious that knowledge not only helps those who have it to more profitably or effectively deal with the things that the knowledge is about, but it also allows them to be more respectfully received in their social circles. The concept appears in the following *haiku:*

Eibutsu no	The peony
shi o kuchizusamu	makes me recite
botan kana	a poem on things
	Buson[18]

This *haiku* encapsulates an almost tautological relationship between the thing (in this case the peony) and the word; in an intellectual's self-conscious musings, the peony reminds the speaker of an object in a poem that s/he knows. The object does not merely evoke a poem; it evokes the *idea* that a poem can be and has been composed about it. It is not just a simple reversal of the order of events that is at work here, but also their placement in a paradoxical spiral, where *causality* as well as chronology becomes ambiguous. The fetishization of knowledge and the textualization of connoisseurship validate and facilitate each other. Crowning this entanglement is the fact that the Japanese poem frames the speaker's act of recitation in Chinese. It has not been determined whether the Chinese or Japanese language was primary in the making of this poem.

Things That You Do, Things That Are You: The Location of the Japanese Self

The practice of nonliterary Chinese arts (an exemplary case of which we will see in Ema Saikō in the next chapter) had been diffused among Japanese intellectuals since the mid-eighteenth century. This is not to deny an earlier exposure of Japanese artists and art lovers to Chinese cultural products in the early Muromachi period, which was known for its intense acquisition and appreciation of "things Chinese," or "Karamono"— noted, for example, among the shogun's attendants in charge of entertainment (*dōbō shū*). The medieval collection and admiration of the Chinese visual arts, however, differs from the case under investigation in two ways. First, a systematic codification of things was yet to be completed, if even begun, and thus things had not been saturated by their marriage with language. Meticulous and profuse documentation and annotation was a concept of the eighteenth century. Second, the acquisition and appreciation of things Chinese in the Muromachi period was limited to the nobility and artists with noble patronage, whereas an expansion of the urban consumer culture in the mid-Tokugawa period provided a much wider clientele for cultural products in fields other than the literary. Patricia C. Graham, inspired by Bourdieu, relates the circumstances as follows:

> The [Tokugawa] government's endorsement of Chinese learning for the masses and encouragement of trade, both domestic and international, led to far-reaching social changes, some of which the bakufu may not have foreseen

or approved. Excelling at learning became a means of moving beyond restrictions imposed by birth into a lower class, for education allowed commoners access to knowledge of the higher culture of China to which they had previously been denied. Similarly, growth in trade resulted in increased wealth for merchants, allowing them to acquire the material goods that were associated with this higher culture. Wealthy merchants and townspeople aspiring to parity with the samurai class sought the material trappings of that class, including Chinese luxury products or Japanese substitutes in similar styles.[19]

The fifth shogun, Tokugawa Tsunayoshi, during whose reign spoken Chinese came to be studied widely (as we saw above), invited the Chinese Buddhist monk Yinyuan and his followers to come to Japan and permitted them to move freely around the country (including Edo); to found a sect called Ōbaku-shū; and to build many temples, which offered venues for intellectual and aesthetic gatherings of the Japanese literati, Ogyū Sorai among them. Yinyuan greatly facilitated the importation of books, paintings, and other artistic artifacts and practices and thus contributed to further the appreciation of Chinese culture.[20]

As in China, kinki shoga (Ch. qinqi shuhua; music, chess, calligraphy, drawing) were considered to be the four essentials that literati must master and practice. Jiezi yuan huazhuan (The mustard seed garden manual of painting, 1679), by Li Yu (Li Liweng, 1611–ca. 1680), was imported soon after its original publication in China and was circulated widely among Japanese painters and artists-to-be as a requisite for the study of correct strokes and other drawing/painting methods.[21] Some of the distinguished masters of the four arts were not from the nobility or gentry, a fact that attests to the wider dissemination of education and the consequent emergence of a large number of connoisseurs. Among them were Ike no Taiga (1723–1776) and Yosa (no) Buson (1716–1783), whose paintings are densely informed by the Chinese poetic tradition and yet are illustrative of the everyday life of commoners.[22] An excellent example of cultural practices that transcend social boundaries is Jūben jūgi zu (Ten conveniences and ten preferences, 1771), a collaborative work by the two artists that was inspired by Li Liweng's poetry.[23] In addition to the aforementioned four essentials, the tea ceremony (specifically sencha, as distinct from cha no yu), seal engraving (tenkoku), flower arrangement, horticulture, incense burning, bird feeding, and goldfish feeding (among others) were celebrated as commendable arts for the cultivated to practice in order to demonstrate their discriminating taste.

Peony viewing was imported from China to Japan as an essential ac-
tivity of the literati. Bai Juyi's criticism of the affluent urban residents' fa-
natic spending on the flower in "Mudan fang" (Peony is beautiful) was
lost on the Japanese audience for the second time (the first had been
when the poem itself had been imported).[24] While the mid-Tang poet's
intended satire may have eluded the Heian court because of the Japanese
emphasis on the lyrical rather than the political, this time, the Japanese
failed to recognize it because of the shift from an ideological to a materialist reception of Chinese culture. The aim of literature was no longer considered to be the crystallization of emotions (rather than social criticism)
but the archiving of information (rather than the promotion of ideas).
The earlier contrast of values may be construed as Japanese versus Chinese definitions of literature, while the newer dyad juxtaposes Qing and
Ming (pro-Tang) criticism. This reveals a much higher degree of, and
broader familiarity with, Chinese thought in Japan, on one hand, and,
ironically, a sense of transgression of the national cultural boundaries, on
the other hand. The latter is distinctly present in the following *haiku*:

Tōin mo	The peony
sukoshi iitaki	Makes me feel like
botan kana	speaking in Chinese
	Kanchō[25]

This *haiku* showcases an entanglement of the Japanese subject, who
views and speaks of the peony, and the Chineseness that he thinks the
peony embodies and that he wishes to embody by muttering in Chinese.
The authentic enunciation of Chinese would transform him into a
quasi-Chinese and thus exoticize him. What is happening along with
the Japanese fashioning themselves on the Chinese model is worth a
closer look. Because the peony is thought to emit Chineseness, the subject feels like exoticizing himself to match it. The flower itself, as Hino
Tatsuo points out, had long ago been brought to the Japanese soil and
was familiar to the Japanese eye. But it had been re-Sinified in order to
symbolically bear the mark of Chineseness.[26] The recognition of the materialist aspects of Chinese culture—such as the cultivation, exhibition,
and appreciation of peonies—was a step short of the inscription of foreignness on China's cultural products, which were also symbolic goods.
The shift from the Chinese art of cultivating and arranging flowers (the
model after which the Japanese had fashioned themselves) to the label-

ing of particular flowers as quintessentially Chinese was a shift from the Japanese adaptation of Chinese connoisseurship to the Japanese objectification of things Chinese. The foreignness was imagined and reinvented so that objects of desire that had already been domesticated could function as embodiments of Chineseness. Chineseness, which had previously been recognized in the *practice* of connoisseurship, was newly inscribed in the *objects* thereof.

The following *haiku* captures a moment of erosion in the image of China as the spiritual and aesthetic model and reveals its material and physical vigor:

Utsukushii	The beautiful face
kao de Yōkihi	of Yang Guifei
buta o kui	reveling in pork
	Senryū[27]

"*Kao*" is represented by a *kokuji,* or a made-in-Japan "Chinese" character, commonly in use in *haiku* and other Tokugawa popular literary texts in *wabun,* suggesting the ambiguous origin of the Japanese cultural practice of inscription. This particular instance is significant, given that the *kokuji* is used to contrast the facade of Yang Guifei, the legendary Chinese beauty, with the vulgar act of eating pork—a dietary practice that had been foreign to the Japanese and is thus connoted with savagery. On a more physical note, the beautiful face and the vulgar act present a contrast between the exterior and the interior (not the psyche, but the literal interior of the body), painting a picture of a gaping hole in the beautiful face and the disappearance of the piece of meat into the darkness of the body.

It is interesting that the objectification of China is a ramification of the very act of the Japanese fashioning themselves after the Chinese model. Be it a scholarly study; vernacularism; or the collection, exhibition, and utilization of objects of art, the Japanese had learned from the Chinese how to establish and maintain a distance from which to valorize the object. That knowledge—and its application—was used for China itself, leading to a Japanese commodification of China, when the Japanese became aware of the national boundaries between China and Japan. Whereas many Japanese literati may have imagined that they had joined the Chinese connoisseurs in their acts of objectification, the Japanese connoisseurship of Chinese products/objects slipped into the objectification of China itself. Consequently, Chineseness became equated with materiality, whereas Japaneseness was concealed in the ostensible neutrality of spectatorship/commentatorship.

The Self-Aware Subject of Objectification

Scholarship in Chinese literature that had begun in the eighteenth century continued with a reorganization of the academic community in the late nineteenth century as Japan adopted the Western institution of the university. As departments in the Faculty of Letters were arranged by language (e.g., the Department of National [i.e., Japanese] Literature, Department of English Literature, Department of French Literature), the standing of *kanshibun* became institutionally ambiguous and affected the formation of the national canon.[28] At the same time, the reciprocal embedding of the textual and the material in Chinese culture continued to thrive as academia was being transformed.

By far the most prominent figure in the study of Chinese material culture is Aoki Masaru (1887–1964), arguably the best scholar of his time in Chinese literature, especially drama. Aoki, who taught such subjects as Chinese theater and poetry at many universities—including his alma mater, which was acclaimed as the center of Sinology—is at least equally if not better known for his studies of the Chinese nonliterary arts.[29] He translated several significant works on Chinese painting (for example, *Jiezi yuan huazhuan*); cuisine (Yuan Mei's *Suiyuan shidan* [Suiyuan's recipes]); and tea (many works, starting with Lu Yu's [?–804] *Chajing* [The classics of tea], a study of tea from the Tang through the Ming dynasties).[30] At the same time, he wrote and published prolifically: on the Chinese art of drinking (*Shuchūshu* [Taste in wines]), on cultural pursuits (*Kinki shoga* [Music, chess, calligraphy, painting]), and on other aspects of Chinese material culture. From these contributions, it is clear that Aoki was a mediator par excellence, informing his Japanese audience of how to evaluate, collect, exhibit, utilize, and appreciate material goods in the Chinese mode. While the direction of the dissemination of knowledge remained the same—China the originator and Japan the recipient—the fact that Chinese material culture began to receive Japanese analytical attention reveals a new phase in the Sino-Japanese entanglement: China was now the object and Japan the subject of cross-cultural analysis.

Aoki's work marks a new phase in the Sino-Japanese entanglement in yet another way: he is among the first Japanese Sinologists whose works were extensively translated into Chinese. Many of his translated works have been printed by Chinese presses and distributed in both mainland China and Taiwan over an extended period.[31] The number of translations, various places of publication, and duration suggest not only Aoki's individual accomplishments or a higher status for Japanese scholarship on things Chinese, but also a change that had occurred in China— namely, Chinese academics were becoming aware that their own culture could be an object for others to study and that the research of other scholars could bring something worthwhile to their study of their own culture. That Chinese students of Chinese culture sought the views of Japanese Sinologists back in the mid-twentieth century signals an awareness and active engagement in the "entanglement" on the part of the Chinese.

Aoki himself reflects upon the attention of the Chinese to Japanese Sinology in an essay, "Shina bungaku kenkyū ni okeru hōjin no tachiba" (The Japanese position on the study of Chinese literature, 1937) in which he recalls that one of his teachers, Naitō Konan (1866–1934), used to say that Chinese students would come to the University of Kyoto to study Chinese in the foreseeable future.[32] However, Naitō's—and Aoki's— focus was the level of scholarship in Japan and not the paradigm change on the part of the Chinese. In other words, Aoki does not seem to have been concerned with the burden of the past, when Japan had no other way to define itself than to compare itself with China. Thus "Chinese literature" in Aoki's title is interchangeable with any national literature, and the scholarship could have pertained to any region.

It is noteworthy that Aoki refers to Chinese literature throughout his short essay as *gaikoku bungaku,* or "foreign literature," whose foreignness makes it difficult for the Japanese to study it. Aoki's term confirms that Chinese literature is no longer an essential part of Japanese literature that the Japanese should learn by heart; rather, it is a subject that individuals can choose to study in institutional settings. It is in this spirit that in "Kanbun chokudoku ron" (A discussion on the straightforward reading of Chinese writings; written in 1920) Aoki firmly renounces the Japanese practice of *kundoku/yomikudashi*—as well as the whole mode of thinking that the practice imprints in the minds of Japanese Sinologists—and advocates solely the Chinese reading of Chinese texts. He praises Ogyū Sorai and Amenomori Hōshū (1668–1755, who was also proficient in spoken Korean) for promoting the mastery of the authentic and original Chinese language.[33]

Aoki continues with the same thesis in an autobiographical essay, "Shina gakusha no uwagoto" (A Sinologist babbling). He reveals that upon entering college, he ceased to recite Chinese poems in *kundoku* and began to recite them instead in the original Beijing dialect and to read in the original word order rather than changing it in order to apply Japanese grammar and syntax to Chinese texts.[34] Aoki is obviously in favor of undomesticating Chinese and cleansing the texts of the residues of Japanese emotional input, which, he claims, increased the spiritual value of the classical Chinese canon. Aoki worked to neutralize the age-old fold within which the Japanese had found themselves and to re-ethnicize Chinese literature. The time when English literature was not in the same league as *wen*, or the Chinese classics (as once judged by Natsume Sōseki), seems to have long passed by the Taishō period; just as the Chinese began to see themselves being defined by Japan, the Japanese began to objectify China, not as a force pertinent to their identity but as nothing more or less than a body of knowledge.[35]

Tourists but not Travelers

Japanese tourism in China is another modern phenomenon that strongly attests to the changing Sino-Japanese entanglement. In the fictional narratives that we saw in chapter 1 Japanese travels to China were centripetal—that is, toward the center of civilization. In the Taishō period, however, the framework was much changed: unlike the privileged and extraordinary fictional heroes earnestly seeking and fortunately earning rare opportunities to visit China, more and more modern Japanese could afford to travel to China. Their trips were often funded by Japanese newspapers, which printed and distributed their travelogues for fellow Japanese to read and enjoy vicariously.

Aoki was one of those travelers to China. *Kōnan shun* (Spring in Jiangnan) is a result of his visit in 1922—a short while after the publication of Tanizaki Jun'ichirō's writings on China, with which I deal next.[36] Aoki recounts his sightseeing tours, visits to theaters, and shopping in Hangzhou, Nanjing, and Yangzhou—literary topoi that Tanizaki had visited earlier and recurrently takes up in his fiction. Whereas Aoki is occasionally surprised by the gap between the fantastic image of China generated by texts he had read and the sobering, if not disillusioning, reality, he does not resort to the cliché that China's great tradition was tarnished by the invasion of modern Western civilization. In response to those who lamented that the West Lake district had been cheapened by the encroachment of Western-style buildings, he is quick to point out that Chinese architecture is not incompatible with, let alone in conflict with, Western architecture and that given the alacrity with which China had been incorporating foreign cultural elements since the Tang dynasty, the Chinese would soon find a way to design the landscape so that old and new elements would be in harmony.[37]

Then Aoki offers a word of caution to the Japanese tourists who seek to see historic China in contemporary China:

> West Lake is not an antique object that is preserved for a small number of curiosity-driven Japanese tourists—West Lake is alive and kicking. It is a site of respite that heaven bestowed upon the Chinese people. It is natural for the modern Chinese to build Western-style restaurants and hotels in order to effectively enjoy the gift—it is a way to augment the gift of nature with artifice. One should not view West Lake simply as a historic site. You should not visit it with such a category in mind, or else you will be upset or repelled by thwarted expectations. Let me advise [those of you who have predetermined notions]: you had better explore West Lake in texts and fantasize about it with your eyes closed.[38]

While maintaining a distance from China as the object of modern scholarly inquiry, Aoki counsels his reader against the fetishistic appreciation of China as a thing of the past. It is not fair, he contends, to contrast the present-day China that tourists see with the historic China gleaned from their reading experience; it would be selfish of privileged connoisseurs to demand what they want to see. China was not a commodity that would add luster to travelers' lives. Unlike the travelers in earlier times, Japanese tourists would not be compelled by their visits to reflect on their cultural identity, much less to revise it. Their tours would be on a prescribed route, and they would return with purchases, pictures imprinted in their minds, and episodes archived and to be retrieved as memories. No traveler returns, but tourists plan to and do return, existentially intact, in possession of things from the distant land, geographically and chronologically. The trajectory of the tourist's mind is by default nostalgic: he or she wants something that will be a reminder of the trip later on—what is prospectively of their past.

Furthermore, the criticism of Japanese tourists regarding China was as much a product of their formulaic definition of what China should and should not be vis-à-vis the West as it was a product of the choices that China was making regarding Westernization. They wanted things of the past in China because for them China belonged to the past. Aoki, though informally and tangentially, questions the platform on which the Japanese tended to judge China's Westernization as a corruption of its cultural heritage—that is, the ground on which the Japanese granted themselves an ostensibly neutral position so as to make unsolicited judgments on behalf of the Chinese.

Land of Extravaganza

The shift from practicing Chinese fetishism to fetishizing China is embodied in a contemporary of Aoki, the renowned novelist Tanizaki Jun'ichirō (1886–1965). Tanizaki's Sinophilia is well documented though relatively unexplored in comparison with his earlier pro-Western stance and later manifest admiration of traditional Japanese culture. Unlike many of his predecessors, Tanizaki did not grow up memorizing classical Confucian texts before being admitted to school. His familiarity with Chinese owes much to coincidence and personal preference. The encouragement of a home room teacher at his elementary school may have led him, at the age of fourteen, to transfer to a private school to study the Chinese classics, as well as to attend another school to study English.[39] The immediate effect of such exposure was that four of Tanizaki's *kanshi* compositions appeared in a high school journal.[40] He did not publish anything in *kanshi* or *kanbun* as a professional writer. *Kanshi* or *kanbun* were never an essential part of his writing—not uncommon among Japanese writers who made their literary debuts in the Taishō period.

Tanizaki's engagement with China flourished in the genre of the travelogue.[41] He published several essays on the two trips that he made, in 1918 and 1926, including "Soshū kikō" (Account of my trip to Suzhou; originally published as "Gabō ki" [Account of a painted vessel, 1919]); "Shinwai no yoru" (Night in Qinhuai, 1919); and "Rozan nikki" (Diary of Lushan, 1921), in which he describes historical sites, restaurants, and brothels in southern China.[42] The topics suggest that Tanizaki's China was the object of nostalgic aestheticization, appetite, or lust. It is true that Tanizaki's gaze and tongue (in its two functions) sensualize China as erotic or edible. However, Tanizaki had an unfailing penchant for material details, objectifying and devouring any place of his infatuation, be it Yokohama, with its quasi-Western urban culture, or Kansai, with its reconstructed Japanese court tradition. Thus one might wonder if in Tanizaki's stories there was anything specific to China, that only China did for him—that is, if Tanizaki differentiated between China and the other objects of his aestheticizing creation.

The historic backdrop of Tanizaki's Sinophilic fiction in the 1910s is as follows: a part of Shanghai was a shared concession among several nations, including Japan, which had intervened to pacify the Boxer Rebellion (1899); in addition, Japan had attained a part of the Liaodong Peninsula in 1905 as part of a pact with Russia, the Portsmouth Treaty, signed after Russia's defeat by Japan. A new power hierarchy was being established, but it had yet to be confirmed by increasing Japanese control over China. The political circumstances created ambiguity in the China-Japan cultural hierarchy, and Tanizaki took advantage of it in writing stories of privileged Japanese travelers and their observations and infatuation with things Chinese. Within such a historical context, the two faces of the Sino-Japanese entanglement resurface: while Tanizaki's narrators appropriate the format of Chinese intellectual travelers (the center viewing the periphery), they also symbolically help colonize China, as a newly imperialist nation would. The dual function of the narrating subject materializes in Tanizaki's eloquent and articulate writing.

In "Shina no ryōri" (Chinese cuisine, 1919), Tanizaki enumerates dishes in the Chinese cuisine (most of which he had tasted); his list is a much shorter version of Yuan Mei's *Suiyuan shidan*. His critique of Chinese food and restaurants is either extremely positive or extremely negative, with no middle ground. Tanizaki is more than willing to admit that the food even in rural restaurants in China was "incomparably more delicious" than Chinese food he had tasted in Japan, that there was a much wider variety of dishes, and that they were much more reasonably priced than in Japan.[43] On the other hand, he was "greatly distressed at the extreme filthiness of rooms and appliances" in restaurants in Manchuria, to the extent that he had to "sanitize old and well-used ivory chopsticks with hot Shaoxing liquor"; moreover, he was disappointed with the quality of Western and Japanese food in China, and there was so much garlic in Chinese food that his "urine reeked until the next morning."[44] Then Tanizaki offers an overarching thesis on how to understand the Chinese:

> If one has read Chinese poetry, which celebrates the divine and the ethereal, and has then eaten those pungent foods, one may feel an insurmountable contradiction. However, I think that China's greatness lies in comprising both of the two extremes. It seems to me that a people who could cook such elaborate

foods and eat them until they are satiated are, any way you look at it, a great nation. I hear that although many Chinese drink more than Japanese, there are very few who would lose consciousness from intoxication. I think it is necessary to eat Chinese cuisine in order to understand the Chinese nation.[45]

The perceived contrast between the divine and the distasteful in Chinese culture is indeed a perfect match for Tanizaki's well-known sensibility, which, while worshiping strikingly beautiful objects, never fails to incorporate elements of vulgarity. The greater the distance between contradictory elements within an object, the more likely it is to capture his attention. The Japanese tended to view Chinese culture as displaying both divine beauty and earthly pleasure, often at the same time (recall the example of Yang Guifei eating pork), and the tendency culminated in Tanizaki.

"Shina-geki o miru ki" (An account of seeing Chinese theater, 1919) similarly offers an intense ambivalence—or, more precisely, a fascination with both the pleasant and the unpleasant. Tanizaki's first experience with Chinese theater, which was in Fengtian, Manchuria, was disastrous: the performance appeared "nightmarishly unpleasant" and sounded clamorous "to deafening effect."[46] The hope that he would fare better in Beijing was soon shattered; he was "distressed with the filthiness of the theaters," in the worst of which he witnessed a whirl of dust each time the actors somersaulted.[47] Also, he was "utterly mystified" when he saw actors, even those in the roles of beaus and beauties, spit on the stage and blow their noses into their hands. He wonders how they could do that when "they were clothed in dazzlingly gorgeous costumes."[48]

While Tanizaki may have preferred more hygienic places and more decorous people on his travels, as a writer he exploited the lower end of the aesthetic spectrum in order to create effective bathos. Harada Chikasada cites a similar sudden turn from the beautiful and theatrical to the filthy and disenchanting in Tanizaki's "Itansha no kanashimi" (The sorrow of the unorthodox, 1917) as the protagonist muses to himself, "Why on earth can't I help being reminded of Bai Letian [Bai Juyi] when I go to the restroom?"[49] Even though the narrator figures out the immediate reason—a scrap of newspaper in the toilet has an article on a hot spring that subconsciously reminds him of the poet's "Changhenge"—still the initial shock holds, perhaps to an even greater degree since the association is made in a place that would seem least evocative of the poem's focus, the beautiful imperial consort Yang Guifei. Tanizaki might take full credit for the connection between the fatal beauty and the toilet, as the juxtaposition of the beautiful and the disgusting is not uncommon in his work.[50] However, the iconicity of the legendary beauty, as well as the hegemony of her country of origin, enhances the effect in a similar way that it does in both Sen'ryū's poem and *Honchō Suikoden.*

The several short stories Tanizaki wrote in the late Taishō, which I will discuss in the balance of this chapter, should illuminate the coexistence of the ethereal and the physical in the Japanese perceptions of China and their ambivalence toward it.[51] As he is always conscious of the positions of the subject and object of analysis, Tanizaki fleshes out the formula with observations on gender, locale, historical period, and other specifics. We will see how China's cultural attributes function to promote fetishism, which borders on sadomasochism, and how miscegenation and transvestism figure into the staging of meaning so as to complicate the subject-object relationship, both in Tanizaki's work and beyond.

Fatal Disease and Fatal Beauty: Chinese Women on the Borderlines

Tanizaki's portraits of Chinese women showcase his ambivalence toward China most eloquently, owing to the observer's relentlessly objectifying gaze and speech. At times a narrator blatantly suggests that Chinese women are somewhat inferior substitutes for Western women. At other times, he loudly praises Chinese women's beauty, which stands out against Japanese women's plainness (which he laments).

"Ningyo no nageki" (The lament of a mermaid), which has no explicitly Japanese characters, serves as a template of Tanizaki's views of China vis-à-vis the West.[52] The story centers on a young millionaire in Nanjing who has grown bored with all the luxuries available in a city in Qing dynasty China. Wine, food, clothes, jewelry, and women have ceased to excite him. While the character is no longer fascinated with what is to him domestic and familiar, the readers are treated to a lavish list of exotic names of all the objects of pleasure. Without a knowledge of what these objects are in substance—or rather precisely because of the lack of knowledge—the catalogued names become objects of fetishism themselves, in a manner not unlike that suggested by Jean Baudrillard in the epigram of this chapter.

What captures the young millionaire's heart at the end of his decadent life is a mermaid in captivity that is brought in from the southern seas by a Dutch merchant. The European, distinctly exotic to the Chinese eye, serves only as a preface to his merchandise, which is even more unusual and imaginative. After purchasing the mysterious creature and keeping her in a glass tank, the Chinese man falls for her—or, more precisely, he falls for her unattainability: her body is semifish, and initially she appears to be mute. The biological boundary between species emphasizes, rather than obliterates, the cultural boundaries between China and Europe. When the mermaid begins to speak, she tells of exotic places well beyond the territory of China; they bear the same value of irreducible foreignness as she does for her Chinese listener. Inspired by her descriptions of her native Netherlands and her ancestors' home in the Mediterranean Sea, the Chinese man comes to yearn for a glimpse of Europe.

In the process of the protagonist's awakening, China is assigned a lower place than the West in the scale of values. Since the story is told in Japanese—and thus implies a Japanese narrator and a Japanese audience— the placement either reflects Japan's views of China and Europe or disguises the perceived hierarchy between Japan and Europe. Whichever may be the case, it is important to note that with the erasure of the body of the narrator (as s/he remains nameless and uninvolved in the story), Japan's position has become ambiguous, while China's and Europe's are articulated as opposing poles. The invisible Japanese can function either as an ostensibly objective observer (as is the case with modern Sinologists and travelogue writers) or as a clandestine impersonator of the Chinese, who vicariously share the Japanese desire for the West.

When Japanese characters step into Tanizaki's fiction on China, they turn a more appreciative gaze on it than its "second best" status might suggest. Though not entirely without echoes of the hierarchy of values noted above, "Seiko no tsuki" (The moon on West Lake) praises the beauty of China's natural landscape and its women in parallel.[53] The story is framed within the first-person narration of an unnamed and yet intradiegetic Japanese male tourist (watakushi) who is stationed in Beijing as a special correspondent for a Tokyo-based newspaper. Having an opportunity to extend a business trip to Shanghai to visit Hangzhou, he spares no praise for the region's natural beauty, which he observes from the window of a train. He makes frequent references to Chinese literary icons whose names the Japanese have long associated with West Lake. Liberally superimposing scenes from Chinese romance onto the landscape before his eye, he aestheticizes southern China as follows:

> It was no wonder one was inspired with such ethereal fancies as those in Li Li- weng's poetic drama if one was born in such a beautiful land with such beautiful residents. "Shenzhong lou" in Shizhongqu presents the mysterious story of

Liu Shijian, who visits the eastern seashores for a vacation, crosses the sea to the illusory tower, and marries Shunhua, a daughter of the Blue Dragon King. Perhaps the eastern seashores where the romance develops are somewhere around here, in Jiangsu or Zhejiang Province. Perhaps *Bimuyu*—a story about Liu Maogu, an actress, and Tan Chuyu, an exceptionally talented scholar, who throw themselves into the river, arm in arm, to transform themselves into sole and flow in the direction of Yanlang—was also automatically conceived in Li-weng's mind. In this vein, I feel that anyone born in this area of southern China could not help becoming a poet. I wish I could show a glimpse of this scenery or local color to those who boast of Japan as the eastern nation of poetry.[54]

Evidently the narrator ahistoricizes and mythologizes what he sees in China. He becomes infatuated with the China of the past, which seems the only thing that he sees while glancing at the present-day landscape. However, his list of Chinese references reveals that he is not necessarily guided by the classical canon. He does not mindlessly celebrate all established writers just for the sake of an abstract value with which they had been imbued; rather, he makes a conscious choice to present his own preference for less austere writers. In the above passage, he goes back at least as far as Li Liweng (Li Yu) of the Qing dynasty. Elsewhere in the same text, the narrator also mentions Su Dongpo (Su Shi; 1036–1101) of the Song dynasty, who used to be governor of Hangzhou and thus is closely associated with West Lake.[55] The narrator further says he feels as if he "had been lured into the poetic world of Yang Tieyai [Weizhen; 1296–1370], Gao Qingqiu [Qi; 1336–1374], and Wang Yuyang [Shizhen; 1634–1711]," poets from the late Yuan and Qing dynasties.[56]

Tanizaki's preference for writers from post-Song periods suggests his proximity to the late Tokugawa literary sensibility, of which we have had a glimpse. Like many of the writers in that era, Tanizaki appreciates the "vulgar," quotidian, less ostensibly ideological and more material dimensions of literature. Even in the case of such a canonized poet as Su Dongpo, the narrator's interest lies not in his accomplishments as a man of letters or a bureaucrat, but in his pursuit of earthly pleasures. One evening the narrator has for supper a dish named after him—*Dongpo rou* (Dongpo meat)—and is reminded of how the poet savored the delicacies and beauties of life while he was governor of Hangzhou:

[*Dongpo rou* is] the equivalent of chateaubriand in Western cuisine. It's a stew of the white meat of pork, as tender as soybean cake, in a fatty and sticky

broth of a brownish color. Though Su Dongpo may appear an extremely reclusive and otherworldly poet, when you think of him drinking, with this
rich-flavored meat as an appetizer, and floating in a boat on West Lake with
his favorite mistress, Chaoyun, in the morning and at night—then you feel as
though you more or less understand the real Chinese flavor of things.[57]

Tanizaki's "positivist desire" (kōtei teki yokubō), to use Kōno Taeko's
phrase—that is, appetite or lust—has found a venue in China.[58] He does
not praise historical figures for enabling him to renounce the experiences of the present. On the contrary, Tanizaki admires those who re-
portedly craved the fullness of life and appreciated the sensual pleasures
of the here and now. Indeed, as we saw Mieke Bal assert in the introduction, quoting is a contemporary art; instead of returning us to the past
from which a quotation is drawn, the quoted text becomes a part of the
present. While in the acts of reading and writing the vector of a quotation may be invisible, in the acts of cooking and eating it is obvious that
the recipe (an archived body of knowledge) is brought into the present
as a physical object, rather than the cook or eater being dragged back
into the past. The sensual effect of the act of cooking and eating—that
is, bodily and contemporaneous—confirms the point.

Another point worth making is that Tanizaki is not so oblivious as
to dismiss regional differences within China: China for him is not just
one big entity. In fact, the north-south contrast within the country plays
an important part in his perceptions. Tanizaki's narrator in "Seiko no
tsuki" embodies the sensibilities of the bureaucrat coming from Beijing
in the north; with these sensibilities he observes the landscape and the
people, who exist for him only as objects of art. Indeed he appropriates
the colonizing gaze of the traveler from the center with which Chinese
travelogues are replete. In this light, the following observations convey
an interesting message:

The first glimpse of the passengers in the train makes it obvious that the South
is much richer than the North. To me, accustomed to the second-rate trains of
the Jing-Feng Line and the Jing-Han Line [in the North], it looks as if the inside of the train is meticulously clean. . . . Passengers in the second-class cars
are as well dressed as only those in the first-class cars in the North. It is also remarkable that there are many female passengers. It is rare to see women go out
in the North, while in the South not only entertainers, but also married and
unmarried women of respectable families frequently walk around hand in

hand with men. . . . Needless to say, the attire of women and children is richer in color and more glamorous than in the North. . . . Indeed, Jiangsu and Zhejiang are known for having produced beauties since ancient times.[59]

In this passage, the railroads running between Beijing and Fengtian (Shenyang) and between Beijing and Hankou (which are of military importance) are deemed aesthetically inferior to those of the South. The narrator also generously praises the economic and cultural success of southern China. While drawing upon the conventional aesthetic hierarchy between the South and the North, which he could have learned from reading, Tanizaki may also be revealing his own preference for the literary and artistic milieu of the South over the industrial and military North.

Not only does the narrator objectify southern China as the beautiful land that inspires poets, but he also gazes at women in much the same way that he observes the natural landscape. He claims that Chinese women have "more delicate fingers than Japanese women"—a new marker of value—and "trim calves and feet comparable to even those of Western women," hinting at the Europe-China hierarchy more prevalent in "The Lament of a Mermaid."[60] Singled out among the Chinese women is Li Xiaojie, an eighteen-year-old, taller than other Chinese women, attired in celadon blue, with skin as fine as "Western paper," delicate fingers, slender legs, small feet, and a graceful face with a "Grecian nose."[61] Her every physical feature appears outstanding to the narrator and is suggestive of "noble origins," as well as of ephemerality; he notes a "pathetic beauty" about her that he thinks might be "typical of Chinese beauties."[62] His premonitions about "pathetic beauty" prove to be well founded, as Li Xiaojie is later found dead, floating on the surface of West Lake; she has committed suicide for fear of an imminent death from tuberculosis. Here the narrator appropriately makes an association with Su Xiaoxiao, a courtesan of the Six Dynasties who died and was buried on the shores of West Lake; he quotes several poems composed by later poets that were inscribed on her tombstone.[63] The narrator also alludes to another iconic figure: Xishi, the fatal beauty sent to the King of Wu as part of the plot by neighboring Yue to divert the king's attention from his duties. Legends have it that Xishi suffered from the same disease as Li Xiaojie.[64] Linked to the legendary Xishi because they share a locale and an illness, Li Xiaojie is granted a higher status than Japanese women, but only in aesthetic terms. While the narrator rides the same train and stays at the same hotel as she, he never speaks with Li Xiaojie or with her female companion (who, though to a lesser degree, as is appropriate for a sidekick, is also beautiful and graceful). The lack of conversation with Chinese women—which is not unlike the remoteness of the mermaid from her Chinese master—helps create and maintain an aesthetic distance from them—a distance that diminishes in the companionship of Japanese women, who share the same language. Chinese women can be objectified into muses, while Japanese women are defined as domestic.[65]

The gender divide also makes it easier for the narrator to aestheticize the Chinese. It is worth noting that he does speak with Chinese men in the story—with a passenger in the train and with a rickshaw puller who takes him from the Hangzhou station to his hotel on the shores of West Lake. The first conversation ends in uncomfortable silence because the Chinese gentleman looks "obnoxious" and even "haughty,"[66] and the second ends in the puller's demand for extra fare. The narrator needs to converse with Chinese men for both social and business reasons; these involve psychological ramifications and make it difficult to aestheticize Chinese men as the Other. Neither with Japanese women nor with Chinese men can the narrator indulge in his objectifying fancies. Thus, Chinese women are the only ones around whom he can weave his web of fantasy.

Travel and gender relations also form an interface in another story by Tanizaki, "Kakurei" (A crane's cries, 1921). A Japanese man called Yasunosuke, who had abandoned his wife Shizuko and daughter Teruko and left for southern China, comes home after several years, begging for his wife's forgiveness. He is not alone on his return, however; he has brought home a Chinese woman and a crane. Instead of settling down in a familiar domestic setting, Yasunosuke has a separate building constructed on the premises of his mansion and confines the woman and himself within it. He names the building Suo Lan Ge (Building That Holds Back Waves), obviously after one of the six picturesque bridges over West Lake, sightseeing spots that the narrator of "Seiko no tsuki" does not fail to visit.[67] The association of the building with the literary topos of West Lake continues with a reference to plum blossoms and cranes. Yasunosuke keeps a crane in a town renowned for plum blossoms. This is a direct allusion to Lin Bu (967–1028), a man of virtue who lived on the shores of West Lake, had two cranes, and cherished plum blossoms at his humble residence, Fang He Ting (Crane-Liberating Arbor). (Lin's property is one of the topoi that the narrator of "Seiko no tsuki" mentions as "must-visits" during his stay in Hangzhou.)[68] Though physically back in Japan, Yasunosuke remains existentially in China; he refuses to speak Japanese and wears Chinese clothes only. He does not assume his duties as master of the house, husband of Shizuko, or father of Teruko. He does nothing but spend time with the Chinese woman in the Chinese arbor.

This is an extreme case of the souvenir as defined by Susan Stewart, who equates the souvenir, the antique, and the exotic in terms of the distance from the "here and now" that the subject establishes: "The location of authenticity becomes whatever is distant to the present time and space; hence we can see the souvenir as attached to the antique and the exotic."[69] In addition to objects Yasunosuke acquires that become temporarily and spatially autonomous of both the context of travel and present domestic life, an artifice is constructed from the archive of cultural memory at home in the present in order for Yasunosuke, the returnee, to transcend geographic and historical boundaries and become a Chinese literary recluse of the Song dynasty. In fact, the traveler has become a souvenir par excellence himself, crystallized in the distance (China) and the past (archive of cultural memory), rejecting if not renouncing the domestic and the present. Geography and history are neutralized in this act of an infinite and misplaced tour.

Yasunosuke's wife and daughter try to adjust to Yasunosuke rather than trying to change him into what he used to be. Shizuko dresses Teruko in Chinese clothes purchased in the Chinatown in Yokohama in the hope that Yasunosuke might at least speak with his daughter. Teruko, for her part, teaches herself how to speak southern-accented Chinese by befriending the Chinese woman, having unintentionally offended her father by speaking to him in Japanese. The mother's and daughter's transethnic efforts, however, fail to persuade Yasunosuke to reunite with them. When Teruko asks him in Chinese, "Father, when will you begin to speak in Japanese again?", Yasunosuke looks upset and says, "I will never again speak in Japanese for the rest of my life."[70] From that moment on, he seems annoyed by Teruko's attempts to approach him. For him there is no room for compromise with the domestic. The story ends melodramatically, as Teruko stabs the Chinese woman to death, calling her "mother's enemy."[71] Her words complete the picture of polarity between the Chinese woman—who is exotic, erotic, nonhuman, and (regardless of her intent, which the text does not discuss) destructive to the Japanese family—and the Japanese housewife, who is domestic, human, and trained for household duties.

The Chinese woman's presence is central to the plot and yet devoid of substance throughout the story. Her name is never disclosed to the

reader, and her speech is never represented either semantically or phonetically (unlike Yang Guifei's speech in *Honchō Suikoden*, which, as we
saw in chapter 1, is transcribed in the text to significant effect). Though
the woman communicates with Teruko, and undoubtedly with Yasunosuke, the conversations are textually absent. Deprived of name and
speech, the Chinese woman is susceptible to exoticization. In fact, her
voice is compared to the crane's, as if to suggest either a lack of human
intelligence or a lack of interest on the part of the Japanese in striking up
a conversation with her. Whereas the comparison of Yang Guifei's
speech to bird chirping in *Honchō Suikoden* shakes up the hierarchy between the Chinese and Japanese languages, the analogy between this
Chinese woman and the crane sets her beneath humans in the Japanese
mind. Rather than a negotiation with the Chinese beauty across languages (however faulty), as happens in *Honchō Suikoden*, no translingual attempts are made in "Kakurei." The purpose is to maintain an
aesthetic distance from the woman so as to fetishize her.[72] The crane as
her alter ego serves to confirm her as a fetish.

Mixed Blood and Mixed Pleasure: "Birōdo no yume"

The aestheticized and stereotyped image of the Chinese woman—either a
virgin or a whore—that emerges from "Seiko no tsuki" and "Kakurei" is
essential to the scheme of fetishization of China. The Chinese woman
thus imagined has no possibility of communicating with the connoisseur/
viewer and is not given a chance to change. She is kept at bay, in contrast
to the Chinese women we saw in chapter 1, who learn from cross-cultural
experience, reflect on themselves vis-à-vis the cultural Other, and grow
wiser and more capable. Another story by Tanizaki, however, compels us
to suspend all the generalizations we have made so far regarding the functions of cultural and gender distinctions in his work. "Birōdo no yume"
(Velvet dreams, 1919) helps undo the neat contrasts between China and
Japan in the previous stories by introducing characters of mixed origin.[73]
Instead of celebrating hybridity as the possession of attributes and skills
informed by universal and local cultures, as we saw in *Hamamatsu
chūnagon monogatari* in chapter 1, however, hybridity here is presented
primarily if not exclusively in anatomical terms, evoking the presence of
a voyeuristic gaze.

Like "Kakurei," this story has connections to "Seiko no tsuki," as it
effectively draws upon literary connotations around West Lake.[74] The

narrative is a Japanese man's partial recounting of a trial in Shanghai's international court. The defendant is a Chinese man who is accused of physically abusing his slaves in his magnificent villa in Hangzhou. The site of the alleged crime—at the foot of Ge Ling (Ge Mountain), north of West Lake—brings to mind Jifang Yuan (Garden of Assembled Beauties), the estate of a legendary villain, Jia Sidao (1213–1275) of the Southern Song period (1127–1279). Jia Sidao had built many houses; collected beauties, beasts, and unusual objects of art; and indulged in sex, gambling, and sadistic acts while neglecting his office.[75] Thus, this story is a product of both Tanizaki's infatuation with the area through his readings and his travels to southern China.

The narrative is multiply framed: the presence of an observer in each layer is made evident. It is prefaced by a short description of the anonymous Japanese narrator's sojourn in Hangzhou, where he is guided by a friend who works for the consulate general of Japan in Shanghai. They encounter a beautiful and apparently spiteful young woman who appears to be "hybrid" (zasshu).[76] The diplomat, who recognizes the girl, decides to fill the narrator in on the sadistic deeds in which she and her master have been engaged in the mansion. Instead of retelling the friend's tale, the narrator chooses to reconstruct scenes in the criminal court to which the couple's case was brought in order to create immediacy for the reader. The journalistic style yields another effect: it makes it possible to describe each witness' appearance anatomically in such a way as to augment the machinery of fetishization.

Among the many slaves called as witnesses, three "relate" their particular experiences in the mansion. Then, the narrator summarizes the testimony of the fourth slave, whose escape from the mansion led to the investigation. The first witness is a sixteen-year-old boy from Shanghai, with dark hair and yellow skin, who does not know his ethnic background because he was sold to a slave merchant as a child. His physical features, which clearly suggest the boy's Mongoloid origins, combined with his lack of identification, signal the ambiguous position of the story regarding ethnicity: it both explores and strives to undo ethnic identity. The boy's job is to watch the mistress nap in an underground bedroom that has a ceiling made of glass; while on duty, he falls in love with the next witness, who is seen from the bedroom through the glass ceiling.

The girl is twelve or thirteen years old, the daughter of a fisherman in Shandong Province, right across the sea from the Japanese territory of Liaodong; she was sold as a slave in Beijing. She is described, without a specified reason, as "a pure Chinese," but in terms of skin color and body proportions she is "almost like a Caucasian."[77] The persistent attention to physical details that are construed in racial terms emphasizes the ethnic ambiguity represented by the first witness while reiterating the author's preference, which we saw in "Seiko no tsuki," for the Chinese as a substitute for the Caucasian. The girl is swimming in a pool whose floor happens to be the ceiling of the bedroom mentioned above when she falls in love with the first witness. Then she is poisoned by the mistress, who has learned of the mutual affection between the two servants, and she drifts out of the residence into West Lake, unconscious and half dead. In the process, she is seen by the third witness, who is a Jewish woman, around twenty years old, a former prostitute in Shanghai, hired in the mansion as a violinist and imprisoned in a tower on the premises.[78]

Throughout the preface and the three testimonies, the narrator's aesthetic approval of hybridity and migration is evident. He uses such terms as *ainoko* or *zasshu,* meaning "mixed blood"—terms that were usually negatively construed in prewar Japanese writings, which promoted the "purity" of the Japanese race—to praise a physical beauty unparalleled by "pure" folks.[79] In other words, ambiguous racial or ethnic origins are valued in this story. The clear preference for the hybrid is further confirmed when the fourth witness is introduced. He is the only one who is of one race and looks "unmixed"—a Japanese boy who looks Japanese. His parents were from Nagasaki, but he was born and worked in Shanghai until he was sold into slavery. There is a reason that his testimony was summarized rather than transcribed in the text: he is mentally challenged. Because of his handicap, he was both mentally and physically abused by the master and mistress. One of his tasks was to count the number of people in a room whose walls, ceiling, and floor were made of mirrors—something that he could not manage to do, so he was brutally punished. The tone with which this information is relayed is not compassionate, and it is obvious that the narrator, though Japanese himself, does not hold the boy in high esteem—and certainly not higher than the others—simply because he is purely Japanese.

This is not to suggest that the Chinese are granted a privileged position vis-à-vis the Japanese. As in many of Tanizaki's works, the narrative authority resides with a Japanese man—in this case, a Japanese man who edits another Japanese man's recounting of the trial. The power of mediation is obvious in the omission of the Chinese couple's response to the charges against them. Whether or not they chose to present a rebuttal in court, one would expect them to have an emotional response, as well as attempt to defend themselves by providing excuses for their actions, if not outrightly denying that they had ever committed any crimes. The Japanese characters are endowed with the power of speech, while the speeches of the Chinese are either framed and mediated by the Japanese or are entirely absent. Thus we must admit that the Chinese sadists are objectified under the gaze of the Japanese observers, who stay out of the story themselves. This is a classic formula of fetishism, where the fetishist stays at a safe distance in order to observe. If we also consider the fact that in Tanizaki's fiction masochists are often in control of the narration—that is, the process of making sense—even while being dominated and tortured by their sadist masters (e.g., *Fūten rōjin nikki* [1961]), then it becomes obvious that the empowerment of and admiration for the Chinese characters serve the aesthetic desires of the Japanese.[80] It is the Japanese who can afford to indulge in dreams that they are inferior and take pleasure in being enslaved. In the debased condition of the mentally handicapped and physically abused Japanese male slave is the utmost triumph of a masochist who has succeeded in elevating his master to the divine and diabolical.[81]

Transnationalism and Transvestism: "Kōjin"

Another story set in a cosmopolitan ambience is "Kōjin" (Mermaids/Mermen).[82] With a Cen Shen (ca. 715–ca. 770) poem on mermen in the southern seas as an epigraph, the story anticipates the reader's desire for Chineseness, as well as a Chinese exoticization of the periphery:

> **Bidding a Farewell to Lieutenant Zhang Leaving for Nanzhou**
> You did not choose to become lieutenant in Nanzhou;
> You have aging parents to leave behind;
> Buildings overlap with illusion;
> And villages house mermen among humans.
> The sea darkens as rain falls on the three mountains
> Blossoms brighten the five ridges in spring
> This region produces many jewels
> Do not loath staying virtuous and frugal.[83]

In quoting this poem, Tanizaki employs *kenten,* a device commonly used in texts in *kanshibun* to stress some characters. Small circles are placed next to the characters in question—in this case, "mermen," or *kōjin*—to draw the reader's attention to the source of the title of the story. The epigraph inscribes an Orientalist motif: a man from the capital travels to a remote area and admires the natural beauty and exotic people, both so antithetical to the civilization of the city that they degenerate the man. A question that remains to be answered at this point is who assumes the role of the Orientalist in the story. The beginning of the story somewhat thwarts the expectation of an unusual setting; the place is 1918 Asakusa, Tokyo, the Japanese version of a center of modernism and popular culture, with theaters, dance halls, cafes, and street performances (among other things).[84] It is out of this bustling cosmopolitan epicenter, however, that the other important topos of the story emerges: southern China, corresponding to the epigraph.

The extant text of "Mermaids," which was never completed, is in four chapters: "A Certain Artist's Yearning," "A Flock of Actors Living in the Park," "Hayashi Shinju," and "People in the Middle of the Night." Each chapter in turn consists of three or four sections. One might deduce from the statement at the end of the fourth chapter, "The first half is completed," that the author intended to write a second half of approximately the same length.[85] The main characters are two Japanese intellectuals without professions and their acquaintances—a group of actors and actresses in Asakusa (one of whom provides the title for the third chapter). The second, third, and fourth chapters are devoted, respectively, to the most popular actress' physical charms and popularity, to unsolved mysteries involving her from a period when her group performed in Shanghai, and to her strange behavior, which now becomes noticed. The following discussion will focus on the first and third chapters, in which China's role is imperative.[86]

In "A Certain Artist's Yearning," a chapter that precedes the appearance of the popular actress, one of the two intellectuals, who has been trained in Western-style oil painting, announces that he plans to take up traditional Chinese painting of the Nanga style (Ch. Nanhua; Southern school of painting). The man, appropriately named Minami (meaning "south"), asserts the superiority of Chinese culture over Western culture and, by extension, over the heavily Western-influenced culture of modern Japan. Minami voices these views when he is alone with the other male intellectual, Hattori, evoking the homosociality that one might say is appropriate for the degendered subject. In recalling a trip to China, Minami reflects as follows:

Though it was autumn, it was as warm as spring in Japan. The incredibly clear sky extended beyond the window [of the train in which Minami is riding]; the river and pools transparent and green, shining in joy; green fields, willow boughs, flocks of geese, hills, castles, pagodas looking blissful in the abundant sunshine—through the whole of Jiangsu Province, in which these scenes kept appearing like the incessant music of rituals. The train ran all day. It's a delightful land, as if from a fairytale—how fortunate he would have been if he had been born in such a land. How early in his life he would have awakened to nature if he had been raised amid such magnificent scenery day and night. What a profound secret his art could have been endowed with by nature. . . . Minami couldn't help feeling so. He felt it was an enormous misfortune that he, a devoted advocate of Chinese thought, had not been born in China. . . . Separated from the invaluable continent that had been an ancestor and source of the Japanese civilization of the past, he was to stay in Japan as a Japanese man. In place of the meditative Beijing, this shallow and unsightly Tokyo before his eyes. . . . An East Asian, Minami would not wish to depart from East Asian art. However, the Japan of today, into which he had been born—haunted by pro-Westernization, underdeveloped pro-Westernization, that is—had a pure nature in which he found beauty destroyed everywhere. How could he seek a landscape in Ni Yunlin's paintings or a place out of Wang Wei's poems when Japan was so small and shabby in comparison with China?[87]

The first half of the above quotation strikes the same chord as the passage cited from "Seiko no tsuki" in praise of the southern Chinese landscape. The author's well-known penchant for the epicurean culture is evident. The second half of the quotation slips into an abstract discussion of values, which is not necessarily relevant to what Minami actually saw while in China. First, Beijing enters the picture out of context, replacing Jiangsu Province, to form a hypothetical contrast with Tokyo. Second, the mention of Wang Wei seems out of context, since the poet, who lived near Chang'an, had little connection to the place Minami visited and was known for his austerity and reclusiveness. For the sake of consistency, Minami should instead have mentioned Li Yu (for example), as did the narrator of "Seiko no tsuki." The local and actual are replaced with the general and mythical in order to present the overarching thesis that Chinese culture and nature are superior to their Japanese counterparts, which mimic the Western.

Minami's impassioned argument is hardly unprecedented. In fact, the text specifically draws upon a predecessor in the formation of the

China-West dichotomy: Natsume Sōseki's *Kusamakura* (1906).[88] Minami mentions Sōseki as an acquaintance of his father and as a source of inspiration for him:

> As you know, my father was a friend of the late Mr. Natsume and often referred to him as an example. . . . In fact, Mr. Natsume is not that great a novelist. If he had been born in China and had established himself as a poet or painter, he may not have been as famous, but he would have been able to explore an area of superior art and would have felt much happier than being born in the Japan of today. (Or so my father maintains.) English scholar though he was, Mr. Natsume preferred classical Chinese literature to English literature. . . . In the East, Li Taibai's five-character quatrain is more precious than *Shuihu zhuan* or *Hong lou meng*. With only twenty characters, Li Taibai could reach the level of Dante or Goethe in a breath. He is still alive with Dante and Goethe in human beings. Perhaps one could even claim that he is more "omni-present" [an English word in the original] than Dante or Goethe; we cannot learn by heart all of *Faust* or *The Divine Comedy*, but we can recite Li Taibai's quatrain any time.[89]

Minami's argument echoes that of the narrator in *Kusamakura*. Parallels are obvious in the following passage from Sōseki's work, which defends Chinese and shorter forms of literature as opposed to Western and longer forms (such as drama and the novel):

> Happily, oriental poets have on occasion gained sufficient insight to enable them to enter the realm of pure poetry.
>
> > Beneath the eastern hedge I choose a chrysanthemum,
> > And my gaze wanders slowly to the southern hills.
>
> Only two lines, but reading them, one is sharply aware of how completely the poet has succeeded in breaking free from this stifling world. . . .
>
> > Seated alone, cloistered amid bamboo
> > I pluck the strings;
> > And from my harp
> > The lingering notes flow leisurely away.
> > Into the dim and unfrequented depths
> > Comes bright moonlight filtering through the leaves.

Within the space of these few short lines, a whole new world has been created. Entering this world is not at all like entering that of such popular novels as *Hototogisu* [Cuckoo, 1898] or *Konjiki yasha* [Gold demon, 1897]. It is like falling into a sound sleep and escaping from the wearying round of steamers, trains, rights, duties, morals, and etiquette. . . .

I am not really a poet by profession, so it is not my intention to preach to modern society in the hope of obtaining converts to the kind of life led by Wang Wei and Tao Yuanming [Qian, 365–427]. Suffice it to say that in my opinion, the inspiration to be gained from their works is a far more effective antidote to the hustle and bustle of modern living than theatricals and dance parties. Moreover, this type of poetry appears to me to be more palatable than *Faust* or *Hamlet*.[90]

Not only do both narrators privilege China over the West, but they also have a higher regard for poetry than prose fiction or drama. In the case of Sōseki, the generic contrast is paralleled with a cultural one: poetic China, prosaic West. Though the narrator does mention works of prose fiction in China, it is only to confirm the hierarchy among the genres. Given that the narrator of "Seiko no tsuki" admires Li Yu, whose name is absent from Minami's list, Tanizaki is making Minami's debt to Sōseki explicit.[91]

The story develops in another direction in the second chapter, unfolding in the quiet, secluded, and homosocial atmosphere in which two intellectual males freely assume the role of unconcerned commentators of cross-cultural comparisons. Enter a young Japanese actress—or a person who so appears—by the name of Hayashi Shinju, and there goes the men's liberty to edit and analyze cultural icons. She is the most popular actress in a theater in Asakusa that specializes in musical versions of Shakespearean plays. Like that of other heroines in Tanizaki's stories, the portrayal of Shinju draws upon the attributes of archetypal Chinese beauties. Some of her traits—frowning attractively, being temperamental and self-absorbed—are reminiscent of Lin Daiyu, one of the heroines of *Hong lou meng*. Shinju's artistic flair and tempestuous disposition are especially evident when she is contrasted with one of her colleagues, whose composure and selflessness recall such qualities in Xue Baochai, another heroine in *Hong lou meng*.

Minami reminisces that Shinju's troupe once toured in Shanghai and, to please the Chinese audience, performed a scene from *Shuihu zhuan*. That the Japanese actors perform a Chinese classic in China is a version of the reversal of the roles in the exchange of cultural capital that we saw in the case of scholarship in Sinology in the 1930s. The original producer of "authentic" cultural capital is turned into the consumer, as the commodities are now reproduced and distributed by those who were initially on the margins of cultural capital. In the performance Shinju played Yan Qing, one of 108 bandits, who is renowned for such fair skin that any woman would envy it. The Japanese woman was cross-dressed so as to become a Chinese man—and very compellingly at that; the audience, except for those who knew her offstage, mistook her for a man.

The performance was interrupted by an old Chinese man who ran up to the stage and claimed that the actor was his son, who had been lost for years. Shinju was visibly shaken by this seemingly absurd claim, and, though she resumed the performance, she lost consciousness on stage. Through the mediation of a Chinese gentleman called Mr. Wang, who introduces himself as a frequent customer of the old man's daughter, a courtesan, the intruder is later invited backstage to see Hayashi Shinju up close. According to Mr. Wang, the old man, a coolie, was originally from a very respectable family, the Lins of Nanjing (the surname and location coincide with those of Lin Daiyu). When the family's fortunes declined, his son was lost without a trace, and his daughter was sold into entertainment/prostitution. His son's name was Lin Zhenzhu—the same three characters as for the name Hayashi Shinju and the reason that he came to see her.[92] Since Shinju looked exactly like Zhenzhu, the father was convinced that she was his son. To grasp that this "Chinese man" was played by a Japanese woman, the old man was allowed to see her half-naked. As in "Birōdo no yume," anatomical truth prevails, and yet ambiguity persists because the marvels of transvestism and transethnicizing remain intact. The reader is still left in some doubt: why is Hayashi Shinju so distraught when first confronted if she had no prior knowledge of the old man or his son? And how does one account for the remarkable resemblance that Shinju bears to Lin Zhenzhu? (When his sister, who is said to look like her brother, is brought in, she and Shinju look like twins.) The reader is not given a solution to this mystery. The lack of closure may serve well for the theme of ambiguous identity. Transvestite and transethnic performances blur the boundaries of gender and ethnicity. Were the story to continue and the mystery to be solved, Hayashi Shinju would have to be identified as either Chinese or Japanese and either male or female, which would ruin what appears to be the whole purpose of the story as it stands: de-essentializing identity. Hayashi Shinju, whose occupation is appropriately that of an actress, who assumes various identities, should not be defined in one way or another in terms of ethnicity or gender.

In light of the performativity of gender and ethnicity, one should note that a peripheral character makes an ostensibly tangential reference to the celebrated historical Chinese transvestite actor Mei Lanfang (1894–1961), whom he seems to view as a competitor of Hayashi Shinju; he suggests that the theater should perform the same pieces as Mei Lanfang's troupe, which is touring Japan at the same time.[93] This hint at national rivalry is predicated upon the fetishization of China, manifest in the consumer interest in the production of Chinese plays. The fascination of Japanese intellectuals with Mei Lanfang has been well documented. Many traveled to China partly in order to see him perform, and he was invited to perform in Japan. In both cases, Mei became a commodity, a souvenir or an imported good, in great demand of the Japanese connoisseurs who craved things Chinese. Aoki Masaru, whose work we saw above, has an essay entitled "Meirō to Konkyoku" (Mr. Mei and the Kun Theater), in which the scholar of Chinese theater regrets that he had to miss Mei's performance in Osaka owing to illness. In Tanizaki's own "Shina-geki o miru ki" the author compares a performance by Mei that he saw earlier at the Teigeki (Imperial Theater) in Tokyo and one he has just seen in Beijing.[94]

According to the essay, Tanizaki's friend, Kinoshita Mokutarō (1885–1945), a renowned exoticist poet and a physician and professor at the South Manchurian School of Medicine, served Tanizaki as a guide in Fengtian. Mokutarō himself authored a travel account and wrote impassioned poems about seeing Mei Lanfang's performance in Beijing in 1916. In "Peking" (1918), he attempts to translate a climactic scene from *Su San qijie* (a.k.a. *Yutangchun*), featuring Mei Lanfang as the title character, a woman falsely arrested and tortured by the authorities. In a poem entitled "Meilang chang Su San" (Mr. Mei performs Su San), Kinoshita offers a much more emotional response to Lanfang's performance, which brought Kinoshita (among other Japanese viewers) to tears.[95] He appealed to both their infatuation with *onnagata*, or male transvestites, and Sinophilia, and he became a phenomenon.[96] Thus, the implied comparison of this legendary actor with Hayashi Shinju works to praise her not only for her talent, but also for her remarkable ability to cross-dress and cross-ethnicize, as she did in the role of Yan Qing, the Chinese man. The comparison implies ambiguity about her gender and ethnic identity, which the Shanghai incident raised.

On a larger scale, the responses evoked by the legendary Chinese actor, and the fictional Japanese actress seem to reconfirm the old aesthetic hierarchy between China the sublime and Japan the subordinate. If we highlight the gender performance here, however, the feminization of China and the masculinization of Japan are rather obvious. Although in Tanizaki's usual formula of worshipping femininity, this may appear to imply China's triumph, we must not forget that it is the masculine sensibility that idolizes the feminine. Thus, China is once again a pawn in the hands of the Japanese connoisseur. Tanizaki's Japanese characters prevail as they objectify the Chinese characters, who aesthetically conquer them within the plot crafted by the Japanese author.

Conclusion

The introduction of vernacular literature and material goods from China into the Japanese market altered the perception that Chinese culture was represented solely by the Chinese classics and poetry. The connoisseur's privilege of evaluating and utilizing Chinese objects was not unrelated to the birth of Japanese scholarship in the Chinese canon. In this multifarious process of the transformation of the Japanese observer, China ceased to claim the center, from which it had judged the cultural values of others. Instead, Japanese consumers and tourists began to offer their aesthetic judgments and even their sensory reactions to the material China.

Rather than putting an end to the textual engagement with China, the Japanese awareness of the material and ethnic China called for an even more intense and sophisticated codification of it. The most prominent example, the Chinese female body, was iconicized as being either superhuman or subhuman as the Japanese observer—voyeur, connoisseur, imperialist—placed her in a web of sadomasochistic relationships. The themes of transvestism and miscegenation prevailed in this context. These could have complicated if not neutralized the polarity, but they were used not so much to expound on the disparities of cultural identity as to accentuate the liminality of an exotic China—in effect further validating the dichotomy.

The equation of the feminine and the physical with Chineseness, however, was in fact itself a challenge to the conventional corollary drawn between Chineseness, the intellectual, and the masculine. We will see another challenge to the tripod, in which Chineseness, the intellectual, and the feminine are linked together. The understanding that literary Chinese was a language meant exclusively for men is a fallacy that I will challenge in the next chapter.

CHAPTER 3
Sliding Doors
Women and Chinese Literature in the Heterosocial Literary Field

> From the point of view of gender as enacted, questions have emerged
> over the fixity of gender identity as an interior depth that is said to be
> externalized in various forms of "expression." . . . Strategies of exclusion
> and hierarchy are also shown to persist in the formulation of the sex/
> gender distinction and its recourse to "sex" as the prediscursive as well
> as the priority of sexuality to culture and, in particular, the cultural
> construction of sexuality as the prediscursive.
> —Judith Butler

The 1990s witnessed a renewed interest in women's literature from the Tokugawa period. Epitomizing this trend is, for example, the 1998 publication of *Edo joryū bungaku no hakken* (Discovery of women's literature in the Edo [i.e., Tokugawa] period), by Kado Reiko.[1] The term "discovery" may not be appropriate, however; women writers from the Tokugawa period—which some characterize as very oppressive toward women—had not entirely been ignored, as is evident in the fairly extensive list in Kado's bibliography. Nonetheless, Tokugawa women's literary works have been only sporadically "discovered": first in the 1910s by Yosano Akiko (1878–1942), among others; then in the 1970s by a *kokubungaku* (national literature) scholar, Yoshida Seiichi, and his colleagues; and again in the 1990s, as noted above.[2] Such "discoveries" are naturally accompanied by the implicit rhetorical question: "How could we have forgotten such talented women of letters?"

It appears as though women's literature from the Tokugawa period has been strategically forgotten in order to demonstrate women's liberation in modern Japan, on one hand, and, on the other, to highlight the parallels between the Heian court culture of the tenth and eleventh centuries, epitomized by Murasaki Shikibu (Lady Murasaki) and her contemporaries, and modern capitalist culture, which conditioned the work of Higuchi Ichiyō (1872–1896), among others.[3] The imperial court came back into the center of attention in the Meiji era, not only in political terms, but also in cultural terms; as is well known, Empress Shōken reestablished literary and artistic salons, in which talented and accomplished women gathered to compose *waka*, intentionally recalling the environment of Heian ladies-in-waiting. This renaissance of courtly culture in the Meiji was even more obvious because of the neglect of literary women's accomplishments in the preceding (Tokugawa) period. The obliteration of Tokugawa women's contributions to the literary field created an illusion of homogeneity and timelessness in the Japanese language and its literature.

The flux of attention to Tokugawa women's literature not only illuminates gender politics, but also raises issues such as contrasts between literary and oral languages; perceived ruptures between modern and traditional literature; contrasts between the transparent representation of the natural and the rhetorical presentation of a preconfigured essence; and, most directly relevant to our topic here, the putative incompatibility of Sino-Japanese and so-called indigenous Japanese literatures. In her informative study of *kokubungaku* scholarship in modern Japan, Suzuki Tomi traces the process in which *joryū nikki bungaku* (memoir literature by female authors)—a category that was not recognized by the premodern audience—was legitimized as a genre and reveals the roles of gender and genre in the construction of the Japanese literary canon.[4] As the ostensibly confessional writings in the "natural," "indigenous" language of classical Japanese was authenticated as representative of the national literature, many Tokugawa women of letters, whose knowledge of Chinese literature rather than personal life experience contributed to their literary output, were perceived as contrived and out of place and thus deserving to be silenced.[5]

Thus Tokugawa women of Chinese letters were not deemed "feminine," "natural," or "native" enough in light of the values projected by the normative study of Japanese literature in the late nineteenth and early twentieth centuries. Although men's exposure to Chinese learning might have been negatively construed by *kokugaku-kokubungaku* standards, male Sinophilia was perceived more authentic than the female version: in the modern view, it was "masculine" to write not in one's own voice but in a "foreign" language, so it was more "natural" for male writers than for female writers. Female Sinophilia presents a radical challenge to the modern concept of Japanese literature.[6] Thus women Sinophile writers of the Tokugawa have stayed in the shadow of Heian and medieval women memoirists, who were viewed as embodying the national identity of Japan.

Given the fluidity of gender definitions, I propose to use the metaphor of "sliding doors" in place of the familiar "glass ceiling," which has been employed to represent hierarchical and static gender distinctions. "Sliding doors," in my terminology, suggest a contingent placement and varying awareness of gender partitions. Unlike other partitions—walls, ceilings, and floors, which are static and stable—sliding doors can be opened and closed with ease, allowing the control of visibility, ventilation, and movement from room to room. It would be unjust to say that there have been no gender-based restrictions in social and cultural practices, but the boundaries have been drawn, withdrawn, and redrawn by various contingent factors. There have in fact been sliding doors that allowed women Sinophiles to enter rooms that some might have thought were for males only. The writers discussed in this chapter have been selected in order to highlight the contingency of the gender-based boundaries and the strategic intent behind them to either over- or underrepresent certain women writers in order to paint a predetermined picture of women's literature as a whole.

I will first briefly examine biographical and bibliographical facts that have been downplayed in, if not left out of, portrayals of Murasaki Shikibu, a female Sinophile in the Heian period, in order to identify the conditions under which she would *not* have been canonized. Her image as either a martyr to the social discrimination of women or a champion of women's literature/indigenous literature is contrived, made possible by the bracketing of certain aspects of her cultural background, compositional practice, and literary accomplishments.

I will then examine two women Sinophiles from the Tokugawa period: Arakida Reijo (Reiko; 1732–1806), an amateur historian and fiction writer, and Ema Saikō (Tao; 1787–1861), a painter, calligrapher, and poet in Chinese verse. I will show that Reijo and Saikō in effect challenged the modern norm of women's literature by choosing (respectively) historical and fantastic narratives (as opposed to quasi-autobiographical narratives or lyric poetry) and the literary Chinese language (as opposed to the native tongue, Japanese). Although Arakida Reijo and Ema Saikō wrote as intelligently and knowledgeably as Murasaki, they have not made their way into the literary canon as she has. I hope to help undo the conventional link among the indigenously Japanese, the feminine, and the natural and redefine both Japanese literature and gender as cultural practices rather than natural entities.

We will then shift gears to consider a man of Chinese letters in Meiji Japan, Mori Ōgai (Rintarō; 1862–1922); his respect for writers who happen to be female qualifies him for the title of a man of letters (bunjin; Ch. wenren), to whom gender is cultural, rather than a male professional writer of modern times (bunshi), to whom gender is natural. Specifically, we will look at his short story "Gyo Genki" (Ch. Yu Xuanji; 1915), in which he paints a poignant picture of the eponymous character, a female intellectual of Tang dynasty China who was both celebrated in the literary circles of Chang'an and rejected by the exclusively male body of government. Her intelligence, independence, and isolation offered a convenient venue for Ōgai to clandestinely praise a Taishō Japanese feminist writer and activist, Hiratsuka Raichō (Haruko; 1886–1971), who, like other talented women, earned his admiration for their cultural merits regardless of their gender. Though Raichō herself does not exhibit her knowledge of Chinese in any conspicuous way, the implicit connection that Ōgai made between her and a Chinese female writer, as well as his own role in supporting contemporary women writers, offers another site on which to reflect on the challenges and opportunities of women of letters in general who are active in heterosocial societies. Though women in medieval China and modern Japan share in the rejection from and resistance to the mainstream, in which the privileged male has claimed natural rights, those who rejected them occupied varied positions vis-à-vis the literary canon. The same is true of their male supporters, who recognized, if did not share in, the women's burdens. Whereas female intellectuals in Tang China were banned from participation in politics in spite of their merits, which were well recognized by the cultural standards of the time, the "New Women" in Taishō Japan were taken to be radical rebels because of their writings, destabilizing the norms of the establishment, literary or otherwise. That Ōgai apparently presented parallels of distinguished women from the two respective groups reveals the displacement of intellectuals in modern Japan, as well as Ōgai's unique view of what the literary norm should be, in contrast to the view held by influential contemporary critics.

Finally, I will take up a contemporary novelist, Kurahashi Yumiko (1935–2005), who has demonstrated a competence not only in classical Chinese, but also in multifarious negotiations with male authors and critics, whose endorsements were relevant to her status in the literary establishment in the early 1960s. She refused to write about her self "naturally," in the "feminine" discourse, and instead endeavored to write out of her reading knowledge and in a headstrong, "masculine" language. As I have discussed elsewhere, her intelligent, cosmopolitan, and erudite writing was often labeled "unnatural."[7] Active in a period in which the modern category of women's literature had been legitimized, Kurahashi was confronted with even harsher criticism than her Tokugawa predecessors for writing like a man. She had to endure unsympathetic and patronizing male critics in her younger days. Given her long and strenuous experience of coping with male critics, it may not be coincidental that Kurahashi's fiction has many precocious young female intellectuals and their male mentors; one such pair is explicitly parallel to Yu Xuanji (J. Gyo Genki) and Wen Tingyun (Feiqing; 812–ca. 872), who had inspired Ōgai earlier. An examination of Kurahashi will reveal a variation on the pattern in women intellectuals' fates and feats in literary production.

Grappling with Lady Murasaki: "A Woman's Hand"?

It seems appropriate to begin our discussion with the following oft-cited remark by Murasaki Shikibu, which is taken to delineate the boundaries of women's field of literature as opposed to men's:

> When my brother, Secretary at the Ministry of Ceremonial, was a young boy learning the Chinese classics, I was in the habit of listening with him and I became unusually proficient at understanding those passages that he found too difficult to grasp and memorize. Father, a most learned man, was always regretting the fact: "Just my luck!" he would say. "What a pity she was not born a man!" But then I gradually realized that people were saying "It's bad enough when a man flaunts his Chinese learning; she will come to no good," and since then I have avoided writing the simplest character.[8]

The passage has usually been interpreted as venting a woman's regret that her learning in Chinese would not be appreciated because she had been born a woman. What we see here is the construction of the image of Murasaki as a phoenix who was first denied a formal education in Chinese and recognition in the public sphere but who nevertheless emerged as a master of "the woman's hand" (*onnade*), or indigenous discourse (*wabun*) by taking advantage of the social constraints that prevented her from publicly utilizing her knowledge in "a man's hand" (*otokode*) or Chinese discourse (*kanbun*).[9]

While it is true that women of the Heian period had to deal with gender-specific social expectations and rules, later readers might have misconstrued the ways that Murasaki negotiated them.[10] There seems to be a deliberate manipulation behind this confirmation of the woman author as a sacrifice to social discrimination against women who took recourse to the indigenous language. The passage quoted above was taken out of context and blown out of proportion, so that the author's other thoughts and emotions could be obliterated. The point that Murasaki makes in the passage is nothing more or less than the fact that women were not admitted to schools and were therefore not provided with the formal education in Chinese that was made available to men. It also suggests that women—at least some of them—were given opportunities to learn Chinese literature informally. Murasaki's statement is thus not the Japanese equivalent of a famous Tang dynasty poem by Yu Xuanji (which we will examine below) lamenting her lack of opportunity to become a civil servant and participate in public and political activities.[11] Murasaki's tone is proud and triumphant rather than defeated and frustrated. Murasaki is not lamenting her lack of opportunity; rather, she is boasting of her brightness, which enabled her to acquire Chinese learning even without institutional instruction. By the very act of retelling how self-effacing she was compelled to be, Murasaki inscribes rather than effaces how learned she was, an act outside of the decorum for which she is known.[12]

A key to understanding Murasaki's position and its *relative* flexibility is the Japanese practice of learning Chinese. The domestication of Chinese sources through annotation, translation, adaptation, and appropriation made Chinese sources accessible to an audience without formal Chinese learning.[13] The best known source of Chinese poetry available to those illiterate (or incompetent) in Chinese is *Wakan rōeishū*, in which *waka* and excerpts from *shi* and *kanshi* are grouped under a given topic. Such a domestication of Chinese sources could mean either that the authors were simply experimenting with translation to determine the degree of stylistic compatibility between the two languages or that they expected some part of the audience not to completely understand Chinese and wanted to disseminate "privileged" texts in a way that was accessible to the less educated. The authors' intentions aside, the effect of the anthology, as well as other reference materials (*ruisho;* Ch. *leishu*), is double-edged, as is always the case with "secondary" materials: it helps to both diminish and confirm the distance between the audience and the "original" sources. Knowledge is handed down in a distinctly altered form; many in the audience would not seek an opportunity to read the "original," and even if they did, they would already be deprived of the unmediated primary encounter with "the original."

That said, the existence of such materials suggests that those without a reading knowledge of Chinese (of whom women would probably have been the majority) could acquire a degree of familiarity with Chinese literature (which some of them relied on in their own writing), often without knowing the exact sources from which they were quoting. Chinese stories were recycled in later periods, reproduced by agents with different levels of competence, desire, intent, and goals. Kawaguchi Hisao, one of the most prolific historians of Sino-Japanese literature to date, rightly argues that *kanshi* poets (or courtiers) and *waka* poets (or ladies-in-waiting) were closely connected, in both familial and social terms and in both the private and public spheres.[14] In *Murasaki Shikibu nikki* (ca. 1009), Murasaki describes the celebration upon the birth of the imperial prince, in which many Chinese texts were recited to the newborn by leading scholars. She and other ladies-in-waiting who served the prince's mother were not formal participants in any of the events but were nonetheless physically present, facilitating procedures by providing necessary items for the courtiers and monks conducting the ritual. Nakajima Wakako cites a section of Sei Shōnagon's *Makura no sōshi* (ca. 1002), in which a prepubescent boy recites Chinese texts, as another example of women's aural reception of *kanshibun*.[15] Similarly, though women may not have been formally invited to Chinese poetic competitions, they were aware of such events and of the fact that Japanese poetic competitions were designed as counterparts.

It is an obvious and yet often understated fact that the editors of and contributors to major collections of Chinese poetry composed by Japanese, such as *Honchō reisō* (Beautiful pieces of poetry of Japan, ca. 1010), are mentioned at length and frequently in Heian women's works, including Murasaki's own memoir (*nikki*) and Sei Shōnagon's *Makura no sōshi*. One of these figures, Fujiwara no Kintō (965–1041), is known not only as a leading *kanshi* poet and critic, but also as the author of important *waka* treatises, such as *Waka kuhon* (Nine gradations of *waka*, 1009), and thus embodies the syncreticism of the imperial court culture in the reign of Emperor Ichijō (r. 986–1011) that evolved around and yet blurred the distinctions between Chinese and Japanese and between male and female.

Women of letters were exposed to incidental and yet fully predictable encounters with male courtiers in the public space, where courtiers would
recite Chinese poetry and allude to Chinese sources. Women could see
through "sliding doors" even when they were closed and occasionally
would even open them and step into the male domain.

It is in light of the heterogeneity in reading knowledge of the Heian
period women, suggested above (and, more extensively, in the inspiring
work by Joshua Mostow), that I wish to reexamine Murasaki Shikibu's intellectual milieu.[16] Some well-documented historical facts were neglected
in the construction of Murasaki as the exceptional woman of letters who,
denied access to the Chinese canon, resorted to the native tongue and
woman's hand and marked the pinnacle of Japanese literature in the indigenous language. As Kawaguchi notes, most of the leading women of
letters in the court of Emperor Ichijō were somehow related to one or
more of the contributors to *Honchō reisō*.[17] Akazome Emon (mid-tenth
century–mid-eleventh century), for one, the alleged author of *Eiga monogatari* (translated as A tale of flowering fortunes, late eleventh century),
was married to Ōe no Masahira (952–1012), one of the best Confucian
scholars of the time, and was the mother of Ōe no Takachika (?–1046), a
poet whose work made its way into *Honchō reisō*.

Murasaki's father, Fujiwara no Tametoki (949?–1029?), studied Chinese with Sugawara no Fumitoki (whose work we saw quoted in
Hamamatsu chūnagon monogatari in chapter 1) and became a renowned
scholar and practitioner of Chinese verse in the circle of Prince Tomohira
(964–1009; also known by the Sinified title Nochi No Chūsho Ō [Later
prince in charge of the office of central affairs]). Tametoki took his
daughter to Echizen (present-day Fukui), where he held an appointment.
Its capital, Tsuruga, was one of the few ports in Japan that maintained international trade with the continent after 894, the year the Japanese government officially discontinued sending envoys to Tang China. A well-
established and yet often ignored fact is that Japan maintained an official
relationship with Parhae (as noted in chapter 1). Envoys from the country, as well as their Japanese hosts (including notable literati such as Shimada no Tadaomi [829–891] and Sugawara no Michizane), contributed
poems to *Bunka shūrei shū* and *Wakan rōeishū*. Kawazoe Fusae counts
thirty-four Parhae envoys from 727 to 919.[18] By Murasaki's time Parhae
had long been taken over by another country called Liao (916–1125),
which was not necessarily on good diplomatic terms with Japan. Nonetheless, Tsuruga retained its international ambience, and many Chinese

books from the continent arrived there. In 995, some seventy Chinese people drifted to the shores of the adjacent prefecture of Wakasa (the western part of Fukui) and then were moved to Echizen, which prompted a man hypothesized as Murasaki's husband-to-be, Fujiwara no Nobutaka, to write to her and hint at a probable visit to Tsuruga in the near future to see the Chinese ("Tōjin mini yukamu").[19] Thus the physical environment surrounding young Murasaki Shikibu was distinctly hybrid and anything but indigenously Japanese.

A well-known speculation by Emperor Ichijō upon reading a part of *Genji monogatari*—namely, "She [Murasaki] must have read the *Chronicles of Japan!*" (Kono hito wa Nihongi o koso yomitaru bekere)[20]—is verified in *Kakaishō* (An abridged account of rivers and seas, 1367), a medieval commentary edited by Yotsutsuji (Minamoto) Yoshinari (1325–1402) and revered by later critics such as Motoori Norinaga as an excellent reference. The commentary attributes references to matters of the imperial court to the *Six Histories of Japan (Rikkokushi)*, as well as to many Chinese texts composed in either Japan or China, in both prose and poetry. Hirokawa Katsumi suggests that not only *Nihongi* (*Nihon shoki*; Chronicles of Japan, 720) but also subsequent books, such as *Nihon kōki* (Later chronicles of Japan, 840) and *Nihon sandai jitsuroku,* were consulted.[21] Needless to say, all of these official historical records are written in *kanbun,* and thus we can conclude that Murasaki was sufficiently competent in Chinese. In addition to her reading knowledge of the language, the range of Murasaki's allusions—for example, to Korean diplomats and on the succession to the throne—attests to her cultural background and political consciousness.

Another well-known but suppressed fact in situating Murasaki in a history of Japanese literature is that the Chinese texts she read with the imperial consort, Fujiwara no Shōshi (Akiko; 988–1074; also known as Jōtō Mon'in), are of a political nature and thus would be conventionally defined as "masculine." One text that is mentioned in *Murasaki Shikibu nikki* is *Xin yuefu* (New rhapsodies), by Bai Juyi, which includes many long poems of social criticism, with subjects ranging from a war veteran who disfigured himself in order to be discharged from the army to an old coal seller exploited by officers to a Chinese hostage of the Tartars who is recaptured and imprisoned by Chinese military forces—topics clearly at odds with the putatively aestheticized poetic topics of *waka.*[22] The readings with the consort took place roughly concurrently with Murasaki's writing of *Genji monogatari,* making it plausible that some of the texts she read found their way into the work of this "paragon" of Japanese aesthetic sensibility.

The references to sources in Chinese, written physically in either Japan or China, suggest that Murasaki was ready to liberally incorporate sources available only in Chinese. Male courtiers no doubt formed a part of her intended audience, and she expected them to realize how knowledgeable she was on texts that were not commonly read by women. While observing social rules specific to women, Murasaki earned respect for her learnedness. She may have suffered from the males-only educational system and from women who conformed to the norm, but she also succeeded in convincing her male associates, as well as some competent women of letters of her time, that she was their intellectual equal.

Contrasts often made between Murasaki and Sei Shōnagon both reveal and conceal various facets about Murasaki. As is widely known, Murasaki presents a negative portrayal of Sei Shōnagon as showy and error-prone: "Sei Shōnagon, for instance, was dreadfully conceited. She thought herself so clever and littered her writings with Chinese characters, but if you examined them closely, they left a great deal to be desired."[23] This observation has led to a hypothesis of rivalry between the two women: the well-behaved and yet mean-spirited Murasaki and the high-flying and yet open-minded Sei.[24] This impression was further confirmed by the fact that they served opposing royal consorts of Emperor Ichijō.

It would be premature to conclude on the basis of Murasaki's passing remark and no equivalent from Sei that the two women represented—either in their own minds or in those of their contemporaries—two extremes in women's self-fulfillment and self-expression. Such a view neglects other women of their time who were fairly knowledgeable of Chinese sources—for example, Akazome Emon, a historian and Murasaki's contemporary, or (though of a slightly later generation) Sugawara no Takasue no musume, the alleged author of many late Heian narratives, including *Hamamatsu chūnagon monogatari,* which we examined in chapter 1.

The idiom of "Sei-Shi" (Sei Shōnagon–Murasaki, "Shi" being another reading of the character for Murasaki) became most conspicuous in the Tokugawa period (as we will see below). According to Miyazaki Sōhei, who has surveyed the parallels drawn between Sei and Murasaki from the medieval period to the modern period, it was not until Andō Tameakira's *Shika shichiron* (Seven treatises on Lady Murasaki; also known as *Shijo shichiron* and as *Genji monogatari shichiron,* 1703) that a radical contrast was made between the two.[25] Since the Meiji period, the contrast has been maintained, in effect providing two possible responses for intellectual women to make to what was perceived as discrimination against women.

Another downplayed aspect of Murasaki Shikibu concerns her vision of the structure of *Genji monogatari*. Her use of Chinese sources is strategic and systematic rather than arbitrary and fragmentary. Nihei Michiaki demonstrates consistent parallels between the first part of *Genji monogatari* (from chapter 1, "Kiritsubo" [The Paulownia Court] to chapter 33, "Fuji no uraba" [Wisteria Leaves]) and "Qinghe wang Qing zhuan" (Biography of Qing, Prince of Qinghe) in *Hou Han shu* (History of the Later Han, 445) that suggest that Murasaki was well aware of how to develop her story, rather than episodically writing one chapter after another without a blueprint.[26] Murasaki's references to then famous Bai Juyi poems such as "Changhenge," "Li Furen," and "Shangyang Baifaren," as well as other Chinese sources, have been annotated by scholars in Japanese literature. They added many footnotes expressing her debt to Chinese literature. However, these did not lead scholars to conclude that Murasaki did more than merely sprinkle her text with excerpts from Chinese works that she happened to know. In fact, quotations from Chinese contributed to the emplotment of the narrative.

In *Shibun yōryō* (Essence of Lady Murasaki's text, 1763), Motoori Norinaga not only renounces the validity of seeking Chinese sources for *Genji monogatari,* but also pays little attention to the book's structural dimensions or to the fact that its complex plot has few logical flaws.[27] The Chinese factor is obliterated for the sake of the image of *Genji monogatari* as quintessentially Japanese and aesthetically homogeneous. Norinaga's praise for its crystallized ethereal essence (*mono no aware,* pathetic beauty), overshadows the remarkable art of storytelling that Murasaki demonstrated using the structure of the Chinese historical tale. Action (*shiwaza*) is considered subordinate to emotions (*kokoro*), which are meant to make the subject feminine and indecisive. Norinaga further argues that *Genji monogatari* functions first and foremost to show the reader the essence of each character or each occasion, rather than to tell us what it does or what is expected of it. Hence Norinaga neglects the dynamics of the narrative and reduces the text to fragmented poetic moments.[28] This position is consistent with Norinaga's view that *Genji monogatari* is primarily useful as a text for *waka* poets:

> The origin of poetry is *mono no aware.* There is no better way to understand *mono no aware* than by reading this narrative. This narrative came out of the

mono no aware that Murasaki understood, and the *mono no aware* that the present-day reader sees comes out of this narrative. Thus, this narrative has no other significance than enumerating instances of *mono no aware* and letting the reader know of it. The reader should not have any other expectation than to understand *mono no aware*. This is the essence of the discipline of poetry. No narrative or discipline of poetry should exist outside the understanding of *mono no aware*. Thus there is no discipline of poetry other than [reading] this narrative. Scholars, do take this into serious consideration and be urged to grasp *mono no aware*. It is exactly to understand this narrative, which is exactly to master the discipline of poetry.[29]

Norinaga emphasizes his point in the contrast he makes between *mono no aware* (represented by *Genji monogatari* and *waka*) and *ima-shime,* or lessons (to be conveyed by Chinese sources), as well as (though not so clearly) in the possible contrast between poetry (a genre to represent an essence and make an immediate impression) and prose (a genre for recounting a story to sustain the reader's interest and make a convincing argument). In addition, Norinaga downplays the importance of the order in which events are arranged in the narrative. This becomes evident in a comparison of his and other commentators' interpretations of the adulterous and quasi-incestuous affair between Genji and Fujitsubo (a.k.a. Usugumo, as Norinaga refers to her). In many preceding commentaries, including the above-mentioned *Shika shichiron* (which Norinaga cites in order to refute), the incident is considered pivotal, as it is the result of Genji's longing for his lost mother and later leads to retribution on the part of Genji's principal wife, who gives birth to an illegitimate child.[30] Norinaga, however, suggests that the point of the affair is to convey *mono no aware* and that the incident is "not significant enough to make a big deal out of it" (daiji to suru ni oyobanu koto nari).[31]

Instead of portraying Murasaki as appropriately feminine, Norinaga equates femininity with the poetic, the natural, and the indigenous, thus defining it as a quality that needs to be restored in both men's and women's Japanese writing:

All in all, the true emotions of human beings are, like girls, silly and full of attachments. The masculine, well-disciplined, and wise state of mind does not reflect true emotions. It is fabrication and false display. However wise one may be, the depth of one's heart is always like a girl's. The only difference is whether or not one is ashamed of it and hides it. Chinese texts are concerned exclusively with fabricated and contrived appearances and neglect to write of true emotions. At a glance they may appear wise, but all is made up and not true. Only because one is accustomed to reading such fabrications do they appear wise. The poetic narratives of Japan describe the depths of true human emotions and demonstrate *mono no aware*. Nothing can compete with poetic narratives in the detailed and thorough description of fine human emotions.[32]

The negative labels that Norinaga attaches to Chinese texts—"fabrications" and "contrived appearances"—seem to apply to the art of storytelling, which consists of an awareness of structure, the control of action, and the sustenance of plot over an extended period. The act of narration thus may well be defined as "masculine," as it requires the "well-disciplined and wise state of mind." Instead of dwelling upon personal sentiments, a storyteller needs to be well aware of the affairs of many characters and stand ostensibly omniscient, rational, and autonomous of those characters. In order to execute the authority of observation, he or she needs to control personal emotions, which are "like a girl's." Norinaga's emphasis on the poetic nature of *Genji monogatari* in effect overlooks Murasaki's skills in what he deems the "masculine" art of storytelling and thus engenders her as feminine. As Norinaga defined *Genji monogatari* as a series of fragmented poetic moments, so he defined Murasaki Shikibu as a champion of Japanese indigenous literature. When Norinaga matched "feminine" attributes with the notion of Japaneseness, he replaced history with myth, and a master narrative was constructed that Japanese national identity was unchangingly present throughout the history of the Chinese intervention. Within the myth, *Genji monogatari* became an epitome of aesthetic indigenousness and homogeneity, rather than a showcase of lingual heterogeneity that it in fact is.

Arakida Reijo, a Woman Historian

Arakida Reijo, a contemporary of Norinaga's, is rightly designated by Furuya Tomoyoshi as "by far the most prolific woman writer of all time in Japan."[33] Indeed, Izuno Tatsu's bibliography of Reijo's works includes forty-nine titles of fiction (mostly multivolume), all completed between 1771 and 1779.[34] Ichikawa Seigaku categorizes her as a *chojutsuka*, or "professional writer," rather than a poet or novelist, as she wrote in several genres, most conspicuously history and fantasy.[35] Nonetheless, few women of letters in later generations cite Reijo as a model who inspired them. Yosano Akiko, a notable exception, was puzzled by Reijo's relative obscurity and tried to redeem Reijo by publishing a two-volume collection of her writings, with summaries and a biographical introduction.[36] This collection, though a small sampling of Reijo's work, is enough to demonstrate the wide range of genres in which she exercised her talent.[37]

Although Akiko's intention is to portray Reijo as a victim of gender discrimination in the "Confucianist" Tokugawa period, the claim is not entirely true.[38] Except for her parents' opposition to her getting an education, Reijo was surrounded by supportive men of letters. Her failure to establish lasting fame seems to have more to do with the fact that she did not write in genres that modern scholars considered more personal than public—and thus suited to women's participation—such as lyrics or memoirs or genres that transcended gender boundaries (such as Chinese poetry). Most women-authored prose narratives that have been canonized in modern times are ostensibly confessional and lyrical, assuming a single persona that is often (intentionally) confused with the author. Reijo's narratives, in contrast, are on public affairs or supernatural incidents and thus are distinct from her own life. Her narrators are not emotive but detached from the stories they recount.

First, a brief glance at Reijo's background is in order.[39] She was born into, then adopted by and married into the families of Shintoist priests in Ise, in relative proximity to Matsuzaka, the town in which Motoori Norinaga lived and taught classical literature. Though her parents discouraged her from getting an education in either Chinese or Japanese, reasoning that it was inappropriate for women, Reijo's four brothers tutored her in their subjects of study and nurtured her academic potential. Her adoptive father taught her to read Chinese classics and poetry. She then studied Chinese poetic composition with Emura Hokkai (1713–1788), a leading poet, critic, and author of *Nihon shishi* (A history of Chinese poetry in Japan, 1771). In the third volume of the work, Hokkai lists Reijo among a handful of women *kanshi* poets of the time.[40]

Reijo did not establish herself as a *kanshi* poet, however. Nor did she excel in *waka* composition. Though her name is included in Aida Hanji and Harada Yoshino's *Kinsei joryū bunjin den* (Biographies of women of letters in the Tokugawa period), the reception to her *waka* poetry was lukewarm; awkward expressions and transitions seem to have troubled some critics.[41] The only area in which she demonstrated poetic skills was *renga*, or linked poetry. Satomura Shōteki (?–1758), her teacher in the genre, stated that women linked poets were rare, implying that he welcomed her for that reason.[42] The fact that women poets were more inclined to compose in isolation and that Reijo was successful and active in linked poetry instead suggests that she was more communicative than self-indulgent and more keen on developing sequences than on capturing a single theme. It thus seems safe to conclude that Reijo's strength lay less in her style than in her ability to build an overarching structure.

Reijo's husband, Yoshishige Ietada (the surname is also read "Keitoku" by some), considered by Nomura Kōdai (1717–1784) to be a descendant of the Heian courtier and *kanbun* writer Yoshishige no Yasutane (?–1002), encouraged her to write historical and fictional narratives.[43] He took an active role in supporting her, exploiting his library privileges at the Great Shrine of Ise to check out books in both Japanese and Chinese for Reijo to read and volunteering to produce clean copies of her manuscripts. Many of her works are thus handed down in his handwriting. Nomura Kōdai notes in his preface to Reijo's *Tsuki no yukue* (The Whereabouts of the Moon, 1771), which he wrote at her husband's request, that "The husband and wife read books together and discussed difficult passages. Together forever, they traveled hand in hand westbound and sojourned among the five provinces."[44] Emura Hokkai in his preface to Reijo's *Ike no mokuzu* (Weeds in the pond, 1771) makes a similar observation on the couple's relationship: "[Reijo] is . . . married to Keitoku Joshō (studio name of Ietada). Joshō also likes to study and knows the classics well. The husband and wife pore over books and scrolls day and night and take pleasure in deciphering the meanings of the texts. They are comparable to Zhao Mingcheng and Li Yi'an [Qingzhao (1084–ca. 1151)] as a couple."[45]

In short, Reijo was first blessed with male family members who were willing to help her grow as a writer. Then her teachers in linked poetry and Chinese learning thought highly of her and bestowed upon her studio names using one character each from the names of Murasaki Shikibu and Sei Shōnagon: Shizan (Purple Hill) and Seisho (Clean Shore). The naming was not only complimentary, but also appropriate, given Reijo's determination to write in the Heian courtly style. Her mastery of classical poetic prose was such that in *Hakubunkan Kokubun sōsho* (1914), a classical literature series, her *Ike no mokuzu* is included in the same volume as *Uji shūi monogatari* (ca. 1222) and *Matsukage no nikki* (Diary in the shade of the pine, ca. 1710), while her *Tsuki no yukue* appears in the volume that contains *Kagerō nikki* (ca. 975), *Sarashina nikki* (ca. 1060), *Hamamatsu chūnagon monogatari, Torikaebaya monogatari* (ca. 1072), and *Hōjōki* (1212). Reijo's work does not seem misplaced as far as its language is concerned, even when it is grouped with historically distant works.[46]

Reijo's first extensive work was an annotation of the twenty-volume *Utsubo monogatari*. As is well known, this early Heian narrative is set partly in China and Persia, as well as in the Japanese mountainside, which gives an exotic feel to the story, and it thus may not be immediately associated with the feminine as equated with the indigenous. The story evolves around several major characters, rather than a single protagonist, and it spans several generations. *Utsubo monogatari* thus has multiple perspectives, several storylines starting independently of one another and converging later, all of which led to confusion in the chronological order of incidents and in the identification and genealogy of the characters. Reijo obtained a copy from her husband, and she was able to study the text carefully and straighten out its chronology, names, and style. Though the contents of *Utsubo monogatari* are fictional, Reijo sought a historiographic consistency within the premises of the text. The choice of this text and the methodology she applied to it attest to her mastery of historical narratives. Indeed, Ogino Yoshiyuki praises her as "the only woman historian," while there are many women poets in Japan.[47]

Among Reijo's best-known works are "Japanese" translations of *kanbun* chronicles of Japanese history. *Ike no mokuzu* is a historical record of the reigns of medieval Japanese emperors. Emura compares Reijo to Murasaki Shikibu in terms of her compositional skills in structuring texts of substantial length and to the authors of the "Four Mirrors"—*Ōkagami* (The great mirror, ca. 1077); *Imakagami* (The present mirror, ca. 1170); *Mizukagami* (The water mirror, ca. 1190); and *Masukagami* (The clear mirror, ca. 1375)—historical narratives written in *wabun*, a tradition that had not been maintained since.[48] In the postscript to *Ike no mokuzu*, also written in *kanbun* by Miyoshi Genmei, Reijo is compared to Dong Hu, a historian from the Warring States period highly regarded by Confucius, and to Cao Dajia and Ban Zhao (45–117), the sister of Ban Gu (32–92) and co-author of *Hanshu* (History of the Han, ca. 82). *Tsuki no yukue*, also a historical narrative, recounts events under Emperors Takakura (r. 1168–1180) and Antoku (r. 1180–1183), whose reigns coincided with the Gen-Pei Civil War (1180–1185). In the preface, Nomura Kōdai also maintains that while there were many women poets, there were few women historians, and he too compares Reijo with Ban Zhao.[49] The author's own postscript to *Tsuki no yukue* states that she completed writing the narrative on the same day that Murasaki is reputed to have begun writing *Genji mono-gatari.* In contrast to medieval Japanese women writers who explicitly molded their characters after figures in *Genji monogatari* (such as Lady Nijō), Reijo made a conscious effort to become a latter-day Murasaki. Reijo refused to embody poetic essence and planned instead to construct *histoire* (in the sense of both history and story).

Confucian and Chinese scholars accepted this unconventionally intellectual woman, while Reijo was isolated from the *kokugakusha,* or nativist scholars. Furuya Tomoyoshi points out that her reworking of Chinese sources in fiction is among the first of its kind, preceded only by Takebe Ayatari's *Honchō Suikoden.*[50] Among her short stories with a debt to Chinese literature are many of the thirty stories collected in *Ayashi no yo gatari* (Tales of the strange reigns, 1778), an anthology inspired by Chinese ghost stories and using sources such as *Sou shen ji,* an Eastern Jin dynasty (317–420) anthology of *zhiguai xiaoshuo* (horror stories) written by Gan Bao; the same is true of "Fuji no iwaya" (The wisteria cave, 1772), a story based on *You xian ku.*[51] These few of the many examples of Reijo's reworking of Chinese literature demonstrate both her wide reading knowledge of the subject and her willingness to incorporate Chinese elements, either directly or by domestication.

It should be obvious by now that Reijo's work does not conform to the norms of transparency, immediacy, and indigenousness—values that began to be legitimated by the *kokugakusha* and then, with the help of modern aestheticism, by *kokubungaku* scholars in modern times. Reijo's many allusions to Chinese references in *Nonaka no shimizu* (The pure stream in the field, 1772) were among the reasons that Motoori Norinaga criticized her work: "Kono dan kaesugaesu Karagoto ni matsuware sugite ito urusashi" (This passage is cumbersome, plagued with too many references to Chinese sources).[52] Indeed *Nonaka no shimizu* is remotely based on *You xian ku,* which, as we saw touched upon in chapter 1, is a classical tale about a male traveler's incidental encounter with two mythical women. Norinaga made unsolicited corrections to the manuscript of *Nonaka no shimizu,* marking words and phrases to be replaced with better choices, whereas Reijo herself was more concerned with the overall structure of the story.[53] In "Keitoku Reijo nanchin" (Statement of complaints by Keitoku Reijo), Reijo called Norinaga "a country bumpkin, a phony student" (inaka no ese shosei) not entitled to criticize her work.[54] Shimizu Hamaomi (1776–1824), a nativist scholar of the Kamo no Mabuchi (1697–1769) lineage, states the following: "This old woman thought so highly of herself that she did not follow others' cautionary advice. Since she did not ask for instruction of Mr. Motoori or Mr. Uji, her writing is often flawed with the misuse of particles, which is regrettable."[55]

It is true that Norinaga was generous with his time and expertise and may have meant well in offering editorial suggestions to someone who was not his student. Indeed, as Ishimura notes, many of his suggestions helped Reijo's text read more smoothly and coherently.[56] But Norinaga may also have had an agenda in voluntarily taking up the task of editing (or anatomizing) her text. Reijo's compositional practice of liberally drawing upon Chinese sources squarely defied Norinaga's conviction that differences between Chinese literature (which was didactic and artificial) and Japanese literature (which was aesthetic and natural) were so essential that readers should not even try to trace references to Chinese texts and that writers should not intentionally allude to them. Furthermore, it is evident that Reijo's purposes in writing—writing history to set the record straight and entertaining readers with well-plotted stories—had little in common with what Norinaga believed were the purposes of prose fiction, which we saw in his guidelines on how to read *Genji monogatari*—namely, to show poetic essence and to move the reader emotionally. Reijo sought to perfect her style according to Murasaki (and may have failed to do so according to Norinaga's philological judgment), and she had no intention of capturing the poetic essence of "feminine" emotions. Rather Reijo planned, developed, and controlled her complex plots rationally. She was more than willing to seek inspiration in Chinese sources in order to achieve her goals. She did not write out of her body; her writing came out of her mind, which was neither "feminine" nor "indigenous" by Norinaga's standards.

In fairness to Norinaga, I should hasten to add that he did not suggest that Reijo should not write the way she did because she was a woman. His criticism of Sinophilic writing is consistent regardless of whether the author in question is male or female. However, when we go beyond Norinaga's critique of Reijo's texts specifically and consider the fact that Reijo is largely dismissed from later histories of Japanese literature—unlike male fantasy writers, such as Ueda Akinari, who also had conflicts with Norinaga—we may suspect that her gender affected her status. When "how women are supposed to write" is equated with "how the Japanese are supposed to write," there is no place for women historians or women Sinophiles. Womanhood and nationality are essentialized and crystallized by masculine observers, who claim to have a monopoly on reason and who resist women's control of time. Women and/or the nation should either embody timeless qualities or succumb to oblivion.

Women were welcome to make spontaneous and improvisational observations (hence the large number of women poets from ancient to modern times who had done so) but were not encouraged or expected to draw pictures on a large scale—an act that requires logical thinking.[57] Nationality, likewise, was taken to be unchanging over time, transforming history into myths that showed only origins and essence. Women with four-dimensional vision, discussing chronology and causality in events and actions, were either reduced to representing the embodiment of momentary beauty, as Murasaki was (in the guise of being elevated to an idol), or erased from literary history, as Reijo nearly was. "Sliding doors" were opened and closed for Reijo by different elements of her contemporary audience and then shut in such a way that few could even see her from behind the closed doors.

Between Transvestism and Essentialism: Ema Saikō, a Muse with a Pen in Hand

Accomplished and productive in Chinese verse, calligraphy, and ink painting—subjects that men of letters were expected to study—rather than excelling in historical fiction or fantasy in classical *wabun* as Reijo did, Ema Saikō faced a challenge of a different kind from Reijo's. Whereas Reijo's negotiations with earlier Chinese sources invited criticism, Saikō did not need to defend her compositional method of quotation from Chinese texts as it was a common and commended practice in her fields of production. Saikō's challenge instead was to cope constantly with comparisons of her work with that of male colleagues, who outnumbered female artists. Her work was received with comments that it was as good as, if not better than, that of her male contemporaries and that she made a unique contribution to the literary tradition by creating it in an unmistakably feminine manner.[58]

Saikō was one of the many women *kanshi* poets (*kanshijin*) who were exceptionally privileged, respected, and successful in this "masculine" genre during the Tokugawa period. As Maeda Yoshi, who has been studying the subject, has pointed out, there were many notable women *kanshi* poets in different regions of Japan but most notably in Kyūshū: Tachibana Gyokuran (?–1794) of Chikugo (present-day Fukuoka); Kamei Shōkin (Tomo; 1798–1857) of Chikuzen (Fukuoka); and Hara Saihin (Michi or

Mitsu; 1798–1859), also of Chikuzen.[59] In 1880, Minakami Roteki compiled and published *Nihon keien ginsō* (Anthology of Japanese women's poetry), which is a proof of the sizable and worthy output of female *kanshijin*. In 1883, thirty-six poets from Minakami's collection, including Saikō as well as Reijo, were further selected by Yu Yue (Quyuan; 1821–1906) to form a volume of women's poetry (*guixiu;* J. *keishū*) in *Dongying shixuan* (Anthology of poems from the eastern sea, 1903).[60] Another anthology that we touched upon above, *Edo Joryū bunjin den,* lists thirty-three major *kanshi* poets (including Saikō, Shōkin, and Saihin), as well as a group of minor ones. The works of Saikō, Saihin, and Yanagawa (nee Chō) Kōran (Kei; 1804–1878) are collected in *Joryū* (The Female School), a volume in the series *Edo kanshi sen* (Anthology of *kanshi* from the Tokugawa period).[61] Thus, women *kanshi* poets were published and established, sometimes even in their lifetimes, and their work remained in print in various editions.

Although the Tokugawa women *kanshi* poets stepped into the "male" territory of composition in Chinese, gender still remained an issue for them and their male colleagues. However, participation in a cultural practice that had been construed as masculine inspired an interesting approach to gender configuration: discursive transvestism and dialogue with the male audience. For example, Hara Saihin, as legends have it, wore men's clothes, carried a sword, and loved to drink in the mode of her favorite poet, Li Bai.[62] Her father, Hara Kosho, was an accomplished Confucian scholar in the Ko-bunjigaku school in Kyūshū with whom Saihin first studied Confucian texts.[63] The following poem by Saihin, addressed to a male friend who apparently had praised her for her talent in *kanshi* composition, offers a qualified acceptance of the conventional gender divide:

> You are a true man, who could slight you? . . .
> I have learned how to sew and have sewn women's jackets and the like. . . .
> I do not wish to take a broom and become someone's wife
> thus have left my humble home with books my late father had left me.[64]

Despite the ostentatious humility, Saihin seems to imply that she is now on a par with male literati in the masculine art of *kanshi* composition. She studied poetry with Rai San'yō (1780–1832), a well-known and arguably the best Sinologist and *kanshi* poet in Kyoto in the late Tokugawa period.[65] She had a chance to show him her "Gengo-shi" (Poems on *The Tale of Genji*), fifty-four poems to match the number of chapters in *Genji*.[66]

Saihin was not the only female disciple that San'yō took on. In fact, he was rather famous for mentoring younger female poets, among whom he named Ema Saikō as the best.[67] San'yō first met Saikō, then twenty-seven years old, at her father's home in 1813. Shortly afterward, her father, Ema Ransai, a physician and scholar of Dutch medicine who worked for the Ōgaki feudal domain, asked San'yō to mentor her in Chinese poetic composition and calligraphy.[68] San'yō not only offered her instruction, but also acted as an agent of sorts, promoting the distribution of her works of art. San'yō would pass Saikō's work on to his friends, inscribing complimentary remarks on her paintings. While not a professional painter, San'yō was an accomplished amateur and was a renowned critic of Ming dynasty paintings. He apparently suggested to Saikō that she abandon the style of Gyokurin, her first painting teacher, who San'yō thought was too technically inclined to be artistic.[69] In 1814, San'yō took the trouble to introduce her to Uragami Shunkin (1779–1846), a son of the renowned Uragami Gyokudō (1745–1820) and himself a leading painter of his day who later taught Saikō.[70] From all these negotiations, we can see the extent of San'yō's commitment to Saikō's education, which necessitated interactions with selected senior male colleagues.

Calligraphy was another venue of communication between this versatile woman and her mentor. San'yō would send Saikō poems for her to inscribe, including his own poems (*yanshi*, "erotic poems") and those of others, such as Cao Zhi's "Luoshen fu," about an erotic encounter with the eponymous beautiful mythical being.[71] Fukushima Riko suggests that San'yō selected the specific poems because he intended to help Saikō become a quintessentially feminine poet.[72] This interpretation would corroborate a part of San'yō's commentary on Saikō's poetry (to be discussed below) but would contradict another part. Fukushima's interpretation is valuable in her resistance to the persistent and yet unfounded speculation about a romantic liaison between the younger female student and her male mentor.

It is true that San'yō was romantically interested in his young student at one point. One of his extant letters, addressed to a close friend, Koishi Genzui, reveals that San'yō was so attracted to Saikō that he seriously considered her as a potential wife; he says that he "wants to edit (J. *tensaku*) her entire body."[73] From the unusual phrasing in this letter and from later remarks that her letters to him evoked the image of her body, it seems that San'yō equated Saikō's texts with her corporeal presence. In other words, he had the propensity to eroticize her literature, which indeed transcended conventional gender distinctions. It is also true, however, that the artistic and intellectual relationship between the two survived the apparent emergence and disappearance of the possibility of marriage or romance. San'yō's putative marriage proposal for Saikō, made to her father, and her father's rejection thereof in 1814 did not stop San'yō from mediating Saikō's acquaintances with distinguished men and women of letters and arts.[74] With his recommendations, Saikō began in 1819 to correspond with people such as Tanomura Chikuden (1777–1835), a literatus who remains famous to date, and Jiang Yige, a Chinese visitor in Nagasaki.[75]

Saikō kept sending her *kanshi* to San'yō for his comments and suggestions until his death. While this practice may appear at first glance to be an example of female subservience to the male cultural standard, it should be noted that male disciples commonly did the same thing as part of their learning. San'yō seems to have taken pride in helping her grow as a poet. His pride is evident in his presentation to her of an abridged and newly annotated version of *Suiyuan nudizi shixuan* (Anthology of poems by the female disciples of Suiyuan; reprinted in Edo, 1830), a work by Yuan Mei (Suiyuan). Yuan is known not only for his famous recipe collections, which we touched upon in chapter 2, but also for mentoring many female poets. Rai San'yō inscribed the following note on the front page of the copy that he gave Saikō: "I too have female disciples. They are not necessarily inferior to some of the female poets whose works are collected in this volume. Though I do not wish [in my own merits] to rival their mentor, Suiyuan, I should be able to parallel him in this regard."[76] San'yō also recommended that Saikō publish her works, especially because she had been so dedicated to poetry that she had allowed herself no distractions. Her refusal to do so, out of humility, meant that she could not show her entire work in print to her mentor during his lifetime. San'yō died within two years of making the suggestion. In a poem she composed upon his death, Saikō compares San'yō to Yuan Mei while humbly stating that she does not have the talent to equal Yuan's best female disciple, Jin Yi (1770–1794).[77]

San'yō's comments on Saikō's poems reveal several distinct outlooks on gender: sometimes he assumes there are essential differences between males and females; at other times he is willing to admit that this woman poet could do much better than his male disciples; and yet at other times he considers it ridiculous to evaluate poems according to an author's gender.[78] For some of Saikō's poems that appeared to deal with sentiments aroused by subtle changes in natural surroundings and domestic incidents, he would add what was meant to be praise: "Every line is gentle—this is truly a feminine tone of speech; men with beards and eyebrows could not imitate it no matter how many tactics they devised";[79] "[this is] truly feminine expression—no one has ever said this yet. Without an astute mind or feminine voice, how could one manage to mold expression like this?";[80] "[this is] truly a distinguished woman's expression."[81] At the same time, he would proclaim her "a female version of Lu Wuguan [You; 1125–1210]," comparing her to the Southern Song poet renowned for his attention to minutiae; in so doing, San'yō would transcend the gender boundaries in poetic composition.[82]

In a similar vein, San'yō's comments on a particular poem by Saikō sound double-edged: "[It is] not accommodating to female language. If it had been composed by a man, it would have been a masterpiece";[83] "I did not expect women to have such knowledge of [Chinese] history; [even] a distinguished male of today may not understand this [reference]."[84] While San'yō seems to have viewed the gap between Saikō's discursive and anatomical gender identities as affecting the quality of the poem in question, he simultaneously admitted that Saikō had mastered the masculine language. Echoing a question frequently asked by feminists, San'yō also wondered, while looking at another poem, "Who could tell this is a woman's work without having asked for the author's identity beforehand?"[85] He also quoted a statement by a male disciple of his who had read her work: "How could she put such complex thoughts so lucidly? Whenever I attempted to do the same, I ended up being scolded by you [San'yō]." (San'yō confided in Saikō that while the male disciple was quite good, his expression could become awkward, a shortcoming from which Saikō did not suffer.) "It was surprising to him that the work was done by a woman."[86] Here again we recognize both the prejudice against women writers and men's willingness to admit that they were prejudiced.

Mastering the masculine discourse to the extent of surpassing male colleagues could mean alienation from other women. San'yō was mindful of such a potentially distressing circumstance and advised Saikō not to be afraid to be different: "If you are qualified to join my poetic circle, you are already unusual."[87] San'yō's advice suggests that he was evaluating Saikō on the basis of her cultural achievements rather than her sex. Yet Saikō deeply felt the isolation from other women. She told younger women with aspirations of following in her footsteps to reconsider: "I have failed to observe any of the three obligations of obedience [that women should exhibit to their fathers, husbands, and sons]," she begins "Jijutsu" (Autobiographically speaking), and she concludes with the following: "I fear lazy women in the world go out of their way to pursue the literary arts and follow in my footsteps."[88] She defied the norms, for which she felt she had to pay the price. Sliding doors might have been opened for her to enter an adjacent room of the masculine hand, but they were closed behind her, allowing her no way back into the conventionally engendered area of femininity.

Saikō was conscious of her divergence not only from the social norms, but also, at times, from the conventional expectations of women poets. Saikō's book collection included *Meien shiki* (Ch. *Mingyuan shigui*; Poems by famous beauties), an anthology of more than two thousand Chinese poems attributed to more than four hundred women from antiquity through the Ming dynasty.[89] On her reading of works in the volume, she wrote: "Why do they all write of loneliness, isolation, and longing for their heartless lovers?"[90] Saikō seems to suggest that women should deal with as wide a range of subject matter as men do, and thus she seemed apprehensive about endorsing the convention of *keien shi* (Ch. *guiyuan shi*; poems on bedchamber regrets). Women's portrayals of themselves as lonely ladies deserted by their husbands or lovers are a choice made in accordance with the male representation of women and are the opposite of another choice available to them—namely, presenting themselves as content, independent, and intellectually engaged and engaging. Saikō's choice was well known and respected among those who knew her, and it is evident from the inscription on her tombstone: "As for her personality, [it was] sincere and graceful, sensible, pious to her father; for some reason never married, [she] indulged in poetry and drawing, though at the same time she was concerned with the fortunes of the nation, lamenting its negative prospects; [such concern] put men with beards to shame. . . . [She was] a woman but not a wife, female but not feminine (Onna ni shite fu ni arazu)."[91]

Saikō's versatility in poetry has been forgotten, if not willfully ignored, by modern critics. Moreover, according to Kado Reiko, contemporary critics and biographers tended to view Saikō's relationship with San'yō in a positive light, whereas in the Meiji and the periods thereafter criticism of her became intense. For example, Morita Sōhei (1881–1949), a one-time lover of Hiratsuka Raichō (Haruko, to whom we will return below), wrote a story entitled "Onna deshi" (Female disciple), which exploited the well-known mentor-disciple relationship between San'yō and Saikō; it was serialized in a women's journal, *Fujin kōron,* in 1931. Without having studied primary sources such as San'yō's letters, Morita changed the mentor-disciple relationship into an adulterous affair and thus was publicly criticized by Kizaki Yoshinao, a biographer of Rai San'yō.[92] Morita eroticized a primarily if not exclusively scholarly relationship and in so doing portrayed the woman poet as essentially erotic and as voicing her female essence rather than representing a culturally formed identity. Also, a popular historical novelist, Yoshikawa Eiji (1892–1962), writes of Saikō in a section on San'yō's mother, Baishi (who herself was well educated and accomplished in *waka;* hence the possession of a pseudonym by which she is known) in his volume of historical stories, *Nihon meifu den* (Biographies of distinguished women in Japan, 1942) as follows: "Baishi was terribly concerned with the rumor that the spinster and self-proclaimed poet took pains to make up her face and dress herself up and shamelessly came to see San'yō in his residence, Suisei-sō. Not only that, [it was said that] the two took advantage of poetic composition meetings to have trysts."[93] Such portrayals of Saikō are at odds with the observations of Saikō, San'yō, his mother, and their friends, whose writings Yoshikawa neglected, if he consulted them at all. Yoshikawa's intent to redefine Saikō as a lascivious, pedantic, and adulterous woman is an image as distant as can be from the portrayal of Saikō as "sincere and graceful," as written on her tombstone.[94]

Morita and Yoshikawa's views of Saikō tell us less about her than about them. While Meiji society may have liberated women on some accounts, it could be less agreeable than Tokugawa society to women intellectuals who did not conform to the institution of marriage. Professional women were accepted only if they were also proper wives—and preferably mothers as well—in the first place. While Tokugawa literati were more willing to accept intellectual women as their colleagues and comrades, rather than as objects of erotic or voyeuristic desire, Meiji men of letters tended to see them in physical terms, as they redefined women's literature as the natural expression of their emotions in their native (and thus naturally given) language.

That it took Saikō many years of training to acquire a reading knowledge of Chinese literary conventions before she could start writing has been largely obliterated, while the fact that she was an unmarried woman who was closely associated with a married man has been emphasized and often blown out of proportion in the modern reception of her poetry. That her work is almost exclusively in literary Chinese has further led to its marginalization, as modern Japanese literature and modern perceptions of classical Japanese literature have increasingly taken the path of homogenization, domestication, and naturalization.[95] Thus fewer women of letters followed her footsteps to become *kanshijin,* and the numbers of readers of her poetry declined. As noted, the modern perception of literature dictates that writers should write as they feel and in their "own" language, which is "natural"—just as Murasaki Shikibu is mistakenly believed to have done. Thus, Saikō is shut out of the room into which she was once warmly invited, although an intense gaze can still be cast upon her from behind the "sliding doors."

Mori Ōgai: Defending "Misfits"

Mori Ōgai seems to have been able to transcend gender boundaries as some Tokugawa literati that we have seen. His support for Meiji and Taishō women writers is well documented: Higuchi Ichiyō's posthumous fame owes much to his positive reviews; Yosano Akiko published some of her poetry in *Subaru,* a journal that Ōgai helped establish; and Hiratsuka Raichō was acquainted with Ōgai (to be discussed below). His short story "Gyo Genki" (1915) features Yu Xuanji (Gyo Genki in the Japanese reading) from Tang China, a legendary beauty and poetess who fell prey to the gender relations of her time. We will first see how Mori Ōgai portrays his heroine and if he does justice to the historically documented facts about her, which he ostensibly knew. The well-known relationship between Yu Xuanji and her mentor, Wen Tingyun, constitutes an important part of this story (with some fictional modifications), and it seems to be an intra-textual model for the relationship between Ōgai and Raichō.

The pairing of the male mentor and the younger female disciple—not unlike the case of San'yō and Saikō—illustrates the art-for-art's-sake of the classical literary canon in women's education. While teaching male students, mentors could be rewarded by these students' success in the bureaucracy or in academia, but mentoring females guaranteed no social reward. However accomplished she may have been, a woman intellectual could not be a government official or a teacher in the scholarly institutions. The mentor's satisfaction thus consisted solely in witnessing the intellectual or artistic growth of the student. One could say that women's mastery of the masculine language was as much of a dead end as the modern intellectuals' reliance on classical language (the subject of chapter 4).

Mori Ōgai is known to have portrayed many historical as well as fictional women of intelligence and integrity. Critics have observed that

Ōgai tended to be more inventive—exhibiting what he termed *rekishi banare* (departures from history)—when it came to the portrayal of women in his historical fiction.[96] The greater degree of free interpretation is attributed to the relative lack of historical documentation about women, a point that precisely corroborates our concern with canonization: women found their place in orthodox history much less than men did. The relative lack of information on women as legitimate authors within the canon often caused them to fall prey to rumors and gossip. The title character of Ōgai's story, Yu Xuanji, is no exception. The legendary courtesan, Daoist nun, and poetess of the late Tang dynasty has been the subject of many anecdotes that are hard to either validate or invalidate. Still, data about her are better preserved than those of many other women in official histories, owing to her associations with male officials, most notably Wen Tingyun. Ōgai lists a considerable number of archival sources at the end of the story, and in part he followed some of them very faithfully. It will thus be even more revealing of his authorial intent for us to examine the space that his invention rather than his research filled.

The story begins with the shocking news that Xuanji has been arrested for murder—an incident that occurred toward the end of her life—and it then turns to a retrospective of her public life. The voyeuristic gaze prevails at the beginning of the story with a description of her physical appearance, suggesting the entire business of the scandal: "Xuanji had long been renowned for her beauty. She was as voluptuous as Yang Guifei rather than as slim as Zhao Feiyan"[97] However, the narrator soon establishes Xuanji as more than just a passive object of observation. She was aware of herself and interested in enhancing and showing off her physical beauty, as is suggested immediately after the above-cited passage: "One might assume that as a Daoist nun she avoided tainting her face with makeup. That was not the case: she was always carefully dressed and made up."[98] Though her background as a courtesan and a concubine might sufficiently account for such habits, this passage precedes Ōgai's description of her days in a pleasure quarter or in her master's residence and thus points more to her will to perform than to the necessity of selling her beauty as a means of earning a living.

Instead, however, of praising her beauty or portraying her as a lonely lady longing for a distant lover—the effect of which would be to aestheticize and objectify her—Ōgai's narrator foregrounds her dignity, learning, and talent:

Xuanji's fame among the men of letters in Chang'an was not solely as a beauty: she was distinguished in poetry. . . . Xuanji was only five years old when Bai Juyi passed away in the first year of Dazhong, in the reign of Yizong, but she was so precocious that she had memorized many poems not only by Bai Juyi, but also by Yuan Weizhi, who was as celebrated as Juyi. The total number of poems, in old and new styles combined, that she had memorized reached several dozen. Xuanji composed her first seven-character quatrain at the age of thirteen. By the time she was fifteen, some connoisseurs had already begun to copy and circulate poems by that girl from the Yu family.[99]

As the detailed studies of Yamazaki Kazuhide and others have shown, Ōgai draws on a number of Chinese sources in this story, including *Taiping guangji* (A wide range of accounts of the great peace, 978), from which the above passage is derived.[100] He is thus not exclusively responsible for the construction of Yu Xuanji as she appears in his story. Nonetheless, his strategic selection and placement of references suggest that he makes his own statement about the poetess. Ōgai's portrait of Xuanji is distinct from those offered by either Karashima Takeshi, a contemporary Japanese scholar in Chinese literature, or Satō Haruo, a Japanese literary man and Sinophile whom we saw in passing as a friend of Tanizaki Jun'ichirō in chapter 2. One fact that Karashima and Satō seem to agree upon—and that Ōgai disregards—is that Yu Xuanji composed poems about longing for her master, Li Yi, who apparently deserted her after traveling with her. Karashima explains how the man and his concubine separated and emphasizes Yu Xuanji's expressions of agony in his annotations to her poems.[101] In a similar vein, Satō includes in his anthology of translations of Chinese women's poems, *Shajin shū* (Anthology of particles of dust from passing vehicles, 1929), only one poem by Yu Xuanji— "Qiuyuan" (Autumn regrets), which concerns the fading beauty of a lonely lady who longs for her former lover.[102] In contrast, the five poems by Xuanji quoted in "Gyo Genki" do not include "Qiuyuan" or any *guiyuan* poetry that concerns a lonely lady's laments.

The omniscient narrator of "Gyo Genki" highlights the presence of the male objectifying gaze upon Xuanji's body and thus in effect invalidates the framework for Karashima and Sato's readings. He/she recounts how men's expectations of physical intimacy with Xuanji are thwarted by her relentless expressions of contempt and by their sense of inferiority when faced with her intelligence and poetic talent: "When visitors with no literary penchant turned up, simply lured by the reputation of the beauty, Xuanji would relentlessly insult them and chase them away. Even if illiterate young men, exploiting their connections with frequent customers, could be spared contempt and curses, they would voluntarily sneak out of the house, convinced of their own deficiencies after witnessing the poetic composition and musical performance of the company."[103] The tone of narration, though detached, clearly mocks male attempts at eroticizing this female intellectual.

Ōgai's narrator observes that Yu Xuanji is not "feminine" in the conventional sense of the word and that she is equal if not superior to the male intellectuals of her day in her scholarly manner and literary talent. The scene in which Wen Tingyun, one of the best poets of the late Tang, first meets her is presented as follows: "Xuanji straightened her collar and received Wen with utmost respect. Wen, predisposed to meet her the same way he would meet courtesans, could not help but change his attitude. An exchange of a few words was enough for Wen to see that Xuanji was no ordinary woman; that fifteen-year-old girl, as pretty as a flower, showed no sign of coquetry and spoke like a man."[104] Subsequently, Wen gives Xuanji a topic on which he suggests that she compose a poem. Her work impresses him: "Wen had been a judge for the civil service examination seven times, and every time he witnessed a presentable man agonizing in vain to finish even one line. No such man could possibly compete with her."[105] The narrator also states that Yu Xuanji has a "masculine soul" within her "feminine appearance"; he cites a famous poem by her, in which she regrets having been born female, and he does so while looking at the signatures that recent successful candidates in the civil service examinations had left on the walls of a Daoist temple during a celebration.[106]

This is not to say, however, that Ōgai did not recognize Yu Xuanji's erotic potential.[107] On the contrary, the story also describes the process of her sexual awakening—but it is not initiated by men. Remaining celibate throughout her career as a courtesan and later as an officer's concubine, Ōgai's Yu Xuanji sexually matures on her own rather than in response to male demands. She refuses to sleep with her master, Li Yi, who then sends her off to a Daoist temple, and as a result of Daoist training, she is finally awakened to sexual pleasure. According to Karashima, neither her biographies nor her poems register this transformation; there is no indication that the liaison between Yu Xuanji and Li Yi was not physically consummated; furthermore, a poem addressed to her next lover explicitly says that she was experienced.[108] Ōgai must then have deliberately rewritten the way in which Yu Xuanji's sexuality comes to the fore so that it would appear as though the process had occurred independently of male desire.

The story goes on to describe further sexual development—a quasi-lesbian relationship with another Daoist nun and Xuanji's invitation to a younger man to spend nights with her—and compellingly paints a picture of Yu Xuanji as taking the initiative in planning her *vita sexualis*. The classical Chinese stereotype of the lonely lady longing for her absent lover is replaced with the image of a woman who is uninhibited in her sexual relationships. Some Japanese scholars have noted that the episode of female companionship in Ōgai's story is not to be found in any biography of Yu Xuanji and that it is thus Ōgai's invention.[109] Ogata Tsutomu maintains that the author must have been inspired by a matter of journalistic interest in contemporary Japan—namely, the allegedly lesbian relationship between Hiratsuka Raichō, the feminist activist who in 1911 founded the feminist association Seitō (Blue Stockings), as well as a journal of the same title, and one of her followers, Otake Kōkichi (Kazue).[110] Raichō was known to her contemporaries as a sexually liberated woman. Earlier in her life, when she was engaged to marry a man, she eloped with another, Morita Sōhei, apparently intending to commit double suicide with him. The lovers parted but were reported to have consummated their relationship while on the road. This incident was further publicized by Morita's ostensibly confessional novel, *Baien* (Soot, 1909), which came out within a year of the breakup and became a best seller. Raichō appears to have inspired not only Morita, but also Natsume Sōseki with the concept of a "New Woman," or *atarashii onna* (or *atarashiki onna*), which Morita portrayed with both awe and repulsion.

In contrast to Sōseki, Ōgai is known to have actively supported the feminist movement. As Kaneko Sachiyo and Watanabe Yoshio (among others) have observed, he attended feminist meetings in Leipzig, where he was a student of hygiene; approved of his wife Shige's affiliation with Seitō; and complied with Raichō's requests for articles to her journal (the requests were usually mediated by her business associate and alleged lover, Otake Kazue).[111] Raichō affectionately recollects her interactions with Ōgai in an essay, "Ōgai sensei" (About Master Ōgai; written in 1962 and published in the following year):

> For one of the earliest examples, I heard from someone that he [Ōgai] had said that the title of the journal *Seitō* was very good. This might perhaps be

the source of the widely spread fallacy that Ōgai gave the title *Seitō*. Natural as it may be, given that his wife, Mori Shige, was an associate member of Seitō and that every issue of the journal was mailed to him, it was still surprising for me to hear more than once, and also see from his comments on me, that he read my writings. I felt as if I, as well as *Seitō*, were being looked after by him for a certain time. How different these things about him are from Sōseki's attitude toward women—his indifference to us and his lack of understanding of women![112]

The hypothesis that Ōgai wrote "Gyo Genki" as an implicit tribute to Raichō is congruent with his outspoken praise for her and with his acclaimed role as a mentor of women of letters in the late Meiji to early Taishō periods. In a special issue of *Chūō kōron* on Yosano Akiko published in June 1912, Ōgai touches upon Raichō as a talent comparable to Akiko's:

> I do not think there is anything new left for me to say. But if I am to recommend a distinguished woman writer, it has to be her, now that Ms. Higuchi Ichiyō is deceased. Akiko does not imitate others in any regard. One cannot miss her distinctive qualities. An American, Percival Lowell, said recently that Far Easterners are unique in their lack of individuality. I wish I could show him Akiko—but she will soon be shown in Paris.
>
> Incidentally, the one I think might equal Akiko is Ms. Hiratsuka Haruko. Though she does not seem to have much talent in poetry, her critical essays, published under the pseudonym "Raichō," make me realize that no male critic could write of philosophical matters as lucidly as she does. Aside from the bases of hypotheses that are yet to be tested, her writing itself is articulate in every corner. In contrast, male critics are not worth consulting on philosophical issues.[113]

The last few lines of the short essay suggest that the sex of an author does not affect Ōgai's reading of his/her work. If female writers such as Hiratsuka Raichō were superior to male writers, then Ōgai was ready to acknowledge it, just as Rai San'yō was.

As is well known, in his historical fiction Ōgai likes to portray women of strong will and intelligence—for example, Sayo in "Yasui fujin" (Mrs. Yasui, 1914), Ichi in "Saigo no ikku" (The last phrase, 1915), and Io in *Shibue Chūsai* (1916), to mention but a few.[114] They were historical persons in Tokugawa Japan from whom the author could maintain a temporal distance (as was the case with Yu Xuanji). Given what we have learned from Mieke Bal, the reworking of the lore does not necessarily confirm a nostalgic penchant on the part of the author; the author must have been motivated to write stories of women of this kind in the early twentieth century, when feminism was rising in Japan, in order to create specifically contemporary effects. If we read "Gyo Genki" partially as a biography of Hiratsuka Raichō under the guise of a biography of Yu Xuanji, the story would convey another message: Ōgai, neither frightened nor repelled by the "New Woman," does not present the figure for the sake of criticism of, or curiosity about, "sexual misfits." The detached and yet respectful tone suggests that he intended to do justice to a woman's independence and intelligence, regardless of who she happened to be or with whom she happened to be involved.

Raichō's position in the Japanese literary establishment was even more peripheral than Yu Xuanji's was in the Tang dynasty. While the Chinese poetess was admired by men for her mastery of "their own" language and cultural practices, Raichō staked out an area of criticism/philosophy that was then considered outside the pale of literature. In contrast to Yu Xuanji's days, when those who were engaged in literary production were all intellectuals, anti-intellectualism was evident in the renunciation of rhetoric, mediation, or structure in modern Japanese literature. Whereas Yu Xuanji's case represents the gender partition that prevented her from political engagement, Raichō's suggests that writing intellectually was a challenge to the entire premise of literature in modern Japan.

The reason for Ōgai's choice of Tang China as the historical backdrop of "Gyo Genki" is completely different from Sōseki's references to archaic China. Ōgai does not try to aesthetically distance, idealize, or immortalize China, as we saw Sōseki do in chapter 2. Instead of equating China with the historical past so as to create and maintain a distance at which a purportedly neutral Japanese commentator can make aesthetic and critical judgments, Ōgai puts incidents of Tang China in the contemporary context, where it becomes relevant to current issues. Ōgai also recognized the double-edged nature of the canonicity of classical Chinese literature; he was not oblivious to the fact that the full benefits of meritocracy, in which individuals' merits were to be measured by their levels of mastery of the Chinese canon and not by family prestige, were not extended to women in Tang China. Knowledge of the canon was an essential and yet insufficient precondition for success in the classical elitist society, and the Chinese meritocracy was not gender neutral. When we consider the fear and rejection of intellectual women in modern Japan, where the classical Chinese canon was actively excluded from the core literature (as we will see in the next chapter), it becomes evident that gender-screening was not intrinsic to the classical Chinese canon alone. Paradoxically, female intellectuals in modern Japan, who were deemed anomalous, could justify their "artificial" writing by exhibiting knowledge of the classical Chinese canon; unlike in the nineteenth century, familiarity with classical Chinese was no longer considered a major threat to the primacy of the native tongue, which was redefined in the twentieth century against European languages of the imperialist nations.

What Ōgai, vicariously through the "New Women," showcased in "Gyo Genki"—the denaturalization of gender identity—resonates in Kurahashi Yumiko's exploitation of her knowledge of classical Chinese literature, though with twists and turns that complicate analogies between Chinese and Japanese, origin and destination, the physical and the spiritual, and the female and male.

Kurahashi Yumiko: Female Sinophile in Contemporary Japan

Classical and "premodern" vernacular Chinese literature found a seemingly unlikely admirer in Kurahashi Yumiko (1935–), who made her literary debut in 1960 with experimental and absurdist stories often compared to Franz Kafka's. Her interest in the classical literature of Japan and Greece became obvious in the late 1960s, and it was followed by her active reworking of Chinese texts in the 1980s. Whereas many critics consider her transformation from experimentalist to classicist the result of maturity (attributed to marriage and motherhood and her first visit to the United States in between), I intend to situate her increasing and sustained use of Chinese texts as a professional and strategic choice.[115]

Given her prominent use of pastiche and preference for elaborately structured texts, premodern Chinese literature seems a natural destination in Kurahashi's bibliophilic tour. Critics did not problematize her quotations from classical Chinese sources, as they did those from French existentialist works, illuminating the ambiguous status of classical Chinese in modern Japan. The Chinese classics were already excluded from the canon of Japanese literature by the beginning of the twentieth century (as we shall see in the next chapter), and Chinese literature was recognized as a foreign national literature in the 1930s (*gaikoku bungaku,* as we saw Aoki Masaru label it in chapter 2). It constituted little threat to the imagined autonomy of the national literature of Japan in the 1960s. Kurahashi thus was able to write as eruditely as she wanted to when negotiating with Chinese literature. Quotations from archaic Chinese sources are of particular importance, as they allow Kurahashi to reject the confessional, native, and feminine without being accused of doing so.

Kurahashi often domesticates Chinese literary or legendary figures. Arakida Reijo did the same, transplanting characters from Chinese stories into Japanese settings, while Mori Ōgai used the original settings so as to disguise his parallels to contemporary Japan. "Kōkan" (1985)—Kurahashi's parody of both "Peach Blossom Spring" (immortalized by Tao Qian of Six Dynasties China in his "Taohuayuan ji") and a story collected in Lu Xun's (1881–1936) *Guxiaoshuo goushen* (Probing the depths of old fiction)—is set in an unspecified location that could quite well be contemporary Japan.[116] The main characters are government officials, as many Chinese literati characters are. One of them looks demonically hideous; the other, who is the "I" narrator of the story, divinely handsome. The first, who has a monstrous face, tells the other that he used to be as good looking as the narrator but was demanded his original face by a man in a dream who had a hideous face. The dream man tells him that the face he now has is not his original face. He once visited a seemingly utopian mountainside village inhabited exclusively by beautiful people; then he discovered many ugly face skins, presumably the residents' real faces, hung on polls to dry. Frightened, he managed to flee from this "paradise," except an ugly face skin got attached to his handsome face like a mask. He then began looking for an attractive face to replace the hideous skin. Having explained that much, the man in the dream demands the dreamer's face. When the dreamer wakes up, he realizes that his original face is gone and has been replaced with the face of the man in the dream. Listening to the story, the narrator begins to fear that the same misfortune will befall him.

Kurahashi's parodies of Chinese stories attest to her erudition. For example, the characters of "Kōkan" explicitly cite "Peach Blossom Spring" (the other source is not mentioned). Such explicit mentions of sources have another and more important function in our context: they foreground the act of quotation, in which an active negotiation with the earlier text makes a new point. The original story in the Lu collection has no psychological descriptions of the parties involved in the trade of faces, and thus it comes across as a simple horror story. Kurahashi's reworking adds a layer of modern self-awareness to it and challenges the conventional divide between essence and appearance and male and female. The men's obsession with their appearance is a reversal of conventional gender stereotypes, as vanity and narcissism have been more persistently attributed to women than to men.[117] In fact the story is entirely devoid of female spectacle; no mention is made of whether or not a given female character is physically attractive, while some female spectators assess the main male characters' appearance. Thus the story subverts the formulaic pattern of the male observer/female object. Most vital in our context, however, is that quotations from archaic Chinese texts, one highlighted and the other subdued, are not tangential but essential to the plot. These factors are all evident in Arakida Reijo's fiction as well, but Kurahashi has successfully escaped any nativist criticism for her use of classical Chinese texts because inspirations from the Chinese were less threatening to the commended autonomy of the indigenous in Kurahashi's time. We might say that the China-Japan entanglement has loosened and that there are other entanglements at work, involving players other than China and Japan.

"China" operates on multiple levels in "Kubi no tobu onna" (1985), another story by Kurahashi. Inspired by Sou shen ji, as was Arakida Reijo, Kurahashi reworks the story of the Feitouman (Flying head savages). In Ayashi no yo gatari, Reijo reworked this same story in "Hitōban" (Flying head savages), precisely the same characters as in Feitouman, only read in Japanese.[118] While Arakida's story is set in Heian Japan as a way to equate Chinese fantasy with courtly Japanese language, Kurahashi's story is set in postwar Japan at a time when Sino-Japanese contact is imminent. The story features two Japanese men, one of whom has returned from continental China after the Fifteen Year War between China and Japan (1931–1945), and one young woman; the Japanese returnee assumed that she was a Chinese orphan and brought her home with him to raise as an adopted daughter. It is this young woman's head that is found to be flying about at night. Observing this, her adoptive father is reminded of the Flying Head Savages that he has read about in Sou shen ji. The story thus evokes exoticism in much the same way that Tanizaki's Sinophilic stories do (as we saw in chapter 2); it capitalizes on a fascination with the supernatural that is also beastly. Thus, Kurahashi's version resonates with the implication of the colonizing gaze of the Japanese upon the Chinese that is of course nonexistent in the original story.

Another prototype for the story—Genji's pseudo-incestuous desire for his adopted daughter Tamakazura—invests the story with a message that transcends the national boundaries between China and Japan and hinges more firmly on the gender divide.[119] The woman, whose head flies away to have nightly trysts with the other Japanese man, with whom she is in love, while her body is violated by her adoptive father night after night, offers an allegory of the perceived divide between the mind and the body of a woman. The pseudo-incest suggests the patriarch's physical control over the female body, or his fantasy of surrender by a woman whom he has symbolically decapitated, whereas the free movement of her head implies the independent mind of the woman, who seeks and establishes an emotional outlet of her own. The marriage of the Flying Head Savages and the quasi-incest thus brings an entirely new perspective to the fore, taking full advantage of quotation.

Kurahashi's persistent choice of Chinese stories about the supernatural, beyond the two sketched above, is more than a simple infatuation with the strange. Chinese fantastic literature is a powerful weapon with which to neutralize the legitimacy of modern medical knowledge, a mission that has concerned her since the earlier stages of her career, when she was labeled an "absurdist" and Europhilic. She has been committed to challenging the autonomy of the body, and in doing so, she has also challenged the autonomy of the text. Regardless of the cultural origins of her inspirations, Kurahashi strategically selects which body of texts to cannibalize in order to demonstrate the contingency of the perceived constitution and delineation of the body. Chinese literature happens to be inspiring for her, and neither its ethnic uniqueness nor its canonicity in Japan concerns her as much as it did earlier writers that we saw.

The works that most clearly showcase Kurahashi's Sinophilia are *Shiro no naka no shiro* (The castle within the castle, 1980) and *Kōkan* (Pleasure exchange, 1989). The chapter titles in both books are four-character compounds taken from or inspired by Chinese verse, including the compositions of Tokugawa Japanese poets. This design is appropriate for the novels as their major characters are Sinophiles. The female protagonist of both novels, Keiko, mentions that her late father, a publisher, edited a volume of *Tangshi sanbai shou* (Three hundred poems from the Tang dynasty, ca. 1763), an anthology of classical Chinese poetry that was well circulated in Japan in the Tokugawa period, although he personally preferred Song dynasty poetry, a penchant that his daughter has inherited. When her beloved cat died, the father consoled Keiko by reciting

Mei Yaochen's (1002–1060) eulogy to a deceased cat, "Simao."[120] Characters in the novels often refer to *jiu cha lun*, or "debates on the merits of wine and tea," hypothetical arguments often made in order to reflect upon the contrasts between Tang and Song cultures, represented by the two beverages respectively. These well-established literary conceits in Kurahashi's fiction serve to divide the characters into two groups: those who are impassioned with ideological, political, religious, or romantic ideals, and those who are emotionally detached and inclined to appreciate the minutiae of everyday life. The two types are also distinguished by their musical preferences, the romantics versus the classicists.

References to Chinese literature are also abundant in another novel by Kurahashi, *Shunposhion* (Symposium, 1985), which alludes to not only texts, but also material products of Chinese and other origin. *Suiyuan shidan* (discussed in chapter 2) is cited as characters experiment with the gastronomical. A specific quotation from Yu Xuanji, by way of Mori Ōgai, is central to the most important storyline in the novel and underlines the considerable entanglement with Chinese texts in Kurahashi's fiction. The novel's focal female character, Satoko, writes a semi-autobiographical story in which Mori Ōgai's "Gyo Genki" is occasionally quoted. The relationship between Yu Xuanji and Wen Tingyun proves to be a perfect vehicle through which Satoko can elaborate on the asymmetrical, hierarchical, and volatile union of intellectuals of the opposite sex that she has experienced. Instead of addressing it directly as her own experience, Satoko uses layers of analogies. Mariko, the heroine of Satoko's story, is a precocious teenager who develops an intensely emotional and intellectual relationship with Mr. Matsudaira, her private tutor in French and Latin and a former lover of her mother; he may have possibly fathered Mariko. Given these circumstances, she compares herself to Tamakazura in *Genji* and Lady Nijō of *Towazu gatari* (1313), both of whom were subject to sexual advances by father figures who used to be involved with their mothers.[121] Indeed, it is Mr. Matsudaira's gaze upon her body that makes Mariko first realize that she exists in the flesh. The theme of the mind/body entanglement, which we saw in "Kubi no tobu onna," recurs in *Shunposhion*, except this time we get the woman's perspective, which was entirely missing in the previous story.

Mariko then turns to Mori Ōgai's "Gyo Genki" in order to compare her relationship with Matsudaira against the relationship between Yu Xuanji and Wen Tingyun. She offers the paradoxical assessment that her relationship with Matsudaira is "problematic because there is nothing improper."[122] Though Mariko has been awakened to her sexuality by her tutor, their liaison is not sexually consummated; they share only intense gazes, occasional cuddling, and intellectual exchanges. We might recall that in Ōgai's account, the male mentor and the female disciple also do not develop a sexual relationship, a situation that might in part have led to Xuanji's liaison with the musician Chen, whom she ends up murdering. Mariko has her own potentially romantic partner, her cousin Hiroshi, who happens to be musically talented. Mariko shares with him her interpretation of Yu's feelings for Wen, implicitly suggesting her own feelings for Matsudaira: "Yu Xuanji may have wished she could become both Wen's disciple and his mistress, devoting her life to composition rather than reproduction."[123] This statement also echoes one interpretation of Ema Saikō's relationship with Rai San'yō. It appears again to focus on a woman's body in a story about a woman's intellectual growth, but because the story comes from the woman herself, it is obviously an attempt to reunite the flying head with the potentially sexually vulnerable body.

Mariko is both disappointed by her incompetence as a seductress—she tries to seduce Matsudaira by pouring *sake* for him and leaning against him, but to no avail—and embarrassed by her secret desire for physical intimacy with her tutor. The sensual thrill she experiences as he strokes her hair contrasts sharply with Yu Xuanji's composure and determination to present herself not as a woman but as an intellectual, an attitude that makes Wen Tingyun immediately alter his behavior toward her. While Ōgai does hint at Yu Xuanji's longing for personal as well as intellectual attention from her mentor, he respects her as an independent, proud, and distinguished poet who would not cross the boundaries of propriety. As a male mentor for many female writers himself, Ōgai may have been keener on drawing the line between the professional and the private. Having been a female disciple, however, Kurahashi portrays Mariko as aware of her own corporeality; she cannot afford to bracket it, while at the same time she refuses to be seen only as a body.

Mariko's unfulfilled wish to fashion herself after Ōgai's Yu Xuanji and then develop a physical relationship with her mentor leaves her confused about her identity, a difficulty women writers faced when they chose to write like men.[124] In the cultural milieu of modern Japan, in which writers, women in particular, were expected to expose their gender identity to public scrutiny, it was difficult to maintain a balance between "masculinity" in the discourse of their choice and the "properly feminine" that was entrenched in the public image.[125] Mariko's choice of

"Gyo Genki" as a site for negotiations on this dilemma is multiply provocative because in Kurahashi's story, erudition meets confession, the intellectual meets the physical, the male meets the female, and the Chinese meets the Japanese. The multifarious entanglement shows that while China is still a powerful factor in the investigation of identity, it may not demand the intense inquiry it used to; investigation of the other polarities is obviously much more pressing. Unlike in early modern Japan, Chinese literature is no longer the canon that commands the attention of all competent readers. One might say that in negotiating with Chinese texts, Kurahashi made the "sliding doors" transparent both to convention-bound fellow women writers in modern Japan and to the Chinese-illiterate modern male critics, even though she may have shut them behind herself.

Conclusion

Just as women have not lived entirely on their own, so has their writing not been independent of discursive and social negotiations with men. The facts that Murasaki grew up in a highly cosmopolitan ambience, studied Chinese literature (especially that of a historical and political nature), and took advantage of the content and form of her reading in her writing have been brushed aside in favor of inaccurately defining her work as "indigenously Japanese" and an expression of naturally felt emotions. The image of Murasaki's work has thus been distorted to accommodate a certain perception of women's literature. That Arakida Reijo—whose strength lies in her ability to plan complex plots, tell coherent stories, and incorporate Chinese sources into her texts—has been largely neglected in the literary history of Japan also suggests that women's literature was taken to represent intuition and indigenousness rather than intellect and information. That Ema Saikō's literature has been interpreted by many modern critics only in association with her marital status rather than in light of her compositional practice demonstrates that women's writing was received on the basis of who the women were rather than on what they did. That in the age of the "New Women" Mori Ōgai's portrait of a Chinese female poet still stood out from other interpretations of her reveals a lack of attention to women's intelligence and intellectual equity, as opposed to women's desires and frustrations, and it has resulted in caricatures of feminists as misfits. Kurahashi Yumiko was active in a period when Chinese literature was no longer relevant as a gender marker, and thus she rewrote Chinese texts without drawing such criticisms as "she writes unnaturally, like a man," as she did when reworking contemporary European literature. Yet the engendered literary standard held just as firmly as in preceding periods, so that Yu Xuanji was still a valid model from which to review gender relations between male and female artists. It is ironic that these women's works tend to be misrepresented, favorably or unfavorably, so that each of the writers can be seen first as a woman rather than as a writer and that a history of women's literature has been constructed in Japan that in effect makes us fail to see that gender (and ethnicity) is a part of cultural identity.

Let me return to the metaphor of "sliding doors." Sometimes women were welcomed and other times denied access to a room that was for men only. Sometimes women of letters were privileged precisely because of the scarcity of women, and they were rare members in the room. Sometimes women were portrayed as though excluded so that they could be idolized by those inside the room. Sometimes points of distinction shifted, and what had mattered before was no longer an issue. Partitions are moved for reasons other than gender relations, including genre definitions, language reforms, or the construction of nation-states. To assume that the doors were always on the same spot and locked is to miss many implications in gender configurations and the Sino-Japanese entanglement, which are too often presented as parallel.

CHAPTER 4

The Transgressive Canon?
Intellectuals on the Margins and the Fate of the "Universal" Language

Classical language is always a persuasive continuum, it postulates the possibility of dialogue, it establishes a universe in which men are not alone, where words never have the terrible weight of things, where speech is always a meeting with the others. Classical language is a bringer of euphoria because it is immediately social. There is no genre, no written work of classicism which does not suppose a collective consumption, akin to speech; classical literary art is an object which circulates among several persons brought together on a class basis.
—Roland Barthes

Literary language (as the product of the educational system) will always mediate between canonical texts (the syllabus of study) and the production of new literary works; but literary language is neither necessarily inhibiting nor enabling in relation to new works. The relation will rather be differently constituted at different times according to the total complex of institutional forms and social/linguistic stratification. Hence, while it is simply (but not trivially) correct to say that literature must be written in the literary language, with its linguistic and generic constraints, it does not necessarily follow that the heteroglossic is the wellspring of the new, but rather that it acts through texts upon the literary language and its genres.
—John Guillory

In chapter 3, we saw how mastery of the Chinese literary canon empowered some of the women of letters in Japan and allowed them admission on the basis of their merits to the intellectual society of their times. However, learning and compositional accomplishments did not qualify the women for positions in the "real world"—the bureaucracy, business, or in most cases even education.[1] The acknowledgment of women's literary talent within artistic and literary circles was considered

reward enough. These distinguished women did not become professionals in the sense of either earning a living or holding an official position.[2]
Cultural merit did not facilitate admission into the polity or economy as
full-fledged members who could participate in decision making and
take responsibility in legislation and administration.

In modern Japan, the classical canon ceased to empower men as well
as women. The disappearance of men of letters from the centers of bureaucracy and commerce is a marker of modernity. Knowledge of the
Chinese classics and poetry, once a requirement for bureaucrats and
scholars in the state schools, became irrelevant to the attainment of
worldly success.[3] Classical elitism, which had entitled the privileged and
educated few to lead in both government and culture, broke down, and
learning was compartmentalized into fields of expertise, to be assumed by
professionals with specialized training. Literature and the arts, no longer
essentials for the elite, became fields of production and consumption in a
capitalist society. In place of literary Chinese, the acquisition of one or
more European languages useful in particular fields of the real world (English for business, French for law, and German for medicine) became imperative and thus compulsory in the educational system.

The effects of this shift were not only domestic. The loss of literary
Chinese affected the ability of the Japanese to correspond with the rest
of East Asia because literary Chinese had long been the lingua franca
among East Asians. (As I mentioned in chapter 2, Ishikawa Jōzan succeeded in communicating with a Korean envoy by writing in literary
Chinese.) Since the mid-Meiji era, however, an increasing number of
Japanese intellectuals who became proficient in one or more of the European languages found it difficult to write in *kanbun*. By the Taishō period, the Chinese literary canon had become a mystery even to many
well-educated Japanese.[4] In addition to the loss of the "universal language," a lack of familiarity with the modern languages of other East
Asian countries increased the barriers for communication. The "one nation, one language" policy of modern nationalism naturally presents an
obstacle to transnational communication, which was possible among
the elite of a common lingual culture. The only way to overcome the obstacle was to master a European language (English or French), the language of an imperialist nation-state. Thus, in lingual terms, nationalism
replaced one civilization (Sinocentric) with another (Anglophone/Fran-
cophone), rather than freeing all from the constraints of literary Chinese, which had symbolized Chinese hegemony.

It should be stressed, however, that the changes did not occur overnight. There was a transitional period during which many Japanese remained conversant in the classical Chinese canon while acquiring a proficiency in European languages and disciplines. Literary Chinese was effectively employed by early Meiji bureaucrats and educators to denote their experiences in Europe or in the modern environment, which obviously had not informed the language until their time. Furthermore, the Chinese literary canon became a useful medium with which to voice resistance to nationalism: in opposition to the nationalist promotion of a spoken language, a common written language was celebrated as a path to transnational networking. The irony of the classical canon becoming a weapon in the hands of discontented literati has inspired the title of this chapter. Against the modern, state-endorsed efforts to identify the "canon" exclusively in the "national language," the classical Chinese canon was given a new role.[5] In the age of globalization, where we constantly reassess the validity of national boundaries, it is useful to revisit some of the earlier opposition to nationalist enterprises.

In this chapter, I will first present an overview of the state of literary Chinese in Meiji Japan. I will then examine how specific applications of classical Chinese in the modern genre of prose fiction (shōsetsu) facilitated communication among intellectuals across national boundaries and presented an alternative to hegemonic modern ideologies such as imperialism, nationalism, and ethnocentrism. The genre of the novel is a product of nationalism, diffused by European imperialism, and it became almost synonymous with literature in modern Japan. However, we will closely examine two shōsetsu that resist the compromising effects of the new definition of literature by liberally incorporating features of premodern literariness, best manifested in the use of literary Chinese. It is interesting to explore how the medium, while invested with nationalism, imperialism, and ethnocentrism, offers a venue for resisting these modern ideologies.

We will begin our journey with a political novel started in the late 1880s, Kajin no kigū (Unexpected encounters with beauties; 1885–1892, incomplete), by Shiba Shirō (1852–1922; studio name: Tōkai Sanshi). In a style highly imbued with wenyan, it relates the unions and separations of male and female intellectuals from four modern nation-states. In terms of its discourse and its mode of production and distribution, Kajin no kigū captures the last glow of an East Asian intellectual community that shared the cultural practices of reading, composition, and recitation in literary

Chinese. The novel also hypothesizes the dissemination of literary Chinese beyond East Asia as a counternarrative to the reality of cultural imperialism. Its reception by critics reveals the value contingencies that worked against literary Chinese in modern Japan.

We will then examine the case of Nakamura Shin'ichirō (1918–1999), whose biography of Rai San'yō we consulted in chapter 3 and who, like Mori Ōgai, was well versed in both modern European and classical Chinese literature. He wrote extensively on Japanese Sinophiles in the Tokugawa period while generously drawing analogies with European and Japanese Europhile intellectuals. The imagined hierarchy between Chinese refugees in Japan and members of their adoptive homes is not unlike that between male and female intellectuals in that the "superior" groups own literary Chinese, which they "graciously" share with the others so as to cultivate them. The implicit aims of enfranchisement are exposed in *Kumo no yukiki* (Traffic of clouds, 1965–1966), an essay-like novel by Nakamura on which I will focus below. We will see many faces of pro-traditionalism in this novel that, unlike the nationalist definition of the ideology, do not conform to the nostalgic image of the nation's past.

Kanshibun in the Meiji Period

The end of the so-called "locking up of the (Japanese) nation" (*sakoku*) and a major expansion of diplomatic and trade relations with European and American nations did not mean that the importance of the Chinese literary and cultural heritage suddenly began to decline. In fact, after the 1850s more Chinese books were imported than in the eighteenth century because the Japanese market was much more widely opened to East Asia as well as to the West. A larger readership developed for classical Chinese literature, as well as for vernacular Chinese fiction, and Chinese literature became more significant than ever in Japan's reading experience in the early Meiji.[6] Moreover, advances in printing techniques allowed for a radical increase in distribution, and thus many literary and scholarly works of the eighteenth and early nineteenth centuries had a larger readership at the end of the nineteenth century than when they were originally produced.

The tradition of *kanshibun* was hardly fading in the early Meiji. Societies of poetic composition, *shisha*, kept being formed after the Meiji Restoration (1868), and commercial journals—a new mode for the dissemination of literary works—offered a new venue for *kanshi* poets, as well as for other types of writers. Among the leading figures in *kanshibun* of the early Meiji period were Ōnuma Chinzan (1818–1891), who was a champion of Song poetry; Mori Shuntō (1819–1889), a proponent of Qing poetry; and Yoda Gakkai (1833–1909), an avid reader of vernacular fiction (as we shall see below).[7]

It was not only the specialists—professional poets and teachers of Chinese literature—who practiced composition in *kanshibun*. Many people whose primary occupations were not in Chinese literature are known to have kept diaries in *kanbun* and to have maintained the practice of *kanshi* composition. Meiji *kanshijin* include some bureaucrats—and prominent ones at that—who were more like literati than technocrats. Takezoe Seisei (Shin'ichirō; 1842–1917), who had quit his career as a diplomat assigned to posts in Tianjin and Beijing, traveled into the depths of Sichuan Province in order to visit literary topoi, a trip that produced his best known work, *San'un kyōu nikki narabini shisō* (Clouds around the bridge, the rain over the valley: A diary and poetry manuscript, 1879).[8] The travel journal, accompanied by many poems by Takezoe himself, pays frequent tribute to such admired poets as Du Fu and Su Shi, who were from Sichuan, and to precedents in the genre of literary travelogue, most notably Lu You's *Ru shu ji* (A journey into Shu, 1170) and Fan Chengda's *Wu chuan lu* (Diary of a boat trip to Wu, 1177).[9] Takezoe's text is prefaced by many Chinese and Japanese political and literary luminaries (the author's associates), including Li Hongzhang (1823–1901), a statesman who oversaw many crucial changes in military, diplomatic, and industrial affairs in the late Qing, and Yu Yue, whom we saw in passing in chapter 3; Yu acknowledges Takezoe's help in collecting Chinese verse composed by Japanese poets in the preface to his anthology (*Dong-ying shixuan*).[10]

Suematsu Kenchō (Seihyō; 1855–1920) was formally educated in England and earned a degree from Cambridge. As a man of letters, he is probably best known for the first (though partial) English translation of *Genji monogatari*;[11] in the preface he promotes what he considered indigenous literature of the Heian period.[12] Despite his nativistic remarks, Suematsu was enough of a *kanshi* poet to edit his own anthology, *Seihyō shū* (Collected poems by Seihyō, 1923). His name is also found in the anthologies of many other writers, as he exchanged poems with them and composed rhyming poems with theirs.

One of Suematsu's poetry friends, Nagai Kagen (Kyūichirō; 1852–1913), was, according to his son, Nagai Kafū (1879–1959), so crazed with Chinese poetry that he performed a ritual to pay respect to his favorite poet, Su Shi.[13] Originally from the feudal domain of Owari (present-day Aichi Prefecture), Nagai moved to Tokyo to pursue a bureaucratic career in the ministries of education and the interior; he married a daughter of Washizu Kidō (1825–1882), a distinguished Sinologist in Owari who had had the opportunity to study at the shogunate school of Shōheikō. Nagai then quit the bureaucracy to join Nihon Yūsen, a shipping and passenger liner company partly operated by the government that sent him to Shanghai to head its branch there. Nagai composed *kanshi* extensively both in and outside China; these are collected in his anthology, *Raiseikaku shishū* (Anthology of poems by Raiseikaku, 1913).[14]

As is obvious from these examples, which are only the tips of the iceberg of the *kanshijin* community, it was not a contradiction to be a man of the rapidly changing "real world" and a writer in the time-honored genre of *kanshibun*. Rather, these "real" men turned to *kanshibun* in order to address worldly matters.

Whereas the literary contributions of Takezoe, Suematsu, and Nagai (among others) did not extend much beyond *kanshibun* and thus did not garner a readership beyond the longevity of the genre, it should be noted that Mori Ōgai, the most accomplished Japanese Europhile of his time, also took *kanshibun* very seriously. Ōgai, whose versatility is well demonstrated in the wide range of genres and styles with which he experimented, composed *kanshi* and kept diaries in *kanbun*. Some of them were written during the time he spent in Germany and thus obviously engage topics that previously had not been explored in classical Chinese vocabulary or rhetoric. *Kōsei nikki* (Diary of a westbound voyage, 1884); *Taimu nikki* (Diary during the term of military duties, 1888); and *Kantō nichijō* (Diary of returning to the east, 1888) are in *kanbun*, as is *Zai Toku ki* (Account of the stay in Germany, 1884–1888), a nonextant text that is now thought to be the original version of what we know as *Doitsu nikki* (German diary), published in 1899 in *bungo*.[15]

Unlike Natsume Sōseki, with whom he is often compared, Ōgai does not polarize literature between the Chinese and the European. As we saw in chapter 2, Sōseki was disillusioned by English literature, which he had previously thought comparable to the Chinese classics,[16] and since that time he was antagonistic toward Western civilization in general, a sentiment Ōgai does not seem to have shared. Instead of hypothesizing an essential dichotomy between the East and the West, Ōgai took to cosmopolitanism: he translated some Western poems in *kanshi;*

he collected these along with his own and others' translations of poems from a range of places in the world (naturally including China, represented here by Gao Qingqiu) in *Omokage* (Lingering images, 1889).[17] Nor did he share Sōseki's inferiority complex of being a nonnative speaker of the language he was studying. He triumphantly records, in *kanbun*, that his command of German proved to be good enough to communicate with the Germans: "As I arrived in Cologne, Germany, I understood German. Thereafter I was cured of deafness and muteness— how pleasant it was!"[18] The mastery of both a modern European language and classical Chinese spared him the pitfall of ethnocentrism, a snare for those whose aspirations for the international currency of their work were thwarted by the asymmetric values between the languages of imperialist nations and their own.

The early Meiji reception of Chinese literature was not confined to classical poetry. One of the best known of Ōgai's works, *Gan* (Wild geese, 1915), offers a glimpse of the addiction of the period's young intellectuals to *kanshi* journals and Chinese vernacular fiction.[19] Moreover, in a plausible episode in Mori Ōgai's fiction, *Vita sekusuarisu*, a *kanbun* teacher—speculatively identified as Yoda Gakkai, a teacher of Ōgai's—is caught red-handed by a student in the act of reading the sexually charged novel *Jinpingmei*.[20] This episode, along with the fact that students at the dormitory of the Tokyo School of Agriculture were prohibited from reading Chinese vernacular fiction, shows the extent of Meiji intellectuals' craving for such "obscene" stories and of unofficial recognition thereof.[21]

Kōda Rohan (1867–1947) articulated the position of Chinese vernacular fiction vis-à-vis European literature in modern Japan. Kōda boasted a high degree of familiarity with genres that had not formed a part of the canon, such as Yuan drama and vernacular fiction, as is evident in his essay on Yuan drama, "Gen jidai no zatsugeki" (Musical theater in the Yuan dynasty). Rohan also translated such monumental fiction as *Shuihu zhuan* (which Okajima Kanzan had translated and Takebe Ayatari had parodied) and co-translated *Hong lou meng* (which had informed Tanizaki's "Kōjin"), both for the prestigious *Kokuyaku kanbun taisei* series.[22]

While eager to make Chinese fiction accessible to general readers, Rohan nonetheless evenhandedly evaluated literary genres according to Chinese standards, which rank prose fiction lowest on the ladder. While he was genre conscious, Rohan was not oblivious to the changing status of prose fiction in world literature. Though he had not had an opportunity to formally study Western literature, he compellingly discussed Chinese literary genres in comparative perspective. In his "Ko-Shina bungaku ni okeru shōsetsu no chii ni tsuite" (On the status of prose fiction in premodern Chinese literature, 1926), Rohan asserts the following:

> There is a tendency in European and American countries to consider prose fiction the primary form of literature—far from despising the genre, they even give it prestige. In China, by contrast, the society not only dispenses with respect for the authors of prose fiction, but it also actively disdains them for doing things inappropriate for literati, even though talented men of letters occasionally author such works. There is no point in trying to come up with a logical reason for this, since it is only natural, given the different manners and customs in different countries. Thus, it would be a ridiculous mistake, quite out of the question, to assume that Chinese prose fiction is Chinese literature.[23]

Although Chinese literature had grown "natural" to him, Rohan was aware that alternative literary judgments could be made according to European standards. In the above-quoted passage he goes on to caution against a generalization of literary conventions across lingual and literary diversity. Without falling into nostalgia or cultural antagonism toward the "foreign," he maintains, in concrete and technical terms, that literary genres are not universal but culturally defined. With his reading experience, although limited on the European language side, Rohan is able to differentiate genres and historical stages in Chinese literature and does not treat everything Chinese as timeless, invariably valuable, and representative of the entire tradition of China or literature.

As is obvious from these examples of Europhiles who were also Sinophiles, the supposed incompatibility of *kanshibun* and Westernness is only an illusion, created by a post-Meiji understanding of Westernness as an autonomous, homogeneous, and tangible entity distinct from Chineseness or Japaneseness. The essentialist contrast between the modern/West and the classical/East is theoretically groundless. Nonetheless, the illusion began to grow as conviction in the autonomy of each nation as a monolingual community replaced faith in the transnational communality facilitated by a universal language. The growing suspicion of the incommensurability of *kanshibun* with modernity/Westernness, however misconceived, coincided with the marginalization of the literati.

Sharing *Kanshibun* with "Barbarians":
Variations on Literary Chinese

Kajin no kigū features four nationalists from different nations who happen to become friends in Philadelphia, where the author, Shiba Shirō, lived from 1882 to 1886: a Japanese man, originally a samurai from the defeated pro-shogunate domain of Aizu (present-day Fukushima Prefecture) who goes by the quasi-Chinese pseudonym of Tōkai Sanshi; an old Chinese man, Tei Hankyō (Ch. Ding Fanqing); a young Spanish woman, Yūran; and an Irish woman, Kōren.[24] The story evolves around their partings and meetings through family or national emergencies, revolutionary activities, arrests, and other trials and tribulations. Owing to frequent interruptions, a potentially romantic relationship between Tōkai Sanshi and Yūran is never consummated, even with the efforts of Kōren, a capable go-between. The threesome seems inspired by the scholar-beauty romance genre of Chinese fiction, *caizi jiaren xiaoshuo* (J. *saishi kajin shōsetsu*).[25] The lovers' devotion to and respect for each other set a dignified tone. Meanwhile, the fourth nationalist, Hankyō remains romantically uninvolved, as is appropriate for an old sage, a role typically found in classical Chinese literature. While the story is distinctly set in the age of nationalism and imperialism and references are made to events and figures of the period, the characterization nonetheless is clearly bound to rhetorical conventions.

Transnational bonding among intellectuals in the age of nationalism is elusive. Having to fight battles at "home," they can share only incidental "encounters" that allow them to give vent to their discontent, with the Chinese literary canon as a source of discursive energy. The premise of the characters' alliance—they are expatriate intellectuals—calls for partings and chance meetings; this status does not allow them to be permanently united as immigrants or refugees, who can establish a common base for new lives in the United States. This is not a story of settlers in one nation; it is a story of transnational wanderers.

The conflict of wishing to belong to different lands and individuals and feeling alienated from all of them is captured by Yūran in a poem sequence she composes in literary Chinese. Four emotions—homesickness, longing for her father, the hope of seeing Japan, and her attachment to a Japanese man (Tōkai Sanshi)—are represented in a pastiche of a four-poem sequence entitled "Sichou shi" (Poems on four sorrows), by Zhang Heng (78–139), collected in *Wenxuan*.[26] The cultural authenticity of the characters' actions and speech is obviously not an issue here; rhetorical perfection within the context of traditional East Asian high-cultural practice is. Insofar as European women are portrayed as major figures who bond with Japanese and Chinese men of letters, they must conform to the textual norms epitomized by the composition of *kanshi*. However unrealistic it may be in light of the extratextual social conditions in Europe in the 1880s for them to be competent in Chinese poetic composition, the law of the scholar-beauty romance genre demands that they should be, in order for them to qualify for their roles as *kajin* (Ch. *jiaren*)—beauties—in this text.[27]

Few critics have failed to point out the consequences of *Kajin no kigū's* style: inaccessibility and the sacrifice of realistic effects. Its diction has long been blamed for its failure to qualify as a piece of "modern Japanese literature." As Donald Keene observes, "The language is ornate, difficult, and exceedingly conventional, borrowing heavily from the stereotypes of Chinese fiction. The characters, regardless of their country, are constantly referring to events in Chinese history, using all the appropriate clichés."[28] It is true that the style is not descriptive but rhetorical, geared less to the mimetic portrayal of people and things than to an observance of the laws of *shūji* (rhetoric) and *bibun* (elaborate discourse). At elevated moments, the text adopts the parallel prose in four and six characters (*shiroku benrei tai*) that was established in the Six Dynasties in such notable examples as Song Yu's "Gaotang fu" and Cao Zhi's "Luoshen fu" (both of which we saw as inspirations for *The Tale of Matsura* in chapter 1); Tao Qian's *Taohuayuan-ji* (which both Natsume Sōseki and Kurahashi Yumiko quote); and Zhang Wencheng's *Youxian ku* (which Arakida Reijo parodied).[29] The text thus obviously does not transcribe "natural" Japanese speech of the 1880s.

Accordingly, the two women are depicted in Chinese rhetorical terms. The following excerpt describes the way Kōren and Yūran first appear to the Japanese male protagonist:

> Sanshi would always regret that Americans lacked aesthetic taste and missed having friends to talk to about blossoms and the moon. However, now that he had met these ethereal ladies, who sang and played stringed instruments among blossoms in the late spring, he admired their refinement and the aesthetic atmosphere about them and was eager to float on the ripples so as to convey his feelings to them on the other shore. He thus thought to himself: Once Wang Zhaojun's fortunes declined in the boundless desert of the Hun

and saddened the heart of the Emperor of Han; and when Yang Taizhen [Guifei] passed away as transiently as a dewdrop in Mawei, the Ming emperor dreamt of past romance in the Pavilion of Longevity. Such things happened for good reason.[30]

Aesthetic appreciation of the moon and blossoms on appropriate occasions alone seem informed of East Asian literary tradition. More specifically, Wang Zhaojun and Yang Guifei are two Chinese literary archetypes that Japanese literature had long ago adopted.[31] The usage of tropes shared within the Sinocentric East Asian civilization confirms the discursive space that the text claims outside the location of the story. The Yang Guifei association continues: as Kōren first approaches Sanshi, she "snaps a twig of the willow" and is compared by Sanshi to "a dewy pear blossom" or to "a crimson lotus soaked in a green pond."[32] They are all tropes conventionally used for Yang Guifei.[33]

The "West," however, does not remain an empty space to be encoded by the literary discourse of East Asia. Yūran and Kōren demonstrate their knowledge of classical Chinese as opportunities present themselves. Thus, in a comment by Tōkai, Kōren immediately recognizes a reference to the *Shijing*, where a man says he has encountered an attractive lady who meets his standards for a spouse:

> There is a beauty
> as curvaceous as a fresh willow;
> I met her by chance
> and she fulfilled my wishes.[34]

Kōren's ability to identify the source and interpret the intent of the quotation is obvious from her prompt response to Sanshi: "I am not your match; you must mean the other one [Yūran] in the shade."[35] Yūran also reveals her knowledge of classical Chinese. When Sanshi first visits Yūran's residence, he notices framed calligraphy:

> The orchid in the distant valley harbors its fragrance for nothing
> Year after year it remains chaste and waits for a phoenix to come.[36]

The couplet, taken from Qu Yuan's (340–257 BC) *Lisao* (Encountering sorrows), is about a virtuous person waiting for the right opportunity; if interpreted in romantic terms, it is about a reserved woman waiting to meet the right man to marry. The upper column commentary of *Kajin no kigū* confirms the effect of the quotation—"The phoenix indeed arrived just at that moment"[37]—suggesting that Yūran's wait is over when she meets Sanshi and that a romance between the two is set to begin. Yūran seems to be able not only to appreciate the Chinese art of calligraphy, but also to understand the Chinese origin of her name represented in the first line.

The way that the Spanish and Irish women's names are transcribed is an instance of entanglement. They are each represented by two Chinese characters that each stand for a concept: Yūran 幽蘭, as we noted, is an idiom in Chinese meaning "an orchid in a deep valley," or, more metaphorically, "a virtuous and reserved woman"; Kōren 紅蓮, literally meaning "crimson lotus," is a Chinese Buddhist term for one of the eight infernos where one's skin cracks from excessive cold, and by extension it is also a metaphor for a flame. Indeed, the meanings of the two names correspond to the two women's personalities: Yūran speaks less and seems the more introspective of the two; Kōren is the more vocal and lively of the two. As a result of their political activities, Yūran is imprisoned and helpless, and Kōren comes to her rescue with a witty plot to seduce the head guard. Yūran is believed to have died in a shipwreck, and Kōren brings Sanshi the news that she is alive. Thus, these names need to be interpreted in light of the East Asian traditional lexicon in order that their bearing to the plot of the novel becomes clear.

Whereas the naming of the two characters ostensibly showcases the versatility of the classical Chinese vocabulary, it in fact suggests a specifically Japanese engagement with the East Asian tradition, which is the focus of this chapter. The two names sound recognizably European only when they are pronounced in Japanese. In their Japanese readings Yūran and Kōren are identifiable with "Jolanda" and "Colleen" respectively. The latter in Chinese reads "Honglian," which could not stand for "Colleen" or any other readily recognizable European female name. Thus, the Chinese characters, connoted in the classical Chinese literary tradition, are able to stand for European names *only* via the Japanese sound. In other words, it is not exactly literary Chinese that manages the discourse here: it is *kanshibun*.

The Japanese mediation of Chinese is obvious in the style of the entire text. It employs *kanbun kundoku (yomikudashi)-tai*, or a Japanese reading of literary Chinese. When characters in the novel quote or compose poems, these are accompanied by *kunten* (signs to direct the reader to the next character according to the word order of Japanese rather than Chinese syntax) and *furigana* (a Japanese reading supplied to Chinese letters).

Another entanglement is evident as the four nationalists get together to compose Chinese verse. The scene purportedly shows the universal canonicity of Chinese poetry. The Spanish and Irish women begin to compose *gushi* (old poem)-style pieces in classical Chinese. They prove to be faster and better in improvisational composition than their East Asian male counterparts, demonstrating a remarkable mastery of the practice.[38] This should put the two East Asian males to shame, as they are supposed to embody the essence of their own culture. The two take it in stride, however. The scene suggests that the author understood poetic composition as a cultural practice rather than the natural manifestation of an essence, and thus it was not gender- or race-specific.

What is unique in this case is the fact that European women write classical Chinese poetry. It would have been not only extraordinary but impossible for European women of the 1880s (and at the tender age of the early twenties) to do what Yūran and Kōren were doing. In our context of reconfiguration of cultural relationships, this hypothetical distribution of the cultural capital of China beyond East Asia could mean either a European fetishization/colonization of the Chinese canon or the East Asian "enfranchisement" (in Stephen Greenblatt's terminology) of the "barbarians."[39] Indeed, the blunt intent of educating the perceived barbarians could be concealed by engendering the subject as female: encountering "beauties," rather than male barbarians—the real threats in the real world—Sanshi and Hankyō can afford to sit back and praise the Western women's accomplishments while taking for granted the hegemony of their own culture.

Whichever the interpretation, the illusion of transnationalism holds only in written form. A transcription alone can tactfully conceal the potentially disruptive effects of European women composing in Chinese and reciting their verse in, presumably, Japanese, because the text silences the voice. Instead of hearing the women's engendered and ethnicized voice, we read what they "say" in *kanbun kundoku,* separate from their bodies, a seemingly neutral and authenticated exclusive version that claims immortality. Reservations, conditions, or modifications that would have been noted if the performance were "real" are suppressed in the text as we are immersed in the illusion of the universality of literary Chinese. The written language thus acquires transnational currency within the text, while orality, an element crucial to the phonocentricism in the European languages, is suffocated.

A similar and yet distinctly different entanglement of European and Chinese languages is evident as Yūran and Kōren sing *La Marseillaise* in Chinese. In place of the original French lyrics, the narrator provides the Chinese translation by Wang Ziquan (Tao; 1828–1897), which is indented to be distinct from the body of the main text.[40] Sanshi and Han-kyō are clearly swept away with the concepts of liberty, equality, and fraternity, separated though they are from the French historical context. At other points in the text, they are blatantly critical of French imperialism, so they are not Francophiles by default. The de-ethnicization of the French national anthem is made possible by using a translation in another language, the one that for the two East Asian intellectuals is the only "universal" language.

The Literary Versus the Literal: Literature's Missions

While the characters of *Kajin no kigū* rely upon *kanshi* as a medium of communication, some critics were troubled by the predominance of *kanshibun* in the novel because the discourse embodied "antimodernity" for them: the premodern and Sino-Japanese form appeared historically and culturally inadequate for representing a modern and Western content. As Morita Shiken (1861–1897) argued in an essay entitled "Nihon bunshō no shōrai" (The future of Japanese writing, 1888), "Chinese rhetorical expressions should be expelled from modern Japanese discourse as the Japanese begin to think in a more complex manner."[41]

Many claimed, however, that there were good reasons for the choice of this particular style. The style effectively defended the cause of literature, in which premodern Japanese writers and readers had faith. A literary critic, Etō Jun, and two literary historians, Ochi Haruo and Seki Ryōichi, have looked into the literary past and situate *Kajin no kigū* in the genealogy of a kind of literature that was distinct from European literature as was understood by Meiji Japan. Etō offers a class-based reevaluation of the rhetorical language that some *seiji shōsetsu* (political novels) used. He contrasts novels descending from *gesaku* (comical works) and those written by *bunjin* (literati) and identifies venues of publication for each. There are two types of newspapers: *ō shinbun* (major papers), in which *seiji shōsetsu*, stylistically more or less confined to *kanbun* or *bungo*, were serialized; and *ko shinbun* (minor papers), in which the remnants of *gesaku* were serialized.[42] They have distinct styles suited to distinct audiences. Although *Kajin no kigū* was never serialized in a newspaper, the contrast Etō draws seems to apply to its position vis-à-vis the more popular styles of fiction. Shiba Shirō was not a professional writer but a literatus. Thus he chose artistic perfection, which readers of his class could appreciate, over descriptive precision, which would appeal to less sophisticated readers.

Ochi Haruo and Seki Ryōichi also note, in somewhat different ways, differences in the definitions of literature, though Tōkai Sanshi himself did not explicitly theorize about literature. The samurai in the Tokugawa era and the ex-samurai in the Meiji era took *bungaku* (literature) to mean learning in the discourse of *kanshibun*. (One exception, Tsubouchi Shōyō [1859–1935], though an ex-samurai himself, represented *gesaku* authors rather than the literati in *Shōsetsu shinzui* [The essence of the novel, 1885]). As Seki discusses, the term *bungaku* or *wenxue* meant studies of the *Shisho* (Ch. *Sishu;* Four books) and *Gokyō* (Ch. *Wujing;* Five classics), as opposed to a mastery of the martial arts:

> Chinese learning and *kanbun* had obviously been validated since the importation of Chinese thought and literature, especially Confucianism. However, this tendency was most predominant in the Tokugawa era. . . . What we call "literature" now consists of poetry, fiction, and theater. In light of the negative view that Confucianism held of fiction and theater, it was thought that *haishi, shōsetsu, jōruri,* and *kabuki* should not be dealt with by respectful literati. Such an idea was also inherited by the modern era. In this light, the history of modern Japanese literature can be described as the history of a movement to upset and change this view of "literature," and to give "civil rights" to fiction and theater. . . .
>
> This is not to say, however, that the tradition of Confucian learning was irrelevant to modern "literature," nor does it mean that the tradition had only negative effects on it. Furthermore, it does not necessarily mean that the Confucian view of "literature" was incorrect. . . . The samurai in the Tokugawa era and the ex-samurai in the modern era believed in Cao Pi's saying, "Literary works are the supreme achievement in the business of state," in *Dianlun* [Authoritative discourses], and tried to discuss all kinds of things literary. In their mind always lay such a view of writing, or "literature."[43]

Many authors of *seiji shōsetsu* were originally samurai and later became members of parliament. For samurai-turned-statesmen, it was only natural to write of political affairs in the highly rhetoricized style of *kanbun*, which had been meant to discuss a variety of issues involving individuals and the government.

Literature as a manifesto becomes more evident in later chapters of *Kajin no kigū,* in which Tōkai Sanshi relates the histories of several nations. An "enlightened" aspect of Tōkai Sanshi's views lies in his understanding of power relations in the world and his refutation of the hierarchy often hypothesized between "civilized" or hegemonic nations (Britain, France, and Russia) and the "undercivilized" (nations whose independence was threatened if not terminated by the imperialist nations). *Kajin no kigū* generously references historical incidents in the latter countries: Poland, Turkey, Egypt, and Korea, countries Shiba Shirō had the opportunity to visit as a government official and a member of parliament. Matsui Sachiko compares volumes 11–16 of the novel, in which Tōkai Sanshi visits these countries, and the diary of Tani Tateki (1837–1911), then minister of agriculture and commerce and head of an entourage in which Shiba Shirō took part, and she points out a significant discrepancy between the two texts: while Tani minutely describes events in Vienna, Florence, Paris, and London (in which the party stayed for longer periods than elsewhere), Shiba Shirō hardly says anything about these cities and instead concentrates on meetings with political leaders in Egypt, Hungary, Poland, and Turkey (whom he met in reality).[44]

Shiba's explicit sympathy toward challenged nations is usually attributed to the fact that Tōkai Sanshi (as well as the author himself) is from Aizu, one of the feudal domains that was steadfastly in favor of the shogunate and against the imperial court in the civil war (1868–1869). Thus he is opposed to the foreign policies of the Meiji government, as Shiba was in an earlier stage of his career.[45] In passages censored from the original manuscript, Tōkai Sanshi liberally criticizes Satsuma (present-day Kagoshima Prefecture) and Chōshū (Yamaguchi Prefecture), the two feudal domains behind the Meiji Restoration, for defeating and exploiting Aizu, and he blames the United Kingdom for the Opium War. Tōkai Sanshi is more preoccupied with affinities between Japan and the nonhegemonic nations than with the much emphasized differences between the West and the East (or Japan, to be specific). With his awareness of the complexity of the world, he does not advocate a Japanese uniqueness, nor does he simplify the foreign (*gaikoku*) as one distinct entity. Donald Keene suggests the following:

> The Wanderer of the Eastern Seas is so proud of being a Japanese that he is moved to copious tears when he hears praise of his country, but there is no suggestion that he finds the Irish, Spanish, Chinese, or Hungarian people he

encounters alien from himself, nor does the wanderer suppose, as many Japanese still suppose, that foreigners, by definition, are incapable of understanding the griefs of a Japanese. For all its childishness, this novel (like *Inspiring Instances of Statesmanship*) is deeply appealing in its idealism, especially its faith in the emergence of Japan as a strong, compassionate, and democratic country.[46]

Similarly highlighting the cosmopolitan solidarity found in *Kajin no kigū*, Maeda Ai calls our attention to different views of Ireland presented by Tōkai Sanshi and Katō Hiroyuki (1836–1916), an enlightenment thinker; in so doing, he puts Sanshi in a positive light because he resists the hegemony of imperialist nations:

> Tōkai Sanshi's *Kajin no kigū* is a book of accusation, on the largest scale, of the Darwinist progressive views of civilization that had captivated "enlightenment" thinkers, ranging from Fukuzawa Yukichi to Katō Hiroyuki. Sanshi has political refugees from Spain, Ireland, Hungary and other countries narrate the tragic histories of their nations, deprived of independence, and compiles a long list of crimes that European hegemonic nations forcibly committed in the name of civilization....
>
> Contemporary readers must have naturally sensed another history, contrasting with that seen from the progressive perspective. While in classrooms they studied Parley's [i.e., Samuel G. Goodrich's] and [William] Swinton's *History of Nations,* which echoes [François] Guizot and [Henry Thomas] Buckle's history of civilization, *Kajin no kigū* demonstrated for the readers another possible version of world history, narrated from the viewpoint of the non-European world.[47]

While Maeda and others do not overlook the imperialist orientation that becomes increasingly evident toward the end of *Kajin no kigū*, the novel nonetheless presents a radically different vision of world history from the "official" versions taught in early Meiji educational institutions and thus suggests other paths that could have been taken by modern Japan.

We could cite Tsubouchi Shōyō's *Shōsetsu shinzui* as the primary standard by which critics came to consider *Kajin no kigū*'s ideological content and traditional rhetoric inappropriate for modern literature. *Kajin no kigū* in effect conflicts directly with the genre, style, and themes recommended by Shōyō, who advocates *shōsetsu* over other genres; *gazoku setchū-tai* or *kusazōshi-tai* over other styles; *ninjō* (human emotions) and *setai* (customs and manners of society) over other themes; and the mode of *shasei* (mimetic representation) over that of *shūji* (rhetorical control over characters, incidents, and settings).

I must hasten to add that Shōyō could not have seen *Kajin no kigū* before the publication of *Shōsetsu shinzui;* the first book (consisting of the first two volumes) of Tōkai Sanshi's novel came out in the same year as *Shōsetsu shinzui.* Nevertheless, the contrasting values of the two authors led to a later and oft-repeated practice of reading *Kajin no kigū* against Shōyō's work. Asukai Masamichi stresses the contrast between Shōyō's and Tōkai Sanshi's views of literature, quoting from an essay by Shōyō, "Shōsetsu o ronjite *Shosei katagi* no shui ni oyobu" (On the novel, with references to the main thesis of *Shosei katagi;* published in August 1885, after the completion of *Shōsetsu shinzui*), in which Shōyō comments that "it is wrong to hold political allegories as the main theme of the *shōsetsu,*" Asukai maintains that Shōyō was witnessing a decline in the civil rights movement and took advantage of it in order to promote his thesis of literature for the sake of literature. Shiba's statement in the preface to volume 5 (in the third book of *Kajin no kigū,* published in 1886), sounds like a counter response to Shōyō: "The novelist's goal is not to play with exquisite devices or to describe customs and human emotions; it is to demonstrate opinions and disciplines and to influence people with ease—in other words, the goal lies outside the text."[48] Though without an explicit mention of Shōyō, this manifesto should be understood in the context of Shōyō's position that literature was independent of ideology.

Notwithstanding the lack of any further exchange of opinions between Shōyō and Shiba, later receptions of Shiba's novel are informed by Shōyō's argument. As readers grew increasingly accustomed to the psychological novel—a genre developed under the aegis of individualism—they came to find the conspicuous dogmatic orientation and stereotyped characterizations in *Kajin no kigū* outdated and unsatisfying.[49] Tokutomi Sohō (1863–1957) was among the first of these critical readers. As early as 1887, in "Kinrai ryūkō no seiji shōsetsu o hyōsu" (A criticism of the political novels recently in vogue), he criticized *seiji shōsetsu* for their lack of "literary qualities"; poorly structured plots; and flat, stereotypical characterization.[50] While Sohō's criticisms were addressed toward the genre as a whole, *Kajin no kigū* must have been on his mind to some extent, given the enthusiastic reception of the novel throughout the country at that time. In further negative reviews along these lines, the "Kanmatsu kaidai" (Appendix to the volume: A guide to readers) in the 1931 Kaizōsha version of

Kajin no kigū, written by Kimura Ki, noted that characters in the novel were nothing but puppets of concepts and lacked individual characteristics.[51] Similarly, Donald Keene's view was that this work "possesses little novelistic merit. At times the plot can hardly be followed because of the digressions and interpolations, and no attempt is made to create believable characters or to describe scenes convincingly."[52]

It is worth taking into account the critical criteria that the novel's contemporary audience applied to the work. What it considered to be literature—or *bungaku*—in terms of suitable themes and authorial intent was radically different from the standards held by Sohō in the 1880s, Kimura in the 1930s, or Keene in the 1980s outside of Japan. The difference between the reception of the work in the mid-Meiji and in later periods compels us to historicize our notion of literature or literariness. The definition of literature was much broader in early modern Japan than after the late Meiji, and the Japanese language encompassed dimensions other than the *genbun itchi* style, the ostensibly speech-oriented discourse that was privileged as modern and authentically native/national. Kōda Rohan defines *kanbun* as an aesthetically and intellectually engaging discourse for the early Meiji literati.[53] As Asukai Masamichi notes, Shiba Shirō had no other choice for his work than *kanbun,* "the only style for the expression of thought"; the choice was "most effective for communication," as "*kanbun* was meant for ideological issues."[54] Indeed, *kanbun* might have been best suited to describe Western thought and affairs during the 1880s—more articulate than *wabun,* more formal than *gesaku buntai,* and more intelligible than the early stages of the *genbun itchi* style.[55] Many readers were well at ease reading about a variety of contemporary issues in *kanbun.*[56]

Sound and/or/of Silence: Orality, Modern and Premodern

While today's readers might find the *kanji*-filled text of *Kajin no kigū* visually intimidating and suited exclusively to a semantic and silent reading, it would be a mistake to assume that readers in the 1880s shared this impression; indeed they took to reciting the text. As George Sansom notes,

> Its literary merit is negligible, but it is of value as evidence of the way in which patriotic Japanese minds were working after some twenty years of international intercourse. It is said that there was not a remote mountain village in Japan in which some young man had not a copy in his pocket, and the Chinese

verses that so freely stud its pages were recited everywhere with great relish. Even its congested prose seems to have been imitated by younger writers, but no doubt its political complexion was what gave it most of its success.[57]

It is not clear where Sansom obtained the above information, but young students' passion for reciting *Kajin no kigū* is noted in Tokutomi Roka's (1868–1927) novel, *Kuroi me to chairo no me* (Dark eyes and hazel eyes, 1914).[58]

While oral literature may often be regarded as "lowbrow," this was not always the case. Tokugawa and Meiji literati used to begin their education with the memorization and recitation of the classics at the ages of four or five—that is, before they were even able to understand what a text meant. Chinese literary discourse was thus primarily orally acquired and then textually interpreted. Even after aspiring literati passed this secondary stage, they would practice *shigin,* or the recitation of poems, either solo or in a group. Such recitations functioned to reaffirm solidarity within a group, college, or prep school and were specific to oral readings, or *ondoku,* and not silent readings *(mokudoku).* While commoners took pleasure in reciting famous passages from *jōruri,* and some samurai or ex-samurai often followed in their footsteps in doing so, the latter also—and more publicly, proudly, and perhaps pedantically—were accustomed to orally performing *kanshibun,* which might appear to us, who have lost the practice of *sodoku* or *shigin,* the least oral and most heavily literate.[59]

Given that the Chinese classics and poetry were not recited in the original pronunciation, however, the effects of recitation became ambiguous, as we observed above in the instances of recitation in *Kajin no kigū.* While ostensibly confirming and celebrating the universal canonicity of these texts, recitation in the *kanbun kundoku* style—a twofold structure of oralizing written and read discourse—inserted a layer of domestication that was naturalized and thus was invisible or negligible to the Japanese intellectuals. What they saw/decided to see as universal—the classical Chinese canon—was in fact already de-ethnicized, deprived of the sound of the native tongue, and re-ethnicized, given the sound of the Japanese poetic language. To flip the coin just one more time, however, the "facade" of transnationalism, supported by the obviously Japan-specific method of reading, may not be as illusory as it seems. It may well be a European phonocentric idea to define as inauthentic an oral performance of a text in any other language than the original native tongue. Reciting the

Chinese literary canon in Japanese may not be an act of domestication but a movement toward transnational fluidity.

Literary Text as Intellectual Property

Given the propensity for intellectuals to bond, transcending the boundaries of nationality, gender, and age, it seems appropriate that Shiba Shirō is reported to have considered translating *Kajin no kigū* into Chinese. Although his own translation did not materialize, a Chinese translation did come out as *Jiaren qiyu*, by Liang Qichao (1873–1929), a distinguished politician and literatus. In light of the heavily Chinese-imbued style of the original, Donald Keene muses, "It could not have been very difficult for the distinguished scholar Liang Ch'i-ch'ao to make the Chinese translation of this work!"[60] Liang's translation became not only a best-selling novel in China, but also a subject of scholarly investigation in studies of modern Chinese literature.[61] According to C. T. Hsia (among others), Liang came across the original novel in 1898, a year after the publication of its last part, as he was headed to Japan as a political refugee. He was so impressed with it that he immediately began to translate it. *Jiaren qiyu* was serialized in *Qingyi bao*, starting in December 1898, in thirty-five segments. Hsia casts some doubt on the accuracy of Liang's translation: "Since he did not seriously study the language until after his arrival in Japan, one may well wonder if he knew enough Japanese at the time to translate the work even though its style was highly Sinicized."[62] The question of accuracy aside, it is undeniable that Liang edited the original extensively, probably for political considerations. Hsü traces the process by which Liang departed from the original in order to erase the anti-Manchurian/pro-Han (*mieman xinghan*) statements made by Ding Fanqing, the Chinese nationalist character; he did so upon the suggestion of his mentor, Kang Youwei (1858–1927), a scholar and political leader. Most surprisingly, in the final version (included in Liang Qichao's collected works) the Chinese character has been completely eliminated, leaving the Japanese man with two "beauties" and making the content ostensibly irrelevant to China.[63]

While the degree of liberty that Liang took does not seem to have provoked any objections from the Japanese author, a variation of *Kajin no kigū* in Japanese became the basis for a lawsuit—a modern medium to which allegedly plagiarized authors could resort in order to reclaim possession of their "own" texts. The book in question, *Tsūzoku Kajin no kigū,* was written under the pseudonym of Daitō Hyōshi and was published in 1887 in two volumes.[64] The copyright page mentions as the book's author a Tsuchida Taizō, a little known commoner *(heimin)* from Tokyo. The work is generally attributed to Hattori Seiichi (Bushō; 1842?–1908), whose name appears as the contributor of the preface to the second volume. Hattori was the defendant, held accountable for the legal liabilities created by the publication of the text.

The story by Hattori reveals unmistakable resemblances to *Kajin no kigū,* but also has drastic alterations. It is set in no place other than Pennsylvania, where a Japanese man called Daitō Hyōshi meets Irish (Maria), Spanish (Alice), and Persian (Sarais) women and subsequently befriends an African American man (Port) and a Chinese man (Ruan Yiquan), both servants for the three women, who live under the same roof. Interspersed with the romance between the Japanese man and the Irish woman are political references, which are at times more detailed and informative than in Shiba Shirō's version. Battles in the U.S. War of Independence, conflicts between Russia and Persia in Central Asia, and the British invasion of Sudan are not to be found in the original and thus must come from Hattori's own sources.[65]

More significant than the alterations to the plot is the choice of a distinctly different style and format. We might recall from chapter 2 that the term *tsūzoku* in a title was used to suggest the popularization of the style. Hattori's language is indeed much more accessible than that of the original: the text is written not in *kanbun kundoku,* but in *gabun,* or quasi-classical Japanese, transcribed in *kanji* and *hiragana,* rather than in *katakana.* Characters often compose poems, but their work is either in *bungo* or its vulgarized version, reminiscent of *zokuyō,* or the popular songs of early modern Japan. Commentaries are added in the upper column of a page, as in the first edition of the original, but the language employed is not *kanbun* in Chinese characters with *kundoku* signs (as in the original) but *kanbun yomikudashi.* In other words, both the main text and the commentaries are written in styles that are slightly more accessible for a mass audience. Hattori claims to have written his version so that ordinary people without *kanbun* learning could read the text—a point well made in light of the civil rights movement that was then at its peak.[66] The inclusion of a mass audience was also crucial to a modern literary author's professional survival in modern capitalist society. While Shiba wrote the original *Kajin no kigū* primarily, if not exclusively, for the people of his class, Hattori was aiming at the emergent mass audience.

These differences between the two texts notwithstanding, similarities were obvious enough to convince Shiba Shirō and the Hakubundō publishing house to file a lawsuit in 1889 against Hattori and his publisher, Shiotani Yoshibei of Dōmei shobō. After three trials, Hattori and Shiotani were found guilty of copyright violation. Thus, the modern concept of the author as the owner of a text was applied and confirmed.[67] As Mark Rose states, "Copyright is founded on the concept of the unique individual who creates something original and is entitled to reap a profit from those labors," a concept that is in fact "a specifically modern institution, the creature of the printing press, the individualization of authorship . . . and the development of the advanced marketplace society."[68] *Kajin no kigū* as printed and marketed was judged to be original enough that *Tsūzoku Kajin no kigū* constituted a legal infringement on its copyright.

Two essential aspects of *Kajin no kigū* were ignored in the process of this legal dispute. First, the "original" text negotiated with even older sources; second, the text was collaboratively written: poems were commissioned, the manuscript was edited, and commentaries were added by readers who saw versions of the manuscript before it came out in print. Since erudition was indispensable in the type of literary composition practiced among men of letters in premodern Japan, resonance with other texts was essential if a text were to qualify as "literary" at all. Literary discourse was "literary" precisely because of the prominence of quotation from the classics. This practice contradicts the modern definition of literary texts as original products of individual authors, an understanding that is necessary for the protection of an author's ownership of intellectual property, a legal category under which literary texts came to be recognized.

Not only the style, but also the format of the printed text of *Kajin no kigū* reflected the communality that prevailed in East Asian texts in pre-Meiji periods. The original Hakubundō edition is multifaceted: the sixteen volumes, published in eight books, are accompanied by prefaces by prominent men with whom the author was associated in real life (for example, Tani Tateki). Often colophons were added by the author himself or his associates, such as the Korean political activist Kim Ok-kyun (1851–1894), who appears as himself in the last volume. Very obvious contributions to the author's text are in the upper column of each page, where readers' commentaries and responses appear—usually positive evaluations of the masterful narration—a feature that, unlike prefaces and postscripts, has somehow escaped the attention of critics.[69] The text thus incorporates reader responses and the author's reflections thereon.

Such a communal production of texts was common among men of letters in premodern Japan. These premodern multivalent features, however, were significantly compromised in the 1931 edition and were completely erased from the 1965 edition. Instead, the text came to represent the linear flow of the story and to demonstrate a single narrative authority at the cost of the other voices from the exterior.

Kajin no kigū is a collaborative effort beyond the sense of communal composition. Shiba Shirō, while from the samurai class, was apparently not proficient enough in literary discourse to complete the manuscript on his own and required help from more competent *kanshi* or *kanbun* writers. In the author's preface to the main text, Shiba (signing himself as "Tōkai Sanshi" there) defensively states that he is "not a specialist in classical poetry or prose" and that his work thus "cannot be without flaws." The preface also shows that the author was fully aware of a range of hypothetical responses to his draft:

> Upon my completion of this piece, a Confucian scholar commented that its style tends to be that of lowbrow fiction *(gesaku shōsetsu)* and that the work also could introduce the noncommendable Western trend of humiliating men and respecting women, which may make women haughty and base. A storyteller *(haishi-ka)* criticized it saying that the reader could grow bored at a glance since there are few erotic passages or romantic emotions and no talk of pleasure quarters or the popular theater, only angst and sorrow [over the nation's fortunes] from beginning to end. A man made of steel regrets that there were not more parallel clauses and that high literary words were not consistently selected, suggesting that it would be perfect if more parallel clauses were used and the style were more polished. A recluse, however, has the following to say: because of the meaningless persistence upon old-style prose *[kobun; Ch. guwen]* from the Han, Wei, and Six Dynasties, [evident in the] parallel clauses and high literary expressions, the work, though figuratively elegant, lacks the spirit that is appreciated by the Western masters—besides, it imitates only the worst of Eastern and Western fiction. Another of flamboyant tastes refutes this, saying that [this author] stands out from the rest of the fiction writers because he has invented a new design, without drawing upon Eastern thought or borrowing from Western structure, with no talk of spirits or demons, responding to current affairs and registering real incidents, all of which results in a fluid style and lofty spirit—every character is a gem. Another man, without reading more than a few lines, closes the book and says that this is another returnee student's thesis on freedom, not worth a look.[70]

Takahashi Taika (1863–?), among others, is often thought to have considerably revised the prose, while Nishimura Tenshū (1865–1924) is thought to have authored poems embedded in the text.[71]

The collaborative nature of the production process, however, was to an extent neutralized when Shiba's manuscript was published by Hakubundō. Although the edition faithfully reproduced the prefaces and postscripts written by individuals other than Shiba Shirō, under their own names, the copyright page bears only Shiba Shirō's name (and emphatically not the literary pseudonym of Tōkai Sanshi), with the domain and class of origin specifically mentioned as *chosakusha ken shuppannin* (author as well as copyright holder) and, for Hakubundō's Harada Shōzaemon, as *seihon ken hatsubainin* (publisher as well as distributor). The text in print thus was defined as belonging neither to the man of letters, who could go by the studio name of his choice, nor to his circle of friends, who had participated in the discursive formation and transformation of the text, but to the modern citizen, identified in bureaucratic terms, and his business partner, who was responsible for the production and circulation of the printed copies. The copyright page also specified the date on which the copyright was acknowledged by Naimu Shō (the Ministry of Internal Affairs)—the mark of a modern legal system, which protects the ownership of cultural capital and recognizes that a text, when in print, should belong to its legally certified author.

Kajin no kigū bears the marks of both modern and premodern literariness at the same time and thus is in its own right a watershed in the history of Japanese literature. Whereas its content celebrates the transnational communion of intellectuals (facilitated by the use of classical Chinese) and its format takes full advantage of the multivalent mode of writing (prefaces, colophons, and peer commentaries), substantive changes in its publication history deny the communality of literature by identifying and legally protecting the autonomy of the text. While the text suggests the productive use of the classical Chinese canon, its publication effectively put an end to the cultural environment in which the heritage of the Chinese literati culture prospered.

"The Garden in the Air": Hybrids and Exiles in Nakamura Shin'ichirō's *Kumo no yukiki*

Nakamura Shin'ichirō exhibited a wide range of interests. He is probably best known for his essays on French literature, the subject he studied at the University of Tokyo, and for French-inspired psychological novels that deal with romantic relationships among Japanese intellectuals. He also wrote extensively on classical Japanese literature, analyzing the psychological dimensions of courtly romantic tales such as *Genji monogatari*.[72] His interest in *kanshibun* is no fleeting matter. He followed up his voluminous biographical study, *Rai San'yō to sono jidai,* with two more equally sizable biographies: *Kakizaki Hakyō no shōgai* (The life and death of Kakizaki Hakyō [1764–1826]) and *Kimura Kenkadō no saron* (The salon of Kimura Kenkadō [1736–1802]; manuscript completed in 1997, serialized in 1995–1998, and published posthumously as a book with the remaining draft in 2000). Nakamura also wrote *Shijin no niwa* (The poets' gardens), a collection of essays on Tokugawa *kanshi* poets.

Nakamura thus belongs to the literary class of "tripod writers." That is, his work extends into three conventionally demarcated areas in Japan: *wa* (Japanese), *yō* (Western), and *chū* (Chinese) literature. One of his mentors was Hori Tatsuo (1904–1953), another Europhile who also extended into the different areas.[73] Hori's literary debut was supported by Akutagawa Ryūnosuke, whose Sinophilic stories are well known.[74] As is more often the case, however, such writers' references to texts in Chinese are discussed more as formative of their careers rather than as reflective of a reconfiguration of the Sino-Japanese relationship. Nakamura's musings on the entanglement of the Japanese subject with Chinese and French literary figures remain and deserve to be explored.

In the following excerpt from a novel by Nakamura Shin'ichirō, *Kūchū teien* (The garden in the air, 1965), Uomi Shūtarō, the protagonist, encapsulates the author's view of Japan's complex cultural position, for which the title of the novel serves as a metaphor:

> They [Tokugawa *kanshi* poets] composed poems in classical Chinese. Many of them did not even know the correct pronunciation in the classical language. Their audience was also limited to the Japanese. Literature that represented their time was not written in their own language, even though the Japanese wrote for themselves. Yet their work was not all trash: Kan Sazan [1748–1827], Rai Kyōhei [1756–1834], Ichikawa Kansai [1749–1820], Kashiwagi Jotei [1763–1819], Fujii Chikugai [1807–1866], Ōkubo Shibutsu [1767–1837], Tachi Ryūwan [1762–1844], Yanagawa Seigan [1789–1858], Kusaba Haisen [1788–1867], etc. . . .
>
> The role that the Japanese assumed in world civilization was not to create, but to adopt and apply. Thus, Japanese literature and art do not encompass the

grandiose universe. When it comes to reception, the Japanese also appreciate minor artists and authors. As the German idealist theory of the 1910s arrived in Taishō Japan, it became something lovely and sophisticated. We are residents in the garden in the air, set apart from the earth.[75]

The *teien* (garden) in the title of the novel is an apt metaphor for the rhetorical elaboration that poets in classical Chinese verse strove for, as opposed to the ostensible spontaneity that scholars often suggest characterizes modern Japanese literature.[76] The *kūchū* (in the air) suggests that Chinese verse composed by Japanese poets does not belong to either China or Japan and thus defies the Sino-Japanese polarity.

Nakamura's metacritical framing of the Sino-Japanese entanglement itself is most evident in *Kumo no yukiki,* a loosely structured novel. Its first-person narrator, who is a Japanese male writer, is interested in the early Tokugawa *kanshi* poet and monk Gensei (1623–1667), and he relates his experience of reading his poetry and other writings. The narrative structure evokes Mori Ōgai's *shiden* (biographies), in that the text relates the project as it develops, as well as the outcome of the narrator's readings. Like Ōgai's biographies, Nakamura's piece thus foregrounds the pre-posterity of history that we discussed in the introduction. The text later recounts the narrator's life after the project and confirms the presentness of the story we follow.

A further echo of Bal and Deleuze is the way the narrator defines his approach:

> Somehow a portrait of the early Tokugawa monk had begun to form within my heart.
>
> It was not consciously sought and built through maneuvers required for "biographical studies." While I read this and that work by him, [such inconsequential things as] incidentally transmitted episodes and tones of speech heard from bits and pieces of the writing emerged from the margins of the pages, so to speak, and silently piled up like ashes from a volcano, without being caught in the net of consciousness. The monk had inhabited me long before I noticed it.[77]

"Rather than the portrait of a person hatched up artificially through materials collected as in 'biographical studies' (though archives helped authenticate the basis of the portrait)," Nakamura goes on to say that the portrait he found inhabiting his mind was "imbued with [his] own scent."[78]

The inseparability of the subject from the object, and the object from the subject, reminds us of the concept of the "fold" in Deleuze's terminology. "I" does not study "him" at a distance; in the act of involvement, "I" is already a part of "him," who is a part of "I."

Gensei's befriending of a late Ming political refugee, Chen Yuanyun (J. Chin Gen'in), presents a case in point in our discussion of the Sino-Japanese literary negotiation. The Chinese man, exchanging poems with Gensei, calls Gensei "a brother" because they both bear the character "Yuan" (J. Gen) in their names.[79] This gesture intrigues, and perhaps slightly annoys, the narrator, who feels "the inflection of the Chinese refugee's complex psyche": "Yuanyun had come from the center of world civilization at that time to Japan, the periphery. The intellectuals on the island on the eastern sea must indeed have had their egos boosted by being deemed 'brothers' by the Chinese intellectual. The refugee must have learned from long-term experience the survival tactics of how to take advantage of the inferiority complex of the Japanese."[80] Yuanyun was being protected and hosted by the feudal lord of Owari and was surrounded by the uncertainty in which every exile finds himself. Yet he had a medium through which to reclaim and exercise power—that is, cultural authority—and he used it to call Gensei a cultural brother and annoint him as quasi-Chinese. Gensei could not have issued the license of brotherhood to Yuanyun, even though Gensei was a member of the host country. The concept of brotherhood is predicated upon the universality of Chinese cultural practices, which automatically situates China in the center and Japan on the margins. The enfranchisement of "barbarians" who understand literary Chinese, conducted by an intellectual in exile, is evidently in operation in Yuanyun's ostensibly friendly remark.[81]

The "I" narrator says that he is reminded of another anecdote involving another refugee—a Russian expatriate, Ilya Ehrenburg, residing in France.[82] Ehrenburg was introduced to a group of French writers by Jules Roman, who, "in order to extend a warm welcome to the barbarian who had fled from the margins of the Latin civilization," said to him, "You are already half French." This remark upset Ehrenburg, who later unleashed his fury in his correspondence from France, entitled "From the Western Front."[83] Clearly the two anecdotes are different in terms of the vector of (dis)placement of the intellectual: one is centrifugal, the other centripetal. Still, the operation of normalized cultural hegemony remains the same. In our context, in which we examine Nakamura Shin'ichirō rather than Chen Yuanyun or Ilya Ehrenburg, I might point out that the narrator's equation of the two entanglements potentially neutralizes him in the position of the observer/judge/comparativist. He manages to avoid the pitfall, however, by later placing himself as a character deeply affected by the entanglements and in effect renouncing the privilege of neutrality (as we will see below).

The narrator then observes a shift that occurred between the eighteenth and nineteenth centuries in Japanese Sinophiles' perspectives on Chinese poetry and poetics. Whereas leading eighteenth-century Sinologists and *kanshi* poets such as Ogyū Sorai and Hattori Nankaku (among others) advocated a strict observance of the conventions set by high Tang poetry, echoing the sentiments of their contemporaries, such as Li Panlong and Wang Shizhen (as we saw in chapter 2), a later generation of Japanese Sinophiles found a comrade in Yuan Mei, who refuted the nostalgic recycling of ancient poetry and proposed more free-spirited composition. The two methods of composition have different origins: *moni* (J. *mogi*; imitation) and *xingling* (J. *seirei*; spirit) respectively.

Nakamura's narrator maintains that Yuan Mei's groundbreaking work of criticism, *Suiyuan shihua*, was a phenomenon in Japanese circles of poetic composition and criticism. He then resorts again to a comparison, this time between Japanese Sinophiles and Japanese Europhiles:

> The Japanese edition of *Suiyuan shihua*, whose impact on Japanese intellectuals was comparable to that of André Breton's Surrealist theory in the interwar period, was published in 1804, thirteen years after its original publication in China, with prefaces by innovative scholars, critics, and poets such as Yamamoto Hokuzan [1752–1812], Ōta Kinjō [1765–1825], Satō Issai [1772–1859], Ōkubo Shibutsu, and Kashiwagi Jotei. Those who initiated a new literary generation praise the released poetic spirit with hardly any reservations.
>
> One can imagine the excitement in the poetry establishment in Japan at that time by wondering [what it would have been like] if [Breton's] "The Manifesto of Surrealism" had been published with provocative prefaces by Haruyama Yukio [1902–1994], an advocate as energetic as Hokuzan; Nishiwaki Junzaburō [1894–1982], who is reminiscent of Kinjō as a theorist and practitioner; Suzuki Shintarō [1895–1970], an academician not unlike Issai; or Kitasono Katsue [1902–1978] and Anzai Fuyue [1898–1965], poets as innovative as Shibutsu and Jotei.[84]

Despite the enthusiasm that Yuan Mei's work ignited, Nakamura's "I" narrator notes that the Japanese poets/critics did not admit their debt to him. Instead of viewing his theory as the origin from which theirs stemmed, they considered him a contemporary who happened to have the same views. In contrast to the eighteenth-century Sinologists, who strictly chastised the domestication of Chinese verse as *washū* (Japanese flavor/custom) and promoted a return to authenticity, the narrator suggests that the nineteenth-century Japanese Sinophile intellectuals neutralized the hierarchy between the origin and the destination/descendant while holding their Chinese comrade's thesis in high esteem. Just as Yuan Mei renounced Tang poetry as the ancestor of all poetry, so contemporary Japanese intellectuals renounced Chinese criticism as the predetermined authority and began to evaluate its achievements on the same basis as they would evaluate their fellow countrymen's.

Prudently, Nakamura's narrator hastens to add that the new generation of Japanese Sinophiles admits to having been inspired with the concept of *xingling* by a Chinese from an earlier period, Yuan Hongdao (1568–1610) of the Ming dynasty.[85] It is thus not that the nineteenth-century Japanese critics claimed to be indigenous and original, but that they considered themselves to be the legitimate descendants of Yuan Hongdao as much as Yuan Mei. The national boundary was not drawn but *withdrawn* in favor of literary communality in East Asia.

Nakamura's narrator comes to realize that Yuan Hongdao is Gensei's favorite poet; he cites a legend that Gensei read Yuan's work twenty times, burned it, and never read any other poet's work after that.[86] Nevertheless, Gensei did not repeat in his own works the erotic and decadent ambience for which Yuan Hongdao's poetry—and late Ming poetry in general—is known. Instead of attributing the serenity of Gensei's poetry exclusively to his Buddhist practice, Nakamura's narrator maintains that a harmonious amalgam of different cultural elements—Confucian, Buddhist, Chinese, and (courtly) Japanese—brought about an equilibrium in Gensei's mind that comes through in his work. The narrator finds a body of Gensei's *waka* poems and a travelogue written in *wabun*; these not only refute the argument that one can only be either a *kanshi* poet or a *waka* poet, but also show Gensei's orderly and systematic reception of diverse cultures, rather than an arbitrary juxtaposition that is often found in the work of dilettantes. As he guides us through Gensei's writings, the narrator alerts us to the parody in which Gensei engages, taking advantage of his erudition. Aware of the boundaries among different rhetorical traditions, Gensei inventively and intentionally crosses the borders in order to enrich the traditional rhetoric of a given genre.

The narrator's study of Gensei is interrupted by his friend's sudden request that he entertain a young film actress. She is visiting Japan en route to Taiwan, where she is to participate in an international film festival. Reluctantly obliging, the narrator soon realizes that the actress, Ms. Yang, is not only well versed in Chinese and European poetry, but is also herself an embodiment of lingual, physical, and cultural hybridity. She has been trained to assume different roles, as any actress would, and she is also a polyglot. Her success has taken her to many countries, and she can speak the language of whatever place she happens to be (recall Abe no Nakamaro's translingual practice, split between China and Japan). Either retrieving attributes from her repertoire or acquiring some new ones, she can represent any identity that is needed.

Ironically, Ms. Yang does not speak Japanese, possibly implying the marginality of the language that has survived Sinocentrism and persists in the age of nationalism. Still, the narrator manages to communicate with her, both by writing down Chinese characters (a scaled-down version of the "brush talk" between Ishikawa Jōzan and the Korean diplomat discussed in chapter 2) and by speaking French, a language the two have in common. Despite their age and gender differences, the unlikely companions realize that they can discuss quite a few poets of different nationalities, including Yuan Mei and Yuan Hongdao. However, the narrator has trouble identifying them when Ms. Yang pronounces Chinese names in the "authentic" Chinese fashion or when European names are phonetically transcribed in Chinese characters.[87] The barrier for communication is thus represented by the modern Chinese language—or the Japanese unfamiliarity therewith. The Japanese narrator knows Chinese names in the domesticated Japanese reading of the characters, according to which they are represented in *katakana*. Their authentic pronunciation may not sound "barbaric" or "like gibberish" to him—as it did to Japanese characters in *Kokusen'ya gassen* and *Honchō Suikoden,* as we saw in chapter 1—but it still is largely unintelligible. The transcription of a European name into Chinese characters is challenging to the narrator for yet another reason: to him, the Chinese script stands not for sound but for meaning, which the Japanese can figure out owing to the shared classical Chinese literary tradition. It baffles him when the Chinese language arrives at him aurally and when the Chinese script is used to transcribe characters that are phonetic.

From this tedious means of communication we can make two observations. First, the phonocentricism of modern languages—their claim to authenticity via phonetic distinction—is dissonant with the traditional East Asian means of identifying names with Chinese characters, which may be pronounced differently and yet mean the same. Second, Chinese script is transformed into, if not reduced to, phonetic signs in order to accommodate European sounds. It should be noted, however, that these phonetic signs are not for recitation; they are to be read silently and deciphered as European names. The orality of classical Chinese, which we saw in the first half of this chapter, is nowhere to be found in the scribblings of Nakamura's narrator and his guest, while the text has become phonocentric. The duality of the classical Chinese texts—ideologemes to be recited orally—is lost both ways.

Ms. Yang's family relationships provide another venue for a reflection on the roles of the universal and national languages in expatriate circumstances. She turns out to be the daughter of the narrator's old acquaintance, Professor Silvermann, a Jewish Sinologist from Germany, and a Chinese woman. The narrator and the professor exchanged language tutorials, though it is not clear which language the professor taught the narrator in return for Japanese. It may have been French, rather than German, as the narrator tells Ms. Yang that Silvermann gave him a copy of the French translation of Simon Fraser's *The Golden Bough*.

The professor taught German to a Japanese woman (a friend of the narrator), who fell in love with him. Later she published a book of poetry in the format inspired by an exchange between Rilke and one of his lovers. The narrator deems this imaginary exchange of poems in Japanese a miserable comparison with the poetic dialogue between Gensei and Chen Yuanyun. According to the narrator, the difference in Japan's reception of Chinese literature and European literature is not owing to the different lengths of exposure but to the fact that European literature was introduced in a time of nationalism, which both by definition and in effect precluded a transnational sharing of a common culture. Premodern Japanese intellectuals did not think of Chinese literature as foreign, whereas in modern times every national literature is foreign to every other, and thus European literature has always been beyond the linguistic boundary and foreign.

Ms. Yang's true motive in coming to Japan was to visit her late father's former lovers, including the amateur poet. The narrator compares Silvermann's constant wandering among languages and women to the behavior of Rilke and Kafka, both of whom were known to do the same. Just as Silvermann felt marginalized and compelled to leave Germany under the

Nazi regime, Rilke and Kafka were made to feel inferior in Vienna because they were Czechs writing in German, the language of a hegemon. The narrator suspects that Rilke turned to another hegemonic language, French, because he felt the lack of authenticity in his use of German. Whether or not one accepts this hypothesis, it is evident that the narrator recognizes a hierarchy among German speakers. His theory also accounts for the inclination of polyglots to move on to yet another language to speak or write. They feel compelled to be out of a place where they feel out of place, and they stay in the place only as long as they are accepted as displaced.[88] Their lack of belonging or authenticity is excused when they attempt to speak/write in another's language and when they have a range of languages that they have "mastered." The quality of language command is replaced by the quantity of languages and the speed at which they change from one language to another.

Thus, Silvermann's polygamy may not be irrelevant to cosmopolitanism. Neither is another piece of his personal history, revealed by Ms. Yang: Silvermann was raised by a possessive mother, whom he resented. The narrator is reminded of how agonized Silvermann looked when the term "mother" was mentioned. Matriphobia is also a fear of origins and the sense of belonging that one cannot overcome. As cultural nostalgia is often compared to attachment to the mother, transnationalism can be paralleled with detachment from the maternal figure. The aspiration to learn other languages may be triggered by the desire to reject the mother tongue, or at least its claim to the cultural authenticity in which one is expected to build and preserve one's identity. Languages, to transnationalists, are cultural products to be learned and practiced, and thus the concept of the mother tongue as naturally given is to be rejected—just as the love for a mother is a cultural construct.

Conclusion

Literary Chinese and the canon written in it presented a medium with which intellectual expatriates could escape the constraints of a national language. The assignment of masculinity to literary Chinese and its various applications, which we saw in chapter 3, elevated the indigenous "mother tongue" as the only legitimate modern language of each nation. Whereas gender is not restrictive, the practice of engendering the contrast between the foreign and the indigenous is. The tradition of *kanshibun*, which thrived on the incidentality of ethnicity and gender, thus had to be brought to a halt in modern Japan. The mediation of Japanese sounds in the transnational reception of literary Chinese was replaced with the orality of modern Chinese, a language that is nation-specific and thus presents an obstacle to the attainment of universal citizenship.

Instead of being rooted in native soil or under the spell of the mother tongue, however, intellectuals sought to soar—on the wings of the literary, transnational language, however imaginary it might have been in their age. They oscillated between the sound (ethnic) and script (universal) of Chinese to defy the mutation of their voice/hand in the name of nationalism.

Coda

Folding the Subject into the Object

> Perception is inappropriate as an instrument of empirical, positive
> knowledge, whereas it simultaneously represents the kind of knowl-
> edge that happens within a baroque point of view. . . . This knowledge
> is legitimate and offers insights into every endeavor of knowledge pro-
> duction which cannot be offered by a positivism that has confidence in
> perception's capacity to yield up knowledge of the object. Perception
> "has no object," but it involves objects; just as white is not a color be-
> cause it is all colors: it reflects them.
> —Mieke Bal

In the preceding chapters, I have tried to challenge the conventional
equation of "China" with a specific kind of spatiality (China as a territory on the continent, as opposed to Japan as an archipelago, each a
geographically defined entity); system of language (the intellectual, the
metaphysical, and the written, as opposed to the material, the physical,
and the oral); gender (writing and reading in Chinese in Japan as associated with masculinity, as though there were no Chinese or Japanese
women writing or reading in Chinese); and temporality (the imagined
"past," which is timeless and homogeneous, with little recognition of the
historical transformations of China). The quadruple equation of reading
China predominates in the modern understanding of Chineseness in
Japanese literature as a given, fixed quality, while what was perceived as
Chinese is in fact entirely contingent upon circumstances (constituted by
artistic, academic, journalistic, social, economic, or political agendas; hierarchies; rivalries; compromises; and conspiracies—in short, dissonance
and its political manifestations, exploitations, and ramifications). As Mieke
Bal has noted, "This is the story of the changing but still vital collusion between privilege and knowledge, possession and display, stereotyping and

realism, exhibition and the repression of history."[1] It is my hope that this statement has come to sound as if it were written about the Sino-Japanese entanglement as seen in Japanese literature.

By telling my version of such a "story" as stipulated by Bal, I hope I have revealed that what is persistent is not "China" as defined by the Japanese in the terms noted above, but the faith in the images of China that the Japanese held. The desire to believe that "nature"—geographically circumscribed space, nationally identified language, biologically anatomized bodies, and chronologically measured time—exists externally to culture is just as much a product of culture as is the opposite desire to claim that there is nothing that has not been constructed. The issue here is not which, if either, of these views is the case, but how culture articulates its relationship to nature, truth, and reality as envisioned in space, language, bodies, and time.[2]

I propose to end this study in a way that may appear to be unusual; instead of summarizing the points that I have made in the preceding chapters, I would like to demonstrate how these premises about what has been taken for granted as natural can cloud our vision to the extent that we fail to see obvious manifestations of their arbitrariness. As the chapters invalidate the predominant myths about China defined in contrast to Japan, we are now at a vantage point from which to apply the thesis of this study to other texts and to see the extent to which it holds.

There seems no one in Japan who better articulates the contingencies of space, language, gender, and time than Tanizaki Jun'ichirō. Various principles that are formative of Sino-Japanese negotiations are eloquently presented in some of Tanizaki Jun'ichirō's stories that are set in Japan and cite traditional Japanese literature and arts. These stories have been either celebrated largely for their "quintessentially Japanese" qualities (unlike those about China that we saw in chapter 2 and that have not been taken seriously in the literary establishment) or criticized for their ostensibly nativistic penchant. Whether positively or negatively construed, these stories have been regarded as evidence of the so-called "return to Japan" (Nihon kaiki), or renativization, that Tanizaki is believed to have made as he advanced into midlife after a stage of infatuation with modern Euro-American literature and arts. In fact, these stories cut across an entanglement of mobile positions that China and Japan took in Japanese literature, rather than fixing on a static Sino-Japanese dialectic. They thus serve my purposes to identify and neutralize those abiding regulatory forces that have dominated the way China has been viewed in Japanese

literature. By using some of Tanizaki's stories as test cases, we can cata-
logue the crucial moments in the Sino-Japanese entanglement and explore the revised ways of reading China/Japan as I have discussed.

While this coda may appear informal as a conclusion, I believe it is
appropriate for both thematic and structural reasons. Tanizaki's well-
known stories are ideal for the thematic purpose, as they have been misconstrued as embodying a Japanese aesthetic essence by the same modern
sensibility that has wrongly formed and maintained the Sino-Japanese dialectics. In structural terms, a standard conclusion summarizing the important points made in this study would reestablish a faith in empiricism
and chronology, whose legitimacy this study set out to modify. Instead, I
aspire to intentionally confuse and complicate the choice, pace, and order
of the events that have been discussed in the preceding chapters by letting
the select stories by Tanizaki speak to many of the points raised. We will
start with the theme of chapter 4 and proceed in reverse order.

Orality and Emotion in the Written Language

The aural/oral method of teaching classical Chinese texts to children at an
early age, without expecting that the learner would understand their
meaning, had been very common in Japan until the nineteenth century
(as discussed in chapter 4). We then saw that as the canonicity of classical
Chinese was renounced in modern Japan, a mastery of the language became a weapon for intellectuals to voice dissatisfaction with and resistance to the barriers created by nationalism. As discontented men and
women of letters took recourse in the commonality of classical Chinese,
however, the issue of orality surfaced and complicated the perceived East
Asian sharing of the same culture. While the oral performance of classical
Chinese poetry allowed for a communal site in which everyone who had
mastered the language could express his or her emotions and publicly re-
spond to another's, it also exposed the barriers of national oral languages,
which are privileged in the modern age of phonocentricism.

The oral recitation of Chinese poems, a common practice among
Heian courtiers that has been ignored in the modern misunderstanding of
the mid- to late-Heian culture as homogeneous and indigenous, surfaces in
Tanizaki's *Shōshō Shigemoto no haha* (1950), a novella that is set in the
early tenth century.[3] The major characters of the story include Fujiwara no
Tokihira (better known in the Sinified reading of his given name, "Shihei";
871–909), the scion of the most powerful aristocratic family in Japan.

Shihei allegedly fabricated a conspiracy against the emperor so as to impli-
cate a rival minister, Sugawara no Michizane, a renowned poet, scholar,
and teacher of the Chinese classics and poetry, and remove him from the
central administration.[4] This widely known turn of events could be construed as signaling a transition from the Sinified meritocracy, which Sugawara no Michizane embodied, to a native aristocratic order. Rather than
squarely dealing with the political transformation, however, Tanizaki focuses on another episode about Shihei that sheds light on the role of classical Chinese poetry in tenth-century Japan. Explicitly drawing upon official
and popular accounts that document Shihei's callow behavior, Tanizaki
elaborates upon the fact that Shihei forcibly married a woman who was the
wife of another courtier. In some of the scenes, the unfortunate courtier, an
old man, misses the wife that he let go but convinces himself that it was for
her good, and he recites poems by Bai Juyi that match his feelings. The
poems are generously quoted within the novella, as the old man teaches his
little son (the eponymous character, Shigemoto), how to recite them: "Son,
let me share with you this Chinese poem. It's composed by a Chinese man
called Bai Letian. It may be too difficult for a child like you to understand
its meaning, but it doesn't matter. It is fine if you can only memorize it as I
give it to you. You will understand the meaning when you are of age."[5]

Obviously, the old man is trying to teach his young son classical Chinese texts orally/aurally rather than semantically. The term "Chinese
poem" is represented as shi 詩, with the Japanese reading instruction of
kara uta on the side, a practice that accentuates the hybridity of Sinified
Japanese. The poems by Bai Juyi (here referred to by his studio name as Bai
Letian) include one about an old man's longing for a pet crane that has
flown away (entitled "Shihe" [Losing a crane]) and another about a man's
yearning for an unattainable object of affection ("Yeyu" [Nocturnal rain-
fall]). Both poems are given in kanbun kundoku-tai (the style employed in
Kajin no kigū) rather than in their original "authentic" forms. Later Shigemoto recalls many other lines, without being able to identify exactly
where they are from; Chinese verse as he knows it has already been domesticated and edited. The domestication of Chinese poetry bears witness
to the entanglement that produces Japaneseness as well as Chineseness in
Japanese literature when quotations are given from Chinese texts.

The father's recitation of Bai Juyi's Chinese poems has an effect similar
to what we saw in Kajin no kigū. He is overcome with emotion, and, instead
of teaching Shigemoto the poems line by line, he recites them rapidly in his
husky voice, pausing only to sip wine and shed tears; the sight and sounds

move the child even though he does not know the texts. That classical Chinese poetry is a venue in which to vent the most strongly felt emotions (the loss of a beloved wife in this case; in *Kajin no kigū*, indignation toward Western imperialism, homesickness, and romantic love) puts into question the legitimacy of the conventional claim that the Chinese language is meant for artificial and intelligent writing and that the Japanese language is suited to the natural and emotional. Indeed, the classical Chinese verse has a dual effect: it is highly charged with meaning and is orally performative.

"Yume no ukihashi" (1959), a story about a son's obsessions with his birth mother and stepmother, similarly defies the divide between the Chinese and Japanese languages along the axis of foreign versus native and written versus oral.[6] The story begins with a quotation from a handwritten poem *(waka)* that has been apparently composed by one of the two mother figures. The poem says that its speaker has finished reading *The Tale of Genji*. Persistent critical attention has been given to the link that the poem establishes between this story by Tanizaki and the Heian classic. Critics have discussed at length the pseudo-incestuous romance between a son and his stepmother, a major storyline in both works. In contrast, the attentive description of the technical and material aspects of the calligraphy as a work of visual art has largely been neglected. The narrator tells us that this work of calligraphy (among others said to have been written by the mother) uses *man'yōgana*, an ancient Japanese mode of transcription using Chinese characters, to represent the sound of each syllable of Japanese words. The transcription system reveals a problem in the Japanese use of Chinese script: it relies upon the phonetic aspect of Chinese characters while neutralizing their semantic aspect, which had established Chinese as the literary language. *Man'yōgana* overwrites the essence of the ideologemes of the Chinese characters. The orality of Chinese is exploited not in order to demonstrate the language's ethnic identity, but to transcribe text in a foreign language, Japanese; Chinese is phonocentralized as Japanese is made literate. Keenly aware of the duality of Japanese writing—sound/script, Japanese/Chinese—as is evident in many of his pieces, Tanizaki takes advantage of the implications of disparity that lie in the system of *man'yōgana*.

Gender, Nationality, and Language

In chapter 3, we saw that Japanese female Sinophiles were acknowledged by their peers as legitimate members of the intellectual/artistic community, while they were either under- or misrepresented by the modern literary community because they did not comply with the norms of the natural and the nativistic attributed especially to the female. Whereas Tanizaki is normally considered keen on the maternal woman or the femme fatale, both catering to the conventional heterosexual economy of gender one way or another, upon careful examination his female characters often prove to be culturally ambiguous. In "Shunkin shō" (1933), the narrator is a historian who collects information on the eponymous female artist, in much the same way as Mori Ōgai writes of Yu Xuanji through an un-identified narrator (as we saw in chapter 3).[7] Shunkin, a professional *shamisen* player and music teacher, keeps a warbler that sings divinely. Her practice of the art of bird feeding, one of the arts learned from China and made popular in Tokugawa Japan (as we saw in chapter 2), qualifies her as a member of the literati community. Since domesticated warblers chirp only out of the sight of humans, they have to be kept in a cage; as a result, humans became obsessed with elaborate cage designs. Shunkin uses a cage imported from China, an exquisite artifact in itself, with a frame of rosewood and a plaque of jade displaying landscapes and build-ings, a prevalent motif in traditional Chinese crafts.[8] Thus the Japanese female artist has assumed a connoisseurship of things Chinese, destabi-lizing the conventional pairings of male subject/female object and Chi-nese/Japanese.

"Yume no ukihashi" also effectively questions the validity of the contrasts between the intellectual and the natural and the masculine and the feminine, the theme of chapter 3. Having given some examples of calligraphy in which the mother employs a writing system replete with Chinese characters, the narrator offers the following observation: "A woman calligrapher, one would expect, should choose *kana* charac-ters, slender and swerving in the Kōzei school style. It is strange that she instead has chosen this plump and pudgy style with many Chinese char-acters, which I feel might reveal peculiar characteristics of this lady."[9] The narrator does not elaborate on the "peculiar characteristics" at this point in the narrative, leaving ambiguous exactly what he intends to convey. Given the contrived nature of the retrospective account, which is prudently designed, the perceived masculinity of the lady's calli-graphic style cannot be dismissed as incidental or inconsequential. Never-theless, critical focus on the quasi-incestuous relationship between the son and the stepmother has required ascribing the maternal to the step-mother. However, it becomes obvious as the story unfolds that the step-mother lacks maternal instinct; she shows absolutely no joy while expecting a child; nor does she seem remorseful or distressed after giving away the newborn for adoption. This unmotherly woman appropriately chooses to use a conventionally masculine style of calligraphy. Whether her choice is in defiance of the conventional definition of the feminine or in compliance with masculine cultural practices, we see here a challenge to the gender divide—similar to the one laid down by the women Sinophiles whom we discussed in chapter 3.

The Material Culture of China in the Japanese Lifestyle

"Yume no ukihashi" enfolds not only the themes of chapters 4 and 3, but also showcases the theme of chapter 2—namely, how early modern Japanese Sinophiles lived with encoded products of the Chinese material culture. The style of calligraphy described above as "plump and pudgy," anticipating the physique of the lady that could comparably be described, cannot but evoke the physicality of the Chinese characters. The specification thus evokes disparate views of the Chinese script: it cannot be reduced to the semantic or the idealistic, as perceived especially when written in *kaisho* (the upright style). In addition to the story's detailed descriptions of paper and methods of mounting it, the "plump and pudgy" style highlights the physicality of Chineseness that we saw in chapter 2.

The narrator paints a colorful picture of his family home, Goi-an (Herons' Hermitage), by detailing the architectural and interior designs. Beyond the references to calligraphy, the story introduces art works that the narrator's father and grandfather have collected, which happen to be mostly written in Chinese or imported from the continent. For example, there are two bamboo tablets with parallel five-character lines on both sides of a gate:

林深禽鳥楽
塵遠竹松清

(The forest being deep, birds take pleasure
The dust being far, bamboos and pines stand pure)

Though the lines are anonymous (the narrator recalls that his father said he did not know who composed or inscribed them) and thus the geographic location of the poet is unknown, the typical Chinese parallel structure hints at classical Chinese literature.

Nature associated with the reclusive lifestyle—the theme of the bamboo tablets above—resurfaces in a work of art that graces the foyer of the main building: Rai San'yō's framed calligraphy of a phrase from the Confucian classic *Zhongyong*, which literally means "kites fly, fish jump" and is a metaphor for the way of all things between heaven and earth, as well as for the virtue of a ruler, which manifests itself in the vigor of the fauna.[10] The fact that it is not the same work of calligraphy that hung in the foyer of Senkan Tei, Tanizaki's own one-time residence and the reported inspiration for Goi-an, only highlights the deliberateness of the choice. The references to birds and fish go well with the natural environment of Goi-an; it was named for the *goi sagi* (black-crowned night heron), which would frequently fly by, and it has a large pond with many carp. These living creatures give a rapturous sensuality to the otherwise quiet, mediated, artistic life of the recluse. Both birds and fish are associated with the mother of the story, the bird immortalized in her *waka*, the fish, in the narrator's memory of the mother feeding them with her feet soaking in the water. A line from a poem by Wei Ye (uncredited in the text; the narrator simply says that he has found the line "somewhere" [*nanikade*]) serves to confirm the cohabitation of human and other living creatures on the secluded premises: "If you washed your ink stone, fish would drink the ink."[11]

The line above suggests the physical proximity of humans and fish and thus neutralizes the binary between nature and culture. While the reference to an ink stone is only appropriate, given that the mother is engaged in calligraphy, it seems misplaced in the present context, in which the narrator describes the mother's feet as looking like white dumplings in the clear water. Indeed, the edible and the edifying, as discussed in chapter 2, converge as a classical Chinese line cuts into a scene where the son has cast his voyeuristic gaze upon the mother's exposed flesh.

Ishikawa Jōzan, an early Tokugawa Sinophile whom we saw in chapters 2 and 4, is mentioned a few times in Tanizaki's story, most significantly in reference to a famed water mortar in his Hall of Poetry Immortals, a copy of which is placed in the garden of Goi-an and becomes a crucial element in the narrator's obsession with his mother. The origin of the mortar, an agricultural device, is recounted in *kanbun* by Jōzan. His recounting reveals an example of the entanglement similar to those we saw in chapter 2: he makes a pun on *sōzu*, which can mean either a water mortar (if represented by the Chinese characters 添水) or a Buddhist priest (僧都), a pun that makes sense only if these Chinese compounds are read in Japanese, as the two words' Chinese pronunciations are distinct.

Fujiwara no Seika (1561–1619), who was a friend of Jōzan, the teacher of Hayashi Razan, and the founding father of Tokugawa Neo-Confucianism, is another Sinophile cited in the text, and he fleshes out the associations of Goi-an within the *kanshibun* discourse (albeit remotely). Just as Ishikawa Jōzan declined the emperor's invitation to the court, expressing his preference for seclusion, so Seika had declined an offer of office extended by the first shogun of the Tokugawa government, Tokugawa Ieyasu (1542–1616; r. 1603–1605) because he was committed to the life of a recluse. The eight picturesque places that he selected around his dwelling along the Kurama River in Kyoto are recalled as points of interest en route to Kurama, where the narrator's newly born brother is sent for adoption. Some of the place names given by Seika (Chin'ryū Dō, or Cave of Laying One's Head on the Stream; Hichō Tan, or Abyss of the Flying Birds"; Ryūriku Kei, or Valley of the Six-Way Stream) resonate with a life in harmony with birds and water and thus establish a parallel between this early Tokugawa Sinophile and the narrator's own family members in the 1930s.

As the two examples of Jōzan and Seika suggest, the location of the story specifically connotes the early Tokugawa Sinophile milieu. Even when Heian cultural products are cited, a layer of Tokugawa aesthetic or scholarly sensibility mediates between the Heian era and the modern characters. A significant example of the Tokugawa framing of Heian society, a quotation from and citation of *Sugawara no denju tenarai no kagami* (1746) reveals other acts of staging as well.[12] This popular *jōruri* play is mentioned as a means of comparing the narrator's half brother and Sugawara no Michizane's son, who are both secretly adopted. First, as a *jidai mono jōruri* (historical play for the traditional puppet theater), *Sugawara* is a Tokugawa reinterpretation of historical incidents that involve Sugawara no Michizane in the Heian period. Second, this play was first performed in Edo, even though the play is set in Kyoto and its suburbs; hence, the Edo framing of Kyoto culture. Third and most relevant to our study, Sugawara no Michizane, the renowned and deified *kanshi* poet and scholar of the Chinese classics and poetry, is portrayed in a popularized and oralized genre, *jōruri*. Again Tanizaki thrives on the hybridity of the Japanese language, which is constituted of various elements, and he puts it under a microscope.

Problematizing Geography

In chapter 1, we saw how some places in Japan became literary topoi owing to Chinese literary associations, to the effect of neutralizing geographic boundaries, and also how the boundaries between China and Japan were envisioned in terms of the sea between the two shores. Tanizaki's story "Ashikari" (1932), which is usually cited as an embodiment of Heian courtly aesthetic values, is set in a topos that historically resonated along Chinese poetic lines.[13] The text opens with the following oft-cited *waka*, which is placed as an epithet in order to emphasize the inspiration for the title:

> Kimi naku te / ashikari keri to / omou ni mo
> itodo Naniwa no / ura wa sumi uki

> (Without you, things have worsened; as I think that way /
> the reed-covered Naniwa Bay area feels even less tolerable to live in)

The subsequent text embeds numerous quotations from and allusions to *waka* and *wabun*. However, they do not overshadow the equally frequent quotations from Chinese verse and prose. The narrator visits Yamazaki, the literary topos that was compared to Heyang (as we saw in chapter 1), where rivers meet and reeds grow (hence the mention of reeds in the epithet). He recites not only Japanese poems, but also lines from well-known classical Chinese poetry such as Su Shi's "Chibi fu" (An ode to the red cliff) and Bai Juyi's "Pipa xing" (Ballad of the p'i-p'a) in order to release the emotions with which the scenery has filled him.[14] The citation of "Chibi fu" enables him to address themes about the moon, recollections of the past, and visitations of supernatural beings, all of which are elements of the story to come. The poem "Pipa xing," on the other hand, brings him closer to the historical connotations of the place because it is about the misfortune of a woman that the poet encountered on a boat. In addition to being the location of an imperial palace, Yamazaki is a site to which courtesans swarmed in ancient Japan. The narrator liberally and effectively uses Heian *kanbun* accounts of female entertainers in the area in order to underpin the connotation of the topos. Among the texts are "Yūjo o miru no jo" (Preface to the viewing of courtesans), by Ōe no Masahira (whose wife, Akazome Emon, was allegedly an unofficial historian in the Heian era, as we saw in chapter 3), and "Yūjo ki" (Account of courtesans), by Ōe no Masafusa, the author of *Gōdanshō*. These references are appropriate homage to the literary topoi of Yamazaki, which was honored in many *kanshi* poems composed in the reign of Emperor Saga, as we saw in chapter 1. If sufficient attention were given to all these quotations, it would paint a new picture of "Ashikari" that resonates with multiple precedents and that undoes the high/low, masculine/feminine, and foreign/indigenous contrasts that are conventionally made between Chinese and Japanese writing in general. One could count on classical Chinese poetry for emotional outlet, as well as for intellectual endeavor. One could write in *kanbun* about the most profane, feminine, and indigenous subjects, as well as the most highbrow, masculine, and universal.

Tanizaki's incomplete picaresque romance, *Rangiku monogatari* (Chrysanthemum in disarray, 1930), puts an interesting and historically important spin on the image of the Chinese and Japanese shores, separated from each other by waves, and it also effectively captures our metaphor of the fold. Thus it is an appropriate choice with which to end this text, even though it is not nearly as well known as the other works mentioned above. The novella is set in politically disordered late medieval Japan. A Ming Chinese merchant, Zhang Huiqing (J. Chō Keikyō), gets a glimpse of Kagerō, a high-profile Japanese courtesan who is stationed in Muronotsu, a port in the Inland Sea, across which mercantile ships navigate to and from China. As Kagerō's name is given in the phonetic signs of *hiragana*, it could mean either "drakefly" or "mirage."[15] We shall return to the significance of the name(s) below. Upon Zhang's request that she spend a night with him, Kagerō demands a special treasure if she, the best Japanese courtesan, is to do such a favor for a foreigner (a derogatory category in this context). Kagerō's demand is inspired by the legend of Hanaurushi (Floral Lacquer) who was alleged to be the first courtesan in Muronotsu, dating back to the reign of Emperor Engi (r. 901–922; the emperor's reign was commonly referred to as the golden age) and who was also sought after by a Chinese customer. Hanaurushi denotes a specific kind of lacquer, filtered with fine paper, that was one of the most renowned Japanese exports and thus is an appropriate name for the courtesan, a rare Japanese "commodity" to be proudly shown to the Chinese. The legend has it that the Chinese man gave Hanaurushi a silk crepe mosquito net *(kaya)* that was large enough to cover the entire space of an eight-mat room and yet was so finely woven that it could be folded into a four-by-four-inch box. The delicacy of the net was such that the imperial court, to which she later gave it as a gift, bestowed upon her an amount of gold sufficient to build five Buddhist temples.

Out of competitiveness, Kagerō demands a mosquito net that is large enough for a sixteen-mat room and that can be folded into a two-inch-square box: twice the size, four times the fineness. Within two years of the request, Zhang manages to have just such a mosquito net crafted in China, stores it in a two-inch-square golden box, and navigates toward Muronotsu through the Inland Sea. However, the rumor of the rare artifact has spread among Japanese pirates and their like, who swarm the area to steal the gift; they think that being Japanese, they are more worthy of Kagerō than the "foreigner." Despite the precautions that Zhang has taken—among other things, he has procured the military guard of Ōuchi, the feudal lord in the area—just a stop short of Muronotsu Zhang's boat is assaulted by an unidentified group of people who look like ghosts. During the commotion the box is first stolen by Kagerō's maid, who met Zhang in advance to welcome him, and then, as someone attacks her, it is lost in the sea. At least so it is believed until a mysterious individual claims in a signpost to have found it. He signs his claim "Kairyū Ō," or "Dragon King."

The course of events is telling of the China-Japan entanglement specifically in physical and material terms. First, unlike Matsura, the ancient topos on the borders of Japan that we looked at in chapter 1, the setting of the story—the Inland Sea—is within the Japanese archipelago. As a legitimate trader from Ming China with a tally (*kangōfu*) issued by the Ashikaga shogunate, Zhang is allowed to navigate through the Inland Sea. In contrast to the two shores divided by the Sea of Japan, representing China and Japan before cartography defined territory (as in the works we saw in chapter 1), the image of the Inland Sea opened to the Chinese is a fold: China does not stand apart from Japan; it is enfolded within Japan.

The ambiguity of Kagerō's role plays a part in the symbolical configuration of the characters. The name, whether it means "drakefly" or "mirage," embodies intangibility in the Japanese poetic lexicon. Indeed, despite the fact that she is a prostitute and thus an embodiment of the profane, Kagerō is affiliated with the Kamo Shrine, one of the two most exalted Shinto institutions in the country; presided over by unmarried imperial princesses, it is thus considered sacred. Furthermore, she rarely sees any of her customers, even though she is by definition a shared property and is expected to make herself available. In short, what is expected to be most exposed and commodified is in fact most secluded and enshrined. This paradox accounts for the extraordinary demand she imposes upon Zhang; it also explains the reaction of the pirates to the projected exchange between the courtesan and her prospective customer; for her to spend a night with a Chinese man is a reversal of the fold, the most esoteric being revealed to the utmost exterior, an ultimate violation of the sacred.

Then comes another reversal: the mosquito net that she demands is to enclose a Japanese room and presumably herself. It would thus be Japan that is enfolded within China—the Japanese body, indigenous, natural, and feminine, enclosed within a Chinese artwork. One after another reversals follow hereafter: the net itself is made of silk, presumably an export from Japan to China, and thus complicates the origin and trajectory of the exchange; the net is folded into a tiny box, shifting its status from container to contained, from large to small; the box is made of gold, which, as Tanizaki has taken the trouble to remind us, is the most important export from Japan to China. The Japanese raw material is exported to China and is crafted into a product that enfolds the Chinese good, which has been commissioned by and is to be given to a Japanese courtesan, who in turn will give herself to the Chinese man who brings it. Then the box with the net in it is stolen by the courtesan's maid, is subsequently lost to the sea, and is then claimed to be found by the Dragon King. The ownership of the box, nominal and virtual, thus becomes as questionable as the origins of the box and its contents in the production and exchange of goods between the two countries.

The oscillation and *mise-en-abyme* of the acts of folding-inside-out and folding-outside-in, the sequences that materialize in *Rangiku monogatari* and are conspicuous in other texts with which we negotiated in the preceding chapters, make it impossible to differentiate the Japanese from the Chinese, origin from destination, or subject from object. One must stop and wonder if it is the act of differentiation and contrasting itself that is wrong. The time-honored dialectic of the *wa/kan,* one might suggest, should be dismissed all together. Yet it is true that the dialectic is not necessarily of the modern academics' making; the texts that we have engaged, mostly literary, all obsess with the contrast, exploit it, and trigger its explosion. Imagined, designed, and constructed as it may be, the Sino-Japanese dialectic has been essential to the organization and definition of cultural elements in Japan. How long will we be treading upon the fine line between the awareness of an arbitrary distinction and an immersion in the binary? We have yet to see.

Notes

Introduction

1. Pollack, *The Fracture of Meaning*, 3.

2. Ibid., 227.

3. "Coordination," as well as "tabulation," is a guiding formula used throughout in LaMarre, *Uncovering Heian Japan*.

4. Imai Yasuko, "Wakon Yōsai, Wakon Kansai, Yamato damashii."

5. S. Tanaka, *Japan's Orient*.

6. Sakai, *Voices of the Past*.

7. LaMarre, *Uncovering Heian Japan*, 2.

8. The following are but a few of the scholarly works in this category: Mizuno, *Haku Rakuten to Nihon bungaku* (Bai Juyi and Japanese literature); Ishizaki, *Kinsei Nihon bungaku ni okeru Shina zokugo bungakushi* (The history of Chinese vernacular literature in early modern Japanese literature); Kaneko Hikojirō, *Heian jidai bungaku to Hakushi monjū* (Literature of the Heian era and the anthology of Bai Juyi's writings); Asō, *Edo bungaku to Shina bungaku* (Literature of the Tokugawa era and Chinese literature; reprinted under the new [and politically correct] title *Edo bungaku to Chūgoku bungaku*); Kawaguchi, *Heianchō Nihon kanbungakushi no kenkyū* (A study of Japanese literature in Chinese in the Heian era); Kojima, *Jōdai Nihon bungaku to Chūgoku bungaku* (Early Japanese literature and Chinese literature), and *Kokufū ankoku jidai no bungaku* (The Dark Ages of Japanese Literature); Kanda Kiichirō, *Nihon ni okeru Chūgoku bungaku* (Chinese literature in Japanese literature); and Ōta, *Nihon kagaku to Chūgoku shigaku* (Japanese poetics and Chinese poetics).

9. Benjamin, "Theses on the Philosophy of History," 263.

10. Hutcheon, "The Pastime of Past Time,'" 490.

11. Benjamin, "Theses on the Philosophy of History," 261.

12. Chino, "Nihon bijutsu no jendā," 235.

13. Bal, *Quoting Caravaggio*, 66.

14. Bal, *Double Exposures*, 69.

15. Bal, *Quoting Caravaggio*, 8–9.

16. Ibid., 9.

17. Ibid., 11. The text by Derrida to which Bal refers is *Limited Inc.*

18. Scott, "Experience," 61.

19. Ibid., 66.

20. Bal, *Double Exposures,* 72–73.

21. Cited in ibid., 67.

22. That is with the notable exception of *Genji monogatari,* which refers to and engenders Korea vis-à-vis China and Japan. See, for example, Kawazoe Fusae, "Kōekishi no naka no *Genji monogatari*" (*The Tale of Genji* in the history of trade), in Kawazoe, *Sei to bunka no* Genji monogatari: *Kaku onna no tanjō* (*The Tale of Genji* in terms of gender and culture: The birth of a writing woman), 107–125.

23. Bal, *Quoting Caravaggio,* 25.

24. Chambers, *Story and Situation,* 3.

25. Deleuze, *The Fold,* 3.

26. Levinas expounds the theory of alterity in many of his writings, including *Time and the Other.*

27. For the texts or translations of these works, see the following: McCullough, "A Tosa Journal" (published in two anthologies); Sugawara, *A Tale of Eleventh-Century Japan;* Fujiwara no Teika, *The Tale of Matsura;* Chikamatsu, *The Battles of Coxinga.*

Chapter 1: Site Unseen

1. I have discussed poetry separately in Sakaki, "Archetypes Unbound," as the rhetoricity of language was explicitly confirmed in that genre by way of composition on, and arrangements according to, topics (*dai*).

2. As Suda Tetsuo notes, courtiers' diaries record the continual arrival of Chinese drifters during the Song dynasty. The books they brought with them to Japan must have provided those who had not visited the continent—possibly including the alleged author of *Hamamatsu*—a degree of geographic knowledge ("Hamamatsu Chūnagon monogatari ni okeru sakusha no Tō chishiki ron" [Discussion on the knowledge of China possessed by the author of *The Tale of Middle Councilor Hamamatsu*], 34).

3. While Matsuo Akira ("Hamamatsu chūnagon monogatari ni okeru Tō no byōsha ni tsuite" [On the descriptions of China in *The Tale of Middle Councilor Hamamatsu*]) enumerates erroneous references to China in *Hamamatsu,* Suda, in the above-cited article, takes a positive view of these "misrepresentations," suggesting that the author's intent was not so much to compare China with Japan as to liberally quote from legends and other preceding sources, including those on China. Suda's stance is somewhat similar to Bal's, which we saw in the introduction, in that discrepancies between the new and the old texts are accounted for by an attempt at building a new meaning rather than misrepresenting the old meaning.

4. Greenblatt, *Marvelous Possessions,* 88.

5. Kawase, "Kara monogatari to Mōgyū waka" (*The tales of China* and *Japanese poems inspired by* Mengqiu), 128. The "author of *Sarashina nikki*" to whom Kawase refers is of course the alleged author of *Hamamatsu chūnagon monogatari,* whom I discuss below in this chapter.

6. Pratt, *Imperial Eyes*, 6–7.

7. A more appropriate analogy might be with those who undertook the Grand Tour, notably the English visiting Italy to immerse themselves in the great cultural heritage of Europe. The English thus had long fantasized about Italy, a cultural superior that only the privileged could afford to visit. However, I do not pursue a comparative analysis here, for the reasons articulated in the introduction.

8. A complete translation of *Tosa Nikki* can be found in McCullough, "A Tosa Journal." All translations here are mine.

9. See, for example, Miyake, "*The Tosa Diary*," and Watanabe Hideo, *Heianchō bungaku to kanbun sekai*, 257–281 ("Kanbun nikki kara nikki bungaku e" [From diaries in *kanbun* to memoirs as a literary genre]).

10. For translations, see Rodd and Henkenius, *Kokinshu*, and McCullough, *Kokin wakashu*.

11. Wixted, "The Kokinshū Prefaces," LaMarre, *Uncovering Heian Japan*, 143–144. For a translation of *Maoshi daxu*, see Owen, "The 'Great Preface.'"

12. Ki no Tsurayuki, *Tosa nikki*, 42. I am following Thomas LaMarre's challenge to the convention that *waka* is broken into five lines in English translations, as I honor the Japanese breakdown of *waka* into two lines (*kami no ku* [upper half] and *shimo no ku* [lower half]).

13. For a biography of Nakamaro and the composition and registration of the poem, see Hayashi, *Honchō ichiniin isshu*, book 10, 300–304, which offers one poem each by Japanese *kanshi* poets.

14. Partial translation in Ōe, "The Ōe Conversations."

15. *Gōdanshō*, book 3, no.1, 63–69.

16. Ibid., book 3, no. 3, 71.

17. Another episode from *Gōdanshō* (book 4, no. 16) on Ono no Takamura (802–852), more renowned for his *waka* composition than Nakamaro, showcases a ground on which *waka* could be irrelevant to Japan's self-definition vis-à-vis China in literary terms. A figure of multiple literary connotations, Takamura was once appointed vice ambassador to Tang China, then removed from and exiled because he composed a satirical poem on the alleged mishandling of embarkation. In the *Gōdanshō* episode, as Bai Juyi was renowned in Japan for his composition, so was Takamura known in China as a great poet in Chinese verse, to the extent that Bai Juyi had a watch tower Wanghai Lou (Seaview Tower) built to monitor Takamura's arrival. For the above-mentioned reasons, Takamura could not make it to China, but Bai Juyi's posthumous poems had lines identical to those in Takamura's compositions (p. 113). There is no reference to Takamura's *waka*, even though he at least allegedly composed *waka* in sufficient numbers to sustain a quasi-biographical poetic tale (*uta monogatari*), *Takamura monogatari* (late twelfth century). This attests not only to the relative indifference of the author of *Gōdanshō* to *waka*, but also to the fact that an emphasis on *waka* composition in the portrayal of a poet is purely contingent.

18. LaMarre, *Uncovering Heian Japan*, 2.

19. Ueda Akinari's (1734–1809) "Kaizoku" (The pirate), a short story collected in Ueda, *Harusame monogatari* (Tales of the spring rain, 1808–1809), paints an unfavorable picture of Ki no Tsurayuki: he is interrogated by an intellectual pirate on his way to the capital—a similar setting to that in the episode of *Tosa nikki* discussed above. The pirate expounds upon Tsurayuki's incompetence in Chinese, ranging from unreliable references to Chinese poetic terminology in his preface to *Kokin wakashū* to the mispronunciation of his name (the correct reading, according to the pirate, is "Tsuranuki"). The model for this unlikely literary critic, who laments the proliferation of love poems in *waka,* was later hypothesized to have been Fun'ya no Akitsu, a historical figure who putatively wasted his talent in alcohol and died in exile. As is obvious from his surname, Akitsu was a descendant of Fun'ya no Yasuhide, one of the six poetic immortals, or *rokkasen,* listed in Tsurayuki's preface to *Kokin wakashū.* His given name, Akitsu, literally means a drake fly, which is an established metaphor for the Japanese archipelago. The fact that the character whose name represents the essence of Japan renounces *waka,* as well as the fact that he does so in the inland Sea of Japan (we shall see more on the implications of the location in the coda as we discuss a modern short story on medieval pirates set in part in the area) suggests Akinari's awareness of the ambiguous origins of Japanese poetry and clumsy attempts at concealing the heterogeneity—an awareness that is also evident in Akinari's critical works on Japanese literature. For what this story suggests about Ueda Akinari's scholarly position, see Hino, "Akinari to fukko" (Akinari and the restoration of tradition), in Hino, *Norinaga to Akinari: Kinsei chūki bungaku no kenkyū* (Norinaga and Akinari: A study of literature in the middle period of early modern Japan), 223–250, and Katsukura, "'Kaizoku' ron no kiso: Sono zōkeisei to hihyō seishin" (A foundation for discussions on "The Pirate": Its typology and critical spirit), in Katsukura, *Ueda Akinari no kotengaku to bungei ni kansuru kenkyū* (A study of Ueda Akinari's literature and scholarship in the classics), 634–660.

20. While, as noted in the introduction, there is a complete English translation of *Hamamatsu* in Sugawara, *A Tale of Eleventh-Century Japan,* all translations here are mine.

21. Matsuo Akira discusses in detail the transformation of the titles. See "Daimei kō" (Reflections on titles).

22. We shall see in chapter 3 that such resources were available to some young girls in the capital, such as Murasaki Shikibu.

23. The memoir is translated in Sugawara no Takasue no musume, *As I Crossed a Bridge of Dreams.*

24. See Kojima, *Kokinshū izen,* 161–171, for more on the topos in *kanshibun* in the Saga reign (809–823).

25. *Bunka shūrei shū,* vol. 3, *Zatsuei* (Compositions on miscellaneous subjects), no. 96–99. Two poems in response were composed by Fujiwara no Fuyutsugu (775–

826), one by Yoshimine no Yasuyo (785–830), four by Nakao Ō (dates unknown), two by Asano no Katori (774–843), and one by Shigeno no Sadanushi (785–852).

26. Narihira's inadequacy in *kanshi/kanbun* composition was documented in *Nihon sandai jitsuroku* (Factual records of three reigns of Japan, 901), vol. 8, 28: "略無才學善作倭歌" (generally no mastery of the canon, skilled at composing *waka*). This oft-quoted phrase contributed to confirming the binary opposition between composition in Chinese, which was a practice requiring intelligence and disciplined study, and composition in Japanese, which, implicitly, was intuitive. For the concealed conversion of Chinese texts in *Ise monogatari,* a mid-Heian poetic tale for which Narihira is conventionally held responsible as either the protagonist or author or both, see Watanabe Hideo: "*Ise monogatari* to kanshibun" (*Tales of Ise* and *kanshibun*) and *Heianchō bungaku to kanbun sekai* ("*Ise monogatari* ni okeru kanshibun juyō" [The reception of *kanshibun* in *Tales of Ise*]), 491–513. *Ise monogatari* is translated in McCullough, *Tales of Ise,* and excerpts are in McCullough, *Classical Japanese Prose,* 38–69.

27. Sugawara, *Hamamatsu,* 13.

28. The original lines by Sugawara no Fumitoki are "蘭蕙苑嵐摧紫後／蓬萊洞月照霜中" (in ibid., 12; the source of the phrase is given in n. 13). They also appear in *Gōdanshō,* vol. 4, no. 36. They are translated in Fujiwara no Kintō, *Japanese and Chinese Poems to Sing,* 91. Incidentally, "Hōraitō no tsuki" (the moon in the Immortals' Palace), from the second line, a phrase is quoted by the Middle Councilor when he recounts the evening for the Japanese emperor and courtiers upon his return to his homeland (Sugawara, *Hamamatsu,* 134).

29. 不是花中偏愛菊此花開後更無花 (It is not that the chrysanthemum is the favorite among all the flowers; it is because there is no flower whatsoever after this one blooms), as is given in Sugawara, *Hamamatsu,* 13, n. 14. See Fujiwara no Kintō, *Japanese and Chinese Poems to Sing,* 90.

30. Sugawara, *Hamamatsu,* 13. The exchange between the Middle Councilor and the consort is evocative of many first encounters in classical Japanese romance, possibly the most prominent one being the encounter of Genji and Yūgao in the beginning of the "Yūgao" (Evening faces) chapter in *Genji monogatari,* where Yūgao's servant offers Genji's attendant a fan with which to carry the flower that he found on the fence of Yūgao's house (Murasaki, *Genji monogatari,* vol. 1, 126–127). Owing to such associations, the reader could relate to the Middle Councilor's impression that the consort's gesture was "Japanese."

31. Sugawara, *Hamamatsu,* 21.

32. Tsukushi is a topos representing the "wandering of the noble" (*kishu ryūri*) in classical Japanese literature and thus is, in its liminality, appropriate for the story of border crossing.

33. Sugawara, *Hamamatsu,* 12.

34. Ibid., 16.

35. Ibid., 15.

36. Murasaki, *Genji monogatari*, vol. 1, 27.

37. For more on these consorts, see Sakaki, "Archetypes Unbound."

38. See Mostow, "Mother Tongue and Father Script" for the history of the concept of *miyabi* (usually translated as "courtly elegance"); Mostow identifies *Ise monogatari* as the origin of the term.

39. See Fukui, "Honji shi to Ise monogatari" *(Poems of tales and Tales of Ise)*, 292–304.

40. The episode is the first tale in *Kara monogatari*, a collection of tales whose complete English translation is in Geddes, *Kara monogatari*. Geddes translates the story in question as "Wang Ziyou Visits Dai Andao" (pp. 70–71).

41. See Sakaki, "Archetypes Unbound," for more on the significance of this anthology in the tradition of *waka* composition.

42. Sugawara, *Hamamatsu*, 28.

43. Ibid., 35. We should note that in this adaptation, the agent of speech has changed from Yang Guifei (as the original has it) to Xuanzong. The lines from "Changhenge" that inspire the Middle Councilor and the emperor are in fact from a speech by Yang Guifei's spirit, addressing the wizard who visits her at Xuanzong's request. In *Hamamatsu*, the Middle Councilor senses the emperor's longing for the consort and reworks this passage from the lonely man's perspective. This is much the same operation as the reversal of perspective seen in adaptations of the same lines in *Genji monogatari*: in the chapters "Kiritsubo" and "Maboroshi" (The wizard), the Kiritsubo Emperor and Genji compose *waka* on their respective longing for the Kiritsubo consort; Murasaki, drawing upon these lines, focuses on the vow from the man left behind by the love of his life. See Murasaki, *Genji monogatari*, vol. 1, 40, and vol. 3, 213.

44. Sugawara, *Hamamatsu*, 15.

45. Ibid., 45.

46. Ibid.

47. Murasaki, *Genji monogatari*, vol. 1, 47.

48. Sugawara, *Hamamatsu*, 48.

49. The prediction comes true, but the protagonist's object of longing is not the fifth daughter but his true love. Ibid., 57.

50. Ibid., 85.

51. Ibid., 86.

52. Ibid., 85.

53. Ibid., 133.

54. Ibid.

55. Ibid., 135.

56. Ibid., 134.

57. Ibid., 135.

58. As noted in the introduction, a complete translation of *Matsura* is in Fujiwara no Teika, *The Tale of Matsura*, 57–162. All translations here are mine.

59. Fujiwara no Teika, *Meigetsuki*, vol. 1, 58.

60. Fujiwara no Teika, *Matsura*, 162.

61. Ibid., 161–162.

62. Ibid., 162.

63. Ibid.

64. The secret teaching of music usually calls for a foreign or supernatural setting. For example, in *Utsubo monogatari* (late tenth century), it first takes place in Persia and later makes the descent of heavenly beings happen. The exotic and supernatural ambience is certainly visible in *Matsura*, as the tradition dictates. For a translation of *Utsubo monogatari*, see Uraki, *The Tale of the Cavern*.

65. Fujiwara no Teika, *Matsura*, 166.

66. Ibid.

67. Ibid., 172.

68. Ibid., 173.

69. Ibid., 171.

70. Ibid., 180.

71. Ibid., 180–181.

72. As we saw, Sumiyoshi also figured in the aforementioned *Gōdanshō* episode on Abe no Nakamaro. Perhaps the best known example of the deity's miraculous power is in a *nō* play by Zeami Motokiyo (1363?–1443?), *Haku Rakuten* (Ch. Bai Letian), where the deity, in the guise of a fisherman, meets the eponymous poet (Bai Juyi), who, also incognito, is visiting Japan. The deity identifies Bai Juyi (much to his surprise), explains that the Japanese are familiar with his poetry, and matches his composition with a *waka* so as to impress him with the level of artistic sophistication in Japan. This play helped to homogenize Japanese poetic practices, which were bilingual at the time of the play's production. It does not reflect the fact that the Zen monks of Japan regarded Su Shi (1036–1101) and Huang Tingjian (1045–1105), rather than Bai Juyi, as the most important of the classical Chinese poets. See Yokomichi and Omote, *Yōkyoku shū*, 305–308, and, for a translation of the play, Waley, *The Nō Plays of Japan*, 207–215.

73. Fujiwara no Teika, *Matsura*, 190.

74. Ibid., 187.

75. Ibid., 192.

76. China has its own deities and mythical figures, which are known to intervene in human affairs, but their presence is conveniently forgotten in this context of contrasting Japan with China.

77. Fujiwara no Teika, *Matsura*, 198.

78. The theme is exemplified by such famous rhapsodies as "Gaotang fu" (A poetic exposition on Gao-tang) and "Shennu fu" (The goddess), by Song Yu (290–223 BC); "Luoshen fu" (The goddess of the Luo), by Cao Zhi (192–232); and "Qiuxing fu" (Autumn delight), by Pan Yue. The prose preface to "Gaotang fu," without the main part, is translated in Owen, *An Anthology of Chinese Litera-*

ture, 189–190. For "Shennu fu" and "Luoshen fu," see ibid., 190–193 and 194–197.

79. The theme of reincarnation also involves the heavens, apart from Japan or China. Shortly before the lieutenant's departure for Japan, the empress confesses to him that she is indeed the mysterious woman. She further reveals that she was a heavenly being who, upon the Heavenly Emperor's command, descended to conquer Yuwen Hui, who was a reincarnation of Ashura (Ch. Axiuluo), a bellicose mythical Buddhist figure, and that the lieutenant was a boy servant to the Heavenly Emperor who was given arms by Sumiyoshi in order to help her. See ibid., 217.

80. A complete translation of *Kokusen'ya gassen* is in Chikamatsu, *The Battles of Coxinga,* 57–131. All translations here are mine.

81. Among these are the following: *Minshin tōki* (An account of Ming-Qing battles), published in Japan in 1661; *Kai hentai* (The transformation of the Chinese and barbarians), edited by shogunate Confucian scholars in 1717; *Kikō shōsetsu* (Merchants' talks in Nagasaki harbor, 1721); *Jing Tai shilu* (The true record of the pacification of Taiwan), edited in China in 1722; and *Taiwan gundan* (Military tales of Taiwan), edited in Japan in 1723.

82. See Suwa, "Kaihi no fūsetsu" (Rumors from beyond the sea) in Suwa and Hino, *Edo bungaku to Chūgoku* (Literature of the Tokugawa era and China), 228. For another account of the circumstances, see Masuda, *Japan and China,* 184–205.

83. See Sakaki, "Archetypes Unbound," for how Wang Zhaojun's marriage to the Xiongnu chieftain is configured in Japanese literature. For more on Wang Zhaojun, see note 31 in chapter 4.

84. Chikamatsu, *Kokusen'ya gassen,* 232.

85. The three characters are 和藤内. The second character is said to be a homophone of "Tō" 唐 ("Tō no koe o katadotte"; ibid., 242), except that the two are phonetically identical only in the Japanese pronunciation; 唐 reads "Tang," as opposed to "Teng" (藤) in Chinese. This is an example of a widely seen domestication of what is thought to be essential to the national identity of China, and it in effect ridicules the phonocentricism in the linguistic confirmation of the nation-state.

86. Ibid., 244.

87. Ibid.

88. Ibid., 245.

89. Ibid.

90. See Sakaki, "Archetypes Unbound."

91. Chikamatsu, *Kokusen'ya,* 245.

92. Bai Juyi, "Changhenge" (The Song of Lasting Sorrow).

93. Chikamatsu, *Kokusen'ya,* 247.

94. Geddes, *Kara monogatari,* 88–89, translates this story as "The Faithful Wife Who Turned to Stone."

95. Chikamatsu, *Kokusen'ya,* 272.

96. Ibid., 263.

97. Ibid., 262.

98. Ibid., 256.

99. Ibid., 260.

100. Ibid., 252.

101. Ibid., 254.

102. Ibid., 255.

103. Ibid., 273.

104. Ibid.

105. Ibid., 272.

106. Ibid., 256.

107. Yonemoto, *Mapping Early Modern Japan*, ch. 4, "Imagining Japan, Inventing the World: Foreign Knowledge and Fictional Journeys in the Eighteenth Century," 101–128.

108. The preface of *Honchō Suikoden*, signed by a Fujiwara no ason Kaneyo, ostensibly minimizes the parodic intent of the author; it ends with a seemingly nonchalant mention that the reference to the Chinese work in the title is attributed to the publisher ("fumiya ga wazani shitsuru to iunaru"). See Takebe, *Honchō Suikoden*, 3.

109. Takebe, *Honchō Suikoden*, 264. All translations are mine.

110. Ibid., 264.

111. The title of the poem was the inspiration for the title of *Hamamatsu*.

112. Takebe, *Honchō Suikoden*, 265.

113. Ibid.

114. Ibid., 268.

115. Ibid.

116. Ibid., 269.

117. I hasten to add that the transcriptions of Chinese in *Honchō Suikoden* do much more justice to the authentic sounds than they do in *Kokusen'ya*, possibly reflecting the distance between the respective authors' relative knowledge of the Chinese language.

118. In the "Tamakazura" (The jeweled chaplet) chapter of *Genji monogatari*, Tamakazura's chaperon claimed that she was physically handicapped in order to protect her from persistent suitors during the time of her wanderings in Kyūshū. See Murasaki, *Genji monogatari*, vol. 2, 333.

119. Takebe, *Honchō Suikoden*, 275, 270. Note the similarity between this instance and one we saw in *Kokusen'ya*, where a Japanese man distanced himself from a Chinese noblewoman in exile.

120. Takebe, *Honchō Suikoden*, 274.

121. Ibid.

122. Ibid., 284.

123. Ibid., 285.

124. Victor Mair's translation of the poem is as follows (from Mair, *The Columbia Anthology of Traditional Chinese Literature*, 300–301):

As clouds think of her clothing, as blossoms think of her face
Spring wind caresses the railings
and dew is thick on the flowers.
If you do not find her by the Mountain of Numerous Jewels
You may head for the Jasper Terrace
to meet her beneath the moon.

125. Takebe, *Honchō Suikoden*, 285.
126. Ibid.
127. Ibid.
128. Ibid.
129. Ibid.
130. Ibid., 287.
131. Ibid., 288–289.
132. Ibid., 289.
133. Ibid.
134. Ibid., 285.
135. Ibid., 300.

Chapter 2: From the Edifying to the Edible

1. Ibi, "Eibutsu no shi: Kanshi to haikai no ichi setten" (Poems on things: A point of contact between *kanshi* and *haikai*), in Ibi, *Edo Shiika ron,* 111; Hino, "Kōshōheki to bunbō shumi: Bunjinteki yūtō" (Penchant for empirical studies and a relish for stationery: Dilettantism typical of literati), in Hino, *Sorai gaku ha* (The school of Ogyū Sorai), 108–122.

2. The incident took place in 1636. See Ueno, *Ishikawa Jōzan Gensei,* 348–352.

3. Ishizaki Matazō, *Kinsei Nihon ni okeru Shina zokugo bungakushi,* chapter 1: Shina gogaku no genryū so no ichi Tō tsūji (The origin of the study of the Chinese language, 1: Interpreters of Chinese), 20.

4. Ibid., esp. 44–50.

5. Ishizaki gives an elaborately annotated list of the seven Chinese language textbooks edited by Okajima Kanzan in ibid., 96–116. See also Aoki, "Okajima Kanzan to Shina hakuwa bungaku," for the corpus of Okajima's work.

6. There was also a host of Japanese writers who translated classical Chinese fiction stories in Tsuga Teishō's *Kokon kidan: Hanabusa zōshi* (1749) and *Kokon kidan: Hanabusa zōshi kōhen: Shigeshige Yawa* (1766) and in Ueda Akinari's *Ugetsu monogatari* (1768; published 1776) and *Harusame monogatari* (1808) are the most prominent examples.

7. Yonemoto, "Narrating Japan: Travel and the Writing of Cultural Difference in the Late Eighteenth and Early Nineteenth Centuries," in Yonemoto, *Mapping Early Modern Japan,* 85.

8. The Chinese, who were confined to specific areas of the port city of Nagasaki, were well documented by their contemporaries. For details, see P. J. Graham, "The Chinese Community in Nagasaki," in P. J. Graham, *Tea of the Sages,* 31–41, and Yonemoto, *Mapping Early Modern Japan,* 69–100.

9. Konrondo is a generic name for black servants working for the Dutch, but it is used as a character's name in this text. See Yonemoto, 77, for an illustration of "Kuronbo" (another term for black servants), with an annotation in the upper column: "also called Konrondo."

10. Although the character 筌 denotes a net to catch fish, it was used interchangeably with 筅, which means a brush made of bamboo that is used for making tea. Given the names of the author (Chagama Sanjin) and editor (Yakan Shi), which play upon tea-making utensils, it would make more sense to translate the *sen* as a tea brush rather than a fishnet.

11. Hino, "*Tōshisen* no yakuwari: Toshi no hanga to Kobunji-ha" (The role of *Tangshixuan:* The burgeoning of the city and the Old Discourse School), in *Sorai gaku ha.*

12. See Sakaki, "Archetypes Unbound."

13. Jōzan became a legend himself; his residence, with portraits of the poetic immortals, has become a topos. For an elaborate account of his accomplishments, see Chaves, "Jōzan and Poetry," in Rimer and Chaves, *Shisendo,* 27–90. A list of works by the thirty-six Chinese poetic immortals is on 58–75.

14. A corpus of such works is reprinted in the series *Wakokubon kanseki shūsei* (published by Kyūko shoin), which includes many of the book-length works mentioned below in this chapter.

15. See Sakai, *Voices of the Past,* ch. 7, for Ogyū Sorai's response to the Japanese custom of reading Chinese texts. For a survey of the scholarly trends, see, for example, Inoguchi, *Nihon kanbungakushi,* or Ōta, *Nihon kagaku to Chūgoku shigaku.*

16. Baudrillard, "The Implosion of Meaning in the Media," 79 and 80.

17. See Hino, "Kōshōheki to bunbō shumi," in Hino, *Sorai gaku ha,* 108–122. Bourdieu, "The Production of Belief: Contribution to an Economy of Symbolic Goods," chapter 2 in Bourdieu, *The Field of Cultural Production,* 75.

18. The original is " 詠物の詩を口すさむ牡丹かな "; it is from one of Buson's anthologies, *Shin hanatsumi* (New flower plucking, 1777). See Yosa Buson, *Shin hanatsumi,* 78.

19. "Mass Consumption of Chinese Goods," in P. J. Graham, *Tea of the Sages,* 42.

20. For a succinct account of the emergence of the Ōbaku sect and its promotion of cultural activities, see P. J. Graham, "Sencha and the Literati Culture of Ōbaku Zen Monks," in P. J. Graham, *Tea of the Sages,* 48–57. Baroni, *Ōbaku Zen,* offers the most extensive study of the Ōbaku sect that is available in English to date.

21. According to Mizuta Norihisa, the book was printed in Japan in 1748 and 1817, followed by a Japanese translation by Kashiwagi Jotei, prior to one by Aoki

Masaru that I will mention below in this chapter. See Mizuta, "Bunjin shumi, 195." For a translation, see Sze, *The Tao of Painting*. For extensive information on Li Yu, see Hanan, *The Invention of Li Yu*.

22. For Ike no Taiga's reception of the Chinese artistic tradition, see Takeuchi, *Taiga's True Views*, esp. 23–36 and 81–98.

23. There are many references to the work. Particularly inspiring are Kobayashi Tadashi and Tokuda Takeshi, "*Jūben jūgi zu* o yomu" (Interpreting *Ten Conveniences and Ten Preferences*) and Tokuda, "*Jūben jūgi zu* o yomu."

24. See Kondō, *Hakushi monjū to kokubungaku*, 195–208, for extensive annotations to the poem. "Mudan fang" was collected in Bai Jui's *Xin yuefu* (New rhapsodies).

25. The original is "唐音も少し云ひたき牡丹かな." This *haiku* appears in Tan Taigi (1709–1771) and Miyake Shōzan (1781–1801), *Haikai shinsen* (1773) and is collected in Shimasue and Yamashita, *Chūkō haikai shū*, 113.

26. Hino, "Kōshō-heki to bunbō shumi: Bunjinteki yūtō," in Hino, *Sorai gaku ha*, 109.

27. The original is "美しい貝で楊貴妃豚を食い" (in Karai, *Haifū Yanagidaru*, 106). In addition to the arts of the literati, popular cultural elements began to be imported: Chinese restaurants opened in Osaka, and Chinese cuisine came into fashion.

28. For more on the modern rearrangement of disciplines within the universities, see Shirane and Suzuki, *Inventing the Classics*, and Suzuki Sadami, *Nihon no "bungaku" gainen*.

29. For references to his work, consult Wixted, *Japanese Scholars of China*, 10. Joshua A. Fogel also has a brief account of Aoki's visit to China in *The Literature of Travel*, 167.

30. *Chajing* is collected in Aoki, *Chūka chasho* (A book on Chinese tea), for which Aoki wrote a substantial introduction, "Chasho nyūmon: Kissa shōshi" (An introduction to books on tea: A concise history of tea tasting). For more on Lu Yu's inaugural role in the study of tea, see P. J. Graham, "Framing a Philosophy for Tea in Early China," in P. J. Graham, *Tea of the Sages*, 10–13.

31. Among these are the following: *Shina kinsei gikyoku-shi* (A history of early modern Chinese theater, 1930; published in Shanghai, 1933, and in Beijing, 1958); *Genjin zatsugeki josetsu* (An introduction to Yuan opera, 1937; in Shanghai, 1941, and in Beijing, 1957); *Nanboku kyokugi genryū kō* (A thesis on the origins of theater in northern and southern China, 1930; in Changsha, 1939); *Pekin fūzoku zufu* (An illustrious record of manners and customs in Beijing, 1964; in Taipei, 1978); *Shindai bungaku hyōron shi* (A history of literary criticism in the Qing dynasty, 1950; in Beijing, 1988); and *Shina bungaku gaisetsu* (An outline of Chinese literature, 1926; in Shanghai, 1938, and in Hong Kong, 1959). Aoki is even mentioned in the film *Farewell, My Concubine,* as a famous Japanese scholar for whom Chinese actors (who were naturally antagonistic toward the Japanese colonizers) felt it was worth performing. I thank Wilt Idema for the information.

32. The essay was originally published in *Tokyo Teidai shinbun* in June 1937. It was reissued in Aoki, *Kōnan shun*, 67–72. For more on Naitō as a Sinologist, see Fogel, *Politics and Sinology*.

33. Aoki, "Kanbun chokudoku ron," 334–341.

34. The essay was originally published in *Tokyo Teidai shinbun* in June 1935. It was reissued in Aoki, *Kōnan shun*, 64–67. It is well known that Ogyū Sorai's refutation of *kundoku* and *kaeriten* did not establish a new practice. See also Sakai, "The Problem of Translation," in Sakai, *Voices of the Past*, ch. 7, 211–239.

35. Sōseki was known to be distressed by the ethnic specificity and presumed universality of Western civilization, which justified its edifying role in non-European regions. Writing in Sino-Japanese—a hitherto "universal" language in East Asia—meant a resistance to the dominance of Western culture. Sōseki wrote as follows:

> As a boy I took pleasure in studying the Chinese classics. Though I had not studied them for a long time, I had acquired a definition of literature, vaguely, in the subconscious, from [reading] *Zuo Zhuan, Guoyu, Shiji,* and *Hanshu.* I thought to myself that English literature must be the same, and that, if so, it would not be regrettable to dedicate one's life to studying it. . . . Having come to think about it, I am not particularly competent in Chinese literature, and yet I am confident that I could fully appreciate the texts. I do not think that my knowledge in English, though not profound, is inferior to that in the Chinese classics. With the same level of competence, I like one much better than the other. This must be for no other reason than the utter difference between the two literatures. In other words, what is meant by literature in Chinese and what is meant by literature in English can never be encompassed under the same definition (Natsume, *Bungakuron* [A thesis on literature], 7–8).

36. Four of the five sections in the current edition of *Kōnan shun* were printed in the journal *Shinagaku* (Sinology) almost concurrently with the trip.

37. Aoki, "Kōshū kashin" (Correspondence of blossoms from Hangzhou), in Aoki, *Kōnan shun*, 6–7.

38. Ibid., 8–9.

39. The teacher, Inaba Seikichi, is portrayed in Tanizaki's "Yōshō jidai," especially the sections entitled "Inaba Seikichi sensei" (Mr. Seikichi Inaba, my teacher, 214–225) and "Shūkō juku to sanmā juku" (Shūkō school and summer school, 231–240); translated in Tanizaki, *Childhood Years*. See also Harada: "Chūgoku bungaku to Tanizaki Jun'ichirō 1," and "Tanizaki Jun'ichirō to Chūgoku bungaku 2," and Nagae, *Tanizaki Jun'ichirō*, 79–80.

40. They are collected in Tanizaki, *Tanizaki Jun'ichirō zenshū*, vol. 24, 52–53. Tanizaki's "Shindō" (Prodigy) also features a prodigy who impresses his teacher by his ability to compose and recite Chinese poems brilliantly.

41. China was the only foreign land that Tanizaki ever visited except for Korea. Korea had been "annexed" and considered a part of Japanese territory by the time of Tanizaki's visit in 1918. Incidentally, Tanizaki's observations on Korea are consistently positive and appreciative, except for his comments on Korean cuisine—an interesting contrast with his usual enthusiasm for Chinese cuisine. His dislike of the Korean cuisine may explain why Tanizaki never wrote a story on Korean culture. See "Chōsen zakkan."

42. Tanizaki's second trip to China in 1926 did not bear more fruit for fiction with an ostensibly Chinese flavor. With the exception of "Tomoda to Matsunaga no hanashi" (The tale of Tomoda and Matsunaga, 1926), a story about a man who lived a double life, partly rooted in Shanghai, Tanizaki ceased to write fiction about China. Tomoda, one of the two title characters, who proves to be the same person as Matsunaga, talks about Shanghai (and by extension China) as the second best thing to Paris (by extension the "West"). An eccentric Europhile, Tomoda visits Paris as a young man and transforms himself into a Frenchman, Jacques Morain, not only in name, but also—fantastically—in appearance. In his later years, he visits Shanghai to continue enjoying a cosmopolitan life, as it is easier for him to visit Shanghai than Paris, both financially and physically. Tanizaki wrote two travel accounts—"Shanhai kenbun roku" (Observations in Shanghai) and "Shanhai kōyūki" (translated as Shanghai friends)—within a year of his return from the second trip to China. In these he reiterated some of the cultural analyses from his first trip and also reminisced about his encounters with up-and-coming Chinese writers and intellectuals, such as Tian Han (1898–1968), Guo Moruo (1892–1978), and Ouyang Yuqian (1889–1962); over a long period, he wrote a few essays about them. It appears that China had ceased to inspire Tanizaki's creative imagination and had become instead a place in the real, if not mundane, world. When the observer begins to speak with the object of his/her observation in person, the imaginary path of "communication," where the hypothetical entanglement had been taking place, is blocked. As much as Tanizaki's formulation of the Chinese was multifarious and nuanced, his fiction ceased to function as a laboratory of negotiation with China. See Fogel, *The Literature of Travel,* 261–265, and Baba, "Tanizaki Jun'ichirō," for circumstances surrounding Tanizaki's visits to China.

43. Tanizaki, "Shina no ryōri," 78.

44. Ibid., 79, 82.

45. Ibid., 83.

46. Tanizaki, "Shina-geki o miru ki," 71.

47. Ibid., 72.

48. Ibid. Akutagawa Ryūnosuke also expresses his dismay at a beautiful transvestite blowing his nose with his hands in "Shina yūki." See Akutagawa, "Travels in China," 24.

49. Harada, "Chūgoku bungaku to Tanizaki Jun'ichirō 1," 53–54.

50. Tanizaki's penchant for the scatological is well known—for example, Jijū's excretion in *Shōshō Shigemoto no haha* (translated as "Captain Shigemoto's Mother").

51. Tanizaki also wrote such explicitly and consistently biographical pieces as "Kirin" (1910), which features Confucius; "Genjō Sanzō" (Xuanjiang Sancang, 1917); and "So Tōba: Arui wa Kojō no shijin" (Su Dongpo, or a poet on the lake, 1920).

52. A complete translation of this story appears in LaMarre, *Shadows on the Screen*. The translation here is mine.

53. The story was originally published as "Seiji iro no onna" (A woman in celadon blue).

54. Tanizaki, "Seiko no tsuki," 338.

55. Ibid., 340–341.

56. Ibid., 337.

57. Ibid., 340–341.

58. As in Kōno, *Tanizaki bungaku to kōtei no yokubō*.

59. Tanizaki, "Seiko no tsuki," 334–335.

60. Ibid., 335, 342.

61. Ibid., 335.

62. Ibid., 342.

63. Ibid., 353–354. Su Xiaoxiao forms an entry in the well-circulated *Xihu youlan zhi yu* (Supplement to an account of West Lake sightseeing), by Tian Rucheng of the Ming dynasty; the latter quotes a poem in *Yutai xinyong* (New songs from the Jade Terrace, 583), which is attributed to her, and to later poems composed about her. The narrator also mentions Shi Yin's *Xihu jiahua* (Fine stories on West Lake), which may have been one of the sources that the author consulted. See Shi Yin, *Xihu jiahua*, vol. 6. For archetypes of female characters in this and other stories by Tanizaki, see Sakaki, "Keshin no mangekyō."

64. This is another reason why Xishi must have been a convenient choice: tuberculosis was the most romanticized disease in the Japanese literary imagination in the period. See Fukuda, *Kekkaku no Nihon bunkashi*, for a survey of literary works that feature characters with this disease.

65. A conversation with a Western woman seems to suggest an inversion of the hierarchy involving the West and China. The narrator sees her on the terrace of the hotel in which the beautiful Chinese women sat earlier. His gaze on this Western woman is definitely unkind: she is "fat" and dressed in an "unfittingly big" jacket that is "roughly striped" and looks like a *dotera*, a Japanese padded gown worn informally at home. It is not incidental that she takes the initiative in talking to him—and significantly in Japanese—nor that the narrator thinks of asking for her company, thinking that "she must be a prostitute" (Tanizaki, "Seiko no tsuki," 345). By downgrading the Western woman, this short episode highlights the Chinese women's inaccessibility, both linguistic and physical, as

well as elevates the aesthetic status of Li Xiaojie, if not that of Chinese women in general.

66. Ibid., 332–333.

67. Tanizaki, "Seiko no tsuki," 350–351.

68. Ibid., 340. The reference to plum trees in "Kakurei" is deemed autobiographical given that the setting of the story is obviously Odawara, a city in which the author once lived and that is famous for its plum blossoms. More autobiographical materials are found in the protagonist's family structure: a subservient wife, a daughter firmly standing by her mother, and a lover who lives with them. The details of the love triangle involving Tanizaki; his first wife, Chiyoko, who gave birth to his only daughter, Ayuko; and Chiyoko's younger sister, Seiko, are often thought to be the bases of plots involving a husband, wife, daughter, and husband's lover, recurring in Tanizaki's stories in the Taishō period. See Sakaki, "Keshin no mangekyō." It is noteworthy that his personal situation did not inspire Tanizaki to write ostensibly autobiographical fiction (shishōsetsu) but a fiction of exoticism and fetishism.

69. Stewart, On Longing, 140.

70. Tanizaki, "Kakurei," 401.

71. Ibid., 402.

72. The Chinese woman is even more dehumanized when her manner of walking is compared to that of the crane. Whereas this is an empirically accurate description, suggesting that she cannot take long strides owing to the premodern Chinese custom of foot binding, the recurrent metaphor of the crane produces its own iconicity.

73. "Birōdo no yume" was first serialized in the Osaka Asahi shinbun.

74. For example, the title, which is not fully explained in the text, can be accounted for by the following statement by the narrator of "Seiko no tsuki":

Though [the water of West Lake] is crystal clear and of the utmost purity, it does not seem light, but instead rather heavy. Such an impression must be partly due to the fine weeds, like green moss, that have grown thickly on the bottom and shimmer in dark green as though [the bottom of the lake were] a floor made of soft velvet. Indeed, no description would be adequate for the bottom other than that of extremely finely woven velvet of an amazingly beautiful gloss and moisture. Moreover, the goddess of the moon in the sky embroiders all over the surface waving serpentine patterns with an infinite number of long silver threads. The surface's beauty was such that I felt I would love to cover my favorite actress, K-ko's, skin with such a texture if there had been one so beautiful in the human world. If there is a fairy in this lake, the shawl she should put on should be of this velvet. (Tanizaki, "Seiko no tsuki," 348)

75. For more information on Jia Sidao, see, for example, Tian, Xihu youlan zhi yu, 85–95.

76. Tanizaki, "Birōdo no yume," 507. Incidentally, this hybrid heroine seems to have made an impact on at least one contemporary reader—Akutagawa Ryūnosuke. In his travel account, "Shina yūki," he mentions that the famous entertainer, Lin Daiyu (doubtless named after the character in *Hong lou meng,* 1763), reminds him of the Tanizaki character: "Such an appearance one does not ordinarily come across in a restaurant. She resembled a character who mixed crime and extravagance in a work by Tanizaki Jun'ichirō, *The Velvet Dream*" (Akutagawa, "Travels in China," 33). For *Hong lou meng,* see Ts'ao, *A Dream of Red Mansions.*

77. Tanizaki, "Birōdo no yume," 520.

78. Some twenty years later, Yokomitsu Riichi noted in his novel *Shanhai* (Shanghai, 1928) that many Russian women refugees engaged in prostitution in the city.

79. In "kaisetsu" (Guide to readers) to the autobiographical fiction *Dankō Reigan ki,* by the activist/litterateur Su Manzhu (J. So Manshu, 1884–1918), Iizuka Akira states that there were many hybrid children, or Xiangzi—including half-Chinese and half-Japanese, such as Su Manzhu was believed to be—in Yokohama in the late Meiji (Iizuka, "Kaisetsu," 289)—a backdrop that may have appealed to Tanizaki.

80. *Fūten rōjin nikki* is translated in Tanizaki, *Diary of a Mad Old Man.*

81. The sadomasochistic struggle for power plays a significant part in ethnographic or, to borrow Mary Louise Pratt's terminology, "autoethnographic" writings (*Imperial Eyes,* 7). While the colonizers exert their power to make sense of and legitimize their definitions of the colonized, the latter strike back, in part by a gestured surrender to the former's idioms, which often functions in effect as a parody of the colonizers' indecency. In the scheme of fetishism, the colonized become the "colonizers" in the dissemination of their cultural products as collectibles (e.g., souvenirs), although these were constructed in order to cater to the colonizers' desires. Thus, the colonial desire and its object are reproduced and counterreproduced, just as in sadomasochistic acts, creating yet another "fold" in the Deleuzean terminology.

82. "Kōjin" was serialized in *Chūō kōron* in 1920.

83. The original reads as follows:

送張子尉南州

不擇南州尉　高堂有老親
櫻台重蜃氣　邑里雜鮫人
海暗三山雨　花明五嶺春
此鄉多寶玉　愼勿厭清貧 (Cited in Tanizaki, "Kōjin," 29.)

84. See Lippit, *Topographies of Japanese Modernism,* for the important role of Asakusa in the Japanese modernist imaginary of space.

85. Tanizaki, "Kōjin," 212. Tanizaki published a short piece entitled "Kōjin no zokkō ni tsuite" (On the continuation of "Mermaids") in November 1920 in

which he stated that he would make no commitment about completing the story by a certain deadline.

86. For the significance of "Kōjin" in the context of the cultural ambience of Japan at that time, see Ito, *Visions of Desire*, 65–74.

87. Tanizaki, "Kōjin," 57–58.

88. For a translation, see Natsume, *The Three-Cornered World*.

89. Tanizaki, "Kōjin," 69–71.

90. Natsume, *The Three-Cornered World*, 20–21. For a translation of *Konjiki yasha*, see Ozaki, *The Gold Demon*.

91. Slight variations between the two writers may be worth noting. While Sōseki prefers reclusive poets such as Tao Qian (Yuanming), Tanizaki had a fondness for Li Bai (Taibai). That the Tang poet's legendary eccentric behavior and celebration of intoxication in his poetry were more attractive to Tanizaki (as they were to some other "dilettante" writers such as Satō Haruo [1892–1964], whose Sinophilic writings began to appear in 1923) is apparent in such works as "Sakana no Ri Taihaku" (Li Taibai, the fish, 1918), a fantasy about communication between a young Japanese woman and a fish made of silk crepe that is the transformation of Li Bai. In his preference for Li Bai, Tanizaki reveals his attachment to human desires, something that Sōseki claims to reject. Tanizaki also mentions other Chinese poets in "Kōjin" (e.g., Liu Tingzhi [651–679] and Song Zhiwen [?–ca. 710], 72–73) and elsewhere (e.g., Wu Meicun [1609–1671] in "Shina shumi to iu koto," 122).

92. Both names are represented in the following three characters: 林真珠.

93. The reference to Mei Lanfang's performance in Tokyo is historically accurate. See Mei, *Tōyūki*, an account of his third visit to Japan in 1956 that touches upon his first visit in 1919.

94. Tanizaki, "Shina-geki o miru ki," 70–74. Tanizaki also comments on the art and behavior of Mei and other actors.

95. See Fogel, *The Literature of Travel*, 157, for Mokutarō's experiences with seeing Mei Lanfang.

96. On the interface of transvestism and transnationalism, see Garber, "Phantoms of the Opera: Actor, Diplomat, Transvestite, Spy," chapter 10 of Garber, *Vested Interests*, 234–266. The interface has many modern and contemporary literary manifestations, such as David Henry Hwang's *M. Butterfly*, which centers on a transvestite actor in Chinese opera who exploits the Orientalist fantasies of a French diplomat.

Chapter 3: Sliding Doors

1. The volume was issued by Fujiwara shoten, a publishing house known for its translations of books on contemporary theories. Kado has also published *Ema Saikō: Kasei-ki no joryū shijin* (Ema Saikō: A female poet of the Kasei period [1804–1830]), a work Kado calls a novel rather than a biography, and, with Iritani Sensuke, a specialist in Song dynasty poetry, has annotated a two-volume anthology, *Ema Saikō shishū*.

2. We must not, of course, forget scholars outside Japan, such as Roger Thomas, who have consistently studied Tokugawa women's literary works.

3. I do not discuss here the other end of this "bridge"—namely, Meiji literary women. For information on the subject, see Copeland, "The Meiji Woman Writer."

4. Suzuki Tomi, "'Joryū nikki bungaku' no kōchiku: Janru, jendā, bungakushi kijutsu" (The establishment of "women's memoirs" as a literary genre: Genre, gender, and the register of literary history). A similar line of argument is in Suzuki's "Gender and Genre."

5. Tokugawa women memoirists and *waka* and *haiku* poets were, of course, less "inadequate" in the modern version of Japanese literary history, as they wrote in *wabun* and more ostensibly in confessional terms than fiction writers (such as Arakida Reijo) and *kanshi* poets (such as Ema Saikō). Still, they remained more or less obscure until recently, perhaps due to the definition of Tokugawa literature as "masculine," as opposed to Heian literature as "feminine," a distinction made in Meiji *kokubungaku* scholarship so as to make Confucian affectation in the period seem more predominant than it was. That there were Tokugawa counterparts to Heian literary women may have conflicted with this en-gendering of Tokugawa literature. See Suzuki Tomi, "'Joryū nikki bungaku' no kōchiku," for details.

6. Nakajima Wakako locates the origin of the en-gendering of *kanshibun* in the Heian rather than in the Tokugawa. She argues that Heian male courtiers were in a precarious position (with a mix of inferiority complexes and pride), and women's increasing command of *kanshibun* threatened the men's reason for existence. Women were distanced from *kanshibun* precisely because of their closeness to the culture. See Nakajima, "'Karafū ankoku jidai' no naka de," 81.

7. See Sakaki, "Kurahashi Yumiko's Negotiations with the Fathers."

8. Murasaki, *The Diary of Lady Murasaki*, 57–58. The original is in Murasaki, *Murasaki Shikibu nikki*, 500.

9. While Murasaki is believed to have turned the tables to her advantage and created a masterpiece in the only language in which she was allowed to write, Ichiyō was strongly urged by her mentor, Nakarai Tōsui, to write in a quasi-classical Japanese, which Seki Reiko rightly calls *josō buntai* (feminized discourse) in order to display feminine attributes. Seki Reiko, "Fude motsu hito e" (For the woman with a pen in hand). It may be easily overlooked—and Seki directs the reader's attention to it—that Tōsui was explicitly aware of gender as cultural practice rather than anatomical essence. His advice was not that Ichiyō should write like a woman because she was a woman but that she should not take it for granted that she could write in a feminine style just because she was a woman. Femininity, in his view, was to be acquired and demonstrated, rather than naturally given or assumed; his metaphor of drag performances in the theater is particularly effective as a manifesto of performative rather than essentialist gender theory. See also Seki Reiko, "Tatakau 'Chichi no musume': Ichiyō tekusuto no seisei" ('Father's daughter' at war: Formation of Ichiyō's text), in Seki Reiko, *Kataru onna tachi no jidai:*

Ichiyō to Meiji josei hyōgen (The age of narrating women: Ichiyō and feminine expression in the Meiji period).

10. It is not as though the criticism of women of Chinese letters is entirely a Tokugawa invention. Nakajima Wakako points out that in the "Biography of Michitaka" in *Ōkagami*, the fall of Fujiwara no Michitaka's wife, Takashina Takako, in later life (after her husband's untimely death, her sons' exile, and her daughter Teishi's humiliation) is attributed to her exposure to and exhibition of Chinese learning. See Nakajima, "'Karafū ankoku jidai' no nakade," 80, and *Ōkagami*, 268–269.

11. Stephen Owen translates Yu Xuanji's poem in *An Anthology of Chinese Literature*, 510; I have provided the translation below. Whereas many legendary Chinese women have embraced the status of celebrity in the Japanese literary imagination, Yu Xuanji—a celebrated poet, Daoist nun, and courtesan—remained a surprisingly neglected figure. This may be a reason to assume that the male/female dichotomy did not have as strong a hold in Japan as it did in China. It of course had a great deal to do with the fact that the Chinese government was much more bureaucratic than social, while the Japanese government was the opposite. See chapter 4 for more.

12. Ichiyō writes of her experience of using a library in a similarly self-effacing way, yet not without pride at being one of few educated and motivated women:

> Whenever I come and look, it is strange that, while there are many men, hardly any women are looking at books. That alone would still be all right. If I am told that I have made a mistake and have to rewrite the form when I have filled it out with the title, looked up the number of the issue, and brought it [to the circulation desk] amid many men, I blush and shudder. It is worse if I am looked at in the face and whispered to—I feel effaced, drenched with sweat, and unmotivated to examine books (in Nishio, ed., *Zenshaku Ichiyō nikki*, vol. 1, 84–85).

13. Nakajima points out that Sei Shōnagon's references to Chinese sources, which we will examine below, are found in secondary reference books, which puts in question the level of her mastery of Chinese. See Nakajima, "'Karafū ankoku jidai' no naka de," 78–79.

14. Kawaguchi, *Heianchō Nihon kanbungakushi no kenkyū*, vol. 2, 663.

15. Murasaki: *Murasaki shikibu nikki*, 453; *Diary of Lady Murasaki*, 14. Nakajima, "'Karafū ankoku jidai' no naka de," 78. Nakajima refers specifically to Section 146, "Utsukushiki mono" (Pretty things). *Makura no sōshi* is translated in Sei, *The Pillow Book of Sei Shōnagon*.

16. Mostow, "Mother Tongue and Father Script."

17. Kawaguchi, *Heian chō Nihon kanbungakushi no kenkyū*, vol. 2, 663.

18. Kawazoe Fusae discusses trade with Parhae in *Genji monogatari*, which forms the material background of the story, in "Kōekishi no naka no *Genji monogatari*," in Kawazoe, *Sei to bunka no Genji monogatari*, 110.

19. Murasaki, *Murasaki Shikibu shū*, 125.

20. Ibid., 96; Murasaki, *The Diary of Lady Murasaki*, 57.

21. Hirokawa, "*Genji monogatari* no rekishi jojutsu to setsuwa."

22. Murasaki: *Murasaki Shikibu nikki*, 501; *The Diary of Lady Murasaki*, 58.

23. Murasaki: *Murasaki Shikibu nikki*, 496; *The Diary of Lady Murasaki*, 54.

24. On the contrast, see Miyazaki, *Sei Shōnagon to Murasaki Shikibu*, for example, lists Higuchi Ichiyō, "Sao no shizuku" (Drops dripping from the rod, 1895), in which Ichiyō sympathizes with Sei Shōnagon for her unhappy familial circumstances; Yosano Akiko, "Sei Shōnagon no koto domo" (On Sei Shōnagon and other things, 1911), in which Akiko confesses that she does not like Sei; Shimazu Hisamoto, *Taiyaku Genji monogatari kōwa* (Lectures on *The Tale of Genji* in original and modern translation, 1950); and Shimizu Yoshiko, "Sei Shōnagon to Murasaki Shikibu" (Sei Shōnagon and Murasaki Shikibu, 1981), to name but a few.

25. Miyazaki, *Sei Shōnagon to Murasaki Shikibu*, 27–28. Among other texts, Miyazaki consulted the following: *Mumyō zōshi* (Anonymous text, 1200–1201; translated in Marra, "Mumyō zōshi"); *Kakaishō, Kachō yosei (yojō)* (Lingering sentiments of flora and fauna, 1472); *Kogetsushō* (An abridged account of the moon in the lake, 1673); *Genji monogatari hyōshaku* (*The Tale of Genji*: Commentary and annotations, 1854, 1861); and Shimazu Hisamoto, *Genji monogatari kōwa* (Lectures on *The Tale of Genji*). The titles that Miyazaki mentions, and many more on the subject, are found in "Sankō bunken nenpyō" (for works from 1868 on).

26. See Nihei, "*Genji monogatari* to *Go Kanjo.*"

27. Motoori Norinaga's *Shibun yōryō* has been incorporated into his best-known critical work on *Genji, Genji monogatari tama no ogushi* and is found in two different editions—*Motoori Norinaga zenshū*, vol. 4, and supplementary vol. 1. References here are based on the latter.

28. Hagiwara Hiromichi, in contrast, explored the structural aspects of *Genji monogatari* in his *Genji monogatari hyōshaku*, applying—important in our context—the terminology of Chinese fiction. Despite the anachronisms (*Genji monogatari* predates the works of Chinese fiction from which Hiromichi's critical theories were drawn), his commentary does justice to the dynamics of the narration, as well as alerting us to the translingual exchange that informed the book's structure.

29. Motoori, *Shibun yōryō*, 480.

30. Andō, *Shijo shichiron*, 13–16.

31. Motoori, *Shibun yōryō*, 457.

32. Ibid., 465.

33. Furuya, "Shogen," 1. In vol. 2 of *Edo jidai joryū bungaku zenshū* (Collected works of women's literature in the Tokugawa period). For the significance of this series in the study of "women's literature," see Ericson, "The Origins of the Concept of 'Women's Literature.'" Also see Ichikawa Seigaku, *Kinsei joryū shoka retsuden*, 59, for a similar statement.

34. Izuno, "Arakida Reijo nenpu" (Biographical chronology of Arakida Reijo), in Izuno, *Arakida Reijo monogatari shūsei*, 1313–1319.

35. Ichikawa Seigaku, *Kinsei joryū shoka retsuden* (Biographies of early modern women calligraphers), 7; also see 59–60.

36. Yosano, "Reijo shōsetsu shū o yo ni susumeru ni tsuite" (Upon recommending the collection of Reijo's stories), in Yosano, *Tokugawa jidai joryū bungaku*, vol. 1, 3. Joan Ericson refers to this collection as well in "The Origins of the Concept of 'Women's Literature.'"

37. Regrettably the collection has some editorial errors because it includes someone else's work.

38. Yosano, *Tokugawa jidai joryū bungaku*, 1.

39. Consult the following for further details: Arakida, "Keitoku Reijo ikō" (Posthumous manuscript of Keitoku Reijo); Yosano, "Arakida Reijo shōden" (Brief biography of Arakida Reijo), 1–12; Aida and Harada, "Arakida Reijo"; Izuno, *Arakida Reijo monogatari shūsei*, and "Arakida Reijo"; and Kado, "Motoori Norinaga to ronsōshita kyōretsuna kosei, Arakida Reijo," ch. 4 of Kado, *Edo joryū bungaku no hakken*, 113–157.

40. Emura, *Nihon shishi*, 82. The book is vol. 65 of *Shin Nihon koten bungaku taikei*.

41. Aida and Harada, "Arakida Reijo," 205.

42. Shōteki was so welcoming that he paid Reijo for the expenses of the ceremonial *haiku* composition, which normally would be paid by a new disciple; described in Arakida, "Keitoku Reijo ikō," 675, and Yosano, "Arakida Reijo shōden," 3.

43. Nomura, "Arakida shi *Tsuki no yukue* jo" (Preface to *The Whereabouts of the Moon*, by Ms. Arakida), 2.

44. Ibid.

45. Emura, "*Ike no mokuzu* jo" (Preface to *Weeds in the Pond*), 2. For more on the intellectual comradeship between Zhao Mingzheng and Li Yi'an, see Owen, *Remembrances*, ch. 5, 80–98. A concise biographical profile of Li and some of her poems can be found in Chang and Saussy, *Women Writers of Traditional China*, 89–99.

46. According to the colophon of *Kōchū kokubun sōsho*, the series was issued to celebrate the publisher's thirty-fifth anniversary and was prepared in consultation with many leading *kokubungaku* scholars of the time. Although the editor of the two volumes, Ikebe Yoshikata, complains of the historical distance among works in each volume—an inevitable consequence of making each book about equal in length (Ikebe, "Kaidai" [Bibliographical accounts], in vol. 12 of *Kōchū kokubun sōsho*, 1)—the inclusion of Reijo's work in the same volumes as such classical narratives seem to be less mechanical than deliberate and mindful of their similarities in style across time. For translations of the works mentioned here and not already cited, see the following: *Uji shūi monogatari*: Mills, *A Collection of tales from Uji*; *Kagerō nikki*: Fujiwara no Michitsuna no Haha: *The Gossamer Years* and *The Kagerō Diary; Tori-*

kaebaya monogatari: Willig, *The Changelings; Hōjōki:* Kamo no Chōmei, *The Ten Foot Square Hut.*

47. Cited in Yosano, "Arakida Reijo shōden," 5. Ogino's statement is, of course, not entirely accurate, given the existence of Akazome Emon, for one.

48. Emura, "*Ike no mokuzu* jo," 1. For translations of the texts mentioned, see McCullough, *The Great Mirror,* and Perkins, *The Clear Mirror.*

49. Nomura, "Arakida-shi *Tsuki no yukue* jo," 2.

50. Furuya, "Shogen," 3.

51. *Ayashi no yo gatari* (also transcribed as *Kaisei dan*) and "Fuji no iwaya" are included in Yosano, *Tokugawa jidai joryū bungaku,* vols. 2 and 1 respectively; in Furuya, *Edo jidai joryū bungaku zenshū,* vols. 2 and 1 respectively; and in Izuno, *Arakida Reijo monogatari shūsei.* For a translation of *Sou shen ji,* see DeWoskin and Crump, *In Search of the supernatural.*

52. Motoori, "*Nonaka no shimizu* tensaku," 372.

53. Ibid. Also see Ishimura, "Motoori Norinaga no bunshō hihyō ni tsuite," 49.

54. Cited in Ishimura, "Motoori Norinaga no bunshō hihyō ni tsuite," 49.

55. Cited in Furuya, "Shogen," iv.

56. Ishimura, "Motoori Norinaga no bunshō hihyō ni tsuite."

57. While there were a number of women poets, few women critics of poetry could be identified, and none was selected to compile imperially commissioned anthologies (*chokusen waka shū),* a mark of recognition for critics of the time. Women were not expected to exercise their intellectual faculties to draw theoretical arguments; they may have been adored as muses or shamanesses, who spontaneously tossed out inspiring words, but not as critics, who were expected to observe and judge—much less editors of anthologies, a task that requires skills in evaluating, classifying, and arranging poems in an appropriate sequence.

58. See Copeland, "The Meiji Woman Writer," 416, for the persistence of two typical gender-based evaluations of women's works: "She-Writes-Like-a-Man" (or She has "transcended her sex") and "She writes like women as she should."

59. See the following by Maeda Yoshi: "Kinsei joryū kanshijin Tachibana Gyokuran: Sono shōgai to sakuhin" (Tachibana Gyokuran, a female *kanshi* poet in early modern Japan: Her life and work); "Kinsei keishū shijin Hara Saihin to Bōsō no tabi: Hara Saihin kenkyū sono 1" (Hara Saihin, a female *kanshi* poet in early modern Japan and her trip to Bōsō: A study of Hara Saihin, no. 1); "Joryū bunjin Kamei Shōkin shōden: Kamei Shōkin kenkyū nōto 1" (Brief biography of Kamei Shōkin, a female literatus: A draft of a study of Kamei Shōkin, no. 1); "Shōkin shikō *Yōchō kō Kinoto i* o megutte: Kamei Shōkin kenkyū nōto 2" (On the private draft of *The Enticing Travel,* by Shōkin). Also see Shiba, "Kinsei nyonin bunjin fudoki 2."

60. Yu, *Dongying shixuan* (J. *Tōei shisen).* Sai Ki (Ch. Cai Yi) recounts the process of compilation of this anthology, in which he notes that the women's poetry volume was separately published in China. See Sai, "Yu Etsu [Ch. Yu Yue] to

ChūNichi kanseki no kōryū" (Yu Yue and the exchange of books in Chinese between China and Japan).

61. Fukushima, *Joryū*.

62. Maeda Yoshi, "Kinsei keishū shijin Hara Saihin to Bōsō no tabi," 14; Fukushima, "Kaisetsu" (Guide for readers), in Fukushima, *Joryū*, 327.

63. Saihin's primary career plan was to become a Confucian scholar. She consulted Matsuzaki Kōdō, who counseled her against the plan, suggesting that a female scholar would invite undue criticism, as the public would suspect that she lacked virtue. See Matsuzaki, *Kōdō nichireki* (Kōdō's diary), vol. 3, 18 (entries for Bunsei 12-nen, 11-gatsu 24-ka and 25-nichi [twenty-fourth and twenty-fifth days, eleventh month, twelfth year of Bunsei]). Kōdō also notes here that he lent Saihin vols. 22–28 of *Xiaocang shichao* (An abridged anthology from Xiaocang), a collection of Yuan Mei's poetry, as Saihin was keen on poetic composition.

64. The original lines are as follows:

君是真男誰敢輕 . . . .
我亦學製裁羅袿 . . . .
不願執帚為人妻
獨抱遺書辭陋屋 (in Aida and Harada, *Kinsei joryū bunjin den,* 16–17).

65. Ibid., 15; Maeda Yoshi, "Kinsei keishū shijin Hara Saihin no Bōsō no tabi," 17; Fukushima, "Kaisetsu," in Fukushima, *Joryū*, 324 and 327–328.

66. San'yō must have been impressed with Saihin's work, as he advised Ema Saikō later that she should also compose fifty-four poems to cover the contents of all the chapters of *Genji*, after she showed him a few poems that corresponded to some of them. This episode also suggests that San'yō viewed *Genji* as a whole, rather than a series of fragments, a view that differed from Norinaga's. Also important to note here is that Murasaki was a model and source of inspiration even for *kanshi* poets. The equation of the gender divide and the language divide prevents us from seeing some of *Genji*'s potentials.

67. In Nakamura Shin'ichirō, "Onna deshi tachi" (Female disciples), in Nakamura Shin'ichirō, *Rai San'yō to sono jidai* (Rai San'yō and his day), 63–81.

68. "Ema Saikō nenpu" (Biographical chronology of Ema Saikō), in Ema monjo (bunsho) hozonkai, *Ema Saikō raikan shū* (Collection of letters addressed to Ema Saikō), 317. Portrayals of the author are also found in the following: Aida, "Ema Saikō"; Fister, "Female *Bunjin*"; Bradstock and Rabinovitch, *An Anthology of Kanshi,* 297–298; and Ema, *Breeze through Bamboo,* 1–27 (introduction by Hiroaki Sato).

69. Ema monjo (bunsho) hozonkai, *Ema Saikō raikan shū,* 6–20, includes nine letters from Gyokurin addressed Saikō.

70. Ibid., 9.

71. Ibid., 30–31 and 34–35. See also Fukushima, "Keishū shijin Ema Saikō" (Ema Saikō, a female poet), 7.

72. Fukushima, "Kaisetsu," in Fukushima, *Joryū,* 7.

73. Cited in Nakamura Shin'ichiro, *Rai San'yō to sono jidai,* 69.

74. "Ema Saikō nenpu," in Ema monjo (bunsho) hozonkai, *Ema Saikō raikan shū,* 317.

75. Ibid., 318. For Jiang's networking with other artists, see P. J. Graham, *Tea of the Sages,* 108. Two poems by Jiang are included in Kikuchi Gozan (1769–1849), *Gozandō shiwa* (Talks on poetry by Gozandō), an anthology that selected more generously from the works of Japanese *kanshijin* and classical Chinese poets than from the contemporary Chinese. See Ibi, "Kasei-ki shidan to hihyōka: *Gozandō shiwa* ron" (Critics and the establishment of poetry in the Kasei period: Discussions on *Talks on Poetry by Gozandō*), 4.

76. Cited in Ibi, "Kasei-ki shidan to hihyōka," 70–71; Kado, *Ema Saikō shishū,* vol. 1, 1.

77. Ema, *Shōmu ikō,* vol. 2, 11; Kado, *Ema Saikō shishū,* vol. 2, 352. Some of the poems Jin Yi composed, along with a short biographical account, are in Chang and Saussy, *Women Writers of Traditional China,* 485–487.

78. San'yō's comments in their (supposed) entirety are found in Ema, *San'yō sensei hiten,* a reproduction of Saikō's handwritten copies of her poetry with San'yō's comments; it covers poems composed between 1814 and 1832, the year of San'yō's death. San'yō's comments are also included in the 1871 edition of Ema, *Shōmu iko,* and in Kado, *Ema Saikō shishū.* Sadako Ohki categorized San'yō's gender-related comments in a paper that I am not at liberty to quote. For her thesis, see Ohki, "Ema Saikō's Kanshi Poetry," 162.

79. 句句柔麗真女人口吻鬚眉男子百計模倣終不可得 (in Ema, *Sanyō sensei hiten,* 27).

80. 真女子語未經道處非慧心香口安能括破 (in ibid., 96).

81. 真女郎聲氣 (in ibid., 150).

82. In ibid., 17. In fact, San'yō's comparison with Lu Wuguan was owing not only to his acceptance of women of letters, but also to a better understanding in Japan of the diversity of Chinese literature (as we saw in chapter 2) and to the Japanese literati's own practice of the domestic arts that had inspired poets such as Lu You.

83. 豪爽不類女子語若出於鬚眉男子真傑作也 (in ibid., 74).

84. 不料閨閣有此史學今代鬚眉名家或不解此 (in ibid., 121).

85. Ibid.

86. Cited in Ema monjo (bunsho) hozonkai, *Ema Saikō raikan shū,* 55.

87. 自命不凡不如此何足以厠山陽社盟哉 (in Ema, *San'yō sensei hiten,* 260–261).

88. 三從總缺一生涯 and 惟恐人間疏懶婦強將風倣吾儕 (in ibid., 281). Hiroaki Sato translates this poem as "Describing Myself" (see Ema, *Breeze through Bamboo,* 115).

89. Noted by Kobayashi Tetsuyuki, "Kaidai," 356.

90. Ema: *San'yō sensei hiten*, 27–28; *Breeze through Bamboo*, 50.

91. 女史為人篤實温雅有卓識事父孝有故不笄筆硯自娛而又慨然有憂國之氣使鬚眉丈夫有愧色 ("Saikō joshi boshimei," in Ema, *Shōmu ikō*, 31). Also in Kado, *Ema Saikō shishū*, vol. 2, 563. Judging from her poems on drinking and on historical topics—such as the Nanjing Treaty (1842), which confirmed the humiliating status of Qing China vis-à-vis Britain and caused Saikō to be deeply concerned about Japan's future—Saikō loved to drink in the company of friends and discuss politics with them, just as male *kanshijin* would.

92. Kado, *Ema Saikō: Kasei-ki no joryū shijin*, 13.

93. Cited in ibid., 13–14.

94. While Saikō's poems record that she stayed overnight at San'yō's residence in Kyoto and that during her visit his wife kept out of their way except to serve tea and provide a lamp and other necessities, there is no confirmation of a sexual relationship between the two. San'yō, even after marrying a woman who was the domestic type, was candid enough to write of his admiration for Saikō and of his dissatisfaction with his wife, who was hardly as educated as Saikō. Saikō, for her part, composed a poem in which she suggested that she had made a mistake in planning a life that would leave her single. In another poem ("Renshi o tsumamite en'ō o utsu" [Throwing a lotus seed at a couple of waterfowl], in Ema, *San'yō sensei hiten*, 96), she envies a pair of waterfowl and tries to separate them by throwing a lotus seed at them; the action is often taken as a suggestion of her jealousy of San'yō's wife. Despite room for speculation on the possibility of a romantic liaison, many who knew both Saikō and San'yō explicitly confirmed that she remained proper. San'yō himself praised her for remaining "unblemished" in a letter written two years before his death.

95. Saikō's first—and posthumous—individual anthology was published in 1871.

96. See Mori Ōgai, "Rekishi sonomama to rekishi banare," 508–511. It is translated in Mori Ōgai, "History as It Is and History Ignored," 179–184.

97. Mori Ōgai, "Gyo Genki," 103. My translation. A translation of this entire story by David Dilworth can be found in Rimer and Dilworth, *The Historical Fiction of Mori Ōgai*, 185–198.

98. Mori Ōgai, "Gyo Genki," 103.

99. Ibid., 103–104.

100. See Yamazaki Kazuhide, "'Gyo Genki' ron" (Discussion of "Gyo Genki").

101. See Karashima, *Gyo Genki, Setsu Tō* (Yu Xuanji, Xue Tao), 80–83, where he annotates, translates, and interprets Yu Xuanji's "Qingshu ji Li Zian" (Love letter to Li Zian [Yi]) and expresses his frustration with what he perceives as Ōgai's desexualization of the female poet.

102. See Yoshikawa Hakki, *Satō Haruo no Shajin shū*, esp. 118–131.

103. Mori Ōgai, "Gyo Genki," 112.

104. Ibid., 106.

105. Ibid.

106. Ibid., 110. The poem by Yu Xuanji mentioned in this passage is translated by Stephen Owen as follows:

Cloud-covered hilltops fill my eyes,
I revel in springtime light,
here clearly ranged are the silver hooks
that grew at their fingertips.
I have bitter regret that skirts of lace
hide the lines of my poems,
and lifting my head in vain I covet
the publicly posted name (*An Anthology of Chinese Literature*, 510).

107. For an example of a critic who thought that Ōgai's Yu Xuanji was desexualized, see Moriyasu, "Ōgai to Gyo Genki" (Ōgai and Yu Xuanji).
108. Karashima, *Gyo Genki, Setsu Tō*, 123–126.
109. Citing the following poem by Yu Xuanji, Ōgai embellishes it with quasi-lesbian sentiments, which are not the established reading of the poem:

"Presented to the Girl Next Door"

Shying from the sun, I shade myself with gauze sleeves,
Made melancholy by spring, too listless to rise and put on my make-up.
It's easy to seek a priceless treasure—
But hard to find a man with a heart.
I let my tears fall unseen on my pillow,
I am secretly downcast among the flowers,
But if I can steal glances at Song Yu,
Why should I regret Wang Chang? (in Chang and Saussy, *Women Writers of Traditional China*, 75).

110. See Ogata, "'Gyo Genki' to 'atarashii onna'-tachi: Sei to bungaku e no kaigan no kiroku" ("Yu Xuanji" and "New Women": A record of awakening to sex and literature).
111. See, Kaneko Sachiyo, "'Atarashiki onna'-tachi no taitō: Nichi-Doku ni okeru josei kaihō to Mori Ōgai" (The emergence of "New Women": Mori Ōgai and women's liberation in Japan and Germany), and Watanabe Yoshio "Josei kaihō to Mori Ōgai: 'Saezuri' no haikei to igi" (Mori Ōgai and women's liberation: The background and significance of "Chirping").
112. Cited in Kaneko Sachiyo, "'Atarashiki onna,'" 44.
113. Mori Ōgai, "Yosano Akiko san ni tsuite." Ōgai's high esteem for Yosano Akiko is reminiscent of his comment on a legendary Chinese female poet, Xiaoqing; he scribbled the comment in the margins of his copy of her anthology. He

was impressed with Xiaoqing's lucid style, in comparison with which contemporary Japanese male writers appeared to him wishy-washy. For details, see Maeda Ai, "Ōgai no Chūgoku shōsetsu shumi" (Ōgai's penchant for Chinese fiction), and Sakaki, *Recontextualizing Texts*, ch. 3, esp. 170–171.

114. Translations of "Yasui fujin" and "Saigo no ikku" appear in Rimer and Dilworth, *The Historical Fiction of Mori Ōgai*, 255–270 and 209–221 respectively. Edwin McClellan has written an account of Shibue Io based upon Mori Ōgai's historical fiction. See McClellan, *Woman in the Crested Kimono*.

115. For more on my argument that Kurahashi's work speaks against the formula of recounting and assessing a given writer's work according to his or her life story, see Sakaki, "Kurahashi Yumiko."

116. For a translation of "Peach Blossom Spring," see Owen, *An Anthology of Chinese Literature*, 309–310. "Kōkan" is translated in Kurahashi, "Trade."

117. For a detailed account of the short story, see Sakaki, "Kurahashi Yumiko no 'Kōkan' o yomu: Shikai hon'an no hōhō o chūshin to shite" (A reading of "Trade" by Kurahashi Yumiko: Centering on the methodology of reworking Chinese horror stories).

118. "Kubi no tobu onna" is translated by Sakaki as "The Woman with the Flying Head." The original reads as follows:

> In Ch'in times, in the south, there lived the Headfall people whose heads were capable of flying about. This particular tribe conducted sacrifices which they named "Insect Fall," and from that ceremony they took their name.
>
> In Wu times, General Chu Huan took a captive maid from there, and each night when he had fallen asleep, her head would suddenly begin to fly about. It would fly in and out of the dog door or the skylight using its ears as wings; toward dawn it would return to its proper place—and this happened many, many times.
>
> Those around General Chu Huan found this very strange, and late one night they came with torches to observe. They found only the body of the girl, the head being missing. Her body was slightly chilled, and her breathing was labored. They covered the body completely with a counterpane, and near dawn the head returned, only to be balked by the bedcovers. Two or three times it attempted to get under the covers with no success; it finally fell to the floor. The sounds it made were piteous indeed, and the body's breathing became agitated. It appeared to be on the brink of death when the men pulled back the covers, and the head rose again to attach itself to the neck. A short while later, her respiration became tranquil.
>
> Chu Huan found their report very strange indeed and, being afraid to keep the girl in his household, released her and returned her to the tribe. Having examined this very carefully, all came to the conclusion that the flying head was a natural attribute of these people.
>
> At that time the commanding general of Yün-nan expeditions frequently came across such tribes. Once someone covered one of the bodies with an inverted

copper bowl, and the head being unable to reach its body, both parts perished (translated in DeWoskin and Crump, *In Search of the Supernatural*, as "The Tribe with Flying Heads," 147).

119. The ostensible mind/body split, manifested in the body of the Chinese woman in association with Japanese males, could be read as analogous to the Japanese reception of the Chinese intellectual heritage and Chinese material products respectively.

120. Translated as "An offering for the Cat" in Watson, *The Columbia Book of Chinese Poetry*, 342–343.

121. For a translation of *Towazu gatari*, see Go-Fukakusa in Nijō, *Confessions of Lady Nijō*.

122. Kurahashi, *Shunposhion*, 302.

123. Ibid., 309.

124. A case in point is Higuchi Ichiyō's relationship with Nakarai Tōsui, who coached her in stylistics. He advised her to learn how to write in a feminine style, rather than assuming that her writing was by default feminine because she was a woman. This suggests that he knew gender was cultural rather than anatomical. She was compelled to leave his tutelage because of rumors of romance between them. See Seki Reiko, "Fude motsu hito e."

125. For more on engendered territories in the field of literary production in modern Japan and Kurahashi's position therein, see Sakaki, "Kurahashi Yumiko's Negotiation with the Fathers."

Chapter 4: The Transgressive Canon?

1. It is known that Matsuzaki Kōdō discouraged Hara Saihin from opening a private school (*juku*) to teach the Chinese classics in 1829, when she was thirty-one years old. See Fukushima, "Kaisetsu" (Guide to readers), 324–325.

2. As noted above, Saikō's paintings were sold via San'yō, but the artist did not rely on the sales as a primary source of income. In a notable exception, the feudal lord of Niwa gave Reijo an official position, though it was not of a regular office but more honorary in nature. See Izuno, "Arakida Reijo," 115.

3. This is not to suggest that there were no men of letters in the "real" world. Moreover, there have been unemployed men of letters through the ages in Japan, as well as in China, who have upheld the purist vision of the canon as an inherent value regardless of its monetary or social value.

4. Yoshida Ken'ichi points out that Akutagawa Ryūnosuke was able to read *kanshibun*, which his Japanese teacher in German could not read. Yoshida uses this anecdote to differentiate generations of readers. See Yoshida Ken'ichi, "Nihongo" (Japanese language), 264. We might also recall Tanizaki Jun'ichirō's limited mastery of the genre (noted in chapter 2).

5. For a study of modernity and the "national canon," see Tomi Suzuki, "Gender and Genre."

6. See Maeda Ai, "Meiji shoki bunjin no chūgoku shōsetsu shumi" (The early Meiji literati's penchant for Chinese fiction), 298.

7. Ōmachi Keigetsu observed that *kanshi* peaked in popularity in the early Meiji and that the genre was revitalized in the second decade of the Meiji (1878–1887), after a period of political unrest. Cited in Ibi, "Meiji kanshi no shuppatsu" (The beginning of Meiji *kanshi*), 5. The article is particularly useful in its account of Mori Shuntō. See also Inoguchi, *Nihon kanbungakushi,* 507–577, for an overview of major *kanshi* poets in the Meiji.

8. For a modern translation with annotations, see Takezoe, *San'un kyōu nikki: Meiji kanshijin no Shisen no tabi* (A diary of clouds around the bridge, the rain over the valley: A Meiji *kanshi* poet's trip to Sichuan). For the ambiguous position of the author and narrator of the text in terms of enfranchisement, see Sakaki, "Transnational Communications in the Classical Language in the Age of Nationalism."

9. Brief excerpts from Lu You's and Fan Chengda's travelogues, with biographical information on the authors, can be found in Strassberg, *Inscribed Landscapes,* 205–212 and 213–218. We saw in chapter 3 that Ema Saikō was compared to Lu You.

10. Sano Masami's "Kaidai," attached to *Dongying shixuan,* relates Takezoe's involvement in the compilation of the volume. For a brief profile of Takezoe, a few of his poems, and an example of his composition in prose, see Kanda Kiichirō, *Meiji kanshibun shū,* 46–48, 247–255, and 410.

11. For a profile of Suematsu and selections of his poetry, see Kanda Kiichirō, *Meiji kanshibun shū,* 416–417 and 77–79.

12. See Suematsu, *The Tale of Genji,* 15–16.

13. See Kanda Kiichiro, *Meiji kanshibun shū,* 418, for a biographical sketch of Nagai Kagen and 87–89 for a sampling of his poetry. Also see Seidensticker, *Kafū, the Scribbler,* for references to Kagen.

14. Raiseikaku was the name of Kagen's residence, which he built in the Chinese mode (his son Kafū demolished it after his death in order to build a European-style house on the premises); Kagen also used "Raiseikaku" as one of his pseudonyms.

15. *Doitsu nikki* covers Ōgai's stay in Germany immediately after the time related in *Kōsei nikki. Zai Toku ki* is imagined to have been kept concurrently. See Nakai, *Ōgai ryūgaku shimatsu,* 50–52, for a discussion of the extensive editing that must have taken place in the writing of *Doitsu nikki.*

16. Natsume, *Bungakuron,* 7–8.

17. The anthology bears two epithets: one, a *waka* from *Man'yō shū;* the other, a five-character couplet from a poem by Su Shi. See Mori, *Omokage,* 2.

18. 達德國歌倫余解德國語来此得免聾啞之病可謂快矣 (Mori Ōgai, *Kōsei nikki,* 83).

19. See Sakaki, *Recontextualizing Texts,* ch. 3, for references in *Gan* to university students' readings of Zhang Chao's *Yuzhu xinzhi, Xiaoqing Zhuan,* and *Jin Ping Mei.* For translations of *Gan,* see Mori Ōgai: *Wild Geese* and *Wild Goose.*

20. See Maeda Ai, "Ōgai no Chūgoku shōsetsu shumi," 76. For a translation of *Vita sekusuarisu*, see Mori Ōgai, *Vita Sexualis*.

21. See Maeda Ai, "Meiji shonen no dokusha zō" (The image of the reader in the early Meiji), 112.

22. For the *Hong lou meng* translation, see Kōda, *Kōrōmu*, and for *Shuihu zhuan*, see Kōda, *Suikoden*. Both are in the literature (*bungaku*) section (preceded by the Confucian classics and history [*keishi*] section) of the series. The publication of the series—both *Kokuyaku kanbun taisei* and its sequel—tells an ambiguous story about the Japanese reception of Chinese literature in the Taishō period. While the breadth of the works included and the size of the series suggest that the publisher anticipated an enthusiastic reception, the very fact that a Japanese translation was needed is an indication of the Japanese loss of proficiency in Chinese. In a different perspective, a sizable audience had emerged out of the hitherto illiterate population.

23. Kōda, "Ko-Shina bungaku ni okeru shōsetsu no chii ni tsuite," 39.

24. Shiba Shirō received financial support from the Iwasaki family to visit the United States to study. He first arrived in San Francisco in 1879 to study at Pacific Business College, then went to Boston to audit some courses at Harvard, and finally went to Philadelphia to enroll in the Wharton School for a Bachelor of Finance degree from the University of Pennsylvania. See Ōnuma, "Zaibei jidai no Tōkai Sanshi: Nimai no shashin kara" (Tōkai Sanshi in his days in the United States: From two photographs).

25. In the early Meiji works of *caizi jiaren xiaoshuo* boasted an unprecedented popularity, which may be accounted for by the fact that Meiji Japan witnessed the emergence of social conditions similar to premodern China's, as Maeda Ai points out in "Gesaku bungaku to *Tōsei shosei katagi*" (Comical literature and *The Essence of Contemporary Students*), 123. The Chinese-style civil service examination had never been firmly rooted in the Japanese bureaucracy, despite its early introduction, until the Meiji era. The loosening of the rigid social hierarchy left young intellectuals in an unreliable yet flexible world in which they had to prove their talent or perish. Thus it was in a sense natural that romance fiction involving scholars and beauties became popular in the early Meiji, including Tsubouchi Shōyō's *Ichidoku santan: Tōsei shosei katagi* (Once read, thrice praised: The essence of contemporary students, 1885), and *Setchūbai*, a political novel. (Shōyō is discussed below.) The title *Kajin no kigū* also suggests its intended genre.

26. Xiao, *Wenxuan*, 638–640.

27. *Kajin no kigū* nonetheless displays signs of modernity that go beyond the expectations of the genre. There are moments in which it goes beyond the rhetorical requirements governing plot and characterization. When Ms. Parnell, a historical activist in the Irish Independence Movement in the United States, humbly describes herself as a woman who has passed her prime, Tōkai Sanshi demurs, challenging the conventional expression *san-go, ni-hachi*—three-five (that is, fifteen) and two-eight (that is, sixteen)—the years at which women were considered most

attractive. This is not an exclusively realistic observation but an observation justified in rhetorical terms, for the moon is full when it is fifteen days old and nearly full when it is sixteen days old. Women were often associated with the moon, and hence they had to be fifteen or sixteen years old to be at their most beautiful. Tōkai Sanshi, however, maintains that age is not an issue in the discussion of female beauty. He claims that he sees beauty in women's intelligence, experience, and social awareness, rather than in a youthful physical appearance, as the former are the qualities that make women delightful conversational companions. He then lists all the aging or aged women from East and West who were known to be beautiful: Helen of Troy, Cleopatra, Wu Zetian, the Queen Mother of the West, and Mrs. En'ya in *Chūshingura* (1748; translated in Takeda, Miyoshi, and Namiki, *Chūshingura [The Treasury of Loyal Retainers]*, 1971). Though the choices might not be readily accepted by every reader, as many of these women were known to have caused their countries trouble rather than to have delighted their friends, the logic is flattering to women and thus strikes us as modern.

28. Keene, *Dawn to the West*, 85–86.

29. See Fujikawa Shin'ichi, "Kajin no kigū to Yusenkutsu" (*Unexpected Encounters with Beauties* and *Excursion to the Cave of the Immortals*), and Yanagida, "Kajin no kigū to Tōkai Sanshi" (*Unexpected encounters with Beauties* and Tōkai Sanshi), 392.

30. Tōkai Sanshi, *Kajin no kigū* (1885), vol. 1, 8. All the translations are mine unless otherwise noted.

31. Wang Zhaojun was a beautiful lady-in-waiting at the court of Emperor Yuan of the Han dynasty. Because she failed to bribe a painter, he did not do justice to her unparalleled beauty in a portrait; on the basis of the portrait, the emperor gave her as a gift to the Xiongnu chieftain. Much to the emperor's regret, he found her to be an extraordinary beauty after making the decision. Yang Guifei, as we know, was a consort of Emperor Xuanzong of the Tang dynasty, who indulged his lust for her to the extent of neglecting his duties and bringing on the catastrophic An Lushan Rebellion. See Sakaki, "Archetypes Unbound," for more.

32. 楊柳折一枝, 梨花露含 and 紅蓮浴緑池 (Tōkai Sanshi, *Kajin no kigū* [1885], vol. 1, 10).

33. Note that two levels of discourse coexist in the text. When the protagonist talks directly to one of the beauties, Kōren of Ireland, he compares her to Helen of Troy and Jane, Queen of Scotland— 妃蓮蘇皇 —apparently in consideration of the reading knowledge of his addressee. Then the author adds a parenthetical annotation to each of the references—"Greek beauty" or "Queen of Scotland who stood out in beauty and intelligence"—presumably for the sake of his readers in 1880s Japan.

34. Tōkai Sanshi says the following:

有美一人
清楊宛兮

邂逅相遇
週我願兮 (Tōkai Sanshi, *Kajin no kigū* [1885], vol. 1, 11).

The original poem in *Shijing*, which is slightly different (艶 for 宛) and longer, is entitled "Yeyou wancao" 野有蔓草 and can be found in Yoshikawa Kōjirō, *Shikyō kokufū*, vol. 2, 84–86.

35. Tōkai Sanshi, *Kajin no kigū* (1885), vol. 1, 11. *Kajin no kigū* uses classical language even for speeches and dialogues: the characters speak as they write.

36. 幽谷蕙蘭空懐香
年年全節待鳳凰 (ibid., 13).

37. Ibid.

38. Ibid., vol. 2, 26–27.

39. Greenblatt, *Marvelous Possessions*.

40. Tōkai Sanshi, *Kajin no kigū* (1885), vol. 2, 24–25.

41. Cited in Hata and Yamada *Kindai I,* 68. It would be unjust to Morita Shiken, however, if we took him to be invariably antagonistic to modern usages of *kanbun*. (As a comment attached to the quotation we cite suggests, Morita was not expected to make a statement for the "pro-compromise school" *[setchū-ha]*.) See "Jibun hyōron" (A critique of current matters). Elsewhere Morita says that he was delighted to see a revival of interest in *kanbun* among the youth, as Chinese compounds could be used for equivalents of new concepts, and as a knowledge of Chinese words was essential even in creating neologisms (in *Kokumin no tomo* [The nation's friend]; cited in "Jibun hyōron").

42. Etō, "Kindai sanbun no keisei to zasetsu" (The formation and demise of modern prose), 26.

43. Seki Ryōichi, "Kindai bungaku no keisei: Dentō to kindai" (The formation of modern literature: Tradition and modernity), 4–5. The translation of the line from *Authoritative Discourses* (Wenzhang jingguo zhi daye; 文章經國大業) is based on Stephen Owen's translation of "Discourse on Literature" [the title of a section of the work in which the line appears] in *Readings in Chinese Literary Thought*, 68. See also Ochi, "'Seiji to bungaku' no tansho" (The inception of the political novel), 126, for a similar argument.

44. See Matsui, "*Kajin no kigū* to 'Yōkō nikki': Shiba Shirō Tani Tateki no seiji ishiki" (*Unexpected Encounters with Beauties* and "Diary of a Visit to the West": The political awareness of Shiba Shirō and Tani Tateki). See also Inoue Hiroshi, "Tōkai Sanshi Shiba Shirō no *Kajin no kigū* to *Tōyō no kajin*" (*Unexpected Encounters with Beauties* and *Beauties in the East,* by Tōkai Sanshi, a.k.a. Shiba Shirō), for another byproduct of this trip. *Beauties in the East* is also an allegory; it was prefaced by Suehiro Tetchō and published in 1888.

45. See Satō Tsuyoshi, "Kindai bungaku shi kōsō no shomondai: Shuppatsuten to shite no seiji shōsetsu" (Problems with the prospectus of a history of modern literature: The political novel as a starting point).

46. Keene, *Dawn to the West*, 86. The political novel which Keene refers, to *Inspiring Instances of Statesmanship,* is *Keikoku bidan* (1883), by Yano Ryūkei (1850–1931).

47. Maeda Ai, "Meiji rekishi bungaku no genzō: seiji shōsetsu no baai" (The original image of Meiji historical fiction: A case of the political novel), 14–15.

48. See Asukai, "Seiji shōsetsu to 'kindai' bungaku: Meiji seiji shōsetsu saihyōka no tameni" (The political novel and "modern" literature: For the sake of reevaluation of the Meiji political novel), 76.

49. In the following I discuss critics mostly different from the ones Matsui mentions in "*Kajin no kigū* to 'Yōkō nikki.'"

50. Cited in Keene, *Dawn to the West,* 86–87.

51. This should not be taken, however, to mean that Kimura was consistently negative about *seiji shōsetsu.* Matsui cites from Kimura's "Seiji shōsetsu wa seinen Nihon no koe" (1934), in which he praises the genre of the political novel as a sign of growth in people's interest in politics, rather than as a sign of underdeveloped literature. See Matsui, "*Kajin no kigū* to 'Yōkō nikki,'" 212–213.

52. Cited in Keene, *Dawn to the West,* 85–86.

53. See, for example, Kōda, "Meiji shoki bungaku-kai" (The literary world of the early Meiji), 308, in which *Kajin no kigū* earns a brief mention.

54. Asukai, "Seiji shōsetsu to 'kindai' bungaku," 72–73.

55. It should also be noted that *kanbun kakikudashi-tai,* and not the so-called indigenous Japanese, was used for legal documents and discussions of stately and other public affairs of the modern nation-state of Japan.

56. However, Ochi notes that *Kajin no kigū* was probably so difficult for ordinary readers to comprehend that it was "vernacularized" as *Tsūzoku Kajin no kigū* ("Suehiro Tetchō," 140). Ochi further elaborates on the mass audience's desire for *seiji shōsetsu,* as well as on stylistic compromises between the audience and the highly ideologically minded authors ("Seiji shōsetsu to taishū" [The political novel and the mass audience]).

57. Sansom, *The Western World and Japan,* 414.

58. Cited in Maeda Ai, "Meiji shonen no dokusha zō," 117.

59. Interestingly enough, in the Japanese intellectual reception of Chinese literature, it was the so-called "high" literature—such as the Confucian classics, historical records, and Tang poetry—that was more often orally received than the "low" literature, such as ghost stories and romances. Unlike classical literary works, passages from the latter stories were not to be read aloud, especially in public, for the sake of propriety. Also, Meiji intellectuals seem to have found it more difficult to read Chinese vernacular fiction than the classics owing to a lack of institutional training. See Maeda Ai, "Ōgai no Chūgoku shōsetsu shumi," 76. These factors made the "low" literature a purely written (or "read") discourse, while "high" literature remained a relatively oral (or "aural") discourse. "High" literature occupied the public space, which was then the very site on which literature as performance took place.

60. Keene, *Dawn to the West,* 85. "Liang Ch'i-ch'ao" is "Liang Qichao" in *ping'yin.*

61. For more on late imperial Chinese political novels, see Willcock, "Meiji Japan and the Late Qing Political Novel."

62. Hsia, "Yen Fu and Liang Ch'i-ch'ao as Advocates of New Fiction," 235–236. See also Hsü, "*Shin gihō dai 4 satsu yakusai no* 'Kajin kigū' [Jiaren qiyu] *ni tsuite*" (On *Unexpected Encounters with Beauties* translated in the fourth issue of *Qingyi bao*); and Yeh, "Zeng Pu's Niehai Hua as a Political Novel," 135–136, for some of the circumstances of Liang Qichao's translation.

63. Hsü, "*Shingihō dai 4 satsu yakusai no Kajin kigū [Jiaren qiyu] no tsuite.*"

64. Daitō Hyōshi [Tsuchida Taizō], *Tsūzoku Kajin no kigū, zen.* A sequel, *Tsūzoku Kajin no kigū, zokuhen,* also prefaced by Hattori Seiichi, was published by Kakuseisha (Tokyo) in 1887. There is at least another volume that purports to be a "vulgarized" version of *Kajin no kigū: Tsūzoku Kajin no kigū,* by Sekishin Tetchōshi. It was originally published by Keihan dōmei shoshi and distributed by Shinshindō (Osaka) in 1887. This version bears little resemblance to the original, however, in terms of either style or plot. It is about romantic and antagonistic relationships among characters, all Japanese, who embody such notions as the police, the civil rights movement, and freedom. The language is that of *kusazōshi,* and the text is not accompanied by commentaries. See Ochi, "Seiji shōsetsu to taishū," 62–63, for more.

65. Kanro Junki points out that the Hattori version takes the War of Independence not as a war between two nations but one between a colony and a colonizer; this position helps establish a more people-oriented (rather than government-oriented) political stance. See "Mō hitotsu no *Kajin no kigū*: Aruiwa mō hitotsu no *Tsūzoku Kajin no kigū*" (Another *Unexpected Encounters with Beauties*: Or, another *Vulgar version of Unexpected Encounters with Beauties*).

66. Daitō Hyōshi, *Tsūzoku kajin no kigū, zen,* postscript; no page number given.

67. See Kurata, *Chosakuken shiwa* (Historical tales about the copyright), 118–122, for a discussion of the trials.

68. Rose, *Authors and Owners,* 2–3.

69. Occasionally two-page wide illustrations are inserted; each is accompanied by a caption in *kanbun kundoku-tai* (like the main text). Given the expected high intellectual level of the audience, illustrations were less for the explication of a complex plot than for the visual presentation of foreign landscapes, manners, and customs.

70. Tōkai Sanshi, "Jijo" (author's preface), in Tōkai, *Kajin no kigū* (1885), 2–3.

71. Ōnuma Toshio, who studies partial manuscripts owned by Keio University Library, suggests that there were at least four versions of the manuscript: Shiba Shirō's original draft, which he wrote soon after returning to Japan and which is without many (if not all) *kanshi;* one with instructions on how to insert *kanshi;* one with most of the *kanshi* and with some repetitive passages, copied partly in a cus-

tom-made writing pad that has Takahashi Taika's studio name printed on it; and one with all the *kanshi* inserted, including those composed by the four nationalists on the occasion discussed above. See Ōnuma, "'Kajin no kigū' seiritsu kōshō josetsu" (An introduction to a historical study of the creation of *Unexpected Encounters with Beauties*). Kinoshita Hyō lists many references to the novel that suspect that Shiba Shirō, who published few other literary works and did not demonstrate a mastery of *kanshibun* in them, was not the author. See Kinoshita Hyō, "*Kajin no kigū* no shi to sono sakusha" (The poems in *Unexpected Encounters with Beauties* and their authors).

72. See Nakamura Shin'ichirō, Ōchō bungaku no sekai (The world of courtly literature).

73. Hori wrote several stories inspired by classical Japanese literature, including "Kagerō no nikki" (A drakefly's diary, 1927) and "Hototogisu" (A cuckoo, 1929); two sequential renditions of the classical female memoir *Kagerō nikki*; "Obasute" (Disposing of elderly women, 1940), a story inspired by another memoir, *Sarashina nikki*; and "Arano" (Wilderness, 1941), based upon a story in *Konjaku monogatari* (for partial translations, see Brower, "The *Konzyaku Monogatarisyu*," and Ury, *Tales of Times Now Past*). Hori also wrote a monograph on Du Fu's poetry, *To Ho shi nōto* (Notes on Du Fu).

74. Among these, see Akutagawa, "To Shishun" (1920; translated in Akutagawa, "Tu Tzu-ch'un") and his travelogues from China (e.g., "Shanhai yūki" and "Pekin nikki shō" [translated in Akutagawa, "Travels in China"]).

75. Nakamura Shin'ichirō, *Kūchū teien*, 374.

76. Nakamura's comparison of designs in poetry with those in gardening is evident in his use of yet another term for "garden," *niwa*, which appears in *Shijin no niwa*.

77. Nakamura Shin'ichirō, *Kūchū teien*, 394.

78. Ibid.

79. The episode is originally related by Gensei in his "Minobu michi no ki" (An account of travels in Minobu). According to the text, Yuanyun was proficient in Japanese, having lived in the country for a long time. See Sano, "Kaidai," 11. For the Gensei-Yuanyun poems, see Gensei and Chen, *Gengen shōwa shū* (Collection of poems exchanged between Gen/Yuan and Gen/Yuan). See also Gensei, *Sōzanshū* (translated in Gensei, *Grass Hill*).

80. Nakamura Shin'ichirō, *Kumo no yukiki*, 384.

81. Nakamura does not note in this text another manifestation of the enfranchisement: Yuanyun wrote a preface to Gensei's anthology, *Sōzanshū*. See Sano, "Kaidai," 5.

82. Ilya Ehrenburg was born into an upper-middle-class Jewish family in Kiev in 1891; he immigrated to France in 1908, stayed in Paris until 1917, and returned to Russia in 1925. See Rollberg, "Il'ia Grigor'evich Erenburg."

83. Nakamura Shin'ichirō, *Kumo no yukiki*, 384.

84. Ibid.

85. In *Sakushi shikō* (Essence of poetic composition, 1783), Yamamoto Hoku-zan claims that Yuan Hongdao conceptualizes *xingling;* thus he is revered by some eighteenth-century Japanese Sinophiles, in contrast to Li Yulin (Li Panlong), whom Ogyū Sorai and the rest of the pro-Tang Sinophiles held as the model. See Matsushita, *Edo jidai no shifū shiron: Min Shin no shiron to sono sesshu* (Poetic trends and theories in the Tokugawa era: Ming-Qing theories on poetry and its reception).

86. Nakamura Shin'ichirō, *Kumo no yukiki*, 386. As Nakamura also notes in passing (p. 385), it was Chen Yuanyun who first informed Gensei of Yuan Hongdao's poetry when they first met in 1659. See Sano, "Kaidai," 4, which quotes both Gensei's letter to Chen Yuanyun and an account of Gensei in Emura, *Nihon shishi*, vol. 3. See also Ueno, *Ishikawa Jōzan Gensei*, 185, for an annotation to one of Gensei's poems rhyming with one by Yuan Hongdao and a similar retelling of Gensei's encounter with Yuan.

87. For example, Goethe is represented as 歌徳 and Eckermann as 愛克曼.

88. See Said, "Intellectual Exile: Expatriates and Marginals," chapter 3 of Said, *Representation of the Intellectual*, 47–64, for an explication of the complex position-ing of intellectual expatriates.

Coda

1. Bal, *Double Exposure*, 49.

2. Bal, *Quoting Caravaggio*, 264.

3. For a translation, see Tanizaki, *Captain Shigemoto's Mother*. All translations here are mine.

4. Robert Borgen's *Sugawara no Michizane and the Early Heian Court* offers the most extensive biographical account in English of Michizane, both as a histor-ical figure and a mythical one in his afterlife.

5. Tanizaki, *Shōshō Shigemoto no haha*, 248.

6. Translated in Tanizaki, "The Bridge of Dreams."

7. Translated in Tanizaki, "A Portrait of Shunkin." I should alert the reader to the fact that Shunkin is a fictional construct, and thus the parallel between "Gyo Genki" and this story is only partial. In fact Tanizaki deliberately and effectively ap-propriates the format of biography used by Ōgai: Tanizaki's narrator frequently draws upon a source entitled "Mozuya Shunkin den" (A biography of Mozuya Shunkin), which is his fabrication. Its style is the typical *kanbun kundoku-tai*, in-formed by both Chinese and Japanese. The material aspects of the publication also manifest hybridity, albeit of a different kind: the text is printed on traditional Japa-nese handmade paper *(washi)* and is typed using the modern printing technology of *4-gō katsuji* (no. 4 letter).

8. Tanizaki, "Shunkin shō," 530.

9. Tanizaki, "Yume no ukihashi," 148.

10. The original compound is 鳶飛魚躍.

11. 洗硯魚吞墨 (in Tanizaki, "Yume no ukihashi," 154–155).

12. For a translation, see Takeda, Miyoshi, and Namiki, *Sugawara and the Secrets of Calligraphy*.

13. For a translation, see Tanizaki, "The Reed Cutter."

14. English translations of "Chibi fu" and its sequel, "Hou chibi fu," have been published as "Red Cliff I" and "Red Cliff II" in Strassberg, *Inscribed Landscapes*, 183–188. An English translation of "Pipa xing" has been published in Levy, *Chinese Narrative Poetry*, 133–138.

15. 蜻蛉 (drakefly); 陽炎 (mirage).

Glossary

Abe no Nakamaro 安部仲麻呂
ainoko 合の子
Akazome Emon 赤染衛門
Amenomori Hōshū 雨森芳洲
Andō Tameakira 安藤為章
Anzai Fuyue 安西冬衛
Aoki Masaru 青木正兒
Arakida Reijo 荒木田麗女
Ariwara no Narihira 在原業平
Asano no Katori 朝野鹿取
"Ashikari" 蘆刈
Asō Isoji 麻生磯次
Asukai Masamichi 飛鳥井雅道
Ayashi no yo gatari 怪世談
Bai Juyi 白居易
Bai Letian 白樂天
baihua 白話
Baishi 梅颺
Ban Gu 班固
Ban Zhao 班昭
Benshi shi 本事詩
benzaiten 辯財天
bibun 美文
Bimuyu 比目魚
"Birōdo no yume" 天鵝絨の夢
Blue Dragon King 青龍王
bunbō aigan 文房愛玩
bungo 文語
Bunka shūrei shū 文華秀麗集
Cai Yi 蔡毅
caizi jiaren xiaoshuo 才子佳人小說 (J. *saishi kajin shōsetsu*)
Cao Dajia 曹大家

Cao Pi 曹丕
Cao Zhi 曹植
Cen Shen 岑參
Chajing 茶經
Chang'an 長安
"Changhenge" 長恨歌
Chaoyun 朝雲
"Chasho nyūmon: Kissa shōshi" 茶書入門喫茶小史
Chen Yuanyun 陳元贇 (J. Chin Gen'in)
"Chibi fu" 赤壁賦
Chikamatsu Monzaemon 近松門左衛門
Chin Gen'in (Ch. Chen Yuanyun 陳元贇)
Chō Keikyō (張惠卿 Ch. Zhang Hui-qing)
chosakusha ken shuppannin 著作者兼出版人
Chōsen tsūshinshi 朝鮮通信使
"Chōsen zakkan" 朝鮮雑観
chū 中
Chūgi Suikoden 忠義水滸伝
Chūka chasho 中華茶書
Daitō Hyōshi 大東萍士
Dankō Reigan ki 斷鴻零雁記
Dianlun 典論
dōbō shū 同朋衆
Doitsu nikki 独逸日記
Dōkyō 道鏡
Dong Hu 董狐
Dong Jin 東晉
Dongpo rou 東坡肉

Dongying shixuan 東瀛詩選 (J. *Tōei shisen*)

eibutsu shi 詠物詩 (Ch. *yongwu shi*)

Eiga monogatari 榮華物語

eikai shi 詠懷詩 (Ch. *yonghuai shi*)

Ema Saikō 江馬細香

Emura Hokkai 江村北海

Engi 延喜

Etō Jun 江藤淳

Fan Chengda 范成大

Fang He Ting 放鶴亭

Feitouman 飛頭蠻

Fengtian 奉天

Fuji no iwaya 藤のいは屋

Fujii Chikugai 藤井竹外

Fujin kōron 婦人公論

Fujiwara no Fuyutsugu 藤原冬嗣

Fujiwara no Kintō 藤原公任

Fujiwara no Kiyokawa 藤原清河

Fujiwara no Seika 藤原惺窩

Fujiwara no Shōshi 藤原彰子

Fujiwara no Tametoki 藤原為時

Fujiwara no Teika 藤原定家

fujo dōmō 婦女童蒙

Fun'ya no Akitsu 文屋秋津

Fun'ya no Yasuhide 文屋康秀

Furukawa Koshōken 古川虎笑軒

Fūryū Shidōken den 風流志道軒傳

"Gabō ki" 畫舫記

Gan Bao 干寶

Gao Qingqiu 高青邱 (Qi 啓)

"Gaotang fu" 高唐賦

gazoku setchū-tai 雅俗折衷体

Ge Ling 葛嶺

"Gen jidai no zatsugeki" 元時代の雑劇

Gengen shōwa shū 元元唱和集

"Gengo-shi" 源語詩

Genji monogatari hyōshaku 源氏物語評釋

Genji monogatari kōwa 源氏物語講話

Genjin zatsugeki josetsu 元人雑劇序説

"Genjō Sanzō" 玄奘三蔵

Gensei 元政

Go Sankei 吳三桂 (Ch. Wu Sangui)

Gōdanshō 江談抄

Gokyō 五經

Gozandō shiwa 五山堂詩話

guixiu 閨秀 (J. *keishū*)

Guo Moruo 郭沫若

gushi 古詩

Guwenci-pai 古文辭派 (J. Kobunji-ha)

Guxiaoshuo goushen 古小說鉤沈

Gyo Genki 魚玄機 (Ch. Yu Xuanji)

Haikai shinsen 俳諧新選

Haku Rakuten 白樂天

Hakubundō 博文堂

Hakubunkan Kokubun sōsho 博文堂國文叢書

hakuwa shōsetsu 白話小說 (Ch. *baihua xiaoshuo*)

Hamamatsu chūnagon monogatari 濱松中納言物語

Hanaurushi 花漆

Hangzhou 杭州

Hankou 漢口

Hanshu 漢書

Hara Kosho 原古處

Hara Saihin 原采蘋

Harusame monogatari 春雨物語

Haruyama Yukio 春山行夫

Hattori Nankaku 服部南郭

Hattori Seiichi (服部誠一; Bushō 撫松)

Hayashi Razan 林羅山

Heyang 河陽

Higuchi Ichiyō 樋口一葉

Hiraga Gennai 平賀源内

Hiratsuka Raichō 平塚雷鳥

"Hitōban" 飛頭蠻

Hōjōki 方丈記

Honchō ichiniin isshu 本朝一人一首

Honchō reisō 本朝麗藻

Honchō Suikoden 本朝水滸伝

Hong lou meng 紅樓夢

Hori Tatsuo 堀辰雄
Hou Hanshu 後漢書
Huang Tingjian 黃庭堅
Huizong 徽宗
Ichikawa Kansai 市川寬齋
Ike no mokuzu 池の藻屑
Ike no Taiga 池大雅
Imakagami 今鏡
"Inaba Seikichi sensei" 稲葉清吉先生
Ingen 隱元 (Ch. Yinyuan)
Ise monogatari 伊勢物語
Ishikawa Jōzan 石川丈山
Ishizaki Matazō 石崎又造
Issan Ichinei 一山一寧
"Itansha no kanashimi" 異端者の悲
   しみ
Jia Sidao 賈似道
Jiang Yige 江藝閣
Jiangsu 江蘇
Jiaren qiyu 佳人奇遇
Jiezi yuan huazhuan 芥子園畫傳
Jifang Yuan 集芳園
jijo 自叙
"Jijutsu" 自述
Jin Yi 金逸
Jing-Feng Line 京奉線
Jing-Han Line 京漢線
Jing Tai shilu 靖臺實錄
Jin Ping Mei 金瓶梅
jiu cha lun 酒茶論
joryū 女流
josō buntai 女裝文體
Jūben jūgi zu 十便十宜圖
Kachō yosei (yojō) 花鳥餘情
Kagerō nikki 蜻蛉日記
Kai hentai 華夷變態
kaisho 楷書
Kaizōsha 改造社
kajin 佳人
Kajin no kigū 佳人之奇遇
Kakaishō 河海抄
Kakizaki Hakyō no shōgai 蠣崎波響

"Kakurei" 鶴唳
Kamei Shōkin 亀井少琴
Kamo no Mabuchi 賀茂真淵
Kan Sanbon 菅三品
Kan Sazan 菅茶山
"Kanbun chokudoku ron" 漢文直讀
   論
kanbun kundoku (yomikudashi)-tai 漢
   文訓讀（讀下し）體
Kanda Kiichirō 神田喜一郎
Kaneko Hikojirō 金子彦次郎
Kang Youwei 康有爲
kangaku 漢學
Kannabi 神奈備
Kantō nichijō 還東日乘
Kara monogatari 唐物語
"Karafū ankoku jidai" 唐風暗黑時代
Karamono 唐物
Kashiwagi Jotei 柏木如亭
Katō Hiroyuki 加藤弘之
Kawaguchi Hisao 川口久雄
"Kayō jūei" 河陽十詠
Kayō Kōshu 華陽公主 (Ch. Huayang
   gongzhu)
Kayō Kyū 河陽宮
Keikoku bidan 經國美談
keishū 閨秀 (Ch. *guixiu*)
"Keitoku Reijo nanchin" 慶德麗女難
   陳
kenten 圈點
Ki no Tsurayuki 紀貫之
Kibi no Makibi 吉備真備
Kikō shōsetsu 崎港商説
Kikuchi Gozan 菊池五山
Kim Ok-kyun 金玉均
Kimura Kenkadō no saron 木村蒹葭堂
Kimura Ki 木村毅
Kin Shōjo 錦祥女
kinki shoga 琴棋書畫 (Ch. *qinqi shu-
   hua*)
Kinoshita Mokutarō 木下杢太郎
"Kirin" 麒麟

kishu ryūri 貴種流離

Kitasono Katsue 北園克衛

Kizaki Yoshinao 木崎好尚

"Ko-Shina bungaku ni okeru shōsetsu no chii ni tsuite" 古支那文學に於ける小説の地位に就て

ko shinbun 小新聞

kobun (Ch. guwen) 古文

Kobunji-ha 古文辭派 (Ch. Guwenci-pai)

Kōda Rohan 幸田露伴

Kogetsushō 湖月抄

Kojima Noriyuki 小島憲之

"Kōjin" 鮫人

"Kōkan" 交換

Kōkan 交歡

Kokin wakashū 古今和歌集

Kokon kidan: Hanabusa zōshi 古今奇談英草紙

Kokon kidan Hanabusa zōshi kōhen: Shigeshige Yawa 古今奇談繁野話

"Kokufū ankoku jidai" 國風暗黒時代

kokuji 國字

Kokusen'ya gassen 國姓爺合戦

Kokusen'ya gonichi gassen 國姓爺後日合戦

Kokuyaku kanbun taisei 國譯漢文大成

Kōnan shun 江南春

Konrondo 昆侖奴

Kōren 紅蓮

Kōsei nikki 航西日記

kōshōgaku 考證學 (Ch. *kaozhengxue*)

"Kōshū kashin" 杭州花信

"Kubi no tobu onna" 首の飛ぶ女

Kūchū teien 空中庭園

Kūkai 空海

Kumo no yukiki 雲のゆき来

kundoku 訓讀

kunko 訓詁 (Ch. *xungu*)

kunten 訓點

kun'yaku 訓譯

Kurahashi Yumiko 倉橋由美子

Kusaba Haisen 草場佩川

kusazōshi-tai 草双紙体

Kwŏn Ch'ik 權佁

Kyokutei Bakin 曲亭馬琴

kyōshi 狂詩

kyōyō 教養

Li Bai 李白

Li Daotian 李蹈天 (J. Ri Tōten)

Li Furen 李夫人

Li Hongzhang 李鴻章

Li Panlong 李攀龍 (Yulin 李于鱗)

Li Xiaojie 酈小姐

Li Yi 李億

Li Yi'an 李易安 (Qingzhao 清照)

Li Yu 李漁 (Li Liweng 笠翁)

Liang 梁

Liang Qichao 梁啓超

Liao 遼

Lin Bu 林逋

Lin Daiyu 林黛玉

Lingyuan Qie 陵園妾

Lisao 離騷

Liu Maogu 劉貌姑

Liu Shijian 柳士肩

Liu Tingzhi 劉廷芝

lixue (J. *rigaku*) 理學

Lu Wuguan 陸務觀 (You 游)

Lu Xun 魯迅

Lu Yu 陸羽

"Luoshen fu" 洛神賦

Maeda Ai 前田愛

Makura no sōshi 枕草子

Man'yō shū 萬葉集

man'yōgana 萬葉假名

Maoshi daxu 毛詩大序

Masukagami 増鏡

Matsukage no nikki 松蔭日記

Matsura no miya monogatari 松浦宮物語

Mei Lanfang 梅蘭芳

Mei Yaochen 梅堯臣

Meien shiki 名媛詩歸 (Ch. *Mingyuan shigui*)

Meigetsuki 明月記

"Meilang chang Su San" 梅郎唱蘇三

"Meirō to Konkyoku" 梅郎と崑曲

Minakami Roteki 水上蘆荻

Minami 南

Minshin tōki 明清闘記

Mitsu no Hamamatsu 御津之濱松

Miyake Shōzan 三宅嘯山

Miyoshi Genmei 三善彦明

Mizukagami 水鏡

Mizuno Heiji 水野平次

moni 模擬 (J. mogi)

Mori Ōgai 森鴎外

Mori Shuntō 森春濤

Morita Shiken 森田思軒

Morita Sōhei 森田草平

Motoori Norinaga 本居宣長

Mu Lanzi 木蘭子

"Mudan fang" 牡丹芳

Mugaku Sogen 無學祖元

Mumyō zōshi 無名草子

Murasaki Shikibu 紫式部

Nagai Kafū 永井荷風

Nagai Kagen 永井禾原 (久一郎 Kyūichirō)

Naimu Shō 内務省

Naitō Konan 内藤湖南

Nakamura Shin'ichirō 中村真一郎

Nakao Ō 仲雄王

Nanboku kyokugi genryū kō 南北曲戲源流考

Nanga 南畫 (Ch. Nanhua)

Nanjing 南京

Ni Yunlin 倪雲林

Nihon keien ginsō 日本閨媛吟藻

Nihon kōki 日本後記

Nihon meifu den 日本名婦傳

Nihon sandai jitsuroku 日本三代實録

Nihon shishi 日本詩史

Nihon shoki 日本書紀

Nihongi 日本紀

"Ningyo no nageki" 人魚の嘆き

ninjō 人情

Nishimura Tenshū 西村天囚

Nishiwaki Junzaburō 西脇順三郎

Nittō no Ri To 日東李杜

Nochi no chūsho ō 後中書王

Nomura Kōdai 野村公臺

"Nonaka no shimizu" 野中の清水

ō shinbun 大新聞

Ōbaku-shū 黄檗宗

Ochi Haruo 越智治夫

Ōchō bungaku no sekai 王朝文學論

Ōe no Masafusa 大江匡房

Ōe no Masahira 大江匡衡

Ōe no Takachika 大江擧周

Ogyū Sorai 荻生徂徠

Ōkagami 大鏡

Okajima Kanzan 岡島冠山

Ōkubo Shibutsu 大窪詩佛

Omokage 於母影

On Shōki 溫鐘馗 (Ch. Wen Zhongkui)

"Onna deshi" 女弟子

Ono no Takamura 小野篁

Ōnuma Chinzan 大沼枕山

Ōta Kinjō 大田錦城

Ōta Nanpo 大田南畝

Ōta Seikyū 太田青丘

Otake Kōkichi 尾竹紅吉 (Kazue 一枝)

Ouyang Yuqian 歐陽予請

Pan Yue 潘岳

Parhae 渤海

"Pekin" 北京

Pekin fūzoku zufu 北京風俗圖譜

"Pekin nikki shō" 北京日記抄

"Pipa xing" 琵琶行

Qing 清

"Qinghe wang Qing zhuan" 清河王慶

"Qingping diao" 清平調

"Qingshu ji Li Zian" 情書寄李自安

Qingyi bao 清議報

"Qiuxing fu" 秋興賦

"Qiuyuan" 秋怨

Qu Yuan 屈原

Rai Kyōhei 賴杏坪
Rai San'yō 賴山陽
Raiseikaku shishū 來青閣詩集
Rangiku monogatari 亂菊物語
Ri Tōten 李蹈天 (Ch. Li Daotian)
Rikkokushi 六國史
rokkasen 六歌仙
"Rozan nikki" 廬山日記
Ru shu ji 入蜀記
Ruan Yiquan 阮義詮
ruisho 類書 (Ch. leishu)
Ryōbu (Ch. Longwu) 龍武大將軍
"Saigo no ikku" 最後の一句
saishi kajin shōsetsu 才子佳人小説
　　(Ch. *caizi jiaren xiaoshuo*)
Saiyū zakki 西遊雑記
"Sakana no Ri Taihaku" 魚の李太白
Sakushi shikō 作詩志殻
San'in 山陰 (Ch. Shan'yin)
Santō Kyōden 山東京傳
San'un kyōu nikki narabini shisō 桟雲
　　峡雨日記並詩草
Sarashina nikki 更級日記
Satō Haruo 佐藤春夫
Satō Issai 佐藤一齋
Satomura Shōteki 里村紹迪
Sei-Shi 清紫
Sei Shōnagon 清少納言
seihon ken hatsubainin 製本兼發賣人
Seihyō shū 青萍集
"Seiji iro no onna" 青瓷色の女
seiji shōsetsu 政治小説
"Seiko no tsuki" 西湖の月
Seisho 清渚
Seitō 青鞜
Seki Ryōichi 關良一
Sendan 栴檀 (Ch. Zhantan)
setai 世態
Shajin shū 車塵集
Shandong 山東
Shangyang Baifaren 上陽白髮人
"Shanhai kenbun roku" 上海見聞録

"Shanhai kōyūki" 上海交遊記
"Shanhai yūki" 上海游記
Shan'yin 山陰 (J. San'in)
sharebon 洒落本
shasei 寫生
"Shennu fu" 神女賦
"Shenzhong lou" 蜃中樓
Shi Yin 石印
Shiba Shirō 柴四朗
Shibue Chūsai 澁江抽齋
Shibun yōryō 紫文要領
shiden 史傳
Shigeno no Sadanushi 滋野貞主
"Shihe" 失鶴
Shijin no niwa 詩人の庭
Shika shichiron 紫家七論
Shimada no Tadaomi 島田忠臣
Shimazu Hisamoto 島津久基
Shimizu Hamaomi 清水濱臣
"Shina bungaku kenkyū ni okeru hōjin
　　no tachiba" 支那文學研究にお
　　ける邦人の立場
"Shina gakusha no uwagoto" 支那學
　　者の囈語
"Shina-geki o miru ki" 支那劇を觀る
　　記
Shina kinsei gikyoku-shi 支那近世戲
　　曲史
"Shina no ryōri" 支那の料理
"Shina shumi to iu koto" 支那趣味と
　　云ふこと
Shindai bungaku hyōron shi 清代文学
　　學評論史
"Shindō" 神童
Shinhanatsumi 新花摘
"Shinwai no yoru" 秦淮の夜
Shiro no naka no shiro 城の中の城
shiroku benrei tai 四六駢儷體
shisen 詩仙
shisha 詩社
Shisho 四書
Shizan 紫山

Shizhongqu 十種曲
Shōheikō 昌平黌
Shoku Sanjin 蜀山人
Shōsetsu shinzui 小説神髄
Shōshō Shigemoto no haha 少將滋幹の母
Shuchūshu 酒中趣
Shuihu zhuan 水滸傳
shūji 修辭
"Shūkō juku to Sanmā juku" 秋香塾とサンマー塾
shumi 趣味
Shunka 舜華 (Ch. Chunhua)
"Shunkin shō" 春琴抄
"Sichou shi" 四愁詩
"Simao" 祀貓
"So Tōba: Arui wa Kojō no shijin" 蘇東坡或は湖上の詩人
sodoku 素讀
Song 宋
Song Yu 宋玉
Song Zhiwen 宋之問
"Soshū kikō" 蘇州紀行
Sou shen ji 搜神記
Sōzanshū 草山集
Su Dongpo 蘇東坡
Su Manzhu 蘇曼珠 (J. So Manshu)
Su San qijie 蘇三起解
Su Shi 蘇軾
Su Xiaoxiao 蘇小小
Suematsu Kenchō 末松謙澄 (Seihyō 青萍)
Sugawara no Fumitoki 菅原文時
Sugawara no Michizane 菅原道真
Suiyuan nudizi shixuan 隨園女弟子詩選
Suiyuan shidan 隨園食單
Sumiyoshi 住吉
Suo Lange 鎖瀾閣
Suzuki Shintarō 鈴木信太郎
Tachi Ryūwan 館柳灣
Tachibana Gyokuran 立花玉蘭

Taimu nikki 隊務日記
Taiping guangji 太平廣記
Taiwan gundan 臺灣軍談
Takahashi Taika 高橋太華
Takebe Ayatari 建部綾足
Takezoe Seisei 竹添井井 (Shin'ichirō 進一郎)
Tan Chuyu 譚楚玉
Tan Taigi 炭太祇
Tangshi sanbai shou 唐詩三百首
Tani Tateki 谷于城
Tanizaki Jun'ichirō 谷崎潤一郎
Tanomura Chikuden 田野村竹田
Tao Qian 陶潛 (Yuanming 淵明)
"Taohuayuan ji" 桃花源記
Tei Hankyō 鼎范卿 (Ch. Ding Fanqing)
Tian Han 田漢
Tian Rucheng 田汝成
Tō Kōgō 鄧皇后 (Ch. Deng Huanghou)
Tōei shisen 東瀛詩選 (Ch. Dongying shixuan)
tōin 唐音
Tōkai Sanshi 東海散士
Tokugawa Tsunayoshi 德川綱吉
Tokugawa Yoshimune 德川吉宗
Tokutomi Roka 德富蘆花
Tokutomi Sohō 德富蘇峰
"Tomoda to Matsunaga no hanashi" 友田と松永の話
Tomohira 具平
Torikaebaya monogatari とりかへはや物語
Tosa nikki 土佐日記
Tōsen banashi ima Kokusen'ya 唐船噺今國姓爺
Tōshisen 唐詩選
Tōshisen ōkai: Gogon zekku 蕩子筌柺解五言絶句
Tōwa san'yō 唐話纂要
Tōyūki 東遊記

Tsubouchi Shōyō 坪内逍遥
Tsuchida Taizō 土田泰蔵
Tsuga Teishō 都賀庭鐘
tsūji 通事
Tsuki no yukue 月のゆくへ
Tsukushi 筑紫
tsūshi 通詞
tsūzoku 通俗
Tsūzoku chūgi Suikoden 通俗忠義水滸伝
Tsūzoku Kajin no kigū 通俗佳人之奇遇
Ubun Kai 宇文會 (Ch. Yuwen Hui)
Ueda Akinari 上田秋成
Ugetsu monogatari 雨月物語
Uji shūi monogatari 宇治拾遺物語
Uragami Gyokudō 浦上玉堂
Uragami Shunkin 浦上春琴
Utsubo monogatari 宇津保物語
wa 和
Wa Tō chinkai 和唐珍解
Waka kuhon 和歌九品
Wakan rōeishū 和漢朗詠集
wakokubon kanseki 和刻本漢籍
wakon kansai 和魂漢才
Wang Shizhen 王世貞
Wang Wei 王維
Wang Yuyang 王漁洋 (Shizhen 士禎)
Wang Ziquan 王紫詮 (Tao 掐)
Wang Ziyou 王子猷
wangfu shan 望夫山
wangfu shi 望夫石
Wanghai Lou 望海樓
Washizu Kidō 鷲津毅堂
washū 和臭 / 習
Wei Ye 魏野
Wen Tingyun 溫庭筠 (Feiqing 飛卿)
Wenxuan 文選
wenyan 文言
Wenyuan yinghua 文苑英華
Wu Meicun 吳梅村
Wu Sangui 吳三桂 (J. Go Sankei)
Wu chuan lu 吳船錄
Wudi 武帝

Wushan 巫山
Wushan 五山
Xiangpu 湘浦
Xiangzi 相子
Xiaocang shichao 小倉詩鈔
Xiaoqing 小青
Xihu jiahua 西湖佳話
Xihu youlan zhi yu 西湖遊覽志餘
Xin yuefu 新樂府
xingling 性靈說
Xishi 西施
Xuanzong 玄宗
Xue Baochai 薛寶釵
xungu 訓詁學 (J. *kunko*)
Yamamoto Hokuzan 山本北山
Yamanoue no Okura 山上憶良
Yamazaki Rikyū 山崎離宮
Yan Qing 燕青
Yanagawa 梁川 (Chō 張) Kōran 紅蘭
Yanagawa Seigan 梁川星巖
Yanagisawa Yoshiyasu 柳澤吉保
Yang Guifei 楊貴妃
Yang Meng 楊蒙
Yang Tieyai 楊鐵崖 (Weizhen 維楨)
Yangzhou 揚州
Yanlang 嚴陵
Yano Ryūkei 矢野龍渓
yanshi 艷詩
"Yasui fujin" 安井夫人
"Yeyu" 夜雨
Yinyuan 隱元 (J. Ingen)
yō 洋
Yoda Gakkai 依田學海
yonghuai shi (詠懷詩; J. *eikai shi*)
yongwu shi 詠物詩 (J. *eibutsu shi*)
Yosa (no) Buson 與謝蕪村
Yosano Akiko 與謝野晶子
Yoshikawa Eiji 吉川英治
Yoshimine no Yasuyo 良峰安世
Yoshishige 慶滋 (Keitoku 慶徳) Ietada 家雅
Yoshishige no Yasutane 慶滋保胤

"Yōshō jidai" 幼少時代
Yotsutsuji (Minamoto) Yoshinari 四辻 (源) 善成
You xian ku 遊仙窟
Yu Xuanji 魚玄機 (J. Gyo Genki)
Yu Yue 俞樾 (Quyuan 曲園)
Yuan 元
Yuan Hongdao 袁宏道
Yuan Mei 袁枚 (Suiyuan 隨園)
Yuan Zhen 元稹
"Yūjo ki" 遊女記
"Yūjo o miru no jo" 見遊女序
"Yume no ukihashi" 夢の浮橋
Yūran 幽蘭
Yutai xinyong 玉臺新詠

Yutangchun 玉堂春
Yuwen Hui 宇文會 (J. Ubun Kai)
Zai Toku ki 在徳記
zasshu 雑種
Zatsuei 雑詠
Zhang Heng 張衡
Zhang Huiqing 張惠卿 (J. Chō Keikyō)
Zhang Wencheng 張文成
Zhantan 栴檀 (J. Sendan)
Zhao Mingcheng 趙明誠
Zhejiang 浙江
Zheng Chenggong 鄭成功
Zheng Zhilong 鄭芝龍
zhiguai xiaoshuo 志怪小說

Bibliography

Aida Hanji and Harada Yoshino. "Arakida Reijo." In Aida and Harada, *Kinsei joryū bunjin den,* 203–205.

———. "Ema Saikō." In Aida and Harada, *Kinsei joryū bunjin den,* 10–14.

———, eds. *Kinsei joryū bunjin den.* Tokyo: Meiji shoin, 1960.

Aitkin, Stuart C., and Leo E. Zonn, eds. *Place, Power, Situation, and Spectacle: A Geography of Film.* Lanham, MD: Rowman and Littlefield, 1994.

Akazome Emon. *A Tale of Flowering Fortune: Annals of Japanese Aristocratic Life in the Heian Period.* 2 vols. Translated by Helen Craig McCullough. Stanford: Stanford University Press, 1980.

Akutagawa Ryūnosuke. *Akutagawa Ryūnosuke zenshū.* Edited by Yoshida Seiichi, Nakamura Shin'ichirō, and Akutagawa Hiroshi. Tokyo: Iwanami shoten, 1977–1978.

———. "Pekin nikki shō." In vol. 10 of Akutagawa, *Akutagawa Ryūnosuke zenshū,* 313–325.

———. "Shanhai yūki." In vol. 5 of Akutagawa, *Akutagawa Ryūnosuke zenshū,* 3–59.

———. "To Shishun." In vol. 4 of Akutagawa, *Akutagawa Ryūnosuke zenshū,* 150–166.

———. "Travels in China." Translated by Joshua A. Fogel and Kiyoko Morita. In Fogel, *Japanese Travelogues of China in the 1920s,* 10–55.

———. "Tu Tzu-ch'un." Translated by James R. Hightower. In *Traditional Chinese Stories: Themes and Variations,* 416–419. Edited by Y. W. Ma and Joseph S. M. Lau. New York: Columbia University Press, 1978.

Amagasaki Akira. *En no bigaku: Uta no michi no shigaku II.* Tokyo: Keisō shobō, 1995.

Ames, Roger T., and David L. Hall, trans. *Focusing the Familiar: A Translation and Philosophical Interpretation of the Zhongyong.* Honolulu: University of Hawai'i Press, 2001.

Anderson, Benedict. *Imagined Communities: Reflections on the Origin and Spread of Nationalism.* Rev. ed. London: Verso, 1991. Originally published 1983.

Andō Tameakira. *Shijo shichiron: Kakai shō, Kachō yosei, Shijo shichiron.* Edited by Muromatsu Iwao. Vol. 3 of *Kokubun chūshaku zensho,* 1–23 (itemized pagination). Tokyo: Kokugakuin daigaku shuppanbu, 1908.

Aoki Masaru. *Aoki Masaru zenshū*. 10 vols. Tokyo: Shunjūsha, 1969–1975.

———, trans. *Chūka chasho*. In vol. 8 of Aoki, *Aoki Masaru zenshū*, 191–395. Originally published 1962.

———, trans. *Kaishien gaden*. In vol. 10 of Aoki, *Aoki Masaru zenshū*, 1–404.

———. "Kanbun chokudoku ron." In vol. 2 of Aoki, *Aoki Masaru zenshū*, 334–341. Originally published 1920; rev. 1927.

———. "Kinki shoga." In vol. 7 of Aoki, *Aoki Masaru zenshū*, 197–419.

———. *Kōnan shun*. Tokyo: Heibonsha, 1972.

———. "Meiran to Konkyoku." In vol. 2 of Aoki, *Aoki Masaru zenshū*, 101–110. Originally published 1919.

———. "Okajima Kanzan to Shina hakuwa bungaku." In vol. 2 of Aoki, *Aoki Masaru zenshū*, 275–286. Originally published 1921; rev. 1927.

———. "Shina bungaku kenkyū ni okeru hōjin no tachiba." In Aoki, *Kōnan shun*, 67–72. Originally published 1937.

———. "Shina gakusha no uwagoto." In Aoki, *Kōnan shun*, 64–67. Originally published 1935.

———. *Shuchūshu*. Vol. 9 of Aoki, *Aoki Masaru zenshū*. Originally published 1962.

———, trans. *Zuien shokutan*. In vol. 8 of Aoki, *Aoki Masaru zenshū*, 399–592. Originally published 1958.

Arakida Reijo. "Fuji no iwaya." In vol. 1 of Furuya, *Edo jidai joryū bungaku zenshū*, 537–580.

———. "Keitoku Reijo ikō." In Ōkawa and Minami, *Kokugakusha denki shūsei*, 674–682. Originally published ca. 1802.

Asō, Isoji. *Edo bungaku to Chūgoku bungaku*. Tokyo, Sanseidō, 1955. Originally published 1946.

Asukai Masamichi. "Seiji shōsetsu to 'kindai' bungaku: Meiji seiji shōsetsu saihyōka no tameni." *Shisō no kagaku* 6 (1959): 62–82.

Baba Yumiko. "Tanizaki Jun'ichirō: Taishō 7 nen no Chūgoku ryokō." *Dōshisha kokubungaku* 44 (March 1996): 47–60.

Bai Juyi. *Haku Rakuten shishū*. Vol. 1. Tokyo: Nihon tosho sentā, 1978. Originally published 1928.

Bal, Mieke. *Double Exposures: The Subject of Cultural Analysis*. New York and London: Routledge, 1996.

———. *Quoting Caravaggio: Contemporary Art, Preposterous History*. Chicago: University of Chicago Press, 1999.

Baroni, Josephine. *Ōbaku Zen: The Emergence of the Third Sect of Zen in Tokugawa Japan*. Honolulu: University of Hawai'i Press, 2000.

Barthes, Roland. *Writing Degree Zero*. Translated by Annette Lavers and Colin Smith. New York: Noonday Press, 1968. Originally published 1953.

Baudrillard, Jean. *For a Critique of the Political Economy of the Sign*. Translated by Charles Levin. St. Louis: Telos Press, 1981.

———. "The Implosion of Meaning in the Media." In Jean Baudrillard, *Simulacra and Simulation,* 79–86. Translated by Sheila Faria Glaser. Ann Arbor: University of Michigan Press, 1994.

Benjamin, Walter. "Theses on the Philosophy of History." In Walter Benjamin, *Illuminations,* 253–264. Written in 1940. First published posthumously in 1950. Edited and introduced by Hannah Arendt. Translated by Harry Zohn. New York: Schocken Books, 1968.

Bhabha, Homi. *The Location of Culture.* London: Routledge, 1993.

———. *Sugawara no Michizane and the Early Heian Court.* Cambridge, MA: Harvard University Press, 1986.

Bourdieu, Pierre. *The Field of Cultural Production: Essays on Art and Literature.* Edited and introduced by Randal Johnson. New York: Columbia University Press, 1993.

Bradstock, Timothy R., and Judith N. Rabinovitch, trans. and eds. *An Anthology of Kanshi (Chinese Verse) by Japanese Poets of the Edo Period.* Lewiston, NY: Edwin Mellen Press, 1997.

Brower, Robert Hopkins. "The *Konzyaku Monogatarisyu:* An Historical and Critical Introduction, with Annotated Translations of Seventy-Eight Tales." PhD diss., University of Michigan, 1952.

Bunka shūrei shū. In *Kaifūsō, Bunka shūrei shū, Honchō monzui.* Edited by Kojima Noriyuki. Vol. 69 of *Nihon koten bungaku taikei.* Tokyo: Iwanami shoten, 1964.

Butler, Judith. *Gender Trouble: Feminism and the Subversion of Identity.* London and New York: Routledge, 1990.

Chambers, Ross. *Story and Situation: Narrative Seduction and the Power of Fiction.* Minneapolis: University of Minnesota Press, 1984.

Chang, Kang-i Sun, and Haun Saussy, eds. *Women Writers of Traditional China: An Anthology of Poetry and Criticism.* Stanford: Stanford University Press, 1999.

Chaves, Jonathan. "Jōzan and Poetry." In Rimer and Chaves, *Shisendo,* 27–90.

Chen Kaige, director. *Ba wang bie ji* [Farewell, my concubine]. 1993.

Chikamatsu Monzaemon. *The Battles of Coxinga.* Translated by Donald Keene. In *Four Plays of Chikamatsu,* 57–131. Edited by Donald Keene. New York: Columbia University Press, 1961.

———. *Kokusen'ya gassen.* In *Chikamatsu jōrurishū 2.* Edited by Shuzui Kenji and Ōkubo Tadakuni. Vol. 50 of *Nihon koten bungaku taikei,* 227–292 and 385–396. Tokyo: Iwanami shoten, 1968. Originally published 1715.

Chino Kaori. "Nihon bijutsu no jendā." *Bijutsushi* 43, no. 2 (March 1994): 235–246.

Copeland, Rebecca L. "The Meiji Woman Writer 'Amidst a Forest of Beards.' " *Harvard Journal of Asiatic Studies* 57, no. 2 (December 1997): 383–418.

Copeland, Rebecca L., and Esperanza Ramirez-Christensen, eds. *The Father/Daughter Plot: Japanese Literary Women.* Honolulu: University of Hawai'i Press, 2001.

Daitō Hyōshi [Tsuchida Taizō]. *Tsūzoku Kajin no kigū, zen.* Preface by Hattori Seiichi. Tokyo: Dōmei shobō, 1887. In *Kokuritsu kokkai toshokan shozō Meiji-ki kankō tosho maikuroban shūsei* DBQ-2046. Tokyo: Maruzen, 1991.

————. *Tsūzoku Kajin no kigūo Zokuhen*. Tokyo: Kakuseisha, 1887.

De Certeau, Michel. *Heterologies: Discourse on the Other*. Translated by Brian Massumi. Vol. 17 of *Theory and History of Literature*. Edited by Wlad Godzich and Jochen Schulte-Sasse. Minneapolis: University of Minnesota Press, 1986.

Deleuze, Gilles. *The Fold: Leibniz and the Baroque*. Translated by Tom Conley. Minneapolis: University of Minnesota Press, 1993. Originally published 1988.

Derrida, Jacques. *Limited Inc*. Translated by Samuel Weber. Evanston, IL: Northwestern University Press, 1988.

DeWoskin, Kenneth, and J. I. Crump Jr., trans. *In Search of the Supernatural: The Written Record*. Stanford: Stanford University Press, 1996.

Duara, Prasenjit. *Rescuing History from the Nation: Questioning Narratives of Modern China*. Chicago: University of Chicago Press, 1995.

Eagleton, Terry. *The Function of Criticism: From the Spectator to Poststructuralism*. London: Verso, 1984.

Ema Saikō. *Breeze through Bamboo: Kanshi of Ema Saikō*. Translated, edited, and introduced by Hiroaki Sato. New York: Columbia University Press, 1997.

————. *San'yō sensei hiten: Shōmu shisō*. Introduced by Kobayashi Tetsuyuki. Tokyo: Kyūko shoin, 1997.

————. *Shōmu ikō*. In *Kokuritsu kokkai toshokan shozō Meijiki kankō tosho Maikuroban shūsei*. DBV-2237. Tokyo: Maruzen, 1991. Originally published 1871.

————. *Shōmu ikō*. In vol. 15 of Fujikawa, Matsushita, and Sano, *Shishū Nihon kanshi*, 145–178.

Ema monjo (bunsho) hozonkai, ed. *Ema Saikō raikan shū*. Kyoto: Shibunkaku, 1988.

Emura Hokkai. "*Ike no mokuzu* jo." In vol. 11 of *Kōchu kokubun sōsho*, 1–2. Edited by Ikebe Yoshikata. Tokyo: Hakubunkan, 1915.

————. *Nihon shishi*. Vol. 65 of *Shin Nihon Koten bungaku taikei*. Edited by Shimizu Shigeru, Ibi Takashi, and Ōtani Masao. Tokyo: Iwanami shoten, 1991.

Ericson, Joan E. "The Origins of the Concept of 'Women's Literature.' " In Schalow and Walker, *The Woman's Hand*, 74–115.

Etō Jun. "Kindai sanbun no keisei to zasetsu." *Bungaku* 26, no. 7 (July 1958): 13–29.

Feldman, Horace Z. "The Growth of the Meiji Novel." PhD diss., Columbia University, 1952.

Fister, Patricia. "Female *Bunjin*: The Life of Poet-Painter Ema Saikō." In *Recreating Japanese Women, 1600–1945*, 108–130. Edited and introduced by Gail Lee Bernstein. Berkeley: University of California Press, 1991.

Fogel, Joshua A., ed. *Japanese Travelogues of China in the 1920s: The Accounts of Akutagawa Ryūnosuke and Tanizaki Jun'ichirō*. *Chinese Studies in History* 30, no. 4 (Summer 1997).

————. *The Literature of Travel in the Japanese Rediscovery of China, 1862–1945*. Stanford: Stanford University Press, 1996.

————. *Politics and Sinology: The Case of Naitō Konan (1866–1934)*. Cambridge, MA: Council on East Asian Studies, 1984.

Fujikawa Hideo, Matsushita Tadashi, and Sano Masami, eds. *Shishū Nihon kanshi*. Tokyo: Kyūko shoin, 1988.

Fujikawa Shin'ichi. "Kajin no kigū to Yusenkutsu." *Kokubo to kokubungaku* 11, no. 12 (December 1934): 105–109.

Fujiwara no Kintō, ed. *Japanese and Chinese Poems to Sing: The Wakan Rōei shū*. Translated and edited by J. Thomas, Rimer, and Jonathan Chaves. New York: Columbia University Press, 1997.

Fujiwara no Michitsuna no Haha. *The Gossamer Years: The Diary of a Noblewoman of Heian Japan*. Translated by Edward Seidensticker. Tokyo and Rutland, VT: C.E. Tuttle, 1964.

————. *The Kagerō Diary: A Woman's Autobiographical Text from Tenth-Century Japan*. Translated, edited, and introduced by Sonja Arntzen. Ann Arbor: Center for Japanese Studies, University of Michigan, 1997.

Fujiwara no Teika. *Matsura no miya monogatari*. Edited by Ichiko Teiji and Misumi Yōichi. Vol. 5 of *Kamakura jidai monogatari shūsei*, 149–228. Edited by Ichiko Teiji and Misumi Yōichi. Tokyo: Kasama shoin, 1992.

————. *Meigetsuki*. Vol. 1. Edited by Tsuji Hikosaburō. Tokyo: Zoku Gunsho ruijū kanseikai, 1971.

————. *The Tale of Matsura: Fujiwara Teika's Experiment in Fiction*. Translated and edited by Wayne Press Lammers. Ann Arbor: Center for Japanese Studies, University of Michigan, 1992.

Fukuda Mahito. *Kekkaku no nihon bunkashi*. Nagoya: Nagoya daigaku shuppan-kyoku, 1996.

Fukui Teisuke. "Honji shi to Ise monogatari." In Fukui Teisuke, *Ise monogatari seisei ron*. Tokyo: Yūseidō, 1965. Originally published 1953.

Fukushima Riko, ed. and introd. *Joryū*. Vol. 3 of *Edo Kanshi sen*. Tokyo: Iwanami shoten, 1995.

————. "Kaisetsu." In Fukushima, *Joryū*, 313–336.

————. "Keishū shijin Ema Saikō." *Gobun* 50 (1988): 3–16.

Furuya, Tomoyoshi, ed. *Edo jidai joryū bungaku zenshū*. Rpt. Tokyo: Nihon tosho sentā, 1979. Originally published 1918.

————. "Shogen." Vol. 2 of Furuya, *Edo jidai joryū bungaku zenshū*, 1–4. Originally published 1918.

Garber, Marjorie. *Vested Interests: Cross-Dressing and Cultural Anxiety*. New York: Routledge, 1992.

Geddes, Ward, trans. and introd. Kara monogatari: *Tales of China*. Tempe: Arizona State University Press, 1984.

Gensei. *Grass Hill: Poems and Prose by the Japanese Monk Gensei*. Translated by Burton Watson. New York: Columbia University Press, 1983.

————. *Sōzanshū*. Introduced by Sano Masami. Vol. 13 of Fujikawa, Matsushita, and Sano, *Shishū Nihon kanshi*. Originally published 1674.

Gensei and Chen Yuanyun. *Gengen shōwa shū*. Introduced by Sano Masami. Vol. 13 of Fujikawa, Matsushita, and Sano, *Shishū Nihon kanshi*, 367–398. Originally published 1663.

Gōdanshō. *Gōdanshō, Chūgaishō, Fūkego*, 3–254 and 457–548. Vol. 32 of *Shin Nihon koten bungaku taikei*. Edited by Gotō Akio, Ikegami Jun'ichi, and Yamane Taisuke. Tokyo: Iwanami shoten, 1997.

Go-Fukakusa in Nijō. *Confessions of Lady Nijō*. Translated by Karen Brazell. Garden City, NY: Anchor Books, 1973.

Graham, Masako Nakagawa. *The Yang Kuei-fei Legend in Japanese Literature*. Lewiston, NY: Edwin Mellen Press, 1998.

Graham, Patricia J. *Tea of the Sages: The Art of Sencha*. Honolulu: University of Hawai'i Press, 1998.

Greenblatt, Stephen. *Marvelous Possessions: The Wonder of the New World*. Chicago: University of Chicago Press, 1991.

Guillory, John. *Cultural Capital: The Problem of Literary Canon Formation*. Chicago: University of Chicago Press, 1993.

Hagiwara Hiromichi. *Kōsei yakuchū Genji monogatari hyōshaku shukan*. In vol. 10 of *Kokubun chūshaku sōsho*, 1–63 (individual pagination). Tokyo: Kokugakuin daigaku shuppanbu, 1909.

Hanan, Patrick. *The Invention of Li Yu*. Cambridge, MA: Harvard University Press, 1988.

Harada Chikasada. "Chūgoku bungaku to Tanizaki Jun'ichirō 1." *Gakuen* 348 (December 1968): 45–60.

————. "Tanizaki Jun'ichirō to Chūgoku bungaku 2." *Gakuen* 350 (February 1969): 15–29.

Hasegawa Michiko. *Karagokoro: Nihon seishin no gyakusetsu*. Tokyo: Chūō kōronsha, 1986.

Hata Yūzō and Yamada Yūsaku, eds. *Kindai I*. Vol. 5 of *Nihon bungei shi: Hyōgen no nagare*. Edited by Furuhashi Nobuyoshi. Tokyo: Kawade shobō shinsha, 1990.

Hayashi Gahō, ed. *Honchō ichinin isshu*. Edited by Kojima Noriyuki. Vol. 63 of *Shin Nihon koten bungaku taikei*. Tokyo: Iwanami shoten, 1994. Originally published 1660.

Hill, Chris. "National History and the World of Nations: Writing Japan, France, the United States, 1870–1900." PhD diss., Columbia University, 1999.

Hino Tatsuo. "Akinari to fukko." In Hino, *Norinaga to Akinari: Kinsei chūki bungaku no kenkyū*, 223–250. Tokyo: Chikuma shobō, 1984. Originally published 1981.

————. *Sorai gaku ha: Jugaku kara bungaku e*. Tokyo: Chikuma shobō, 1975.

Hiraga Gennai. *Fūryū shidōken den*. In vol. 1 of *Hiraga Gennai zenshū*, 481–558. Tokyo: Hagiwara Seibunkan, 1935. Originally published 1763.

Hirokawa Katsumi. "*Genji monogatari no rekishi jojutsu to setsuwa.*" In Suzuki Hideo, *Bungaku shijō no* Genji monogatari, 20–33.

Hori Tatsuo. *Hori Tatsuo zenshū.* 10 vols. Tokyo: Kadokawa shoten, 1963–1966.

———. *To Ho shi nōto.* Tokyo: Mokujisha, 1975.

Hsia, C. T. "Yen Fu and Liang Ch'i-ch'ao as Advocates of New Fiction." In *Chinese Approaches to Literature from Confucius to Liang Ch'i-ch'ao,* 221–257. Edited by Adele Rickett. Princeton, NJ: Princeton University Press, 1978.

Hsü Ch'ang An. "*Shin gihō dai 4 satsu yakusai no 'Kajin kigū' [Jiaren qiyu] ni tsuite.*" *Nippon Chūgoku gakkai hō* 24 (1972): 193–208.

Hutcheon, Linda. " 'The Pastime of Past Time': Fiction, History, Historiographical Metafiction." In *Essentials of the Theory of Fiction,* 2nd ed., 473–495. Edited by Michael J. Hoffman and Patrick D. Murphy. Durham, NC: Duke University Press, 1996. Originally published 1989.

Hwang, David Henry. *M. Butterfly.* Harmondsworth, Middlesex: Penguin, 1986.

Ibi Takashi. *Edo shiika ron.* Tokyo: Kyūko shoin, 1998.

———. "Kasei-ki shidan to hihyōka: *Gozandō shiwa* ron." *Bungaku* 43, no. 7 (July 1975): 1–20.

———. "Meiji kanshi no shuppatsu: Mori Shuntō shiron." In *Meiji 10-nendai no Edo.* Edited by Robert Campbell. *Edo bungaku* 21 (December 1999): 5–20.

Ichikawa Seigaku. *Kinsei joryū shoka retsuden.* Rpt. Tokyo: Nihon tosho sentā, 1991. Originally published 1935.

Iizuka Akira. "Kaisetsu." In So Manshu, *Dankō Reigan ki,* 271–335.

Ikebe Yoshikata. "Kaidai." In vol. 11 of *Kōchū kokubun sōsho,* 1–8. Edited by Ikebe Yoshikata. Tokyo: Hakubunkan, 1915.

———. "Kaidai." In vol. 12 of *Kōchū kokubun sōsho,* 1–15. Edited by Ikebe Yoshikata. Tokyo: Hakubunkan, 1918.

Ikeda Toshio. *Nitchū hikaku bungaku no kisoteki kenkyū: Hon'yaku setsuwa to sono tenkyo.* Tokyo: Kasama shoin, 1974.

———. *Sarashina nikki Hamamatsu chūnagon kō.* Tokyo: Musashino shoin, 1989.

Imai Yasuko. "Wakon Yōsai, Wakon Kansai, Yamato damashii." *Bungaku* 43, no. 7 (July 1975): 101–113, and 43, no. 9 (September 1975): 29–42.

Inoguchi Atsushi. *Nihon kanbungakushi.* Tokyo: Kadokawa shoten, 1984.

Inoue Hiroshi. "Tōkai Sanshi Shiba Shirō no *Kajin no kigū* to *Tōyō no kajin.*" *Shizuoka joshi daigaku kenkyū kiyō* 21 (1988): 130–114.

Ishimura Yōko. "Motoori Norinaga no bunshō hihyō ni tsuite." *Nihon bungaku* 7, no. 8 (August 1958): 45–55.

Ishizaki Matazō. *Kinsei Nihon ni okeru Shina zokugo bungakushi.* Tokyo: Kōbundō, 1933. Originally published 1930.

Ito, Ken. *Visions of Desire: Tanizaki's Fictional Worlds.* Stanford: Stanford University Press, 1991.

Izuno Tatsu. "Arakida Reijo." In *Kinsei kindai hen,* 105–122. Edited by Yoshida

Seiichi. Vol. 2 of *Nihon joryū bungaku shi.* Edited by Hisamatsu Sen'ichi and Yoshida Seiichi. Tokyo: Dōbun shoin, 1969.

———. *Arakida Reijo monogatari shūsei.* Tokyo: Ōfūsha, 1982.

"Jibun hyōron." *Waseda bungaku* 1 (1st series, 1st cycle) (October 1891): 7–8.

Johnson, Regine Diane. "Fantastic Voyage: Refractions of the Real, Re-Visions of the Imagined in Hiraga Gennai's *Fūryū Shidōken den.*" PhD diss., Harvard University, 1989.

Kado Reiko. *Edo joryū bungaku no hakken: Hikari aru mi koso kurushiki omoi nare.* Tokyo: Fujiwara shoten, 1998.

———. *Ema Saikō: Kasei-ki no joryū shijin.* Tokyo: BOC shuppan, 1984. Originally published 1979.

Kado Reiko, with Iritani Sensuke. *Ema Saikō shishū: Shōmu ikō.* 2 vols. Kyoto: Kyūko shoin, 1992, 1994.

Kamo no Chōmei. *The Ten Foot Square Hut.* Translated by A. L. Sadler. In *The Ten Foot Square Hut, and Tales of the Heike; Being Two Thirteenth Century Japanese Classics, "The Hojoki" and Selections from "The Heike Monogatari."* Westport, CT: Greenwood Press, 1970.

Kanda Kiichirō, ed. *Meiji kanshibun shū.* Vol. 62 of *Meiji bungaku zenshū.* Tokyo: Chikuma shobō, 1983.

———. *Nihon ni okeru Chūgoku bungaku: Nihon tenshi shiwa.* 2 vols. Tokyo: Nigensha, 1965, 1967.

Kaneko Hikojirō. *Heian jidai bungaku to Hakushi monjū.* Tokyo: Baifūkan, 1943.

Kaneko Sachiyo, " 'Atarashiki onna'-tachi no taitō: Nichi-Doku ni okeru josei kaihō to Mori Ōgai." *Shakai bungaku* 2 (July 1988): 37–52.

Kanro Junki. "Mō hitotsu no *Kajin no kigū:* Aruiwa mō hitotsu no *Tsūzoku Kajin no kigū.*" *Nihon bungaku* 46, no. 12 (December 1995): 24–32.

Karai Senryū. *Haifū Yanagidaru. Senryū kyōka shū.* Vol. 57 of *Nihon koten bungaku taikei.* Tokyo: Iwanami shoten, 1958. Originally published 1765.

Karashima Takeshi, ed. and introd. *Gyo Genki, Setsu Tō.* Vol. 15 of *Kanshi taikei.* Edited by Aoki Masaru and Takada Shinji. Tokyo: Shūeisha, 1964.

Katsukura Toshikazu. " 'Kaizoku' ron no kiso: Sono zōkeisei to hihyō seishin." In Katsukura Toshikazu, *Ueda Akinari no kotengaku to bungei ni kansuru kenkyū,* 634–660. Tokyo: Kazama shobō, 1994.

Kawaguchi Hisao. *Heianchō Nihon kanbungakushi no kenkyū.* 3rd ed. 3 vols. Tokyo: Meiji shoin, 1982–1988. Originally published 1961.

Kawase Kazuma. "Kara monogatari to Mōgyū waka." *Kokugo* 1 (July 1936): 128–146.

Kawazoe Fusae. *Sei to bunka no Genji monogatari: Kaku onna no tanjō.* Tokyo: Chikuma shobō, 1998.

Keene, Donald. *Dawn to the West: Japanese Literature of the Modern Era, Fiction.* New York: Holt, Rinehart and Winston, 1984.

———, ed. *Twenty Plays of the Nō Theatre.* New York: Columbia University Press, 1970.

Kikuchi Gozan. *Gozandō shiwa*. In *Nihon shishi Gozandō shiwa*, 155–230. Edited by Shimizu Shigeru, Ibi Takashi, and Ōtani Masao, vol. 65 of *Shin Nihon koten bungaku taikei*. Originally published 1807–1832?

Kimura Ki. "Kanmatsu kaidai." In *Meiji kaikaki bungaku shū*, 608–622. Edited by Yamamoto Mitsuo, vol. 1 of *Gendai Nihon bungaku zenshū*. Tokyo: Kaizōsha, 1931.

Ki no Tsurayuki. *Tosa nikki*. Edited by Suzuki Tomotarō. Vol. 20 of *Nihon koten bungaku taikei*, 3–82. Tokyo: Iwanami shoten, 1957.

Kinoshita Hyō. "*Kajin no kigū* no shi to sono sakusha." *Bungaku* 53, no. 9 (September 1985): 21–30.

Kinoshita Mokutarō. "Meilang chang Su San." In vol. 1 of *Kinoshita Mokutarō zenshū*, 340–341. Tokyo: Iwanami shoten, 1950. Originally published 1917.

———. "Peking." In vol. 9 of *Kinoshita Mokutarō zenshū*, 70–95. Tokyo: Iwanami shoten, 1950. Originally published 1918.

Kleeman, Faye Yuan. *Under an Imperial Sun: Japanese Colonial Literature of Taiwan and the South*. Honolulu: University of Hawai'i Press, 2003.

Ko, Dorothy. *Teachers of the Inner Chambers: Women and Culture in Seventeenth-Century China*. Stanford: Stanford University Press, 1994.

Kobayashi Tadashi and Tokuda Takeshi. "*Jūben jūgi zu* o yomu: Taiga Buson no shi sho ga sanzetsu." In *Bunjinga to kanshijin* I. Edited by Tokuda Takeshi and Kobayashi Tadashi. *Edo bungaku* 17 (June 1997): 2–17.

Kobayashi Tetsuyuki. "Kaidai." In Ema, *San'yō sensei hiten: Shōmu shisō*, 353–372.

Kōda Rohan. "Gen jidai no zatsugeki." In vol. 15 of *Kōda Rohan zenshū*, 49–128. Tokyo: Iwanami shoten, 1952. Originally published 1895.

———, trans. *Kōrōmu*. Translation of *Hong lou meng*. Vols. 14–16 of *Kokuyaku kanbun taisei*. Bungaku bu. Tokyo: Kokumin bunko kankōkai, 1920–1922.

———. "Ko-Shina bungaku ni okeru shōsetsu no chii ni tsuite." In vol. 18 of *Kōda Rohan zenshū*, 39–44. Tokyo: Iwanami shoten, 1949. Originally published 1926.

———. "Meiji shoki bungaku-kai." In vol. 18 of *Kōda Rohan zenshū*, 289–308. Tokyo: Iwanami shoten, 1949; rpt. 1979. Originally published 1933.

———. *Suikoden*. Translation of *Shuihu zhuan*. Vols. 18–20 of *Kokuyaku kanbun taisei*. Bungaku bu. Tokyo: Kokumin bunko kankōkai, 1923–1924.

Kojima Noriyuki. *Jōdai Nihon bungaku to Chūgoku bungaku: Shutten ron o chūshin to suru hikaku bungakuteki kōsatsu*. Tokyo: Hanawa shobō, 1962–1971.

———. *Kokinshū izen*. Tokyo: Hanawa shobō, 1976.

———. *Kokufū ankoku jidai no bungaku*. Tokyo: Hanawa shobō, 1968–1998.

———. *Ōchō kanshi sen*. Tokyo: Iwanami bunko, 1987.

Kokuryūkai, ed. *Tōa senkaku shishi kiden*. Vol. 1 (jō). Reprinted in vols. 22–24 of *Meiji hyakunen shi sōsho*. Edited by Kuzuu Yoshihisa. Tokyo: Hara shobō, 1966. Originally published 1933.

Kondō Haruo. *Hakushi monjū to kokubungaku: Shin gafu Shinchū gin no kenkyū*. Tokyo: Meiji shoin, 1990.

Kōno Taeko. *Tanizaki bungaku to kōtei no yokubō.* Tokyo: Bungei shunjūsha, 1976.

Kuge Haruyasu. *Heian Kōki monogatari no kenkyū: Sagoromo Hamamatsu.* Vol. 10 of *Shintensha kenkyū sōsho.* Tokyo: Shintensha, 1984.

Kurahashi Yumiko. "Kōkan." In Kurahashi, *Kurahashi Yumiko no kaiki shōhen,* 129–138. Originally published 1985.

———. *Kōkan.* Tokyo: Shinchō bunko, 1993. Originally published 1989.

———. "Kubi no tobu onna." In Kurahashi, *Kurahashi Yumiko no kaiki shōhen,* 29–38. Originally published 1985.

———. *Kurahashi Yumiko no kaiki shōhen.* Tokyo: Shinchō bunko, 1988.

———. *Shiro no naka no shiro.* Tokyo: Shinchōsha, 1980.

———. *Shunposhion.* Tokyo: Fukutake shoten, 1985.

———. "Trade." In Sakaki, *The Woman with the Flying Head and Other Stories by Kurahashi Yumiko,* 53–58.

———. "The Woman with the Flying Head." In Sakaki, *The Woman with the Flying Head and Other Stories by Kurahashi Yumiko,* 45–51.

Kurata Yoshihiro. *Chosakuken shiwa.* Tokyo: Senninsha, 1980.

LaMarre, Thomas. *Shadows on the Screen: Tanizaki Jun'ichirō on Cinema and "Oriental" Aesthetics.* Forthcoming.

———. *Uncovering Heian Japan: An Archaeology of Sensation and Inscription.* Durham, NC: Duke University Press, 2000.

Levinas, Emmanuel. *Time and the Other.* Translated by Richard A. Cohen. Pittsburgh: Duquesne University Press, 1987. Originally published 1979.

Levy, Dore J. *Chinese Narrative Poetry: The Late Han through T'ang Dynasties.* Durham, NC: Duke University Press, 1988.

Liang Qichao, trans. *Zhengzhi xiaoshuo: Jiaren qiyu.* In vol. 19 of Liang Qichao, *Yinbingshi heji,* 1–220. Shanghai: Zhonghua shuju, 1941.

Lippit, Seiji M. *Topographies of Japanese Modernism.* New York: Columbia University Press, 2002.

Lu Xun. *Guxiaosho goushen.* Vol. 8 of *Lu Xun quanji.* Beijing: Renmin wenxue chubanshe, 1973. Originally published 1939.

McClellan, Edwin. *Woman in the Crested Kimono: The Life of Shibue Io and Her Family.* New Haven: Yale University Press, 1985.

McCullough, Helen Craig, ed. *Classical Japanese Prose: An Anthology.* Stanford: Stanford University Press, 1990.

———, trans. *The Great Mirror, Fujiwara Michinaga (966–1027) and His Times: A Study and Translation.* Princeton, NJ: Princeton University Press, 1980.

———, trans. *Kokin wakashū: The First Imperial Anthology of Japanese Poetry with Tosa nikki and Shinsen waka.* Stanford: Stanford University Press, 1985.

———. *Tales of Ise: Lyrical Episodes from Tenth-Century Japan.* Stanford: Stanford University Press, 1968.

———, trans. "A Tosa Journal." In McCullough, *Classical Japanese Prose,* 73–102. Also in McCullough, *Kokin wakashū,* 264–291.

Mackerras, Colin. *Western Images of China.* Hong Kong: Oxford University Press, 1989.

Maeda Ai. "Gesaku bungaku to *Tōsei shosei katagi.*" In Maeda Ai, *Kindai Nihon no bungaku kūkan,* 116–133. Originally published 1965.

———. *Kindai dokusha no seiritsu.* Vol. 2 of *Maeda Ai chosaku shū.* Tokyo: Chikuma shobō, 1989.

———. *Kindai Nihon no bungaku kūkan: Rekishi, kotoba, jōkyō.* Tokyo: Shin'yōsha, 1983.

———. "Meiji rekishi bungaku no genzō: Seiji shōsetsu no baai." In Maeda Ai, *Kindai Nihon no bungaku kūkan,* 2–41. Originally published 1976.

———. "Meiji shoki bunjin no Chūgoku shōsetsu shumi." In Maeda Ai, *Kindai dokusha no seiritsu,* 90–304. Originally published 1967.

———. "Meiji shonen no dokusha zō." In Maeda Ai, *Kindai dokusha no seiritsu,* 108–121. Originally published 1969.

———. "Ōgai no Chūgoku shōsetsu shumi." In Maeda Ai, *Kindai dokusha no seiritsu,* 74–87. Originally published 1965.

Maeda Yoshi. "Joryū bunjin Kamei Shōkin shōden: Kamei Shōkin kenkyū nōto 1." *Fukuoka jogakuin tanki daigaku kiyō* 16 (1980): 1–21.

———. "Kinsei joryū kanshijin Tachibana Gyokuran: Sono shōgai to sakuhin." *Fukuoka jogakuin tanki daigaku kiyō* 4 (1968): 29–58.

———. "Kinsei keishū shijin Hara Saihin to Bōsō no tabi: Hara Saihin kenkyū sono 1." *Fukuoka jogakuin tanki daigaku kiyō* 12 (1976): 13–29.

———. "Shōkin shikō *Yōchō kō Kinoto i* o megutte: Kamei Shōkin kenkyū nōto 2." *Fukuoka jogakuin tanki daigaku kiyō* 17 (1981): 1–17.

Mair, Victor, ed. *The Columbia Anthology of Traditional Chinese Literature.* New York: Columbia University Press, 1994.

Marceau, Lawrence Edward. "Literati Consciousness in Early Modern Japan: Takebe Ayatari and the Bunjin." PhD diss., Harvard University, 1989.

———. *Takebe Ayatari: A Bunjin Bohemian in Early Modern Japan.* Ann Arbor: Center for Japanese Studies, University of Michigan, 2004.

Marra, Michele. "Mumyōzōshi, Introduction and Translation." *Monumenta Nipponica* 39, nos. 2–4 (1984): 115–145, 281–305, and 409–434.

Masuda Itaru. *Japan and China: Mutual Representations in the Modern Era.* Translated by Joshua A. Fogel. Richmond: Curzon, 2000.

Matsui Sachiko. "*Kajin no kigū* to 'Yōkō nikki': Shiba Shirō Tani Tateki no seiji ishiki." In Matsui Sachiko, *Seiji shōsetsu no ron,* 116–132. Tokyo: Ōfūsha, 1979.

Matsuo Akira. "Daimei kō." In Matsuo Akira, *Heian jidai monogatari ronkō,* 431–442. Tokyo: Kasama shoin, 1968. Originally published 1936.

———. "Hamamatsu chūnagon monogatari ni okeru Tō no byōsha ni tsuite." *Bungaku* 1, no. 7 (October 1933): 106–111.

Matsushita Tadashi. *Edo jidai no shifū shiron: Min Shin no shiron to sono sesshu.* Tokyo: Meiji shoin, 1969.

Matsuzaki Kōdō. *Kōdō nichireki.* 6 vols. Edited by Yamada Taku. Vols. 235–240 of *Tōyō bunko.* Tokyo: Heibonsha, 1973.

Mei Lanfang. *Tōyūki.* Translated by Okazaki Toshio. Tokyo: Asahi shimbunsha, 1959.

Mills, D. E., trans. *A Collection of Tales from Uji: A Study and Translation of Uji shūi monogatari.* Cambridge: Cambridge University Press, 1970.

Minakami Roteki. *Nihon keien ginsō.* In *Kokuritsu kokkai toshokan shozō Meijiki kankō tosho maikuroban shūsei.* Edited by Kokuritsu kokkai toshokan. DBV-1306. Tokyo: Maruzen, 1991. Originally published 1880.

Miyake, Lynne. "*The Tosa Diary:* In the Interstices of Gender and Criticism." In Schalow and Walker, *The Woman's Hand,* 41–73.

Miyazaki Sōhei. *Sei Shōnagon to Murasaki Shikibu: Sono taihi-ron josetsu.* Tokyo: Chōbunsha, 1993.

Mizuno Heiji. *Haku Rakuten to Nihon bungaku.* 1930. Tokyo: Daigakudō shoten, 1982.

Mizuta Norihisa. "Bunjin shumi." Edited by Suwa Haruo and Hino Tatsuo. *Edo bungaku to Chūgoku.* Tokyo: Mainichi shinbunsha, 1977. 185–204.

Mori Ōgai. "Gyo Genki." In vol. 16 of Mori, *Ōgai zenshū,* 101–119. Originally published 1915.

———. "Gyo Genki." Translated by David Dilworth. In Rimer and Dilworth, *The Historical Fiction of Mori Ōgai,* 185–198.

———. "History as It Is and History Ignored." Translated by Darcy Murray. In Rimer and Dilworth, *The Historical Fiction of Mori Ōgai,* 179–184.

———. *Kōsei nikki.* In vol. 35 of Mori Ōgai, *Ōgai zenshū,* 73–83. Originally published 1884.

———. "The Last Phrase." Translated by David Dilworth and J. Thomas Rimer. In Rimer and Dilworth, *The Historical Fiction of Mori Ōgai,* 209–221.

———. *Ōgai zenshū.* Tokyo: Iwanami shoten, 1971–1975.

———, trans. and ed. *Omokage.* Vol. 19 of Mori Ōgai, *Ōgai zenshū,* 1–68. Originally published 1889.

———. "Rekishi sonomama to rekishi banare." In vol. 26 of Mori Ōgai, *Ōgai zenshū,* 508–511. Originally published 1915.

———. "Saigo no ikku." In vol. 16 of Mori Ōgai, *Ōgai zenshū,* 159–175. Originally published 1915.

———. *Vita sekusuarisu.* In vol. 5 of Mori Ōgai, *Ōgai zenshū,* 83–179. Originally published 1909.

———. *Vita Sexualis.* Translated by Kazuji Ninomiya and Sanford Goldstein. Tokyo: Tuttle, 1972.

———. *Wild Geese.* Translated by Kingo Ochiai and Sanford Goldstein. Tokyo: Tuttle, 1959.

———. *Wild Goose.* Translated by Burton Watson. Ann Arbor: Center for Japanese Studies, University of Michigan, 1995.

———. "Yasui fujin." In vol. 15 of Mori Ōgai, Ōgai zenshū, 545–565. Originally published 1914.

———. "Yasui fujin." 1971. Translated by David Dilworth and J. Thomas Rimer. In Rimer and Dilworth, The Historical Fiction of Mori Ōgai, 255–270.

———. "Yosano Akiko san ni tsuite." In vol. 26 of Mori Ōgai, Ōgai zenshū, 433. Originally published 1912.

Moriyasu Masabumi. "Ōgai to Gyo Genki." Kanshi taikei Geppō 15 (October 1964): 1.

Mostow, Joshua S. "Mother Tongue and Father Script: The Relationship of Sei Shōnagon and Murasaki Shikibu to Their Fathers of Chinese Letters." In Copeland and Ramirez-Christensen, The Father/Daughter Plot, 115–142.

Motoori Norinaga. Motoori Norinaga zenshū. Tokyo: Chikuma shobō, 1968–1993.

———. "Nonaka no shimizu tensaku." In supplementary vol. 2 of Motoori, Motoori Norinaga zenshū, 341–386.

———. Shibun yōryō. In supplementary vol. 1 of Motoori, Motoori Norinaga zenshū, 379–482.

Murasaki Shikibu. The Diary of Lady Murasaki. Translated by Richard Bowring. Harmondsworth, Middlesex: Penguin Books, 1996.

———. Genji monogatari. Edited by Yamagishi Tokuhei. Vols. 14–18 of Nihon koten bungaku taikei. Tokyo: Iwanami shoten, 1958–1963.

———. Murasaki Shikibu nikki. Edited by Ikeda Kikan and Akiyama Ken. In Makura no sōshi, Murasaki Shikibu nikki, 443–509. Vol. 19 of Nihon koten bungaku taikei. Tokyo: Iwanami shoten, 1958.

———. Murasaki Shikibu shū. In Murasaki Shikibu nikki Murasaki Shikibu shū. Vol. 35 of Shinchō koten shūsei. Tokyo: Shinchōsha, 1980.

———. The Tale of Genji. Translated by Edward Seidensticker. New York: Knopf, 1976.

Nagae Hironobu. Tanizaki Jun'ichirō: Shiryō to dōkō. Tokyo: Kyōiku shuppan sentā, 1984.

Nagai Kagen (Kyūichirō). Raiseikaku shishū. In vol. 19 of Fujikawa, Matsushita, and Sano, Shishū Nihon kanshi, 405–525.

Nakai Yoshiyuki. Ōgai ryūgaku shimatsu. Tokyo: Iwanami shoten, 1999.

Nakajima Wakako. " 'Karafū ankoku jidai' no naka de." In "Heian bungaku" to iu ideologii, 58–87. Vol. 1 of Sōsho Sōzōsuru Heian bungaku. Edited by Kawazoe Fusae, Kobayashi Masaaki, Kanda Tatsumi, Fukazawa Tōru, Kojima Naoko, and Yoshii Miyako. Tokyo: Bensei shuppan, 1999.

Nakamoto Dai. "Matsura no miya monogatari ni okeru kanseki riyō ni kansuru ikutsuka no mondai." Shirin 15 (April 1994): 61–66.

Nakamura Mitsuo. "Futatabi seiji shōsetsu o: Shōsetsu shinzui o hitei suru." Chūō kōron 74, no. 6 (May 1959): 281–291.

———. "Hihyō no shimei." In vol. 8 of Nakamura Mitsuo zenshū. Tokyo: Chikuma shobō, 1972. Originally published 1959.

————. "Sakuhin kaisetsu." In *Seiji shōsetsu shū*, 395–400. Edited by Itō Sei, vol. 3 of *Nihon gendai bungaku zenshū*. Tokyo: Kōdansha, 1965.

Nakamura Shin'ichirō. *Kimura Kenkadō no saron*. Tokyo: Shinchōsha, 2000.

————. *Kūchū teien*. In vol. 3 of Nakamura Shin'ichirō, *Nakamura Shin'ichirō chōhen zenshū*, 161–374. Originally published 1965.

————. *Kumo no yukiki*. In vol. 3 of Nakamura Shin'ichirō, *Nakamura Shin'ichirō chōhen zenshū*, 375–464. Originally published 1965–1966.

————. *Nakamura Shin'ichirō chōhen zenshū*. Tokyo: Kawade shobō shinsha, 1970.

————. *Ōchō bungaku no sekai*. Tokyo: Shinchōsha, 1963.

————. *Rai San'yō to sono jidai*. Tokyo: Chūō kōronsha, 1971.

————. *Shijin no niwa*. Tokyo: Shūeisha, 1976.

Natsume Sōseki. *Bungakuron*. In vol. 16 of *Sōseki zenshū*. Tokyo: Iwanami shoten, 1995. Originally published 1907.

————. *The Three-Cornered World*. Translated by Alan Turney. London: Peter Owen, 1965.

Nihei Michiaki. "*Genji monogatari* to *Go Kanjo*: Hikaru Genji no monogatari to Seika-ō Kei den." In Suzuki, *Bungaku shijō no* Genji monogatari, 47–58.

Nishio Yoshihito, ed. *Zenshaku Ichiyō nikki*. 3 vols. Tokyo: Ōfūsha, 1973–1976.

Nomura Kōdai. "Arakida shi *Tsuki no yukue* jo." In Ikebe, *Kōchū kokubun sōsho*, vol. 12, 1–2.

Ōba Osamu. *Edo jidai ni okeru Tōsen mochiwatari sho no kenkyū*. Osaka: Kansai daigaku shuppanbu, 1967.

Ochi Haruo. "Seiji shōsetsu to taishū." *Bungaku* 32, no. 5 (May 1964): 61–73.

————. " 'Seiji to bungaku' no tansho." In Ochi Haruo, *Bungaku no kindai*, 126–133. Vol. 1 of Ochi Haruo, *Bungaku ronshū*. Tokyo: Isagoya shobō, 1986. Originally published 1967.

————. "Suehiro Tetchō." In *Hito to sakuhin: Gendai bungaku kōza, Meiji-hen I*. Edited by Kimata Osamu, Kawazoe Kunimoto, and Hasegawa Izumi, 140. Tokyo: Meiji shoin, 1961.

Ōe Masafusa. "The Ōe Conversations." Translated and introduced by Marian Ury. *Monumenta Nipponica* 48, no. 3 (Autumn 1993): 359–380.

Ogata Tsutomu. " 'Gyo Genki' to 'atarashii onna'-tachi: Sei to bungaku e no kaigan no kiroku." In Ogata Tsutomu, *Mori Ōgai no rekishi shōsetsu: Shiryō to hōhō*, 213–229. Tokyo: Chikuma shobō, 1979. Originally published 1963.

Ohki, Sadako. "Ema Saiko's Kanshi Poetry: Irrelevance of Sex/Gender Categories." In *Abstracts of the 1998 Annual Meeting*, 162. Ann Arbor: Association for Asian Studies, 1998.

Ōkagami. Vol. 20 of *Nihon koten bungaku zenshū*. Edited by Tachibana Kenji. Tokyo: Shōgakkan, 1974.

Ōkawa Shigeo and Minami Shigeki, eds. *Kokugakusha denki shūsei*. Tokyo: Dainihon tosho kabushikigaisha, 1904.

Onizuka Takaaki. "Genji monogatari to Shiki [Shiji]." In Wakan hikaku bungaku kai, *Chūko bungaku to kanbungaku* II, 119–142.

Ōnuma Toshio. " 'Kajin no kigū' seiritsu kōshō josetsu: Keiō Gijuku Toshokan-zō kōhon to kankōbon." *Bungaku* 51, no. 9 (September 1983): 73–90.

———. "Zaibei jidai no Tōkai Sanshi: Nimai no shashin kara." *Nihon kindai bungaku* 32 (1984): 103–108.

Ōta Seikyū. *Nihon kagaku to Chūgoku shigaku*. Tokyo: Shimizu kōbundō, 1968.

Owen, Stephen. *An Anthology of Chinese Literature: Beginnings to 1911*. New York: Norton, 1996.

———. "Discourse on Literature." In Owen, *Readings*, 57–72.

———. "The 'Great Preface.' " In Owen, *Readings*, 37–56.

———. *Readings in Chinese Literary Thought*. Cambridge, MA: Harvard University Press, 1992.

———. *Remembrances*. Cambridge, MA: Harvard University Press, 1986.

Ozaki Kōyō. *The Gold Demon*. Translated by A. and M. Lloyd. Tokyo: Yurakusha, 1905–1909.

Perkins, George W., trans. *The Clear Mirror: A Chronicle of the Japanese Court during the Kamakura Period (1185–1333)*. Stanford: Stanford University Press, 1998.

Pollack, David. *The Fracture of Meaning: Japan's Synthesis of China from the Eighth through the Eighteenth Centuries*. Princeton, NJ: Princeton University Press, 1986.

Porter, Dennis. *Haunted Journeys: Desire and Transgression in European Travel Writing*. Princeton, NJ: Princeton University Press, 1991.

Pratt, Mary Louise. *Imperial Eyes: Travel Writing and Transculturation*. New York and London: Routledge, 1992.

Rimer, J. Thomas, and Jonathan Chaves, eds. and trans. *Shisendō: Hall of the Poetry Immortals*. New York: Weatherhill, 1991.

Rimer, J. Thomas, and David Dilworth, eds. *The Historical Fiction of Mori Ōgai*. Honolulu: University of Hawai'i Press, 1977.

Rodd, Laurel Rasplica, and Mary Catherine Henkenius, eds. *Kokinshū: A Collection of Poems Ancient and Modern*. Princeton, NJ: Princeton University Press, 1984.

Rollberg, Peter. "Il'ia Grigor'evich Erenburg." In *Reference Guide to Russian Literature*, 277–279. Edited by Neil Cornwell. London and Chicago: Fitzroy Dearborn, 1998.

Rose, Mark. *Authors and Owners: The Invention of Copyright*. Cambridge, MA: Harvard University Press, 1993.

Sai Ki (Ch. Cai Yi). "Yu Etsu [Ch. Yu Yue] to ChūNichi kanseki no kōryū." In *Tenseki*, 311–331. Edited by Ōba Osamu and Ō Yū (Ch. Wang Yong). Vol. 9 of *Nitchū bunka kōryū shi sōsho*. Tokyo: Taishūkan shoten, 1996.

Said, Edward W. *Culture and Imperialism*. New York: Vintage, 1994. Originally published 1993.

———. *Orientalism*. New York: Vintage, 1979. Originally published 1978.

————. *Representations of the Intellectual: The 1993 Reith Lectures.* New York: Pantheon, 1994.

Saitō Mareshi. "Meiji no yūki: Kanbunmyaku no arika." In *Meiji bungaku no ga to zoku,* 47–57. Special issue of *Bungaku.* Tokyo: Iwanami shoten, 2001.

Sakai, Naoki. *Voices of the Past: The Status of Language in Eighteenth-Century Japanese Discourse.* Ithaca, NY: Cornell University Press, 1991.

Sakaki, Atsuko. "Archetypes Unbound: Domestication of the Five Chinese Imperial Consorts." In *Acts of Writing.* Edited by Rebecca L. Copeland. *Proceedings of the Association for Japanese Literary Studies* 2 (Summer 2001): 85–100.

————. "Keshin no mangekyō: Tanizaki Jun'ichirō no Taishō kōki shōhin-gun o meguru ichi kōsatsu." *Hikaku bungaku kenkyū* 55 (May 1989): 1–31.

————. "Kurahashi Yumiko." In *Modern Japanese Writers,* 185–198. Edited by Jay Rubin. New York: Scribners and Sons, 2000.

————. "Kurahashi Yumiko no 'Kōkan' o yomu: Shikai hon'an no hōhō o chūshin to shite." In *Takeda Akira sensei taikan kinen higashi ajia bunka ronshū,* 487–498. Edited by Kotajima Yūsuke. Tokyo: Kyūko shoin, 1991.

————. "Kurahashi Yumiko's Negotiations with the Fathers." Chapter 11 of Copeland and Ramirez-Christensen, *The Father/Daughter Plot,* 292–326.

————. *Recontextualizing Texts: Narrative Performance in Modern Japanese Fiction.* Cambridge, MA: Harvard Asia Center, 1999.

————. "Transnational Communications in the Classical Language in the Age of Nationalism." Paper presented at third bi-annual meeting of the International Congress for Asian Scholars. Singapore, August 21, 2003.

————, trans. and ed. *The Woman with the Flying Head and Other Stories by Kurahashi Yumiko.* Armonk, NY: M. E. Sharpe, 1998.

"Sankō bunken nenpyō." In *Genji monogatari ge,* 462–531. Edited by Abe Akio, Oka Kazuo, and Yamagishi Tokuhei. Vol. 4 of *Zōho kokugo kokubungaku kenkyūshi taisei.* Tokyo: Sanseidō, 1977.

Sano Masami. "Kaidai." In vol. 13 of Fujikawa, Matsushita, and Sano, *Shishū Nihon kanshi,* 3–13.

Sansom, George Bailey. *The Western World and Japan: A Study in the Interaction of European and Asiatic Cultures.* New York: Knopf, 1950.

Sasaki Nobutsuna, ed. *Nihon kagaku taikei.* Tokyo: Kazama shobō, 1963.

Satō Tsuyoshi. "Kindai bungaku shi kōsō no shomondai: Shuppatsuten to shite no seiji shōsetsu." *Nihon bungaku kenkyū no genzai.* Special issue of *Kokugakuin zasshi* 92, no. 1 (January 1991): 431–444.

Schalow, Paul Gordon, and Janet A. Walker, eds. *The Woman's Hand: Gender and Theory in Japanese Women's Writing.* Stanford: Stanford University Press, 1996.

Scott, Joan. "Experience." In *Women, Autobiography, Theory: A Reader,* 57–71. Edited by Sidonie Smith and Julia Watson. Madison: University of Wisconsin Press, 1998. Originally published 1991.

Sei Shōnagon. *Makura no sōshi.* Edited by Ikeda Kikan and Kishigami Shinji. In

Makura no sōshi, *Murasaki Shikibu nikki*, 43–332. Vol. 19 of *Nihon koten bungaku taikei*. Tokyo: Iwanami shoten, 1958.

———. *The Pillow Book of Sei Shōnagon*. Translated and edited by Ivan Morris. Oxford: Oxford University Press, 1967.

Seidensticker, Edward. *Kafū, the Scribbler: The Life and Writings of Nagai Kafū, 1879–1959*. Stanford: Stanford University Press, 1965.

Seki Reiko. "Fude motsu hito e." Chapter 4 of Seki Reiko, *Ane no chikara Higuchi Ichiyō*, 127–162. Tokyo: Chikuma shobō, 1993.

———. "Tatakau 'Chichi no musume': Ichiyō tekusuto no seisei." In Seki Reiko, *Kataru onna tachi no jidai: Ichiyō to Meiji josei hyōgen*, 140–162. Tokyo: Shin'yōsha, 1997.

Seki Ryōichi. "Kindai bungaku no keisei: Dentō to kindai." In Seki Ryōichi, *Shōyō, Ōgai: Kōshō to shiron*. Tokyo: Yūseidō, 1971. Originally published 1959.

Sekishin Tetchōshi. *Tsūzoku Kajin no kigū*. Preface by Zuifū Hisanshi. In *Kokuritsu kokkai toshokan shozō Meijiki kankō tosho maikuroban shūsei*. DBQ-2046. Tokyo: Maruzen, 1991. Originally published 1887.

Shi Yin. *Xihu jiahua*. Edited by Mu Lanzi. Tian'yi chuban sha, 1985.

Shiba Keiko. "Kinsei nyonin bunjin fudoki 2: Chikuzen, Chikugo, Buzen no maki (Fukuoka ken)." *Shiryō to jinbutsu: Edo-ki onna kō* 2 (1991): 138–141.

Shih Nai-an. *Water Margin*. Translated by J. H. Jackson. Edited by Fang Lo-tien. Shanghai: Commercial Press, 1937.

Shimasue Kiyoshi and Yamashita Kazumi, eds. *Chūkō haikai shū*. Vol. 13 of *Koten haibungaku taikei*. Tokyo: Shūeisha, 1970.

Shimizu Hamaomi. *Kara monogatari teiyō*. In vol. 16 of *Kokubun chūshaku zensho*, 130–162. Edited by Motoori Toyokai, Kimura Masakoto, and Inoue Yorikuni. Tokyo: Kokugakuin daigaku shuppanbu, 1910. Originally published 1809.

Shirane, Haruo, and Tomi Suzuki, eds. *Inventing the Classics: Modernity, National Identity, and Japanese Literature*. Stanford: Stanford University Press, 2000.

Silverman, Kaja. *World Spectators*. Stanford: Stanford University Press, 2000.

So Manshu [Su Manshu]. *Dankō Reigan ki*. Tokyo: Heibonsha, 1972.

Spence, Jonathan D. *The Chan's Great Continent: China in Western Minds*. New York: Norton, 1998.

Stewart, Susan. *On Longing: Narratives of the Miniature, the Gigantic, the Souvenir, the Collection*. Baltimore: Johns Hopkins University Press, 1984.

Strassberg, Richard E. *Inscribed Landscapes: Travel Writing from Imperial China*. Berkeley: University of California Press, 1994.

Suda Tetsuo. "Hamamatsu Chūnagon monogatari ni okeru sakusha no Tō chishiki ron." *Kikan Bungaku gogaku* (September 1957): 34–43.

Suematsu Kenchō, trans. and introd. *The Tale of Genji*. Boston: Tuttle, 2000. Originally published 1882.

Sugawara no Takasue no musume. *As I Crossed a Bridge of Dreams: Recollections of* a Woman in Eleventh-Century Japan. Translated by Ivan Morris. London: Oxford University Press, 1971.

———. Hamamatsu chūnagon monogatari. Edited by Kuge Haruyasu. Tokyo: Ōfūsha, 1988.

———. A Tale of Eleventh-Century Japan: "Hamamatsu Chūnagon Monogatari." Translated and edited by Thomas H. Rohlich. Princeton, NJ: Princeton University Press, 1983.

Suwa Haruo. "Kaihi no fūsetsu." In Suwa and Hino, Edo bungaku to Chūgoku, 226–244.

Suwa Haruo and Hino Tatsuo, eds. Edo bungaku to Chūgoku. Tokyo: Mainichi shinbunsha, 1977.

Suzuki Hideo, ed. Bungaku shijō no Genji monogatari: Kokubungaku kaishaku to kanshō bessatsu. Tokyo: Shibundō, 1998.

Suzuki Sadami. Nihon no "bungaku" gainen. Tokyo: Sakuhinsha, 1998.

Suzuki, Tomi. "Gender and Genre: Modern Literary Histories and Women's Diary Literature." In Shirane and Suzuki, Inventing the Classics, 71–95.

———. " 'Joryū nikki bungaku' no kōchiku: Janru, jendā, bungakushi kijutsu." Bungaku 9, no. 4 (1998): 13–27.

Sze, Mai-mai. The Tao of Painting, a Study of the Ritual Disposition of Chinese Painting; with a Translation of the Chieh tzu yüan hua chuan; or Mustard Seed Garden Manual of Painting, 1679–1701. New York: Pantheon Books, 1956.

Takebe Ayatari. Honchō Suikoden. In vol. 79 of Shin Nihon koten bungaku taikei. Edited by Takada Mamoru and Kigoshi Osamu, 3–301. Tokyo: Iwanami shoten, 1992. Originally published 1773.

Takeda Izumo, Miyoshi Shōraku, and Namiki Senryū. Chūshingura (The Treasury of Loyal Retainers): A Puppet Play by Takeda Izumo. Translated by Donald Keene. New York: Columbia University Press, 1971.

———. Sugawara and the Secrets of Calligraphy. Translated and edited by Stanley H. Jones Jr. New York: Columbia University Press, 1985.

Takeuchi, Melinda. Taiga's True Views: The Language of Landscape Painting in Eighteenth-Century Japan. Stanford: Stanford University Press, 1992.

Takezoe Seisei. San'un kyōu nikki: Meiji kanshijin no Shisen no tabi. Translated and edited by Iwaki Hideo. Tokyo: Heibonsha tōyō bunko, 2000.

———. San'un kyōu nikki narabini shisō. Vol. 18 of Fujikawa, Matsushita, and Sano, Shishū Nihon kanshi, 23–95.

Tan Taigi and Miyake Shōzan, eds. Haikai shinsen. In Shimasue and Yamashita, Chūkō haikai shū.

Tanaka Mikiko. "Kanshi rōei no denshō to Ō Shōkun setsuwa: Mirukarani kagami no kage no tsuraki kana' uta no haikei to hensen." In Inbun bungaku 'uta' no sekai, 335–359. Edited by Manabe Masahiro, Kamioka Yūji, and Mashimo Atsushi. Vol. 2 of Kōza Nihon no denshō bungaku. Tokyo: Miyai shoten, 1995.

Tanaka, Stefan. *Japan's Orient: Rendering Pasts into History*. Berkeley: University of California Press, 1993.

Tanizaki Jun'ichirō. "Birōdo no yume." In vol. 6 of Tanizaki, *Tanizaki Jun'ichirō zenshū*, 503–550. Originally published 1919.

———. "The Bridge of Dreams." In Tanizaki, *Seven Japanese Tales*, 95–159.

———. *Captain Shigemoto's Mother*. In Tanizaki, *The Reed Cutter and Captain Shigemoto's Mother*, 55–180.

———. *Childhood Years: A Memoir*. Translated by Paul McCarthy. Tokyo and New York: Kodansha International, 1988.

———. "Chōsen zakkan." In vol. 22 of Tanizaki, *Tanizaki Jun'ichirō zenshū*, 61–64.

———. *Diary of a Mad Old Man*. Translated by Howard Hibbett. New York: Knopf, 1965.

———. *Fūten rōjin nikki*. Vol. 19 of Tanizaki, *Tanizaki Jun'ichirō zenshū*. Originally published 1961.

———. "Gakuyūkai zasshi." In vol. 24 of Tanizaki, *Tanizaki Jun'ichirō zenshū*, 52–53. Originally published 1901.

———. "Genjō Sanzō." In vol. 4 of Tanizaki, *Tanizaki Jun'ichirō zenshū*, 329–357.

———. "Itansha no kanashimi." In vol. 4 of Tanizaki, *Tanizaki Jun'ichirō zenshū*, 377–452. Originally published 1917.

———. "Kakurei." In vol. 7 of Tanizaki, *Tanizaki Jun'ichirō zenshū*, 379–402. Originally published 1921.

———. "Kirin." In vol. 1 of Tanizaki, *Tanizaki Jun'ichirō zenshū*, 3–90.

———. "Kōjin." In vol. 7 of Tanizaki, *Tanizaki Jun'ichirō zenshū*, 27–212. Originally published 1920.

———. "Kōjin no zokkō ni tsuite." *Chūō kōron* (November 1920): 54–55.

———. "Ningyo no nageki." In vol. 4 of Tanizaki, *Tanizaki Jun'ichirō zenshū*, 185–212. Originally published 1917.

———. "A Portrait of Shunkin." In Tanizaki, *Seven Japanese Tales*, 3–84.

———. *Rangiku monogatari*. In vol. 12 of Tanizaki, *Tanizaki Jun'ichirō zenshū*, 215–557. Originally published 1930.

———. "The Reed Cutter." In Tanizaki, *The Reed Cutter and Captain Shigemoto's Mother*, 1–53.

———. *The Reed Cutter and Captain Shigemoto's Mother: Two Novellas*. Translated by Anthony H. Chambers. New York: Knopf, 1993.

———. "Rozan nikki." In vol. 7 of Tanizaki, *Tanizaki Jun'ichirō zenshū*, 461–470. Originally published 1921.

———. "Sakana no Ri Taihaku." In vol. 6 of Tanizaki, *Tanizaki Jun'ichirō zenshū*, 39–54. Originally published 1918.

———. "Seiko no tsuki." In vol. 6 of Tanizaki, *Tanizaki Jun'ichirō zenshū*, 329–354. Originally published 1917.

———. *Seven Japanese Tales*. Translated by Howard Hibbett. New York: Knopf, 1963, 1991.

———. "Shanghai Friends." Translated by Paul D. Scott. In Fogel, *Japanese Travelogues of China in the 1920s*, 71–103.

———. "Shanhai kenbun roku." In vol. 10 of Tanizaki, *Tanizaki Jun'ichirō zenshū*, 551–559. Originally published 1926.

———. "Shanhai kōyūki." In vol. 10 of Tanizaki, *Tanizaki Jun'ichirō zenshū*, 561–598. Originally published 1926.

———. "Shina-geki o miru ki." In vol 22 of Tanizaki, *Tanizaki Jun'ichirō zenshū*, 70–74. Originally published 1919.

———. "Shina no ryōri." In vol. 22 of Tanizaki, *Tanizaki Jun'ichirō zenshū*, 78–83. Originally published 1919.

———. "Shina shumi to iu koto." In vol. 22 of Tanizaki, *Tanizaki Jun'ichirō zenshū*, 121–123. Originally published 1922.

———. "Shindō." In vol. 3 of Tanizaki, *Tanizaki Jun'ichirō zenshū*, 275–367. Originally published 1916.

———. "Shinwai no yoru." In vol. 6 of Tanizaki, *Tanizaki Jun'ichirō zenshū*, 245–270. Originally published 1919.

———. *Shōshō Shigemoto no haha*. In vol. 16 of Tanizaki, *Tanizaki Jun'ichirō zenshū*, 153–282.

———. "Shunkin shō." In vol. 13 of Tanizaki, *Tanizaki Jun'ichirō zenshū*, 493–555.

———. "So Tōba Aruiwa kojō no shijin." In vol. 7 of Tanizaki, *Tanizaki Jun'ichirō zenshū*, 213–264.

———. "Soshū kikō." In vol. 6 of Tanizaki, *Tanizaki Jun'ichirō zenshū*, 221–243. Originally published 1919.

———. *Tanizaki Jun'ichirō zenshū*. Tokyo: Chūō kōronsha, 1966–1970.

———. "Tomoda to Matsunaga no hanashi." In vol. 10 of Tanizaki, *Tanizaki Jun'ichirō zenshū*, 409–493. Originally published 1926.

———. "Yōshō jidai." In vol. 17 of Tanizaki, *Tanizaki Jun'ichirō zenshū*, 41–253. Originally published 1955–1956.

———. "Yume no ukihashi." In vol. 18 of Tanizaki, *Tanizaki Jun'ichirō zenshū*, 145–211. Originally published 1959.

Tian Rucheng. *Xihu youlan zhi yu*. Shanghai: Shanghai guji chubanshe, 1980.

Tōkai Sanshi. *Kajin no kigū*. 16 vols. Tokyo: Hakubunkan, 1885–1892.

———. *Kajin no kigū*. In *Meiji kaikaki bungaku shū*, 139–326. Edited by Yamamoto Mitsuo. Vol. 1 of *Gendai Nihon bungaku zenshū*. Tokyo: Kaizōsha, 1931.

———. *Kajin no kigū*. In *Seiji shōsetsu shū*, 85–252. Vol. 3 of *Gendai Nihon bungaku zenshū*. Tokyo: Kōdansha, 1965.

Tokuda Takeshi. "Jūben jūgi zu o yomu." In *Bunjinga to kanshibun II*. Edited by Tokuda Takeshi and Kobayashi Tadashi. *Edo bungaku* 18 (Autumn 1997): 16–34.

Tōrai Sanwa. *Watō chinkai*. Vol. 6 of *Sharebon taikei*, 173–200. Edited by Takagi Kōji, Yamamoto Renzō, and Watanabe Kō. Tokyo: Rikugōkan, 1931.

———. *Watō chinkai*. In vol. 13 of *Sharebon taisei*, 87–112. Edited by Mizuno Minoru, Nakamura Yukihiko, Jinbo Itsuya, Hamada Keisuke, Uetani Hajime, and Nakano Mitsutoshi. Tokyo: Chūō kōronsha, 1981.

Tōshisen ōkai: Gogon zekku. In vol. 5 of *Sharebon taisei,* 9–65. Tokyo: Chūō kōronsha, 1979.

Ts'ao Hsueh-chin. *A Dream of Red Mansions.* Translated by Yang Hsien-yi and Gladys Yang. Peking: Foreign Language Press, 1978–1980.

Ueno Yōzō, ed. *Ishikawa Jōzan Gensei.* Vol. 1 of *Edo shijin senshū.* Tokyo: Iwanami shoten, 1991.

Uraki, Ziro, trans. and introd. *The Tale of the Cavern.* Tokyo: Shinozaki shorin, 1984.

Ury, Marian, trans. and introd. *Tales of Times Now Past: Sixty-two Stories from a Medieval Japanese Collection.* Berkeley : University of California Press, 1979.

Wakan hikaku bungaku kai, ed. *Chūko bungaku to kanbungaku II.* Vol. 4 of *Wakan hikaku bungaku sōsho.* Tokyo: Kyūko shoin, 1987.

Waley, Arthur. *The Nō Plays of Japan.* Tokyo: Tuttle, 1976. Originally published 1921.

Watanabe Hideo. *Heianchō bungaku to kanbun sekai.* Tokyo: Benseisha, 1991.

———. "Ise monogatari to kanshibun." In *Issatsu no kōza: Ise monogatari,* 121–127. Edited by "Issatsu no kōza" henshubū. Vol. 2 of *Nihon no koten bungaku.* Tokyo: Yūseidō, 1983.

Watanabe Yoshio. "Josei kaihō to Mori Ōgai: 'Saezuri' no haikei to igi." *Hikaku bungaku* 31 (1988): 83–97.

Watson, Burton, trans. and ed. *The Columbia Book of Chinese Poetry: From Early Times to the Thirteenth Century.* New York: Columbia University Press, 1984.

Willcock, Hiroko. "Meiji Japan and the Late Qing Political Novel." *Journal of Oriental Studies* 33, no. 1 (1995): 1–28.

Willig, Rosette F., trans. and introd. *The Changelings: A Classical Japanese Court Tale.* Stanford: Stanford University Press, 1983.

Wixted, Timothy John. *Japanese Scholars of China: A Bibliographical Handbook.* Lewiston, NY: Edwin Mellon Press, 1992.

———. "The Kokinshū Prefaces: Another Perspective." *Harvard Journal of Asiatic Studies* 43, no. 1 (June 1983): 215–238.

Xiao Tong. *Wenxuan.* 2 vols. Edited by Li Shan. Hong Kong: Shangwu yinshugan, 1973.

Yamada Yoshio, Yamada Tadao, Yamada Hideo, and Yamada Toshio, eds. *Konjaku monogatari: Shina hen.* Vol. 23 of *Nihon koten bungaku taikei.* Tokyo: Iwanami shoten, 1960.

Yamaguchi Takeshi, ed. *Sharebonshū.* Vol. 12 of *Nihon meicho zenshū: Edo bungei no bu.* Tokyo: Nihon meicho zenshū kankōkai, 1926.

Yamazaki Kazuhide. " 'Gyo Genki' ron." In Yamazaki Kazuhide, *Mori Ōgai: Rekishi shōsetsu kenkyū,* 211–226. Tokyo: Ōfūsha, 1981. Originally published 1964.

Yanagida Izumi. "Kajin no kigū to Tōkai Sanshi." In Yanagida Izumi, *Seiji shōsetsu kenkyū* jō, 361–483. Vol. 8 of Yanagida Izumi, *Meiji bungaku kenkyū.* Tokyo: Shunjūsha, 1967.

Yeh, Catharine Vance. "Zeng Pu's Niehai Hua as a Political Novel: A World Genre in a Chinese Form." PhD diss., Harvard University, 1990.

Yokomichi Mario and Omote Akira, eds. *Yōkyoku shū.* Vol. 40 of *Nihon koten bungaku taikei.* Tokyo: Iwanami shoten, 1960.

Yonemoto, Marcia. *Mapping Early Modern Japan: Space, Place, and Culture in the Tokugawa Period (1603–1868).* Berkeley: University of California Press, 2003.

Yosa Buson. *Shin hanatsumi.* Edited by Okada Rihei, Ōtani Tokuzō, and Shimasue Kiyoshi. Vol. 12 of *Koten haibungaku taikei.* Tokyo: Shūeisha, 1972.

Yosano Akiko. "Arakida Reijo shōden." In vol. 1 of Yosano, *Tokugawa jidai joryū bungaku,* 1–12.

———, ed. and introd. *Tokugawa jidai joryū bungaku: Reijo shōsetsu shū.* Tokyo: Fuzanbō, 1915.

Yoshida Ken'ichi. "Nihongo." In vol. 24 of *Yoshida Ken'ichi chosakushū,* 255–270. Tokyo: Shūeisha, 1980. Originally published 1974.

Yoshikawa Hakki. *Satō Haruo no* Shajin shū: *Chūgoku rekichō meien-shi no hikaku kenkyū.* Tokyo: Shintensha, 1990.

Yoshikawa, Kōjirō, ed. *Shikyō kokufū.* Vol. 2 of *Chūgoku shijin senshū.* Edited by Yoshikawa Kōjirō and Ogawa Tamaki. Tokyo: Iwanami shoten, 1958.

Yotsutsuji Yoshinari. *Kakaishō.* Vol. 3 of *Kokubun chūshaku zenshō.* Edited by Muromatsu Iwao. Tokyo: Kokugakuin daigaku shuppanbu, 1908.

Yu Yue. *Dongying shixuan.* Edited and introduced by Sano Masami. Tokyo: Kyūko shoin, 1981. Originally published 1903.

Zeami Motokiyo. "Lady Han." Translated by Royall Tyler. In Keene, *Twenty Plays of the Nō Theatre,* 129–145.

Zheng, Guohe. "From Patriotism to Imperialism: A Study of the Political Ideals of *Kajin no kigū,* a Meiji Political Novel." PhD diss., Ohio State University, 1997.

Index

Abe no Nakamaro, 23–27, 37, 39, 57–58, 193n.13, 197n.72
ainoko, 94. *See also* hybridity; *xiangzi; zasshu*
Akazome Emon, 110, 112, 186, 213n.47; *Eiga monogatari*, 110
Akutagawa (Ryūnosuke), 168, 204n.48, 207n.76, 219n.4; "Pekin nikki shō," 226n.74; "Shanhai yūki," 226n.74
ancestors, 9, 31–32, 86, 97, 172. *See also* origin/descendant
anthropology/anthropological/anthropologist, 9–11, 13–14, 19–21
Anderson, Benedict, 4, 26
Andō Tameakira, 112, 211n.30; *Shika shichiron*, 112, 114
Aoki Masaru, 15, 78–82, 101, 136, 201n.21, 202nn.29, 31, 203n.34; *Chasho nyūmon: Chūka chasho*, 202n.30; "Gen jidai no zatsugeki," 149; *Genjin zatsugeki josetsu*, 202n.31; "Kanbun chokudoku ron," 79, 203n.33; *Kissa shōshi*, 202n.30; *Kōnan shun*, 80, 203n.32, 203n.34; "Ko-Shina bungaku ni okeru shōsetsu no chii ni tsuite," 150; "Kōshū kashin," 203n.73; "Meirō to Konkyoku," 101; *Nanboku kyokugi genryū kō*, 202n.81; *Pekin fūzoku zufu*, 202n.31; "Shina bungaku kenkyū ni okeru hōjin no tachiba," 79; "Shina gakusha no uwagoto," 79; *Shina kinsei gikyoku-shi*, 202n.31; *Shindai bungaku hyōron shi*, 202n.31; *Shuchūshu*, 78

Arakida Reijo, 15, 105, 115–121, 136–137, 152, 209n.5, 212nn.42, 46, 219n.2; *Ayashi no yo gatari*, 119, 137; "Fuji no iwaya," 119; "Hitōban," 137; *Ike no mokuzu*, 117–118, 212n.45; "Keitoku Reijo nanchin," 119; "Nonaka no shimizu," 119; *Tsuki no yukue*, 117, 118
Ariwara no Narihira, 29, 33
aural, 67–69, 109, 173, 179–180, 224n.59
authentic/authenticity, 9–10, 20, 28, 47, 52, 67, 69–70, 76, 79, 91, 100, 104, 151–152, 162, 170–175, 180, 199n.117, 206n.68
autobiographical, 79, 105, 126, 139, 140–141, 206n.68, 207n.79. *See also* confessional

baihua, 65, 68. *See also* vernacular Chinese
Bai Juyi, 34–35, 54, 62, 71, 76, 84, 111, 113, 130, 180, 186, 191n.8, 193n.17, 197n.72; "Changhenge," 34, 62, 84; "Mudan fang," 76; "Pipa xing," 186; "Shihe," 180; *Xin yuefu*, 111, 202n.24; "Yeyu," 180. *See also* Bai Letian
Bai Letian, 84, 180, 197n.72. *See also* Bai Juyi
Bal, Mieke, 1, 2, 7–8, 10, 12–13, 58, 88, 134, 169, 177–178, 192n.3
Ban Gu, 118; *Hanshu*, 118
Ban Zhao, 118; *Hanshu*, 118

barbarian/barbaric, 48–49, 59, 67, 151, 155, 170, 173
Baudrillard, Jean, 65, 73, 85
Bhabha, Homi, 1, 14
binary, 2–3, 5, 10, 11–13, 22–23, 41, 53, 56, 64, 183, 189. See also dialectics, dichotomy, dyad, polarity, rivalry
boundaries, 3, 15, 16, 21, 25–26, 27, 45–46, 54, 60, 75–77, 86, 91, 100, 105, 107, 125, 128, 138, 140, 145, 163, 172, 186. See also interface
brush talk, 67, 173
bungo, 69, 148, 156, 164. See also literary language

canon, classical Chinese, 4, 5, 15, 16–17, 64, 65, 68–71, 72, 80, 87, 102, 110, 128, 134–135, 143–146, 151, 155, 162–163, 167, 175, 179
Cao Pi, 157; "Luoshen fu," 123, 152, 197n.78
Cao Zhi, 123, 152, 197n.78; "Luoshen fu," 123, 152, 197n.78
Cen Shen, i, 95
Chang'an, 58, 97, 106, 130
Chen Yuanyun (J. Chin Gen'in), 170, 174, 226nn.79, 81, 227n.86; Gengen shōwa shū, 226n.79
Chikamatsu Monzaemon, 47–48, 51, 69. See also Kokusen'ya gassen
Chineseness, 1–3, 13, 15, 16, 18, 21, 31, 34, 66, 76–77, 95, 102, 150, 177, 180, 183
communality, 150, 165–167, 172
comparative, 11–14, 23, 53, 150
confessional, 10, 104, 116, 132, 146, 209n.5. See also autobiographical
connoisseur, 15, 21, 66, 73–74, 75–77, 81, 92, 101–102, 130, 143–144, 182, 184
contact zone, 21–22
contrast, 1–4, 11–14, 22, 24, 27, 30–31, 34, 40, 41, 52–53, 76–77, 84, 88, 92, 97, 99, 104, 112–113, 114, 139, 150, 156, 160–161, 171, 175–176, 181, 182, 187–189

coordination, 3, 23, 191n.3
cultural capital, 100, 155, 167

Deleuze, Gilles, 1, 12, 29–30, 169–170, 207n.81
dialectics, 2–3, 179. See also binary, dichotomy, dyad, polarity, rivalry
dichotomy, 2, 29–30, 36, 56, 98, 102, 148, 210n.11. See also binary, dialectics, dyad, rivalry, polarity
domestication, 54, 68, 70, 108, 119, 128, 136, 162–163, 172–173, 180, 198n.85
dyad, 2–3, 11–14, 16, 63, 76. See also binary, dialectics, dichotomy, polarity, rivalry

Ehrenburg, Ilya, 170, 226n.82
Ema Saikō, 15, 73, 105, 121–128, 140, 141, 209n.5, 214n.66, 214n.69, 215n.78, 216nn.94, 95, 219n.2, 220n.9; "Jijutsu," 126
Emperor Saga, 29, 186, 194n.24; Bunka shūrei shū, 29
Emura Hokkai, 116, 117, 118, 227n.86; Nihon shishi, 116, 227n.86
entanglement, 12–13, 15, 20, 23, 29–30, 39, 41, 47, 50, 60, 65, 74, 76, 78–79, 80, 83, 139, 141, 142, 154–156, 168–169, 171, 178–179, 180, 184, 188, 204n.42
essentialism, 11, 15, 121, 150, 209n.9
ethnocentrism, 66, 145, 148
Europhile, 148, 150, 168, 204n.42
exoticism, 19, 40, 63, 101, 137, 206n.68
exoticize/exoticization, 18, 21, 29, 64, 70, 76, 92, 95

Fan Chengda, 147, 220n.9; Wu chuan lu, 147
femininity, 53, 102, 114, 126, 131, 209n.9. See also gender divide/-partition; guixiu; joryū
Fengtian, 84, 89, 101
fetish(ization), 15, 65, 73–74, 81, 82, 85, 92–95, 101, 155, 206n.68, 207n.81

fold, 7, 11, 12–13, 22, 29–31, 80, 169–
170, 187–189, 207n.81
foreign, 16, 19–20, 22, 28, 35, 37–40, 43,
45–46, 52, 54, 61, 63–64, 68–69, 76–
77, 79, 81, 86, 105, 135–136, 138,
150, 158–159, 174, 176, 181, 187
Fujiwara no Kintō, 109; *Waka kuhon,*
109. See also *Wakan rōeishū*
Fujiwara no Kiyokawa, 57–63
Fujiwara no Seika, 185
Fujiwara no Teika, 41; *Meigetsuki,* 41.
See also *Matsura no miya monogatari*
Furukawa Koshōken, 69; *Saiyū zakki,* 69

Gan Bao, 119; *Sou shen ji,* 119, 137
Gao Qingqiu, 87, 149
gender/-divide/ partition, 92, 103, 105.
See also femininity; masculinity
Gensei, 169–170, 172–174, 226nn.79,
226n.81, 86; *Gengen shōwa shū,*
226n.79; *Sōzanshū,* 226n.81
geography, 14, 19, 21–22, 91, 185–189
Graham, Patricia, 74, 201nn.8, 20,
202n.30, 215n.75
Greenblatt, Stephen, 19–20, 155
guixiu (J. *keishū*), 122. *See also* femininity; *joryū*
Guwenci (J. Kobunji), 67, 72

Hagiwara Hiromichi, 211n.28; *Genji
monogatari hyōshaku,* 211nn.25, 28
Haku Rakuten, 54, 197n.72
Hamamatsu chūnagon monogatari, 14,
27–40, 42, 43, 44, 46, 52, 54, 55, 63,
92, 110, 112, 117–118, 192nn.2, 3,
5, 194n.20, 195nn.28, 29, 30,
196nn.43, 49, 199n.111. See also
Mitsu no Hamamatsu
Han, 42, 48–49, 50, 53, 55, 153, 163,
166, 222n.31
Hangzhou, 80, 86, 87, 90, 93
Hara Saihin, 121, 122–123, 213n.59,
214nn.62–66, 219n.1; "Gengo-shi,"
122
Hattori Nankaku, 72, 171
Hattori Seiichi (Bushō), 164–165,

225n.64; *Tsūzoku Kajin no kigū,*
163–165, 224n.56, 225n.64. *See also*
Daitō Hyōshi
Hayashi Razan, 72, 185
hegemon/hegemony, 21, 64, 85, 144–
145, 155, 158–159, 170, 175
heterogeneity/heterogeneous, 2, 64, 110,
115, 194n.19
Heyang, 28–37, 40, 44, 186
hierarchy/hierarchization, 8, 11, 24, 31,
37, 40, 44, 49, 56, 59, 83, 84, 86, 89,
92, 99, 102, 103, 146, 158, 172, 175,
205n.65, 221n.25
High-Tang, 67, 72–73, 171
Higuchi Ichiyō, 104, 128, 133, 209n.9,
211n.24, 219n.124
Hino Tatsuo, 66, 71, 73, 76, 194n.19
Hiraga Gennai, 55; *Fūryū Shidōken den,*
55
Hiratsuka Raichō, 106, 128, 132–134
historicism, 1, 6, 9
historiography, 6, 118
homogeneity/homogeneous, 4, 6–7, 15,
22, 88, 104, 113, 115, 128, 150, 177,
179
Honchō reisō, 109–110
Honchō Suikoden, 14, 55–64, 68–69, 85,
92, 119, 173, 199nn.108, 117, 119,
Hong lou meng, 98, 99, 149, 207n.76,
221n.22
Hori Tatsuo, 168
hybrid/hybriditity, 14, 32, 35, 40, 54, 59,
92–94, 111, 167–168, 173, 180, 185,
207n.76, 79, 227n.7. See also *ainoko; xiangzi; zasshu*

Ibi Takashi, 65, 215n.75, 220n.7
Ike no Taiga, 75, 202n.22; *Jūben jūgi zu,*
75, 202n.23
Indigenous, 4, 16, 23, 26, 104–106, 107–
108, 110, 111, 114–115, 118, 119–
120, 137, 141, 147, 172, 175, 179,
187, 189, 224n.55. *See also* native/
nativity
influence(s), 2, 7, 13, 23, 96. *See also* ancestor; origin/descendant; quotation

interface, 90, 208n.96. *See also* boundaries
Ise monogatari, 33, 195n.26, 196n.38
Ishikawa Jōzan, 67, 72, 144, 173, 200n.2,
  201n.13

Japaneseness, 2–3, 13, 15, 21–22, 34, 38,
  78, 115, 150, 180
Jiangsu, 87, 89, 97
Jia Sidao, 93, 206n.75
Jin Yi, 124, 215n.77
jingoism/jingoistic, 41, 55. *See also* nationalism
Jinpingmei, 149
joryū, 103–105, 209n.4, 211n.33,
  212n.36. *See also* femininity; *guixiu*

Kado, Reiko, 103, 126, 208n.1
Kafka, Franz, 135, 174–175
Kajin no kigū, 16, 145–146, 151–167,
  180–181, 221nn.25, 27, 223nn.35,
  40, 44, 224nn.53, 56, 225nn.64, 65,
  71
Kamei Shōkin, 121, 213n.59
kanbun, 41, 82, 111, 117, 118, 144, 147–
  149, 156–157, 161, 164, 166, 184,
  186–187, 195n.26, 223n.41
Kan Sanbon, 29. *See also* Sugawara no
  Fumitoki
kanshi, 24, 29–30, 49, 82, 108–109, 116,
  121–122, 124, 146–149, 152, 156,
  166, 168, 171, 172, 185, 195n.26,
  209n.5, 214n.66, 215n.75, 220n.7,
  225n.71
kanshibun, 4, 78, 95, 109, 151, 154, 162,
  168, 175, 185, 194n.24, 209n.6,
  219n.4, 225n.71; incommensurability with Westernness, 146–150,
  156–157
Kara monogatari, 34, 53, 196n.40
Kashiwagi Jotei, 168, 171, 201n.21
Kawaguchi Hisao, 109–110, 191n.8
Kawase Kazuma, 20, 192n.5
Kawazoe Fusae, 110, 210n.18
Keene, Donald, 152, 158–159, 161, 163
kenten, 95

Kibi no Makibi, 25, 27
Kikuchi Gozan, 215n.75; *Gozandō shiwa,*
  215n.75
kinki shoga (Ch. *qinqi shuhua*), 75, 78
Kinoshita Mokutarō, 101, 208n.95; "Mei-
  lang chang Su San," 101; "Peking,"
  101
Ki no Tsurayuki, 22, 194n.19. See also
  Tosa nikki
Kōda Rohan, 149–150, 161, 221n.22
Kokin wakashū, 22, 49, 57
Kokuji, 77
Kokusen'ya gassen, 14, 47–55, 59–60, 69,
  173, 198nn.80, 85
Kokuyaku kanbun taisei, 149, 221n.22
Konrondo, 70, 201n.9
kundoku, 67, 69–70, 72, 79–80, 155, 164.
  See also *yomikudashi*
kunten, 154
kun'yaku, 68
Kurahashi Yumiko, 16, 106–107, 135–
  141, 152, 218nn.115, 118,
  219n.125; "Kōkan," 136–137; *Kōkan,* 138; "Kubi no tobu onna,"
  137–138; *Shiro no naka no shiro,* 138

LaMarre, Thomas, 3–4, 22–23, 26, 191n.3
Liang Qichao, 163, 225nn.60, 62; *Jiaren
  qiyu,* 163
Li Bai, 25, 60–61, 62, 67, 72, 122,
  208n.91; "Qingping diao," 61, 62
Li Daotian (J. Ri Tōten), 49–50, 69–70
Li Furen, 40, 113
Lin Bu, 90
Lin Daiyu, 99, 100, 207n.76
Li Panlong (Yulin), 70, 72, 171, 227n.85
literary language, 19, 52, 60, 63–64, 65,
  67–68, 143, 181. See also *bungo;
  wenyan*
literati, 25–26, 64, 71, 75–77, 110, 122,
  127, 128, 136, 145, 147, 150, 156–
  157, 161, 162, 167, 182, 202n.27,
  215n.82
Li Yi'an (Qingzhao), 117, 212n.45
Li Yu (Li Liweng), 75, 87, 97, 99,
  201n.21; *Bimuyu,* 87; *Jiezi yuan hua-*

zhuan, 75; *Shenzhong lou*, 86–87; *Shizhongqu*, 86
Lu Wuguan (You), 125, 147, 215n.82, 220n.9
Lu Xun, 136; *Guxiaoshuo goushen*, 136
Lu You, 147; *Ru shu ji*, 147
Lu Yu, 78, 202n.30; *Chajing*, 78, 202n.30

Maeda Ai, 159, 221n.25
man'yōgana, 181
Man'yō shū, 57, 220n.17
Maoshi daxu, 22
masculinity, 16, 102, 140, 175, 177, 182. *See also* gender divide/-partition
material/materiality, 3–5, 8, 15, 66, 68, 75, 77–78, 82, 87–88, 102, 139, 167, 177, 181, 183–185, 187–189, 219n.119
Matsui, Sachiko, 158, 224nn.49, 51
Matsura no miya monogatari, 14, 27, 40–47, 48, 49–50, 55, 63, 152, 196n.58
Mei Lanfang, 101, 208nn.93, 95; *Tōyūki*, 208n.93
Meien shiki (Ch. Mingyuan shigui), 126. *See also guixiu*
Mei Yaochen, 138–139; "Simao," 139
mentor-disciple, 26, 72, 107, 123–127, 128, 130–131, 133, 139–140, 209n.9, 212n.42
Minakami Roteki, 122; *Nihon keien ginsō*, 122
Ming dynasty, 48–50, 54–55, 56, 69–70, 72, 76, 78, 123, 126, 170, 172, 188, 205n.63
Mitsu no Hamamatsu, 27, 58. See also *Hamamatsu chūnagon monogatari*
Mori Ōgai, 16, 106, 107, 128–135, 136, 139–140, 141, 146, 148–149, 169, 216nn.97, 101, 217nn.107, 109, 113, 218n.114, 220n.15; *Doitsu nikki*, 148; "Gyo Genki," 106, 128–134, 139–141, 227n.7; *Kantō nichijō*, 148; *Kōsei nikki*, 148, 220nn.15, 18; *Omokage*, 149; "Rekishi sonomama to rekishi banare," 216n.96; "Saigo no ikku," 133; *Shibue Chūsai*, 133;

Taimu nikki, 148; "Yasui fujin," 133, 218n.114; *Zai Toku ki*, 148
Mori Shuntō, 147, 220n.7
Morita Shiken, 156, 223n.41
Morita Sōhei, 126, 132; "Onna deshi," 126
Mostow, Joshua, 110
mother tongue, 17, 175–176, 196n.38
Motoori Norinaga, 56, 111, 113–115, 116, 119–120, 211n.27, 214n.66; "Nonaka no shimizu tensaku," 213n.52; *Shibun yōryō*, 113, 211n.27
Murasaki Shikibu, 15, 104, 105, 107–115, 117, 118–119, 120–121, 128, 141, 209n.9, 211n.24, 214n.66

Nagai Kafū, 147, 220nn.13, 14
Nagai Kagen (Kyūichirō), 147–148, 220nn.13, 14; *Raiseikaku shishū*, 148
Naitō Konan, 79, 203n.32
Nakajima, Wakako, 3–4, 109, 209n.6, 210n.10, 13
Nakamura Shin'ichirō, 16, 146, 167–175, 226nn.76, 81, 227n.86; *Kimura Ken-kadō no saron*, 168; *Ōchō bungaku no sekai*, 226n.72; *Kūchū teien*, 168–169; *Kumo no yukiki*, 16, 146, 167, 169–175, 227n.86; *Shijin no niwa*, 168, 226n.76
Nanjing, 48, 51, 80, 85, 100
national boundaries, 16, 21, 25–26, 45, 54, 60, 76–77, 138, 145, 163, 172
national identities, 2, 6, 34, 54, 105, 115, 198n.85
nationalism, 5, 14, 15–16, 17, 21, 55, 144–146, 151, 173–174, 176
national language, 78–79, 104, 135, 145, 174, 175, 178, 179
nation-state, 17, 142, 144–145, 198n.85
native/nativity, 2, 15, 27, 29, 34, 39, 41–42, 45–46, 51, 54, 56–57, 64, 68, 86, 104–105, 110, 119, 127, 135, 136–137, 144, 147, 148, 162, 176, 178, 180–181, 182. *See also* indigenous

Natsume Sōseki, 80, 98–99, 132–133, 134, 148–149, 152, 203n.35, 208n.91
"New Women," 106, 135, 141
Nishimura Tenshū, 167
Nomura Kōdai, 117, 118

Ōbaku-shū, 75
objectifying/objectification, 4, 8, 10, 12, 15, 20–22, 77, 78–80, 82, 85, 89–90, 95, 102, 129–130
Ochi Haruo, 156–157, 224n.56
Ōe no Masafusa, 25, 186; *Gōdanshō*, 25–27, 30, 186, 193n.17, 195n.28, 197n.72; "Yūjo ki," 186
Ōe no Masahira, 110, 186; "Yūjo o miru no jo," 186
Ogyū Sorai, 4, 67–68, 70, 72, 75, 79, 171, 201n.15, 203n.34, 227n.85
Okajima Kanzan, 68, 149, 200n.5; *Chūgi Suikoden*, 68; *Tōwa san'yō*, 68; *Tsūzoku chūgi Suikoden*, 68
Ōnuma Chinzan, 147
oral/orality, 3, 60–61, 67–80, 104, 155, 161–162, 174, 176, 177, 179–181, 182, 185, 224n.59. *See also* recitation
original, 4, 30, 32–33, 56, 57, 58, 61, 68–69, 75, 79–80, 100, 108–109, 136–137, 148, 158, 162, 163–166, 172, 180, 196n.43, 225nn.64, 71. *See also* quotation
origin/descendant, 3, 7–8, 21, 42, 56, 77, 78, 89, 92–94, 113–114, 118, 121, 171–172, 175, 184, 194n.19, 196n.38, 209n.6. *See also* influence(s); quotation
origin/destination, 21, 38, 43, 44–45, 57, 85, 135, 139, 154, 171–172, 189. *See also* vector

perception, 1, 4, 8–9, 11, 13, 64, 85, 88, 127–128, 141–142, 177
phonocentricism, 162, 173–174, 179, 198n.85
polarity/polarization, 2, 11, 13, 91, 102, 169. *See also* binary; dialectics; dichotomy; dyad; rivalry
Pollack, David, 2
polyglot, 173, 175. *See also* transnational
popular, 35, 54, 63, 68, 71, 77, 96, 99, 157, 162, 164, 166, 180, 182, 185, 202n.27, 220n.7, 221n.25. See also *tsūzoku*
Pratt, Mary Louise, 21, 207n.81

Qing dynasty, 18–19, 48, 66, 71, 72–73, 76, 85, 87, 147, 227n.85
quotation, 8, 9, 17, 35, 88, 112–113, 121, 135–139, 153–154, 165, 180–181, 185, 186. *See also* influence(s); origin/descendant
Qu Yuan, 153; *Lisao*, 153

Rai San'yō, 122–127, 128, 133, 140, 146, 184, 214n.66, 215nn.78, 82, 216n.94, 219n.2
recitation, 29–30, 69, 74, 82, 109, 145–146, 162–163, 174, 179–181. *See also* oral/orality; *sodoku*
rhetoric/rhetorical, 1, 3, 5, 11, 15, 16, 19–22, 33, 48, 51–52, 66, 71, 72–73, 89, 103–104, 134, 148, 151–152, 156–157, 159–160, 169, 172, 192n.1, 221n.27. See also *shūji*
Rilke, Rainer Maria, 174–175
Rimer, J. Thomas, 201n.13, 216n.97, 218n.114
rivalry, 25–26, 47, 101, 112. *See also* binary, dialectics, dichotomy, dyad, polarity
ruisho (Ch. *leishu*), 108–109

Said, Edward, 227n.88
saishi kajin shōsetsu (Ch. *caizi jiaren xiaoshuo*), 151
Sakai, Naoki, 4, 201n.15, 203n.34
Sakaki, Atsuko, 13, 196n.41, 198n.83, 205n.63, 217n.113, 219n.125, 222n.31
Sano Masami, 220n.10, 226nn.79, 81
Satō Haruo, 130, 208n.91; *Shajin shū*, 130

scholarship, 4, 7, 15, 28, 71–72, 78–79, 99–100, 102, 104, 144, 209n.5
Scott, Joan, 9
seiji shōsetsu, 156–157, 160–161, 224n.51, 57
Seitō, 132–133
Shangyang Baifaren, 33, 40, 113
Shiba Shirō, 16, 145, 151, 157–158, 161, 163, 164–167, 221n.24, 225n.71. See also *Kajin no kigū*; Tōkai Sanshi
Shimada no Tadaomi, 110
Shimizu Hamaomi, 119
Shi Yin, 205n.63; *Xihu jiahua*, 205n.63
Shōheikō, 71, 148
Shuihu zhuan, 14, 55, 98, 99, 149, 221n.22
shūji, 152, 160. See also rhetoric/rhetorical
Sinophile, 5, 15–16, 26, 59, 67, 82–83, 105, 120, 130, 135, 137–138, 146, 150, 168, 171–172, 181, 183, 184–185, 227n.85
Six dynasties, 89, 136, 152, 166
sodoku, 69, 162. See also recitation
Song dynasty, 18–19, 41, 55, 73, 87, 91, 93, 138–139, 147, 192n.2
Song Yu, 152, 197n.78, 217n.109; "Gaotang fu," 152, 197n.78; "Shennu fu," 197n.78
souvenir, 91, 101, 207n.81
Stewart, Susan, 65, 91
style, 3–4, 36, 56, 67, 68, 75, 79, 80–81, 93, 96, 117–118, 120, 123, 130, 145, 148, 152, 154–155, 156–159, 161, 162, 163–166, 180, 182–183, 209n.9, 212n.46, 217n.113, 219n.124, 221n.25, 225n.64, 227n.7
Suematsu Kenchō (Seihyō), 147–148; *Seihyō shū*, 147
Sugawara no Fumitoki, 29, 110, 195n.28. See also Kan Sanbon
Sugawara no Michizane, 28, 110, 180, 185, 227n.4
Sugawara no Takasue no musume, 28, 112; *Sarashina nikki*, 20, 28, 117, 192n.5, 226n.73

Su Manzhu (J. So Manshu), 207n.79; *Dankō Reigan ki*, 207n.79
Sumiyoshi, 25, 45, 46, 47, 54, 197n.72, 198n.79
Su Shi (Dongpo), 87, 88, 147, 148, 186, 197n.72, 205n.51, 220n.17; "Chibi fu," 186
Su Xiaoxiao, 89, 205n.63
Suzuki, Tomi, 104, 202n.28, 209n.5, 219n.5

Takahashi Taika, 167
Takebe Ayatari, 56–57, 59, 68, 119, 149. See also *Honchō Suikoden*
Takezoe Seisei (Shin'ichirō), 147–148, 220n.10; *San'un kyōu nikki narabini shisō*, 147
Tanaka, Stefan, 4
Tangshi sanbai shou, 138
Tani Tateki, 158, 165
Tanizaki Jun'ichirō, 15, 17, 80, 82–90, 92–93, 95–96, 99–102, 130, 137, 149, 178–179, 181, 184–185, 187, 189, 203nn.39, 40, 204nn.41, 42, 205nn.50, 51, 206n.68, 207nn.76, 79, 85, 208n.91, 219n.4, 227n.7; "Ashikari," 186–187; "Birōdo no yume," 92–95, 100; "Chōsen zakkan," 204n.41; "Gabō ki," 82; "Genjō Sanzō," 205n.51; "Inaba Seikichi sensei," 203n.39; "Itansha no kanashimi," 84; "Kakurei," 90–92, 206n.68; "Kirin," 205n.51; "Kōjin," 95–102, 149, 207n.85, 208nn.82, 86; "Ningyo no nageki," 85–86; *Rangiku monogatari*, 187–189; "Rozan nikki," 82; "Sakana no Ri Taihaku," 208n.91; "Seiji iro no onna," 205n.53; "Seiko no tsuki," 86; "Shanhai kenbun roku," 204n.42; "Shanhai kōyūki," 204n.42; "Shina-geki o miru ki," 84, 101; "Shina no ryōri," 83–84; "Shina shumi to iu koto," 208n.91; "Shindō," 203n.40; "Shinwai no yoru," 82; *Shōshō Shigemoto no haha*,

179, 205n.50; "Shūkō juku to
Sanmā juku," 203n.39; "Shunkin
shō," 182, 227n.7; "Soshū kikō," 82;
"So Tōba: Arui wa Kojō no shijin,"
205n.51; "Tomoda to Matsunaga no
hanashi," 204n.42; "Yōshō jidai,"
203n.39?; "Yume no ukihashi,"
181–183
Tanomura Chikuden, 124
Tao Yuanming (Qian), 99, 136, 152,
208n.91; "Taohuayuan ji," 136, 152
territoriality, 26, 188
Tian Rucheng, 205n.63; *Xihu youlan zhi
yu,* 205n.63
tōin, 67, 76. *See also* authentic/authenticity
Tōkai Sanshi, 145, 151, 153, 157–160,
166–167, 221n.27; *Jijo,* 225n.70. *See
also Kajin no kigū;* Shiba Shirō
Tokutomi Roka, 162
Tokutomi Sohō, 160
Tomohira, 110
Tosa nikki, 14, 22, 25–26, 27, 57, 193n.8,
194n.19
Tōshisen (Ch. *Tangshixuan*), 70
Tōshisen ōkai: Gogon zekku, 70
tourism, 15, 80–81, 86, 102
translation, 20, 56, 58, 68–71, 78–79,
108, 118, 130, 147, 149, 156, 163,
174, 221n.22
transnational, 16–17, 27, 47, 53–54, 56,
63, 66, 95, 144–145, 150, 151, 155,
162–163, 167, 174–176, 209n.96.
See also polyglot
transvestism, 53, 85, 95, 100–102, 121–
122
travel, 14–15, 19–21, 24, 27, 32, 33, 42,
45, 47, 56–57, 64, 66, 80–81, 82–84,
88, 90–91, 93, 96, 101, 147, 172,
204n.42, 207n.76, 220n.9
Tsubouchi Shōyō, 157, 159–161, 221n.25;
Shōsetsu shinzui, 157, 159–161
Tsuga Teishō, 56, 200n.6; *Kokon kidan:
Hanabusa zōshi,* 200n.6; *Kokon
kidan Hanabusa zōshi kōhen:
Shigeshige Yawa,* 200n.6
Tsukushi, 32, 195n.32

tsūzoku, 68, 164. *See also* popular

Ueda Akinari, 56, 120, 194n.19, 200n.6;
Harusame monogatari, 194n.19,
200n.6;
Ugetsu monogatari, 200n.6
universal language, 30, 43, 144, 150. *See
also* transnational
Utsubo monogatari, 118, 197n.64

vector, 7, 12, 39, 88, 170. *See also* origin/
destination
vernacular Chinese, 56, 63–64, 68, 135,
146. *See also baihua*

Wakan rōeishū, 30, 108, 110
wakokubon kanseki, 72, 201n.14
wakon kansai, 2–3
Wang Wei, 25, 97, 99
Wang Yuyang (Shizhen), 72, 87, 171
washū, 172. *See also* domestication
Wa Tō chinkai, 69
Wei Ye, 184
Wen Tingyun (Feiqing), 107, 128, 129,
131, 139–140
Wenxuan, 25, 151
wenyan, 65, 145. *See also* literary lan-
guage
Wenyuan yinghua, 25
Wixted, John Timothy, 22, 202n.29
Wu Sangui (J. Go Sankei), 49, 70
Wushan, 46, 55

xiangzi, 207n.79. *See also ainoko;* hybridity; *zasshu*
Xiaoqing, 217n.113
xingling, 72, 171–172, 227n.85
Xishi, 89, 205n.64
Xuanzong, 23, 32, 35, 55, 57, 61–63,
196n.43, 222n.31

Yamamoto Hokuzan, 171, 227n.85;
Sakushi shikō, 227n.85
Yamanoue no Okura, 57
Yanagawa (nee Chō) Kōran (Kei), 122
Yanagawa Seigan, 168

Yang Guifei, 32–35, 40, 51, 58–63, 69, 77, 84, 92, 129, 153, 196n.43
Yang Tieyai (Weizhen), 87
Yan Qing, 101
Yinyuan (J. Ingen), 19, 75
Yoda Gakkai, 147, 149
yomi kudashi, 79, 154–155, 162, 164, 225n.69. See also *kundoku*
Yonemoto, Marcia, 55, 69, 201n.9
yonghuai shi (J. *eikai shi*), 73
yongwu shi (J. *eibutsu shi*), 66
Yosa Buson, 73, 75, 201n.18; *Jūben jūgi zu*, 75, 202n.23; *Shin hanatsumi*, 201n.18
Yosano Akiko, 103, 116, 128, 133, 217n.113
Yoshikawa Eiji, 127; *Nihon meifu den*, 127
Yotsutsuji (Minamoto) Yoshinari, 111; *Kakaishō*, 111
You xian ku, 33, 119, 152
Yuan dynasty, 18–19, 87, 149

Yuan Hongdao, 172–173, 227nn.85, 86
Yuan Mei (Suiyuan), 72, 78, 83, 124, 171–173, 214n.63; *Suiyuan nudizi shixuan*, 124; *Suiyuan shidan*, 78, 83, 139; *Xiaocang shichao*, 214n.63
Yuan Zhen, 30
Yu Xuanji (J. Gyo Genki), 106, 107, 108, 128–132, 134, 139–140, 142, 182, 210n.11, 217nn.106, 107, 109; "Qingshu ji Li Zian," 216n.101; "Qiuyuan," 130
Yu Yue (Quyuan), 122, 147; *Dongying shixuan* (J. *Tōei shisen*), 122, 147, 213n.60, 220n.10

zasshu, 93–94. See also *ainoko*; hybridity; xiangzi
Zhang Heng, 151; "Sichou shi," 151
Zhejiang, 87, 89
Zheng Chenggong, 48–51
Zheng Zhilong, 48–51, 53, 54

About the Author

Atsuko Sakaki is a professor in the Department of East Asian Studies and associate member of the Centre for Comparative Literature at the University of Toronto. Her previous books include a translation, *The Woman with the Flying Head and Other Stories by Kurahashi Yumiko* (1998), and *Recontextualizing Texts: Narrative Performance in Modern Japanese Fiction* (1999). Her current research is a book project on "Corporeality and Spatiality in Modern Japanese Literature."